D1037354

Red Internationalism

In *Red Internationalism*, Salar Mohandesi returns to the Vietnam War to offer a new interpretation of the transnational left's most transformative years. In the 1960s, radicals mobilized ideas from the early twentieth century to reinvent a critique of imperialism that promised not only to end the war but also to overthrow the global system that made such wars possible. Focusing on encounters between French, American, and Vietnamese radicals, Mohandesi explores how their struggles did change the world, but in unexpected ways that allowed human rights to increasingly displace anti-imperialism as the dominant idiom of internationalism. When anti-imperialism collapsed in the 1970s, human rights emerged as a hegemonic alternative channeling anti-imperialism's aspirations while rejecting systemic change. Approaching human rights as neither transhistorical truth nor cynical imperialist ruse but instead as a symptom of anti-imperialism's epochal crisis, *Red Internationalism* dramatizes a shift that continues to affect prospects for emancipatory political change in the future.

Salar Mohandesi is the Marvin H. Green, Jr. Assistant Professor of History at Bowdoin College. He is the co-editor of *Voices of 1968: Documents from the Global North*.

Human Rights in History

Edited by

Stefan-Ludwig Hoffmann, *University of California, Berkeley*
Samuel Moyn, *Yale University, Connecticut*

This series showcases new scholarship exploring the backgrounds of human rights today. With an open-ended chronology and international perspective, the series seeks works attentive to the surprises and contingencies in the historical origins and legacies of human rights ideals and interventions. Books in the series will focus not only on the intellectual antecedents and foundations of human rights, but also on the incorporation of the concept by movements, nation-states, international governance, and transnational law.

A full list of titles in the series can be found at:
www.cambridge.org/human-rights-history

Red Internationalism

*Anti-Imperialism and Human Rights
in the Global Sixties and Seventies*

Salar Mohandesi

Bowdoin College, Maine

CAMBRIDGE
UNIVERSITY PRESS

Shaftesbury Road, Cambridge CB2 8EA, United Kingdom

One Liberty Plaza, 20th Floor, New York, NY 10006, USA

477 Williamstown Road, Port Melbourne, VIC 3207, Australia

314–321, 3rd Floor, Plot 3, Splendor Forum, Jasola District Centre, New Delhi – 110025, India

103 Penang Road, #05–06/07, Visioncrest Commercial, Singapore 238467

Cambridge University Press is part of Cambridge University Press & Assessment, a department of the University of Cambridge.

We share the University's mission to contribute to society through the pursuit of education, learning and research at the highest international levels of excellence.

www.cambridge.org
Information on this title: www.cambridge.org/9781316513798

DOI: 10.1017/9781009076128

© Salar Mohandesi 2023

This publication is in copyright. Subject to statutory exception and to the provisions of relevant collective licensing agreements, no reproduction of any part may take place without the written permission of Cambridge University Press & Assessment.

First published 2023

Printed in the United Kingdom by TJ Books Limited, Padstow Cornwall

A catalogue record for this publication is available from the British Library

A Cataloging-in-Publication data record for this book is available from the Library of Congress

ISBN 978-1-316-51379-8 Hardback

Cambridge University Press & Assessment has no responsibility for the persistence or accuracy of URLs for external or third-party internet websites referred to in this publication and does not guarantee that any content on such websites is, or will remain, accurate or appropriate.

Material from Chapters 1, 2, and 3 was previously published in Salar Mohandesi, "Bringing Vietnam Home: The Vietnam War, Internationalism, and May '68," in *French Historical Studies* 41, no. 2, pp. 219–251. Copyright 2018, Society for French Historical Studies. All rights reserved. Republished by permission of the publisher. www.dukepress.edu.

To
Amir Houshang Aryanpour and Assadolah Aghazadeh Mohandesi

Contents

Figures

Acknowledgments

Intellectual production is a collaborative process from beginning to end. Behind my name lie the efforts of hundreds of individuals.

Some of the ideas that would motivate this book first took shape in the fall of 2007 when William Fisher and Simon Joyce invited me to help them launch a new interdisciplinary course at the College of William and Mary on "1968" in its international dimensions. I think it is only fitting to start by thanking them, as well as Varun Begley, Tuska Benes, Cindy Hahamovitch, Scott Reynolds Nelson, and my other teachers at William and Mary for setting me down the academic path.

The project itself began as a dissertation at the University of Pennsylvania, and so I wish to thank my many students, friends, colleagues, and advisors there. I am particularly indebted to Thomas Childers, who taught me the power of narrative; Roger Chartier, who encouraged my passion for theory; and above all Warren Breckman, who accommodated my interests, challenged me when necessary, and gave me a chance by accepting me as his advisee when no one else did.

If the history of this book begins at UPenn, it ends at Bowdoin College. I never expected to find myself in Maine, but now I can't think of another place to call home. It is impossible to describe the monumental support I have received from all levels of the College. I wish to thank my students for inspiring me to think harder, my colleagues for giving me the support needed to succeed, and my department for going to bat for me countless times. Thanks go to Rebecca Banks, Connie Chiang, Sakura Christmas, Javier Cikota, Dallas Denery, David Gordon, David Hecht, Page Herrlinger, Matthew Klingle, Sarah McMahon, Brian Purnell, Patrick Rael, Meghan Roberts, Strother Roberts, Rachel Sturman, Allen Wells, and Ya Zuo.

Between Pennsylvania and Maine lie a decade, dozens of research trips crisscrossing the globe, and a mountain of enormous personal debts. I thank the many librarians and archivists in France, the United States, Canada, Cuba, and Vietnam who graciously offered their assistance. I thank the scholars who invited me to present my research at such venues as the Western Society for French History, the International History Workshop at Yale University, and a workshop organized by the editors of a special issue of *French Historical Studies* on the fiftieth anniversary of May '68. And I thank Bowdoin College, the University of Pennsylvania, and the Council for European Studies for supporting my work with generous awards, grants, and fellowships.

I wish to thank Coleman Donaldson and Dave Mesing for their help with translations. I am indebted to John Palattella for his incisive editing. I would like to thank Pierre Asselin, Michael Scott Christofferson, Eleanor Davey, Gerd-Rainer Horn, Bethany Keenan, Harish C. Mehta, Nguyệt Thị Minh Nguyễn, Nick Pas, Donald Reid, and Daniel J. Sherman for offering advice, sharing materials, and making possible opportunities to develop my work. I have been lucky to have Mark Philip Bradley, Timothy Scott Brown, Kristin Ross, and the three anonymous readers at Cambridge University Press review drafts of the manuscript. And I owe a particular debt of gratitude to Samuel Moyn for his sustained encouragement throughout this process, from his role as outside dissertation reader to series editor. This book would not have seen the light of day without his tireless assistance at every stage.

I am indebted to all the close friends who helped make this book. Thanks to all my colleagues in graduate school, especially my union comrades, who were only too happy to talk over beer and pizza after a hard day of organizing. I wish to thank Ben Webster for helping me think through many of the ideas in this book. I would also like to thank Casey Wellock for years of stimulating conversations and for kindly reviewing parts of the manuscript. Special thanks to Emma Teitelman, who saw this project through from the very beginning. Without her edits, questions, and comments, to say nothing of our invigorating discussions, this book would have never come to fruition.

My thinking has developed in deep dialogue with all my comrades at *Viewpoint*. The many years of writing, editing, thinking, marching, organizing, laughing, dreaming, and commiserating together made this book possible. I am especially grateful to Robert Cavooris, Patrick King, and Ben Mabie for workshopping the entire manuscript with unmatched rigor and insight. I am profoundly indebted to Asad Haider, with whom I began an incredibly rich intellectual collaboration over a decade ago. Our partnership has powerfully shaped my intellectual trajectory. While life has taken us in different directions, we always seem to find ourselves on the same page.

I could have never completed this project without the support of loved ones. I want to thank Jenn So for her kindness, thoughtfulness, and unwavering commitment. A pillar of support during one of the most difficult times in my life, Jenn not only helped me bounce back, but also taught me to see the world differently, with renewed fascination. I am eternally grateful to my family. I lack the words to describe how much I appreciate everything Mom and Dad, Bababozorg and Madar, Mitra and Ken, and Jasmine and Adam have done for me over the years, a statement they may find ironic, because they know me as someone who never stops talking. But the truth is, I don't know how I can ever adequately thank people who taught me how to speak, think, and live in the first place. I will just say here – thank you all for being there for me, supporting my interests, and patiently listening to my ideas, even if they seem bizarre, outrageous, or incomprehensible. Without you, nothing would have been possible.

I am especially grateful to my grandfathers for providing me with a model of a life well lived. Amir Houshang Aryanpour committed himself to fighting injustice and was forced to flee Iran in the turmoil of the 1979 revolution, but never lost hope in a brighter future. The first to inspire my curiosity about the world, he taught me to always ask questions, take sides, and remain true to my convictions, whatever the cost. Assad-olah Aghazadeh Mohandesi committed himself to building an egalitarian future in the Soviet Union and was forced to flee in the turmoil of the 1930s, but also refused to lose hope. Both men lived through countless defeats but never allowed their internationalist commitments to waver. Neither lived to see this book, but their presence animates its pages. I dedicate this book to them, and the millions like them, who fought, and continue to fight, for a new world.

Note on Translations

Anglophone scholarship is surprisingly idiosyncratic when it comes to translating names from other languages. For example, scholars always retain diacritical marks when referring to French individuals, but most writers drop them with Vietnamese names. Thus, "Madeleine Rebérioux" remains unchanged, but "Hồ Chí Minh" becomes "Ho Chi Minh." The matter becomes even more confusing with organizations. Scholars tend to leave untranslated the names of French organizations, but Vietnamese ones are automatically translated into English. Thus, "Gauche prolétarienne" is rarely translated as "Proletarian Left," but "Mặt trận Dân tộc Giải phóng miền Nam Việt Nam" is often written simply as the "National Liberation Front." Moreover, when scholars abbreviate these organizations, they generally derive the acronyms of Vietnamese organizations from their English translations, whereas French ones are rooted in their original names. Thus, "Gauche prolétarienne" is "GP" but "Mặt trận Dân tộc Giải phóng miền Nam Việt Nam" is "NLF."

Whatever its merits, this approach has several limitations. First, it is inconsistent, applying different standards to two languages that nevertheless share the same basic script. Second, it is relatively inaccessible, because it leaves untranslated important words, names, and phrases that not all readers will understand. Third, it is inequitable, because it naturalizes French – and European languages more broadly – while denying that privilege to others like Vietnamese. In light of these limitations, it is unsurprising that some writers have experimented with alternatives. One possibility is to simply leave everything in its original language. Although certainly consistent, this approach would lead to even greater inaccessibility, especially in a book like mine, which draws on materials from French, Italian, German, and Vietnamese.

Another option is to go in the opposite direction by translating everything into English. Although consistent, equitable, and far more accessible, this approach is also not without drawbacks. For example, to remain consistent, one would have to derive all abbreviations from the

English names of organizations. Thus, "Gauche prolétarienne" becomes "PL" instead of "GP." But this would in turn lead to new problems. To begin with, most contemporaries, even those who did not know French, referred to the "Gauche prolétarienne" as the "GP." In addition, the vast majority of the Anglophone scholarship has already come to associate the "Gauche prolétarienne" with the abbreviation "GP" and not "PL." Moreover, most scholars of transnational radical politics in the 1960s and 1970s already associate "PL" not with the "Gauche prolétarienne" but another radical group known as "Progressive Labor." The issue becomes especially thorny with widely recognized groups such as "Médecins Sans Frontières," or "Doctors Without Borders." Millions of people – even those completely unfamiliar with French – refer to this organization as "MSF." Although consistent, replacing "MSF" with "DWB" can only cause confusion.

Because there is no perfect way to balance consistency, equitability, accessibility, common usage, scholarly habits, and academic conventions, I have chosen a compromise. Out of respect, I have written the names of all individuals in their own language, and I have used diacritical marks throughout, except when I reference original sources that omitted these marks – for example, when reproducing direct quotations that did not use them, the titles of texts that ignored them, or the names of authors who chose to remove them, as was often the case with Vietnamese materials published in English for foreign audiences in the 1960s and 1970s. I have also kept the titles of all publications in their original language, unless they were translated into an English version, such as the *Vietnam Courier*. But in order to make the book as accessible as possible, I have translated the names of all places, governments, and organizations into English. I have also tried to use abbreviations derived from those English translations, particularly when referring to political groups that are familiar to only a handful of specialists, such as the "Indochina Solidarity Front." Unfortunately, there were instances where inventing new acronyms would have led to incomprehension. In these cases, I have either foregone acronyms altogether, as with the "Proletarian Left," or I have decided to retain the internationally accepted and standardized abbreviations, as with "Doctors Without Borders," which nearly everyone refers to as "MSF."

sent a sense of possibility flashing out over the airwaves all around the globe," recalls antiwar activist Sheila Rowbotham. "If the Vietnamese could take on the mightiest power in the world, what about us?"[4]

As Vietnamese fighters pressed their offensive, tens of thousands of radicals across North America and Western Europe raced to West Berlin to do their part in bringing the Vietnamese revolution to victory. On February 17, 1968, they overwhelmed the giant auditorium of the Technical University of Berlin, assembling beneath a gigantic flag of the National Liberation Front inscribed with the famous injunction: "The Duty of Every Revolutionary is to Make the Revolution." As one participant explained, it was the "first real gathering of the clans," uniting such groups as the Socialist German Student League, the British Vietnam Solidarity Campaign, the French National Vietnam Committee, and the American Student Nonviolent Coordinating Committee.[5] What brought them together was a shared commitment to not only ending US aggression in Vietnam but also joining with their Vietnamese comrades to overthrow the "imperialist system." This is what inspired them to collaborate across borders in one of the largest radical antiwar convergences of the decade: the determination to make a contribution to the anti-imperialist struggles exploding across Asia, Africa, and Latin America, and hopefully soon in North America and Western Europe as well.[6]

Huddled in that auditorium, where acrid cigarette smoke mixed with the stench of sweat, the anti-imperialists set to work. Faced with American escalation of the war, radicals called for a parallel escalation of their own efforts. They argued that the best way to support the Vietnamese people was to open a "second front" in the North Atlantic. Internationalism meant building a united global movement against imperialism, led by the heroic guerrillas of Vietnam. In France, their efforts to translate the Vietnamese example into a domestic idiom would help to bring about the largest general strike in history. And the unprecedented events of May '68, which seemed to prove that revolution was possible in the capitalist North Atlantic, in turn inspired radicals elsewhere. For a moment, world revolution appeared to be on the agenda.[7]

A decade later, in 1978, veteran antiwar radicals returned their attention to Southeast Asia. Although the war had ended in US defeat, with Vietnam reunified as an independent country embarking on the promised path to socialism, things had not turned out as expected. Reeducation camps were packed with suspects. Poorly planned economic policies exacerbated the challenges created by wartime destruction. State repression forced many to emigrate. Most astonishingly of all, Vietnam was again at war. But instead of locking arms with their neighbors against imperialism, Vietnamese revolutionaries fought against them. Vietnam, Cambodia, and China, all nominally socialist states, all former allies against imperialism, all onetime beacons of international solidarity, were slaughtering each other in an unprecedented internecine war.[8]

The Third Indochina War aggravated existing hardships, prompting even more refugees to flee Southeast Asia, often in dilapidated vessels that drifted across the South China Sea. Creaky fishing boats capsized. Refugees fell prey to pirates. Food ran out. Those who survived the harrowing passage found themselves herded into camps in neighboring Southeast Asian countries and tried their best to find meaning, care for each other, and create a new life. But eventually the host countries began to refuse entry to refugees, even forcing them back to sea. By early 1979, the region was engulfed in a humanitarian crisis.[9]

Many former North American and Western European antiwar radicals watched these images of suffering in dismay. Working with anticommunist Vietnamese living abroad, some erstwhile radicals organized a vast campaign to save the "boat people." Initially hoping to cross into Vietnamese waters to rescue refugees from the sea, they settled instead on chartering a ship, appropriately named the *Isle of Light*, and navigating it to the coast of Malaysia to serve as a floating hospital. As they worked under a scorching sun to save the refugees, their comrades internationalized the campaign, even winning the support of the US government, which was only too happy to use the crisis to rewrite the history of the war, rebrand itself as a virtuous nation, and shine a harsh spotlight on the Socialist Republic of Vietnam.[10] Activists who once joined Vietnamese communists in an international anti-imperialist struggle against the United States now found themselves allied with the United States in a massive international campaign against "human rights violations" in Vietnam.[11]

They had come to champion a very different kind of internationalism. Instead of politics, they preached morality. Instead of advocating the right of nations to self-determination, they promoted the rights of the individual. Instead of struggling to build a new world, they aimed to alleviate suffering in the imperfect one that existed. Instead of looking to the leadership of heroic guerrillas abroad, they claimed to save helpless victims. Instead of anti-imperialism, they spoke of human rights. By the end of the decade, anti-imperialism was in crisis, and human rights were on their way to securing the hegemony that they enjoy today. This book explains how that happened. Tracing the history of international antiwar activism from the early 1960s through the late 1970s, it shows how and why human rights displaced anti-imperialism as the dominant way that leftist activists in the North Atlantic imagined making the world a better place.

Scope

Although activists across the globe came to exchange anti-imperialism for human rights, nowhere was the shift more dramatic than in France. The French, and Parisians in particular, began the 1960s as some of the most engaged militants, sophisticated theorists, and uncompromising advocates of anti-imperialism, yet ended the 1970s as some of the most ferocious anticommunists, unabashed cheerleaders of interventionism, and vociferous proponents of human rights. In the colorful words of one contemporary observer, although once enjoying a "cosmopolitan paramountcy in the general Marxist universe," Paris is "today the capital of European intellectual reaction."[12] More recently, historian Robert Brier has declared the whole episode to be "one of the more spectacular reversals of intellectual history."[13]

What made this reversal so stunning was not just its intensity but also its international repercussions. France had long exercised a cultural, political, and intellectual hegemony over the global left. A beacon for radicals everywhere, the country's revolutionary history held enormous attraction. From Karl Marx to V. I. Lenin, Hồ Chí Minh to Zhou Enlai, Messali Hadj to Frantz Fanon, countless anti-imperialists had walked the cobblestone streets of its capital.[14] After the Second World War, France became a hub for cutting-edge political theory. Because of this unique international status, developments in France could not help but have a significant impact elsewhere, particularly on the rest of the North Atlantic. No other group of figures played so decisive a role in propelling this shift in how activists in North America and Western Europe more broadly approached internationalism.[15]

Although French radicals acted as a driving force, the story of how human rights displaced anti-imperialism cannot be told from a strictly national perspective because the activism of the 1960s and 1970s was thoroughly interconnected. As consummate internationalists, French radicals were in continuous dialogue with comrades not only in neighboring European countries but also across the Atlantic. Indeed, their most important contacts were often Americans, whose unique location inside the imperialist superpower of the era, or what they called the "belly of the beast," lent their struggles great international credibility, turning them into a vanguard of sorts. The French closely followed events in the United States, learned from them, and were profoundly transformed by them. For that reason, while I focus on French radicals, this book also tracks developments in the United States, drawing the two into a single story.

But as important as these connections between French radicals and their peers in the other capitalist countries of the North Atlantic were, relationships with what was then called the "Third World" were at times even more consequential. Struggles abroad not only furnished activists with a wealth of new ideas, tactics, and models but also served as powerful examples of change. This was especially true in France. Once the second largest maritime empire in the world, the hexagon's link to its colonies was so tight that decolonization boomeranged back into France with terrible velocity, effectively sparking a civil war at home that led to the collapse of the Fourth Republic. In this context, French activists were exceptionally attuned to developments abroad. They cut their teeth in solidarity movements, traveled abroad to see revolutions firsthand, and enthusiastically followed events in Asia, Africa, and Latin America.[16]

Much the same can be said about the United States. Although the United States never possessed as large an overseas empire as the French and experienced decolonization differently, the country's legacies of settler colonialism and chattel slavery, its pernicious role in Latin America, and its postwar status as leader of the "free world" provoked substantial domestic concern. The government's string of military bases, incessant interventions, and obsession with annihilating communism in the "Third World" compelled many Americans to look abroad. As citizens of the most powerful imperialist state on the planet, American activists felt especially responsible for the fate of the "Third World." Many took a keen interest in foreign policy, participated in solidarity movements, and made connections between struggles abroad and those of oppressed people inside the United States. Both in France and the United States, then, links with Asia, Africa, and Latin America were fundamental to the radical left.[17]

Radicals in France, the United States, and elsewhere in the North Atlantic turned to many struggles, yet it was the war in Vietnam, a former French colony and now the focus of US intervention, that became their most important international point of reference in the 1960s and 1970s. Many activists concurred with Che Guevara's assessment that Vietnam was the "focal point of all contradictions."[18] Vietnam, they believed, was the key to the entire world situation. The stakes were incredibly high, the struggle was live, and its future undecided. What is more, Vietnamese revolutionaries were fighting back, and it appeared as if solidarity could have a real impact on the outcome. More than any other struggle, the Vietnamese revolution shaped the meaning of internationalism for radicals, if not their very identity. Countless radicals of all ages would have agreed with the final editorial of the famous anti-imperialist journal *Partisans* when it declared: "Our generation is the generation of the Vietnam War."[19] For these reasons, I have focused on the internationalist struggles around Vietnam as a window into exploring the dramatic shifts in global politics that took place in those years.[20]

But if Vietnam played an important role for activists abroad, those movements also played an important role for Vietnamese revolutionaries. Hungry for allies, Vietnamese communists devoted considerable effort to connecting with movements across the globe, including those in the North Atlantic, which they felt could play a strategic role behind enemy lines. Since the United States was the main aggressor in Southeast Asia, Vietnamese revolutionaries unsurprisingly prioritized strong relations with American activists. Even more important than the United States, however, was France. Vietnamese communists had a longer history of organizing there, enjoyed the support of the largest community of overseas Vietnamese, relied on the solidarity of some of the most dynamic leftist movements in the capitalist world, and skillfully took advantage of the French government's outspoken criticism of the American War to turn Paris into their internationalist base of operations for the entire North Atlantic. But Vietnamese communists viewed connections with activists in countries like France and the United States as more than just means to fighting the US government. Like radicals in the North Atlantic, they also viewed their struggles as fundamentally linked to others in a grand project to change the world. As Lê Duẩn – arguably the single most important revolutionary leader during the American War – publicly explained in 1967, "The Vietnamese revolution is a component of world revolution and its successes have never been separated from the latter's."[21] In this way, radicals in France, the United States, and Vietnam were not simply connected to one another politically, intellectually, and affectively. In the 1960s, they came to see themselves as different fronts in the same international revolutionary process, which is why this book focuses on their interrelationships.[22]

History is neither a continuous stream nor a series of neatly bounded periods; it is instead the consequence of contingent encounters, some of which take hold in unforeseen combinations whose accretions may produce what can only later be seen as important shifts. By zeroing in on these "contingent encounters" between developments in France, the United States, and Vietnam, this book explains how human rights displaced anti-imperialism among activists in the North Atlantic. In the mid-1960s, American intervention in Vietnam, activist efforts to internationalize the war, and the Vietnamese strategy to sway public opinion against the United States led radicals to create a new international whose primary objective was to win the ideological war. In the late 1960s, unrest in France, the militancy of Black struggles in the United States, and the audacity of the Tet Offensive in Vietnam led radicals to argue that the best way to help the Vietnamese people was to "bring the war home." In the early 1970s, domestic experiences with incarceration, President

Richard Nixon's new focus on prisoners of war, and South Vietnam's repression of political dissenters led them to reframe antiwar solidarity around civil liberties in South Vietnam. And in the late 1970s, the decline of radicalism, a new foreign policy in the United States, and a humanitarian catastrophe in Southeast Asia helped create the conditions that led internationalists to shift their allegiance from anti-imperialism to human rights.[23]

Of course, events outside France, the United States, and Vietnam also influenced how activists in North America and Western Europe reimagined internationalism. Within the North Atlantic itself, Italy, Great Britain, and West Germany, but also smaller countries such as Belgium, played a role. In addition, while Vietnam was certainly decisive, radicals in the North Atlantic were also influenced by many crosscurrents elsewhere: social movements in Latin America, the aftermath of the Prague Spring in Czechoslovakia, the complexities of the Cultural Revolution in China, the writings of Soviet dissidents, the long struggle of the Palestinian people, the persistent campaign against apartheid in South Africa, the opportunities of the Nicaraguan revolution, the seeming paradoxes of the Iranian Islamic Revolution, the unique rise of Solidarity in Poland, and especially the turn to authoritarianism in Brazil, Chile, Uruguay, and Argentina. Moreover, in some cases other ways of conceptualizing internationalism proved quite important, particularly those organized principally around race, gender, religion, or geography, as well as many smaller radical internationalisms, which dissented from both the hegemonic models of anti-imperialism and human rights.[24]

While I certainly touch on a number of these experiences in this book, trying to include in a single comprehensive narrative everything that may have contributed to the shift from anti-imperialism to human rights would have resulted in an account that was superficial, disorienting, and incapable of conveying change over time in a consistent manner. Instead of jumping from one region, struggle, activist milieu, or solidarity campaign to another, I have chosen to concentrate here on the triangle of France, the United States, and Vietnam. To follow the trajectory of one current of internationalist activists, two ways of practicing internationalism, and linkages between three countries makes for a more coherent narrative about who changed, in which direction, and exactly why.

Overview

US aggression in Vietnam soon drew widespread condemnation in North America and Western Europe. So diverse was this opposition that one cannot speak of a single coherent antiwar movement but rather a cacophonous collection of initiatives spanning the political spectrum. This book focuses on one set of antiwar actors: the "radicals." Although consciously distinguishing themselves from others in the larger antiwar scene, radicals were by no means homogenous. They came from many backgrounds, subscribed to competing traditions, advocated diverse tactics, and displayed wildly different levels of engagement. While a small core memorized Marx and Lenin, developed a comprehensive theory of the world situation, and dedicated their lives to making change, many others were driven by personal concerns, motivated by local problems, and had only a vague desire to do good in the world.

Despite their differences, the radicals all shared the same general approach to opposing the war. While some arrived at it intuitively, and others processed it into an explicit principle, they all believed that the war was not caused by this or that politician, but by a broader "system" that made such wars possible in the first place. Ending the war, then, necessarily meant changing the system. This is why I have called them radicals; true to the word's etymology, they sought to grasp the problem at what they perceived to be its "root."[25] While the term may seem generic, it captures how tens of thousands of antiwar activists from all walks of life came to adopt the same politics of systemic change, together contributing to its rise and fall, even if they personally experienced this history in different ways. In calling them radicals, then, I aim to name a kind of collective character that emerged through a shared process of political subjectivation.[26]

Radicals soon recognized that the system they sought to change exceeded the territorial frontiers of a single state, which led them to coordinate their efforts. In deference to historical tradition, they adopted the term "internationalism" to name their belief that the only way to realize their political project was to unite across borders. At the same time, they took another page from the past by defining the global system they wished to transform as "imperialism." In this way, radicals came to see their project as "anti-imperialist internationalism." Anti-imperialist internationalism allowed radicals to designate a common enemy, link the domestic and the foreign, and think politics at a global level. But it did not in itself offer a concrete path to changing the world. There were potentially many different ways to overthrow the global system of imperialism.[27]

But in the 1960s, most anti-imperialist radicals more or less adopted a single approach. This was the Leninist problematic. If "anti-imperialist internationalism" was a way to frame the problem of uniting across borders in a struggle to change the world, then a "problematic" was the theoretical, practical, and strategic system that promised to actually solve that problem. To be sure, what came to be codified in the early twentieth century as "Leninism," and later as "Marxism-Leninism," was more than just a way to practice international solidarity. As both a development of Marxist thinking and a mode of communist politics, it claimed to unite theory and practice into a comprehensive whole that could provide answers to just about everything, from ideology to strategy, the party to the state, the seizure of power to revolutionary culture, economic planning to socialist construction. The problematic's architects deliberately assembled it into a unitary system, even if they recognized that it would be interpreted, applied, or adapted differently. This book, however, is not about Leninism as such, but rather the competition between the various ways that activists imagined coming together across borders to change the world. For that reason, while I certainly engage with other elements of Leninism when necessary, this study focuses primarily on those dimensions of the Leninist problematic that relate directly to the question of internationalism.[28]

At the heart of the Leninist problematic's solution to the problem posed by anti-imperialist internationalism was the right of nations to self-determination. According to this idea, nations exist, they oppress one another, and oppressed nations have the right to define their political future, which came to mean the struggle to win independence as nation-states. As for anti-imperialist radicals living in the oppressor nations, it was their duty to do whatever possible to lend a hand. Backed by solidarity movements in the imperialist core, oppressed nations would overthrow imperial rule, build strong states at home, and collaborate internationally to construct a socialist system that could facilitate the transition to communism, which they defined as a truly egalitarian world free from inequality, oppression, or domination.

Of course, anti-imperialism was not the only kind of internationalist politics available in the progressive milieus of the North Atlantic. Despite similar aspirations, occasional alliances, and notable cross-fertilizations on the ground, radicals fought to make the world a better place under competing internationalist banners. Some suggested that the best way forward was through religious faith. Others proposed unity on the basis of racial identity. Still others looked to the idea of international sisterhood in the struggle against global patriarchy. Although the explosive political context of the 1960s boosted many of these competing internationalisms, none benefited more than anti-imperialism. The many revolutions, decolonization movements, and national liberation struggles rocking the planet in those years allowed ideas associated with anti-imperialist internationalism to extend far beyond the relatively small circle of committed Leninist radicals in North America and Western Europe.

Anti-imperialism did not just win over many hardened activists sympathetic to these other internationalisms; it even achieved authority across the wider ecosystem of progressives who were concerned with issues like the Vietnam War but did not consider themselves militants, infrequently participated in actions, and only occasionally joined organizations. Although anxious about Leninism, opposed to revolution, and distrustful of Vietnamese communists, countless progressives hoping to transform the world in an egalitarian direction nevertheless came to see the problem as imperialism, the solution as national self-determination, and their task as organizing solidarity with national liberation movements while pushing for change at home. If one measure of a political project's strength is the degree to which it can win the support of the broader population, then anti-imperialism's ability to inform how millions understood, thought about, and acted in the world in the late 1960s was a clear sign of success.

But all that changed in the 1970s. People across North America and Western Europe deserted leftist campaigns, lost faith in national liberation struggles abroad, and abandoned the prospect of comprehensive change. Searching for a viable alternative, they turned to what was once a marginal notion in the leftist milieus of the North Atlantic: human rights. Of course, "human rights" meant different things to different people. But in the same way that radicals equated anti-imperialism with the right of nations to self-determination, so too did many rights activists in the North Atlantic reduce human rights to a single definition: the rights of individuals. According to this idea, individuals exist, they are endowed with certain inalienable rights, and they have the right to demand those rights. As for rights advocates in the North Atlantic, it was their duty to do whatever possible to lend a hand to secure human rights, which came to mean guaranteeing civil liberties against the encroachments of states. By making moral claims, advocating for suffering victims wherever they may be, and pressuring states to grant individuals their rights, humans everywhere would gradually come to enjoy the same universal rights, ultimately alleviating suffering in this world.

Like those radicals who embraced Leninist anti-imperialism, the activists who turned to individualist human rights imagined change at a global level, preached a commitment to universalism, and promoted human rights as an internationalist project that could make the world a better place. But their vision of change was drastically different. If anti-imperialism aimed to help people transform themselves into subjects, human rights viewed them as victims whose only ambition was to survive. If anti-imperialism saw people in the "Third World" as leaders in a struggle for change, human rights looked to professionals in the "First

World" as the active force in minimizing suffering throughout the world. If anti-imperialism declared that the only way to make the world better was through politics, human rights claimed that politics were external impositions to be avoided at all costs. If anti-imperialism insisted that lasting change depended on transforming a global system, human rights suggested that any such attempt would cause more harm. Indeed, human rights activists argued that one of the main reasons why the victims they hoped to save were suffering so badly was because anti-imperialists had foolishly tried to revolutionize the world. For quite a few of these rights activists, the only real way to change the world was to prevent it from getting worse.[29]

Although there was never a singular breakthrough, a definitive moment in which this specific vision of human rights emerged triumphant for everyone across the globe once and for all, by the late 1970s many people in the North Atlantic were not only abandoning anti-imperialism for some kind of individualist human rights, but also coming to see the latter as the only possible way to improve the world. Some historians have interpreted this dramatic transformation as one of evolution. According to this telling, radicals became humanitarians, revolution became ethics, and anti-imperialism became human rights. In its most teleological version, the end is said to be already present in the beginning, only waiting to be realized.[30] While there was certainly a degree of metamorphosis, especially when one turns to the biographies of individuals who traded the Little Red Book for government portfolios, the shift was more complex. As historian Samuel Moyn has argued, human rights succeeded not because they were implicit in all that came before, but because they survived while their rivals failed.[31] Following this approach, I reject the model of "evolution" in favor of "displacement." Anti-imperialism did not mutate into human rights: it entered into crisis in the 1970s, creating a space for human rights to overtake it as the dominant way of doing internationalism.

How did this happen? Much of it had to do with the collapse of the North American and Western European radical left. This decline had many causes, from state repression to an inability to build unity in difference, but I argue that since the trajectory of the radical left was so powerfully defined by events abroad, political developments in the rest of the world were a crucial factor in the collapse of anti-imperialism in the North Atlantic. By the late 1970s, national liberation struggles had fallen short of expectations. Instead of creating a new egalitarian world, they spawned nation-states that repressed their own people, accommodated themselves to capitalism, or fought shooting wars with each other. There was perhaps no greater symbol of this reversal than the Third Indochina War. Once a source of inspiration, the proof of anti-imperialist internationalism's success, Southeast Asia soon became a source of disillusionment, the proof of its failure. In China, anti-imperialists looked to capitalism, realigned with the United States, and turned on their allies. In Cambodia, anti-imperialists harassed their neighbors, constructed an autocracy, and massacred countless innocent people. In Vietnam, they curtailed democratic self-activity, targeted the ethnic Chinese minority, and occupied Cambodia.

Of course, anti-imperialism did not vanish overnight. Some activists in the North Atlantic continued to fight under its flag. Others tried to reinvent radical internationalism in light of new struggles in places like Nicaragua. Nevertheless, radicals were undeniably far fewer in number, anti-imperialism was much less popular, and inherited ideas such as the party, the dictatorship of the proletariat, and even the right of nations to self-determination had become suspect. This spelled disaster for the entire anti-imperialist left: Because anti-imperialism had aligned itself so closely with the Leninist problematic, the terrifying failures of movements tied to that problematic threw anti-imperialist internationalism itself into crisis, which in turn cleared the space for alternative ways of thinking global change. By advocating individual rights instead of national liberation, morality instead of politics, and reform instead of revolution, human rights not only survived this decade unscathed but also capitalized on a growing dissatisfaction with anti-imperialism to propose a different path. The very conditions that triggered the decline of anti-imperialism made possible the rise of human rights.

But a central argument of this book is that this explanation is not enough. Human rights succeeded not simply because anti-imperialism failed, as if in a hydraulic fashion, but rather because its partisans were able to convincingly market human rights as a legitimate successor to anti-imperialism. This involved striking a delicate balance. Human rights had to be presented as distinct from anti-imperialism. But if human rights were framed as too different, they could not have resonated with the desires of activists searching for a new home during the crisis of anti-imperialism. Proponents therefore had to make human rights appear as if they operated on the same continuum as their great rival. Human rights, to put it differently, had to be framed as sharing the same progressive goals of anti-imperialism without suffering from any of its weaknesses.

Taking the example of international solidarity with Vietnam, I show how this was made possible in at least three ways. First, even though anti-imperialism and human rights, differed from one another, the particular form of anti-imperialism that radicals adopted in the 1960s shared many "elective affinities" with the rival human rights internationalism. Activists supporting the idea of national self-determination often treated nations as essentialist subjects, much as rights activists viewed individuals. They saw the nation as endowed with inherent rights, mirroring the flat universalism of human rights. And while they did develop a different tactical repertoire, some radicals nevertheless made moral appeals, pointed to international law, or highlighted the suffering of Vietnamese as victims – all of which were hallmarks of human rights activism.

Second, anti-imperialist radicals and human rights activists converged on a series of projects in the early 1970s, such as the exemplary campaign to save political prisoners in South Vietnam. Although still working within the framework of anti-imperialism, antiwar radicals increasingly demanded the release of individuals imprisoned by the dictatorship in South Vietnam, making possible a tactical alliance with rights activists. Collaborations of this kind introduced the more marginal human rights internationalism to larger activist milieus, boosted its progressive credentials, and helped create a cultural, political, and intellectual terrain that was more favorable to rights talk. The unexpected convergence allowed human rights to appear as emancipatory as anti-imperialism. Consequently, when anti-imperialism slid into crisis in the late 1970s, activists could interpret human rights as simply a better way to realize their shared goal of making positive change in the world.

Lastly, human rights internationalism superseded anti-imperialism because it benefited from the defection of some radicals in the 1970s. To truly compete with anti-imperialism, human rights activists had to do more than just present themselves as an alternative; they needed to match the kind of dynamic activist energy that had helped make anti-imperialism so popular. One solution came in the form of radicals who jumped ship, and in the process brought with them skills, experience, and a repertoire of exciting forms of solidarity. This transfer was largely made possible through the encounter between human rights and a new kind of humanitarianism. In places like France, many of these defectors did not leap directly to human rights. The internal contradictions of anti-imperialism led them to develop a kind of radical humanitarianism that carried forward Leninism's activist aura while rejecting its overall framework. Their search for a new way to frame their militant internationalist practice led them into the arms of human rights. In fusing humanitarianism and human rights, these renegade radicals helped elevate human rights internationalism into a force that could not merely compete with anti-imperialism, but perhaps even beat it at its own game.

Contributions

In order to tell this history of the rivalry between different ways of thinking internationalism, I spent nearly a decade working with a wide range of materials. I pored over the newspapers, manifestos, internal bulletins, and political programs of countless organizations housed in over a dozen archives and libraries in five countries. I relied on hundreds of published primary sources in several languages. And I learned much from the work of fellow scholars working in a number of intersecting disciplines.

This book draws on, and aims to contribute to, three fields of inquiry in particular. One is the vast literature on the antiwar movements of the Vietnam War years. The book begins by arguing that antiwar activism was far more than some liberal, single-issue, American campaign to bring the boys home.[32] It leans on Bethany Keenan's research to demonstrate how antiwar activism was a crucial part of political life in countries like France.[33] It continues the work of Niek Pas by drawing attention to those radicals who saw antiwar activism as part of a much larger project of change.[34] It takes a cue from Sabine Rousseau by stretching the timeline of the war in order to make new discoveries about comparatively less studied topics such as refugees, political prisoners, and the Third Indochina War.[35] It develops the findings of historians like Harish C. Mehta to restore the agency of Vietnamese figures in shaping international antiwar activism.[36] And it takes inspiration from scholars like Judy Tzu-Chun Wu to illuminate the ways that political actors made sense of their internationalism.[37] Indeed, this book hopes not only to provide a richer history of how radicals in the North Atlantic related to struggles in Vietnam, but also to use that history to explore how radical activists imagined anti-imperialist internationalism in the 1960s and 1970s.

To study the meaning of anti-imperialism among radicals in the North Atlantic, this book engages with the burgeoning field of the "Global Sixties." Leaning on scholars like Robin D. G. Kelley, it uncovers the forgotten dreams of activists in the North Atlantic.[38] Like Gerd-Rainer Horn it documents how activists turned those dreams into egalitarian innovations.[39] Like Martin Klimke, it emphasizes the interconnected nature of this transformational activism, doing for the United States and France what he did for the USA and West Germany.[40] Like Christoph Kalter, it sheds light on the centrality of the "Third World" to the trajectory of this interconnected anti-imperialist left in the North Atlantic.[41] Like Cynthia A. Young, it dissects the complex processes of adaptation, projection, and translation that characterized the internationalism of those years.[42] And like Kristin Ross, this book not only reconstructs the radical anti-imperialist experiments of the 1960s and 1970s, but also seeks to explain how they were mutilated, distorted, and replaced by competing internationalist projects like human rights.[43]

This book takes special inspiration from figures like Alessandro Russo who insist that we approach the radical emancipatory projects of the "Sixties" on their own terms.[44] Consequently, it argues that the only way to grasp the political significance of anti-imperialist internationalism is to look at its founding assumptions, internal contradictions, and the historical processes that led to its exhaustion. This means explaining not only why anti-imperialism succeeded but also, more importantly, why it failed, and searching for the reasons for that failure within that mode of politics itself. After all, as important as external factors were to anti-imperialism's demise, millions abandoned it because they believed it fell short of its own promises. This book therefore aims to deepen our understanding of anti-imperialism in the "Global Sixties" not only by tracking its rise, consolidation, and transformation but also by offering a sober investigation of its inherent limits, the reasons why people willingly switched their allegiance to other internationalisms, and how internationalist alternatives like human rights capitalized on its failures in the 1970s.

This leads directly to the third major scholarly field: human rights. This book expands on Samuel Moyn's revisionist arguments that human rights were only one way to improve the world, that until recently they were not very popular among activists, and that their surprising successes had a great deal to do with the fate of other internationalisms.[45] It takes to heart Mark Philip Bradley's insights about the diversity of human rights vernaculars to show how a specifically individualist variant of rights discourse began to cohere in the 1960s and 1970s.[46] It confirms Jan Eckel's claim that developments within the left in those years played an important role in the general rise of this individualist conception of human rights.[47] It develops Barbara Keys's work to show how these rights activists found themselves allied with a US government that appropriated this vision of human rights during a crucial moment of imperialist crisis.[48] And it draws on Eleanor Davey's study of radical humanitarianism to show how France served as a crucible for these dramatic shifts in the way people thought about changing the world.[49]

But if Davey's project adopts the vantage point of human rights to explain how "sans-frontiérisme" replaced "Third Worldism" as the major way of "approaching suffering" in the rest of the world, this book offers an interpretation from the other side. After all, radicals did not conceptualize internationalism as addressing "suffering" but instead as collectively organizing international revolution against capitalist imperialism. Anti-imperialists did not even call themselves "Third Worldists," which is what human rights crusaders hostile to anti-imperialism labeled them. Nor did they see their internationalism as so unidirectional. For them, internationalism was not about how they in North America and Western Europe should approach suffering in the rest of the globe, but rather about how radicals everywhere could collaborate to build a new world altogether, with revolutionaries abroad, like

Vietnamese communists, playing leading roles. My book, then, complements Davey's important study by firmly centering the perspective of the anti-imperialists themselves.

The key innovation of this book, then, is to weave together original findings from archival research, new interpretations of published sources, and insights from a number of scholarly fields into a single, granular, coherent, synthetic, and accessible narrative about international antiwar activism in the 1960s and 1970s that explores the transformative competition between the two dominant ways that activists imagined the international goal of making the world a better place. The Overture sets the scene by returning to the early twentieth century to uncover the construction of the Leninist problematic, explain its international appeal, and show how Vietnam came to be perceived as its prime test case. Chapter 1 begins the story proper by tracking the emergence of a radical antiwar international in the 1960s. Chapter 2 explains why so many radicals followed the lead of Vietnamese revolutionaries by embracing Leninist anti-imperialism over other internationalist projects such as human rights. Chapter 3 discusses why radicals turned to revolution in the late 1960s. Chapter 4 demonstrates how in the early 1970s widespread repression prompted radicals to focus on incarceration, reassess civil liberties, and forge alliances with human rights activists. Chapter 5 surveys the collapse of radicalism, the apostasy of former radicals, and the meltdown of anti-imperialist internationalism in the context of the Third Indochina War. Chapter 6 turns to the international campaigns to save refugees in Southeast Asia to explain how the crisis of anti-imperialism created an important opportunity for human rights internationalism to take the lead in the late 1970s. Lastly, the Coda brings the story to the present by reflecting on the meaning of emancipatory internationalist politics in the wake of human rights internationalism's own crisis.

Stakes

Every history is a history of the present. Even when scholars refuse to acknowledge the presence of the present, all historical studies are shaped by the questions, assumptions, personal convictions, and especially the political stakes of their time. This book began with a conviction that this imperialist world order of systemic inequality, exploitation, and domination is intolerable. Its founding assumption is that this world is not necessary, that a better one is possible, and that ordinary people have the capacity to unite across borders, divisions, and differences to build an emancipatory future.

At the same time, it recognizes that we live in an era haunted by the undeniable failures, and in some cases horrific disasters, of previous attempts to radically change the world. For that reason, it argues that any attempt to think emancipatory internationalist politics today depends on our ability to take stock of prior cycles of struggle. For those of us living in the North Atlantic, that means confronting the internationalist campaigns that emerged across North America and Western Europe in concert with anti-imperialist struggles across the globe in the 1960s and 1970s. Those years witnessed the highest concentration of interconnected anti-imperialist struggles in world history, generated an extraordinarily rich laboratory of political invention that raised new questions that continue to preoccupy us, and brought about sweeping changes that have shaped the world we live in today.

Most of all, they marked a turning point when the very political matrix that had made possible this remarkable political experimentation collapsed. In the 1970s, a set of concepts came apart, a general problematic unraveled, a theoretical system disintegrated, a conceptual language decomposed, a revolutionary culture crumbled, and a mode of politics reached its point of saturation. All this allowed human rights to emerge as an alternative that channeled anti-imperialism's universalist aspirations but rejected its commitment to radical political change. If anti-imperialism enabled millions to organize unprecedented struggles for universal emancipation, then human rights refocused attention to the millions who suffered from the botched emancipatory projects of those very anti-imperialists. In this way, human rights succeeded precisely because they made visible, responded to, and took advantage of anti-imperialism's indisputable failures. The collapse of anti-imperialism, particularly its Leninist variant, and the rise of human rights were completely linked.

If thinking emancipatory internationalist politics today depends on explaining why anti-imperialism failed, and if human rights were historically tied to the sequence that led to anti-imperialism's exhaustion, then it is imperative that we understand their complex relationship. The wager of this book, then, is that taking anti-imperialism seriously sheds new light on human rights, and taking human rights seriously tells us a great deal about the appeal, trajectory, contradictions, and failure of anti-imperialism. As it should be clear, this approach does not presuppose neutrality, and still less any desire to somehow get the best of both worlds, but instead is rooted in the belief that taking each side seriously on its own terms is necessary to understanding the internationalist politics that defined the twentieth century. It is only by contending with this history that we can grasp the consequential transformations of the past, make sense of our own moment of crisis, and find ways to act in the turbulent years that lie ahead.

Overture
Lenin's Shadow

After years of traveling the globe, a young Vietnamese man with lustrous eyes and burning ambition hurried through Paris one hot summer day in 1919. As Europe struggled to recover from the devastation of total war, a flock of diplomats was planning a new world order at the Palace of Versailles, transforming the nearby French capital into the center of international attention. Encouraged by US President Woodrow Wilson's public support for the principle of self-determination, Nguyễn Tất Thành, a staunch critic of French colonial rule in Southeast Asia, sensed an opportunity.[1]

Working with other Vietnamese anticolonialists living in France, he drafted a letter to Wilson, urging him to extend the principle of self-determination to the colonized peoples of the world, many of whom had done their part in the war.[2] Eager for "the principle of national self-determination to pass from ideal to reality," they issued a list of demands, which called not for outright independence from France, but for equal treatment.[3] Wilson's senior advisor acknowledged receipt of the letter, but the initiative went nowhere. Despite Wilson's grandiose rhetoric, the United States remained committed to preserving the imperial order, something the incorrigibly optimistic Nguyễn Tất Thành would learn time and again in the years to come.

Undaunted, he stayed in Paris and searched for an alternative.[4] His breakthrough finally came in July 1920, when he discovered V. I. Lenin's recently published "Draft Theses on the National and the Colonial Questions." It came as a revelation:

In those Theses, there were political terms that were difficult to understand. But reading them again and again finally I was able to grasp the essential part. What emotion, enthusiasm, enlightenment and confidence they communicated to me! I wept for joy. Sitting by myself in my room, I would shout as if I were addressing large crowds: "Dear martyr compatriots! This is what we need, this is our path to liberation!"

"Since then," he added, "I had entire confidence in Lenin, in the Third International." Reborn as a Leninist, he dedicated his life to propagating

18

this new anti-imperialist internationalist project, eventually changing his name to Hồ Chí Minh, which means "Bringer of Light."[5]

In the coming years, other Vietnamese anticolonialists would follow in his footsteps by espousing the Leninist problematic as the best way to bring about political change. In 1930, they founded a unified communist party to guide their efforts. To everyone's surprise, the communists would become the leading force in the national liberation struggle, eventually outfoxing their nationalist rivals, overthrowing the old regime, abolishing French colonial rule, and even fighting an internationalized struggle of epochal proportions against the United States. Their successes against these foes would galvanize some of the most vibrant international solidarity campaigns of the era, inspire numerous anti-imperialist movements across the globe, and supercharge the struggles of millions. By the late 1960s, many came to see Vietnam as the vanguard of an international wave of anti-imperialist revolutions. The fate of the imperialist world order seemed to hang in the balance.

Although there were many reasons for this remarkable outcome, Vietnamese communists themselves insisted that Leninism was a decisive factor. It gave them a framework to analyze the present, provided them with a strategy, bound them together into a disciplined party, furnished them with a blueprint for organizing a new polity, and connected them to an internationalist movement that supplied invaluable aid of all kinds. Leninism also came to play a very important role in the radical solidarity movements that took shape across the world to support the Vietnamese revolution. For a moment in the 1960s and 1970s, radicals everywhere saw themselves as part of a universal struggle conceptualized in explicitly Leninist terms. This is not to say that anti-imperialists did not disagree with one another, interpret Leninism in different ways, fuse it with other ideas, or put it to different uses, but that millions of people came to share something like a common language that allowed them to act in a changing world. In this way, Leninism was central to the rise – and fall – of the interconnected anti-imperialist struggles that rocked the globe in those extraordinary years.[6]

For these reasons, to understand the Vietnamese revolution, the radical international solidarity movements of the Vietnam War years, and the very trajectory of anti-imperialist internationalism in the twentieth century, one must take a serious look at Leninism. The following pages therefore survey the Leninist problematic in its internationalist dimensions. They reconstruct how it coalesced in the early twentieth century, explain why Vietnamese revolutionaries came to adopt it, and show how its internal contradictions would create significant challenges for revolutionaries in the decades to come.[7]

Problems

In 1883, commandant Henri Rivière led an expeditionary force to extend French influence beyond its small foothold in the south to the whole of the country we now call Vietnam. Although he fell in battle, Rivière's death created a stir back in Paris. A passionate imperialist, Prime Minister Jules Ferry used the opportunity to demand the conquest of Vietnam in its entirety.

In July of that year, he announced to thunderous applause, "something else is needed for France: that she cannot be merely a free country, that she must also be a great country, exercising all of her rightful influence over the destiny of Europe, that she ought to propagate this influence throughout the world and carry everywhere that she can her language, her customs, her flag, her arms, and her genius."[8] The same liberal Republicans transforming France into a coherent nation through railroads, conscription, secular education, and language standardization enthused over imperial expansion, seeing nation-building at home and imperial conquest abroad as part of the same modernizing process.[9]

A decade later, French forces subdued the Vietnamese resistance, subsumed all of Vietnam, Cambodia, and Laos into a new colonial entity known as "French Indochina," and conquered a dozen new territories across the globe.[10] According to one estimate, between 1880 and 1910, France's overseas empire grew over twelvefold in area, from approximately 350,000 square miles to 4.6 million, and over sixteen times in population, from 3 to 50 million.[11] But the French were by no means alone. Their European rivals also extended their reach, snatching up new colonies and exerting control over nominally independent countries, especially in Latin America. By the first decade of the twentieth century, these European powers, along with Japan and the United States, dominated nearly the entire planet. But since there was only so much of the globe to carve up, the headlong drive for colonies began to heighten antagonisms between the expanding empires. Although they tried to regulate their competition, coordinate the division of the globe, and stave off war, tensions continued to rise.

Hoping to make sense of these bewildering developments, North Americans and Europeans from across the political spectrum turned to the concept of "imperialism." Initially a rough synonym for the kind of state constructed by Napoleon III in France after 1848, the words "impérialisme," "Imperialismus," and "imperialism" assumed a range of new meanings in the late nineteenth century, referring to phenomenon as diverse as military aggression, colonial conquest, formal annexation, protective tariffs, economic dominance, or rivalry between great powers. Despite the concept's ambiguity, "imperialism" quickly became a central topic of conversation, debated by proponents and opponents alike.

Nowhere did this debate play out more vigorously than in the emerging international socialist movement. "Imperialism" became such a burning issue for social democrats and socialists not simply because it named an important global development, nor even because the core parties of the socialist movement operated in the heart of the most rapacious empires, and so felt a particular responsibility to address it, but because the word focused many questions about socialism itself. It pushed social democrats and socialists to better theorize the global conjuncture, further clarify their goals, make more explicit their strategies, and more thoroughly interrogate the declared universalism of their project.

It is no coincidence, for example, that one of the most famous debates in the international socialist movement, the so-called "revisionist debate," played out in part over imperialism.[12] Advocating moderation, steady reform, and legislative campaigning over revolution at home, reformists like Eduard Bernstein supported various forms of imperial domination abroad, openly suggesting that European colonialism helped "savages" and "barbarians" by pushing them along the natural evolutionary path to "higher civilization."[13] By contrast, revolutionaries like Rosa Luxemburg vehemently insisted that socialism meant the abolition of all oppression, including imperialism in all its varieties.

The showdown came in 1900 when the various socialist and social democratic parties that made up the Second International met in Paris. Repudiating Bernstein, delegates acclaimed a resolution from Luxemburg that condemned imperialism, calling on socialists everywhere to organize an internationalist struggle to overthrow it.[14] To do that, the International decided that social democratic and socialist parties had to undertake a serious "study of the colonial question," do everything possible to further the "formation of socialist parties in the colonies," and actively facilitate "relations between the socialist parties of the different colonies."[15] Bernstein and his followers fought back, proposing a procolonialist resolution at the Stuttgart Congress in 1907, but were defeated again. Commenting on the failed efforts of Bernstein's wing, the British socialist Belfort Bax reported that "the Congress resolutely rejected them in favour of an uncompromising, anti-imperialist, anti-colonial counter-resolution."[16]

Through this contested process, socialists across the planet invented a new way to change the world: anti-imperialist internationalism. The emancipation of humanity had to be global, that meant confronting what they were now calling imperialism, and this could only be done by uniting across borders. As Bax put it, "The great practical problem before Social-Democracy at the present moment is the combating of Imperialism in all countries in the interests of International Solidarity."[17] This was much easier said than done. Although anti-imperialist internationalism offered socialists a way to frame the political problem of building an emancipatory future together, it did not offer a concrete solution. To find one, socialists first had to answer some hard questions: Who would change the world? How could imperialism be overthrown? And what was imperialism?

Imperialism

Ironically, when the international socialist movement vowed to combat imperialism in 1900, socialists had yet to define it in any systematic manner. Most people, socialist or otherwise, used the term in inconsistent ways, prompting many contemporaries to complain about its frustrating vagueness. What, exactly, was this imperialism that everyone kept talking about?[18]

It was in this context that a British journalist named John A. Hobson published one of the first full-length studies of imperialism in 1902. According to Hobson, the rapid growth of monopolies in the capitalist countries contracted workers' disposable income. This in turn had led to a fall in consumption, which foreshadowed economic catastrophe at home. In response to this crisis of underconsumption, Hobson claimed, capitalists had begun to search for other investment opportunities, ultimately exporting their surplus capital to the rest of the world, with states acting as the pliable tools of ravenous firms. It was precisely this insatiable search for profits that had led the European powers to divide the planet. For Hobson, then, "imperialism" referred to a specific policy: aggressive actions by one state against another, which often took the form of conquest. But it was a bad policy, he added, because it would exacerbate tensions between competing imperial powers, increasing the likelihood of world war.[19]

Although not the first to do so, Hobson made a strong case for linking imperialism to capitalism, establishing an important line of inquiry that would be taken up most enthusiastically by the Marxist theorists of the international socialist movement, such as Rudolf Hilferding and Rosa Luxemburg.[20] But while most Marxists believed imperialism was connected to capitalism, they disagreed about the exact relationship between the two.[21] These differences had enormous consequences because how one defined imperialism informed one's stance on what to do about it. Nowhere was this clearer than in the controversy that erupted around Karl Kautsky, one of the most respected theorists of the Second International. Kautsky suggested that although capitalism had led to aggressive foreign policies, world war was avoidable. A nonimperialist capitalism was not merely possible but would be better for capitalists themselves since imperialism was so dangerous. Social democratic and socialist parties should therefore work with progressive elements of the bourgeoisie to organize peace campaigns. Capitalists could reform their ways, curb their belligerent policies, and pursue a kind of "ultra-imperialism" without war. In the longer term, he wrote in a 1914 article, the competing imperialists of the world might even come together in a "holy alliance" to peacefully rule the globe.[22]

Kautsky's arguments elicited violent criticism from the left. Luxemburg, Lenin, and others accused Kautsky of promoting class collaboration, which could only lead to ruin. As it happened, just weeks after he penned his article war erupted between the European empires, and the Second International effectively collapsed when its leading parties supported "their" respective national governments instead of uniting in international opposition to war. With his usual vitriol, Lenin drew a direct line between Kautsky's theories and this colossal betrayal. By proposing the possibility of "ultra-imperialism," Lenin charged, Kautsky opened the door to capitulation. As Lenin fumed, the "significance of Kautsky's 'theory' is this: it is a most reactionary method of consoling the masses with hopes of permanent peace being possible under capitalism, by distracting their attention from the sharp antagonisms and acute problems of the present times, and directing it towards illusory prospects of an imaginary 'ultra-imperialism' of the future."[23]

To refute Kautsky's reformism, Lenin attempted to show that imperialism was the inevitable consequence of capitalist development. In his pamphlet, *Imperialism: The Highest Stage of Capitalism*, Lenin drew on both Hobson and Hilferding to argue that since the 1870s, capitalism had entered a distinctly new stage. The concentration of production, the rise of monopolies, the need to export capital, and the influence of financial oligarchies over the state, Lenin argued, pushed individual countries to pursue reckless imperialist policies.[24] Territorial annexation, informal control over independent countries, and rivalries between empires would lead inevitably to war. Imperialism, then, was the unavoidable product of this stage of capitalism, and therefore one that could only be overcome by destroying capitalism as such. Significantly, Lenin's attempt to retheorize imperialism in order to justify the political need for revolution ended up redefining the term itself, shifting its meaning away from a specific policy to a stage of capitalism that made such policy necessary. As Lenin explained in a cryptic formulation, "imperialism is the monopoly stage of capitalism."[25]

As a theoretical text, Lenin's pamphlet was far from faultless. It over-estimated the importance of monopolies, exaggerated the role of capi-tal export as the driver of imperialism, downplayed other noneconomic aspects of imperialism, and tended to reduce the state to a transparent instrument of capitalist monopolies. Explaining the actions of states, and therefore imperialist policy as such, with exclusive reference to the pur-ported needs of capitalism led Lenin into a kind of functionalist economic reductionism. Worst of all, the theory treated capitalist history as a linear sequence of discrete, bounded, homogenous stages. Its claim that capital-ism had reached a "stage" where empires would necessarily always go to war with one another not only was difficult to sustain in theory but also would be challenged by historical events after the Second World War.[26]

That said, Lenin never intended to produce a flawless theory of impe-rialism true for all time; his primary goal was to use the theory to sub-stantiate his political cause of revolution over reformism. In this, he succeeded. Despite its limitations, his work offered a political analysis of recent events that made a strong case for why only revolution could stop imperialism, and, even more importantly, why revolution was a real possibility at that precise moment. Whatever the theoretical merits of their competing approaches, the dramatic events of those years – world war, crisis, mass unrest, and state collapse – only seemed to discredit Kautsky's theory, along with its reformist implications, while confirming Lenin's theory of an inevitable worldwide inter-imperialist conflagration leading to a period of widespread revolutionary struggles.

Self-Determination

The first major debates between socialists over fighting imperialism focused on the massive land empires of Europe. About half the peo-ple living in the Russian Empire, for example, were not native Rus-sian speakers, and many did not identify as Russian at all. Subjected to "Russification," these minorities – such as Armenians, Tajiks, Poles, and Jews – were not only politically dominated by St. Petersburg but also forced to learn Russian, renounce their local customs, and embrace aspects of Russian culture. Perhaps unsurprisingly, socialists in these diverse empires were some of the first to identify this kind of oppres-sion as a central issue. In trying to explain this imperialist violence, they coded these subject populations as "nations," their oppression as "national oppression," and the political problem of their emancipation as the "national question."

While they discussed many possible solutions, a few Marxists, espe-cially those in the borderlands of Russia, argued that the best way to combat "national oppression" was to struggle for "the right of nations to self-determination." Though a vague formula, self-determination soon came to mean the right of oppressed nations to secede from the empire that dominated them to form independent nation-states, if they so desired.[27] Although relatively unpopular, borderlands socialists eventually convinced Bolshevik leaders such as Lenin to embrace a version of the concept.[28] But even then, it was one of many possible solutions, and faced intense opposition, including from socialists in those oppressed nations. Indeed, the most forceful critic was Rosa Luxemburg, a Polish Jew born in the Russian Empire. Beginning in 1908, she wrote a series of blistering articles shredding the core concepts at the foundation of the idea of the right of nations to self-determination.[29]

Luxemburg began by targeting the "nation." She claimed it was a fiction that deliberately obscures irreconcilable divisions within a social formation. One could therefore never speak of a single coherent national will that could determine itself. Instead, one political force would appoint itself as spokesperson for everyone else. In almost all cases, this would not be the toiling masses but the nascent bourgeoisie. Internally, this ruling class would use the language of the nation to dominate other classes, consolidate its power, and reinforce class hierarchies. Externally, it would make the nation an "efficient tool of conquest" against other nations.[30] It was no coincidence, Luxemburg pointed out, that national liberation movements in places like South America had created new states that almost immediately fought each other. If anything, she suggested, the idea of the right of nations to self-determination was a recipe for more conflict: Dividing the existing heterogeneous polities of the world into neatly bounded nations, each with its own territorially coherent state, would be a "completely hopeless" endeavor, leading to resentment, irredentism, and war. For a socialist, the subject of emancipation can never be the "nation."[31]

As for "self-determination," it, too, was fantastical. Winning formal independence amounted to little, she claimed, because larger empires would simply continue to oppress weaker states, if not through overt violence, then through economic pressure. An oppressed nation might win its own flag, language, or government, but would almost certainly remain subordinate to the capitalist market, geopolitical pressures, and foreign imperialist powers.[32] National self-determination was powerless to stop imperialism as such. It might even be harmful to the larger goal of overthrowing imperialism. On the off chance that an oppressed nation succeeded in determining its own fate, how should socialists respond if that nation chose to pursue not socialism, but capitalism? What if that nation's self-determination led to a dictatorship that murdered socialists at home and conquered other people abroad? Would socialists elsewhere still have to respect that nation's right to determine its future?[33]

These questions led to the problem of "rights." Why did Marxists feel obliged to articulate their struggles in the language of "rights," Luxemburg wondered. In her view, their fight against national oppression did not arise from any "special 'right of nations,'" just as their fight for "the social and political equality of sexes does not at all result from any special 'rights of women' which the movement of the bourgeois emancipationists refer to."[34] The duty to combat national oppression, she continued, stems "solely" from a general opposition to "every form of social inequality and social domination, in a word, from the basic position of socialism."[35] Because socialism by definition meant combating all oppression, rights talk was unnecessary. It was also confusing because it implied a single solution, valid in all contexts – a "metaphysical cliché" no different from the "rights of man" and "rights of citizen" peddled by the bourgeoisie.[36] The crude universalism of the "right to self-determination," in other words, would compel socialists to defend national aspirations to statehood anywhere, ignoring the specific historical context, the opposite of what she thought Marxism entailed. In fact, Luxemburg concluded, the language of rights risked undermining the very basis of revolutionary socialism – it could wrongly encourage socialists to seek reforms on terms set by the "existing system" rather than striving for the abolition of the very system itself. Instead of speaking about rights, she argued, socialists should fight for the elimination of every condition of oppression that stirred up talk about rights in the first place.

Not merely were the concepts flawed, she contended, but the very strategy of national self-determination was contrary to the course of history. In Luxemburg's view, capitalism was inevitably moving toward higher levels of global concentration, erasing local economies, unique cultures, and individual nation-states. This unstoppable march was a progressive development, and the socialist movement, which she called the "legitimate child of capitalist development," would simply take over and complete the capitalist tendency toward centralization with an interconnected economy, a single international culture, and the disappearance of individual nations.[37] In this context, the idea of national self-determination, which implied small national units, the illusion of self-contained economies, and the preservation of cultural particularities, stood "in direct contradiction to the tendency of capitalist development," and therefore, "historically speaking," was a "reactionary undertaking."[38] For Luxemburg, the task was not to step backward but to push this natural development along toward socialism.

The most thorough rebuttal of Luxemburg's position came from none other than Lenin. Although initially lukewarm about national self-determination, Lenin became one of its most recognizable international champions during the First World War. He began by arguing that the issue at hand was not cultural, psychological, or economic, but political. Luxemburg's assertion that independent nations were impotent in the face of global capitalism, he wrote, was "just as intelligent as if someone, in discussing the programmatic demand for the supremacy of parliament, i.e., the assembly of people's representatives, in a bourgeois state, were to expound the perfectly correct conviction that big capital dominates in a bourgeois country, whatever the regime in it."[39] In other words, although it is true that capitalist interests would severely limit the power of any representative government, contesting elections nevertheless had important political effects, just as fighting for self-determination did.

One of the most important of these, Lenin continued, was establishing the preconditions for unity between what he was now calling "oppressor nations" and "oppressed nations." By adopting the idea of national self-determination, the workers of an oppressor nation would demonstrate their commitment to equality, eliminate hostility between themselves and the workers of the oppressed nation, and build mutual trust. Granting oppressed nations the right to freely secede was therefore the only way to build a voluntary union. In this, Lenin compared the right of nations to self-determination to the right to divorce. The right to separation did not mean that women should automatically always break their marriages. But it was only by ensuring that they had the right to divorce whenever they wished that marriage could become a voluntary partnership between equals. In the same way, if oppressed nationalities did not have the right to independence, no international union could be considered equal.[40]

The right to self-determination, in other words, was a key political strategy for revolution, especially in peripheral countries like Russia. There, capitalism was less developed, the industrial working class was miniscule, peasants made up the vast majority of the population, legal action was highly restricted, and the Tsar governed one of the most ethnically, linguistically, and religiously diverse countries in Eurasia. Unevenness was the order of the day, which meant that revolution would be highly complex, if not downright contradictory. "Whoever expects a 'pure' social revolution," Lenin later wrote, "will *never* live to see it. Such a person pays lip-service to revolution without understanding what revolution is."[41] In the unique conditions of Russia, socialists had to ally with other forces, forge diverse coalitions, and endorse struggles that might not be overtly socialist.[42] By striking blows against tsarist autocracy, national liberation struggles would play a decisive part in the revolutionary process.

This idea was rooted in Lenin's belief that, before any country could build socialism, it would first have to complete what he called a "bourgeois-democratic revolution," which would lead to a constitution, national assembly, territorial unification, agrarian reform, and a domestic market – in short, a coherent nation-state.[43] Although achieved in most of North America and Western Europe, this process was only beginning to unfold in the rest of the world. "In Eastern Europe and Asia the period of bourgeois-democratic revolutions did not begin until 1905. The revolutions in Russia, Persia, Turkey and China, the Balkan wars – such is the chain of world events of *our* period in our 'Orient,'" Lenin explained. "It is precisely and solely because Russia and the neighbouring countries are passing through this period that we must have a clause in our programme on the right of nations to self-determination."[44] The right of nations to self-determination, then, named the historically specific kind of revolution that these countries first had to pass through before attempting the fight for socialism proper. In this way, Lenin counterposed his own philosophy of history to Luxemburg's. While Luxemburg believed that capitalist development would force individual nations to gradually disappear into more homogenous imperial units, Lenin maintained that capitalism would actually lead to the rapid disintegration of those massive empires into many new nations. In his view, "independent national states" did not inhibit capitalism, but ensured the "best conditions" for its development.[45] Fighting for the right of nations to self-determination, therefore, was to swim with the tide of history.

While both approaches certainly had their flaws, Lenin's possessed several clear political advantages over Luxemburg's. He addressed the unevenness of capitalist development, reframed the debate in strategic terms, and opened the space for building political unity. In this, he centered the agency of colonized peoples, a weakness of Luxemburg's position. While some of her criticisms of self-determination were quite prescient, her philosophy of history lacked a satisfactory political alternative. Effectively tabling the issue, she maintained that "Socialism alone" could solve the problem of national oppression.[46] As for what to do until then, Luxemburg never proposed a coherent plan. Sometimes she intimated that independence was futile. At times she seemed to suggest that only a proletarian revolution in the capitalist core could liberate oppressed nations. In still other cases, she argued that imperialism could be brought down by uniting the proletariat of all countries, but this left one wondering about Asia, Africa, or Latin America where the industrial proletariat often composed only a small percentage of the population.

By contrast, one of Lenin's greatest strengths was that he deliberately enlarged the debate beyond Europe to the entire world. During the First World War, Lenin combined the "national question" with the "colonial question," recasting all imperialist powers as "oppressor nations," the people who suffered from imperialism as "oppressed nations," and imperialist domination as "national oppression." The global antagonism between oppressor and oppressed nations, he wrote, was the *"essence* of imperialism."[47] In this way, he came to define imperialism as both "the progressively mounting oppression of the nations of the world by a handful of Great Powers" *and* "a period of wars between the latter to extend and consolidate the oppression of nations." For this reason, he argued, "the focal point in the Social-Democratic programme must be that division of nations into oppressor and oppressed."[48]

This approach allowed Lenin to redefine revolution as the coordination of multiple struggles across the globe. As he explained, "socialist revolution is not a single act, it is not one single battle on one front," but a "whole epoch" of "battles on all fronts," on all terrains, everywhere, across the world, that could be concentrated into a united force.[49] Even if they were not purely socialist, Lenin argued, national liberation movements were *"progressive* and *revolutionary,"* and therefore formed an integral part of this global process.[50] Lenin's insistence on self-determination, then, gave anti-imperialist internationalism real bite. Instead of waiting until proletarians in the imperial metropole freed them, which is what many socialists effectively advised, colonized peoples could have a decisive hand in making world socialism.

Here, again, Lenin's uncanny ability to capture the moment tipped the scales in his favor.[51] As Lenin predicted, the First World War would unleash a wave of national liberation movements that shook the old imperial order. In Europe, four empires collapsed overnight, giving rise to a host of new nations and redrawing the map of the continent. Outside Europe, millions of oppressed people in places like Egypt, China, India, Korea, Persia, and Vietnam clamored for change, in some cases through force of arms. In this period of cataclysmic crisis, with liberation movements on the rise, Lenin's vision could not help but resonate.

Internationalism

The Bolsheviks never believed they could independently build socialism in a "backwards" country like Russia. Lenin, however, gambled that prematurely taking power might inspire socialist revolutions in the more developed capitalist heartlands, and that these more powerful revolutionary forces could in turn aid the Bolsheviks in constructing socialism. Together, revolutionaries everywhere could make the long transition to full communism: an imagined world of peace, freedom, and equality beyond all oppression, exploitation, and domination. For Lenin, then, revolution at home had to be conceptualized within a fully internationalist framework. Its very fate depended on internationalism.

Despite strong objections from his comrades, Lenin exhorted the party to make preparations for insurrection. Against the odds, in October 1917 the Bolsheviks shocked the world by seizing control of the largest land empire on the planet. With the October Revolution, the abstract debates of the socialist movement suddenly became the basis of actionable policies in the first explicitly socialist government in history. Immediately after the storming of the Winter Palace, Lenin issued the Decree on Peace, which called for peace without annexations, an end to secret diplomacy, and the equality of all nations.[52] It was the first time any government had made national self-determination the center of its foreign policy, and the Bolsheviks made clear they wanted nothing less than to break the logic of imperialism itself.

The capitalist empires raced to contain the menace. For President Wilson, the best tactic was to co-opt the idea of self-determination for a different project. Whereas Lenin extended the idea to the colonies, Wilson focused on Europe. Whereas Lenin demanded the immediate liberation of the colonies, Wilson advocated the gradual emancipation of subject peoples through the tutelage of allegedly more civilized empires. And whereas Lenin saw self-determination as part of a mass, internationalist, revolutionary struggle against imperialism, Wilson limited it to an elitist League of Nations bent on preserving imperial rule.[53]

Although the Bolshevik position was more radical, it was Wilson who initially captured global attention. While the Bolsheviks found themselves barred from the peace talks at Versailles, unrecognized by the great powers, and locked in a civil war inflamed by the capitalist empires, the United States emerged from the First World War stronger than ever. Wilson projected confidence, and a sophisticated propaganda machine popularized his message internationally, leading many to believe that he had not only the will but also the capacity to realize his promises. To many observers, the world was being remade not in Moscow but Versailles, and it was not Lenin but Wilson who had the combination of vision, influence, and political capital to help the colonized.[54]

Although they looked to the United States, anticolonial activists like the young Hồ Chí Minh did not wait passively for Wilson to free them. They tried to make the most of the moment by projecting an expanded conception of self-determination back onto the US president. Wilson found himself bombarded by messages from anticolonial figures imploring him to make self-determination a reality. But to their chagrin, Wilson retreated, and Britain and France used his counterrevolutionary vision to expand their imperial rule to unprecedented levels. In the end, the "Wilsonian moment" created a world even more imperialist than before the war.[55] This betrayal radicalized activists like Hồ, who would turn instead to the Bolsheviks.[56]

For their part, the Bolsheviks welcomed these new radicals with open arms. Aiming to separate themselves from the old socialist movement, regroup these new revolutionary forces, and organize the struggle for world communism, the Bolsheviks created the Communist International (Comintern). In the summer of 1920, over 200 delegates met in Moscow to formalize its operations. One of the most pressing tasks was to determine the Comintern's official line on the international struggle against imperialism. Given his stature, Lenin prepared a text for discussion, the famous "Draft Theses on the National and the Colonial Questions." He laid out the specific tasks of anti-imperialist internationalism through a comparison with the imperialist internationalism of the League of Nations. Just as inequality could not be resolved through abstract declarations about the formal "equality of individuals" under the law but only by abolishing the capitalist conditions that necessarily created inequality between classes, Lenin argued, so too could imperialism not be overcome through abstract declarations about the formal "equality of nations" but only by overthrowing the imperialist system that created national oppression in the first place.

Like most Marxists, Lenin believed that the only subject who could lead the struggle against this system was the proletariat, and since this imperialist system was fully global, anti-imperialism necessitated the international union of proletarians in all nations. One of the major problems, however, was that the colonies and "semicolonies" – those countries not formally colonized but still subject to imperialist domination – often lacked robust states, developed capitalist relations, and a sizeable proletariat, the alleged bearer of the emancipatory project. For that reason, Lenin argued, anti-imperialist revolution would have to look different in the colonies and semicolonies. There, the communist parties would have to unite the miniscule proletariat with the peasantry, petty bourgeoisie, and even the nationalist bourgeoisie in a vast struggle for national self-determination. While communists would have to maintain their autonomy, advance a communist perspective, and combat competing internationalisms such as Pan-Islamism, Lenin assumed that this first phase could not be socialist. Only after the successful realization of national liberation, and with it the completion of the fundamental tasks of the "bourgeois-democratic" revolution, could the communist party build a properly socialist system, the precondition for the transition to communism.[57]

Although his draft was favorably received, a few delegates, in particular the Indian Marxist M. N. Roy, insisted on several revisions. Roy convinced the Comintern to treat national liberation movements as equal to revolutionary movements in the imperialist metropoles. He also doubted that national bourgeoisies could be trusted, leading the Comintern to a compromise: While communists should oppose the "reformist," or what was now called the "bourgeois-democratic," wing of the bourgeoisie, they should support the "revolutionary," or the "national-revolutionary," wing. And he pressured Lenin to consider the possibility that revolutions in these "backwards" countries could bypass capitalism. Lenin conceded, explaining that "the Communist International should advance the proposition, with the appropriate theoretical grounding, that the backwards countries, aided by the proletariat of the advanced countries, can go over to the soviet system and, through certain stages of development, to communism, without having to pass through the capitalist stage."[58] But this depended entirely on certain conditions. If met, then national liberation movements could transform into almost continual revolutions; if not, then revolutionaries would have to adhere to the two-stage model, one in which, Roy himself clarified, the "revolution in the colonies will not be a communist revolution in its first stages."[59]

While the colonized would lead the liberation struggle, it was the duty of every militant in the imperialist core to assist.[60] In sharp contrast to the half-hearted solidarity of the Second International, Lenin commanded that any party wishing to join the Comintern would have to "ruthlessly expose the colonial machinations of the imperialists of its 'own' country," and had to "support – in deed, not merely in word – every colonial liberation movement, demand the expulsion of its compatriot imperialists from the colonies, inculcate in the hearts of the workers of its own country an attitude of true brotherhood with the working population of the colonies and the oppressed nations, and conduct systematic agitation among the armed forces against all oppression of the colonial peoples."[61] The anti-imperialist struggles in the colonies, semicolonies, and imperialist metropoles were parts of a much larger revolutionary process. All sides were expected to subordinate themselves to the interests of the worldwide communist revolution. Every struggle had to fight for the liberation not only of its own people but also of the entire world, and every successful revolution had a duty to use the resources of its new state to assist others. The whole was more important than the parts. This was called "proletarian internationalism."

It is not difficult to see why this way of thinking internationalism would have such wide appeal. It was certainly enough to win over Hồ Chí Minh, who in 1923 traveled to the newly formed Union of Soviet Socialist Republics (USSR), studied Lenin's ideas in Moscow, participated in Comintern meetings, and was tasked with building this new anti-imperialist international in Asia. That said, much about this internationalist vision remained vague. It was unclear, for example, how the two stages related to one

another, eventually leading to sharp interpretive disputes between Maoists, who would insist on two discrete stages, and Trotskyists, who would
demand a single continuous revolutionary process. It was also unclear how
exactly the proletariat figured in this approach to internationalism. After all,
the proletariat was so tiny in most of these colonies and semicolonies that
"proletarian internationalism" could not really be about the unity of proletarians across borders, but rather the alliance of party intellectuals claiming
to have adopted the viewpoint of a class that barely existed according to
their own criteria. Instead of an internationalism of proletarians, this was
an internationalism of parties.

Then there was the vexing problem of the nation. Although the Comintern claimed that the ultimate goal was to create an egalitarian future free
of all national borders, indeed of all nations themselves, the means to
achieving this end was an internationalist struggle that was still framed
around the centrality of the nation. Communist parties tended to be
national parties. Their struggles unfolded within the parameters set by
national borders. And their immediate task was to win national independence, construct socialism within the boundaries of the nation, use their
new national state to assist other movements, and unite these socialist
national states into federations that could lay the groundwork for complete unity in the distant future. This, then, was a kind of "nationalist"
internationalism in which the constituent units were nations.[62]

Although emphasizing the "inter-national" aspect of internationalism certainly had its advantages, it raised just as many questions. How
can one be certain that the fight for national liberation will connect to
the larger project of building world communism? What is to stop newly
independent nations from pursuing their own national interests against
internationalism? And, perhaps most urgently, what even is a nation?

Nationalism

The rise of nationalism in the late nineteenth century troubled many
socialists. In 1907, Otto Bauer offered one of the first Marxist interpretations.[63] Prioritizing consciousness, he defined the nation as a "community of character."[64] The political corollary to this culturalist approach
was "cultural national autonomy," the proposition that all members of
a nation should participate in the state, as a coherent nation, regardless
of where they lived.

Whatever the merits of Bauer's approach, Lenin believed it ceded
too much. In his view, nationalism had a dual character. On the one
hand, he recognized its appeal, valued its strategic importance, and even
admired its emancipatory content. On the other, he felt that nationalism

could easily slide into a divisive essentialism that would undermine the internationalist struggle for an egalitarian future. Marxists, then, had to play a delicate balancing act: channeling nationalism's potential for universal liberation without giving in to its potential for fragmentation. If Luxemburg made the mistake of dismissing nationalism outright, Lenin thought Bauer bent the stick too far the other way. "As regards to nationalism," Lenin wrote to Maxim Gorky in 1913, "we have to bear down harder." Thankfully, Lenin added, he had a "wonderful Georgian" working on the problem.[65]

In need of allies, Lenin had turned to a Georgian Bolshevik named Iosif Djugashvili who spoke Russian with a heavy accent and wrote in his native language until he was twenty-eight. Promoted as the party's expert on nationalities, Djugashvili published his first major work, *The National Question and Social Democracy*, in 1913.[66] Instead of checking nationalism, Djugashvili argued, Bauer's proposal would only deepen people's identification with an imagined nation, inciting them to disaggregate unified parties into smaller national organizations. In fact, at that very moment, the Jewish Bund was drawing on Bauer's work to not only seek formal recognition as the sole representative of Jewish workers everywhere, but also demand that the Bolsheviks federalize the party. Djugashvili countered this challenge by developing a new theory of the nation: "A nation is a historically constituted, stable community of people, formed on the basis of a common language, territory, economic life, and psychological make-up manifested in a common culture."[67] Defining the nation in this way allowed him to counter the Bund's demands. Since Jews possessed no contiguous territory of their own, they were not a nation, and since they were not a nation, they could not have their own national organization within the larger movement.

While the pamphlet helped win a political struggle, it introduced new problems. On the one hand, Djugashvili rejected racist, idealist, and naturalist approaches, viewing the nation as a historical construct.[68] Far from some ancient essence, the nation was a recent invention made possible by sweeping transformations such as industrialization, migration, and the fissuring of empires. On the other hand, his opposition to the culturalist conception led him to flirt with positivism. His rigid definition of the nation took the form of an enumeration of attributes that could be empirically measured, which seemed to naturalize the nation as an objective substance. This would have grave consequences: Although his definition was intended to play a short-term tactical function in a polemical text, the pamphlet's popularity eventually turned it into the standard take, helping to cement a positivist way of seeing the nation. It is also worth noting that it simultaneously solidified the author's own

identity – the pamphlet's success helped convince Djugashvili to commit
to the Slavic pseudonym he happened to write it under: Stalin.[69]

Leon Trotsky, who despised the author but praised the pamphlet,
later alleged that it was actually Lenin's work.[70] While there is no evidence to prove this claim, Lenin did discuss the ideas with Stalin, and
seemed to approve of his lieutenant's approach to the "national question." Their partnership on this issue only deepened after the October
Revolution in 1917. Civil war, imperialist encirclement, and the collapse
of the Austro-Hungarian Empire terrified the new leaders. The Bolsheviks had to formulate a coherent policy to contain the fires of nationalism raging within a crumbling empire.[71] Lenin again took the lead,
with substantial aid from Stalin, resident maven, commissar of nationality affairs, and soon to be general secretary of the party. While the two
had their disagreements, they together decided – against opposition from
within their own party – that the best way to confront nationalism was to
preempt it by promoting a massive state-centric project of non-Russian
nation-building.[72]

According to historian Terry Martin, Lenin and Stalin aimed to accomplish several goals. First, they reasoned that granting minorities forms of
nationhood would unmask nationalist movements, sharpen papered-over
class differences, and allow the Bolsheviks to win over the lower classes
of minority nations to the cause of communism. Second, they assumed
that nationalism was a necessary stage in the historical development of
peoples, and so an accelerated program of nation-building would mod-
ernize the country as a whole. Third, believing that non-Russian nationalism was a justifiable reaction to Great Russian chauvinism, they argued
that championing nationhood among minorities would be the best way
to defuse defensive local nationalism. Lastly, they hoped that such a
generous approach to the nationalities question might win the support
of other oppressed nations outside the former Russian Empire. To be
sure, as communists, Lenin and Stalin aimed to ultimately transcend the
nation, but they wagered that the way to do that was to use the state to
promote nation-building.[73]

In 1923, the year before Lenin's death, the Bolsheviks confirmed
the policy. They divided the newly formed Soviet Union into national
republics, and each republic into many smaller national regions, territories, and districts. Under the rubric of "korenizatsiia," or "indigenization," the state fostered national identities by creating bounded national
territories, constructing national administrations, promoting national
elites, and encouraging national culture through the celebration of local
dress, food, folklore, and language. In some cases, the Bolsheviks fashioned national identities where none had existed before, creating written

alphabets, inventing traditions, and grouping diverse peoples into new categories. The state went even further by giving these non-Russian nationalities preferential treatment in the largest affirmative action program in history. While the Bolsheviks instructed Russians to learn other languages, seized their territory, and stigmatized chauvinist aspects of their culture, they promoted non-Russians to the highest levels of the state.[74]

This ambitious project helped channel nationalist demands, stabilize the Soviet state, train loyal cadres, and prove to anticolonialists across the world that the USSR was serious about finding concrete answers to national oppression. The developments impressed Hồ Chí Minh, who was living in the USSR at the time. "Lenin's solution of the very complex question of nationalities in Soviet Russia is an excellent propaganda weapon for the colonies," he wrote.[75] Despite these accomplishments, Lenin's approach had its drawbacks, perhaps the most important of which was the further naturalization of the nation. Linking nationality to the administration of a specific territory nationalized political life. Relocating minorities into national territories led to segregation.[76] Discouraging voluntary assimilation engendered closed communities. Recasting invented rituals as ancient traditions encouraged minorities to see nations as prehistoric forces. Dispatching thousands of ethnographer-consultants armed with the census and the map ethnicized the nation.[77] And including nationality in internal documents convinced many that nationality was inherited biologically. As a result, people came to see nationality as one of the most defining attributes of their subjectivity. Those who once defined themselves in terms of clan, religion, birthplace, profession, or language increasingly saw themselves as members of some objective nation. Instead of a fabricated historical category, the nation became a kind of primordial ethnic identity.[78]

This process was made possible by an extreme statism. Initially, Lenin believed that the soviets, red guards, committees, and factory councils created during the revolution were new forms of counterpower that would encircle the existing state, erode its apparatuses, farm off its functions, and prepare the ground to "smash" the old state altogether. In its place, the Bolsheviks would construct a kind of "nonstate" state rooted in this vast constellation of extraparliamentary self-activity, the so-called "dictatorship of the proletariat," which would build socialism and oversee the transition to the new world. After completing its tasks, it would disappear.[79] But, after seizing power, the Bolsheviks found themselves confronted with a series of monumental existential challenges – famine, disease, civil war, economic collapse, and imperialist intervention – that they were not prepared to tackle. They decided that the only way to survive this state of emergency was to transform their party into a governing body with expansive authoritarian powers. This new "party-state" curtailed civil liberties, narrowed the space for democratic activity, and reactivated the bureaucracy of the old empire. Instead of helping these autonomous mass organizations create the new world from below, the party-state assumed primary responsibility for constructing communism from above. Just as the nation did not dissolve but grew even more real, the dictatorship of the proletariat became a full-blown state in its own right, more expansive than anything that had come before.

The system that the Bolsheviks crafted eludes neat categorization. If one defines the "nation-state" as a kind of polity in which a single nation and a single state are meant to coincide as perfectly as possible, then the USSR was not a nation-state. But by fusing a deeply substantialist nationalism with a thoroughly expansive statism, the USSR can be understood as a species of "nationalism-statism." This became even more apparent in the late 1920s with the turn to what was called "socialism in one country." When it became clear that the revolutions in capitalist Europe had ended in defeat, and that the USSR was isolated, encircled, and deprived of the internationalist assistance that Lenin once thought necessary for making socialism, communists like Stalin argued that the Soviet Union should simply make socialism on its own.[80] Although still interested in international struggles, and insistent that the transition to full communism could never succeed without revolutionary victories in other countries, Soviet leaders increasingly saw the defense, development, and modernization of the USSR as the basis for overthrowing imperialism, surpassing capitalism, and creating an egalitarian future. As a result, Stalin came to place an inordinate emphasis on hard work, self-reliance, national pride, state defense, and economic development.[81] And while he eventually abandoned some of the "indigenization" policies of the 1920s, Stalin continued to deepen the "nationalism-statism" of the USSR through such measures as adding nationality to all internal passports and fashioning a kind of patriotic Soviet national culture.[82] In the end, internationalist revolution became even more closely identified with national-statist development.[83]

Leninism

In January 1924, the ailing leader of the Soviet Union succumbed to a final stroke. Tens of thousands of people braved freezing temperatures to pay their respects. "Lenin lives on in our deeds," a frostbitten and grief-stricken Hồ Chí Minh wrote from Moscow. "He is immortal."[84] Against Lenin's wishes, the Bolshevik leadership embalmed his body, preserving it for permanent public display. At the same time that they consecrated his corpse into a holy object, they stitched his scattered ideas into a holistic system.[85] Over the next decade, Bolshevik theorists invented "Leninism" by formally synthesizing Lenin's short, fragmentary, polemical interventions – each of which had unique stakes, responded to distinct conjunctural debates, and followed discontinuous timelines – into a problematic that could guide the communist movement for years to come. As Stalin, one of the most important figures in this process, famously explained, "Leninism is Marxism in the era of imperialism and proletarian revolution."[86] Leninism, in other words, was more than just a response to "peculiar" Russian conditions. It was by definition a universally applicable anti-imperialism. In fact, Stalin argued, it was the only mode of truly revolutionary, internationalist, anti-imperialist politics possible in the present imperialist era.

Although presented as a premeditated, coherent, general strategy true for all cases, the Bolsheviks constructed this problematic by assembling the jagged pieces left over from a series of heated political debates rooted in the specific conjuncture of the early twentieth century. These fragments were never meant to act as comprehensive disquisitions on the world. Take Lenin's thinking on imperialism. As its subtitle made clear, his text was a "popular outline," a hastily written pamphlet designed to intervene in a political debate. Lenin himself acknowledged its partial and one-sided nature, implying that it should not be read as an exhaustive analysis of imperialism.[87] Yet by the 1920s, it would be codified as not only a general theory of imperialism, but also *the* orthodox Marxist theory of imperialism for the international communist movement. Or consider Lenin's thinking on self-determination, which emerged as a strategic response to a political problem in the context of a decomposing multinational empire, with Lenin himself refusing to treat it as a metaphysical principle. Its solidification as the dominant response to imperialism was purely contingent, only achieving hegemony after the surprise of the October Revolution. Much the same can be said about Lenin's thinking on the nation, which stemmed not from abstract rumination but concrete political challenges such as protecting the coherency of the party, building internationalist unity, channeling the universalist ambitions of liberation struggles, or preserving the multinational Soviet Union. But like his other ideas, this instrumentalist approach to defining the nation was soon codified as the only possible way to conceptualize it.

The positions that came to be the Leninist problematic were not simply contingent inventions; they were never the only way to do anti-imperialism. Just as there were different ways to theorize imperialism, ones that did not see states as mere instruments, treat imperialism as an automatic reflex of capitalism, or construct philosophies of history that occluded the possible cooperation between imperialist powers, so too were there different ways to imagine the struggle against imperialism, ones that did not force this complex reality through the conceptual grid of the "nation," classify the dominating imperial powers as "oppressor nations" and the dominated peoples as "oppressed nations," or rely on the language of national rights. After all, many of those suffering from imperialism did not see themselves as nations at all and used other concepts to construct their subjectivity. But the Leninist approach imposed a straitjacket on the messy process of subjectivation, classifying subjects as nations, often in a language that treated them as objective substances, rather than historical inventions. In this way, it encouraged the oppressed to interpret imperialist violence as "national oppression," rather than something else; see themselves as "oppressed nations" that had always existed, instead of some other kind of subject; define their resistance to imperialism as "national liberation," as opposed to framing their struggle beyond nationalist terms; and set their goal as winning independent nation-states, as opposed to some other political configuration. Anti-imperialism, in other words, did not necessarily have to be conjugated with the idea of national liberation.

The Leninist problematic was not just one of many possible ways to practice anti-imperialism; it was not even necessarily the best. It tended to calcify the party, reduce imperialism to capitalism, glorify a strong interventionist state, naturalize the nation as a primordial entity, objectify classes as fixed social categories, root internationalism in nationalist units, tolerate questionable political alliances with nationalists who pursued different aims, and universalize as a fundamental right what was in fact a contingent strategy. Most of all, there lay a profound contradiction at the very heart of the problematic: Its ambition was to build an emancipatory future by transcending such categories as class, state, work, party, and nation, but it proposed to do so by radicalizing these very categories. The goal was to abolish the state, but the way to do that was to erect a special governing body that took over state functions. The goal was to abolish work, but the way to do that was to encourage everyone to work harder. The goal was to abolish party politics, but the way to do that was to merge the vanguard party into the state. The goal was to abolish classes, but the way to do that was to think in class terms, lionize the working class, and evaluate all political change according to class criteria. The goal was to abolish nations, but the way to do that was to hypostatize nations, win national independence, and build strong nation-states. Far from an anomaly, the seemingly paradoxical coupling of nationalism with communism was built into the problematic.[88]

For Leninism, then, the only way out of this world was through its categories, and not just through them, but by doubling down on them.[89]

All that said, there were legitimate reasons why this problematic became so successful. It named an enemy, validated a real desire for freedom, popularized a language of political change, presented a plan for winning liberation from imperial domination, promoted the agency of oppressed peoples in their own emancipation, provided a convincing way to build internationalism, offered an interpretation of history that could explain current events, and projected an electrifying vision of the future. At a time when a handful of imperialist powers controlled the destinies of millions, the old order was becoming intolerable, and people everywhere were searching for some way out, these strengths made the Leninist problematic exceedingly attractive.

Lenin in Vietnam

In February 1927, 174 delegates gathered in Brussels for the founding congress of the League against Imperialism.[90] Organized by Leninists affiliated with the Comintern, the event crystalized a number of overlapping anti-imperialist networks, drawing together organizations as distinct as the Chinese Nationalist Party, the Indian National Congress, the African National Congress, the North African Star, and the Committee for the Defense of the Negro Race. Few of the delegates were dedicated communists, and in fact most drew on a wide range of competing anti-imperialist models.[91] Nevertheless, they saw real value in the Leninist problematic, the Comintern's efforts, and the Soviet Union more broadly.[92]

Although the USSR sometimes elevated its own interests over its internationalist commitments, making deals with capitalist powers, invading neighbors, and even allying with reactionary regimes at the expense of liberation movements, many anti-imperialists felt that the Bolsheviks had done more to combat imperialism than any other governing party in the world.[93] Their comparatively progressive nationalities policies, intransigent opposition to the imperialist powers, and enviable successes in repelling foreign intervention in order to pursue an independent path turned the Soviet Union into a kind of anti-imperialist prototype.

In addition to inspiring liberation movements, influencing their strategies, and supplying them with a model, the Bolsheviks went a step further by concretely aiding them. The Bolsheviks sponsored conferences, funded organizations, sent advisors abroad, and trained generations of anti-imperialists in Soviet institutions. Jawaharlal Nehru, a member of the League's executive committee, traveled to the Soviet Union.

Albert Nzula of South Africa, Jomo Kenyatta of Kenya, Harry Haywood of the United States, Liu Shaoqi of China, and many others studied in Moscow. And a few of these alums went on to work for the Comintern as professional revolutionaries. Hồ Chí Minh, for example, was sent to southern China to teach Vietnamese radicals there how to build a future communist party in Vietnam.

Even anticommunist nationalists in Asia, Africa, and Latin America found Leninism valuable. Chiang Kai-shek, for example, was inspired by the October Revolution, read Marxist publications, toured the USSR, accepted Soviet aid, and collaborated with Comintern agents to reorganize the Nationalist Party along Leninist lines. Of course, he opposed the communists in his own country and had no intention of building world communism. He simply wanted to use Leninism, the communists, and the USSR for his own ends. Indeed, anticolonial nationalists often took what they found useful from the communists and adapted it for different contexts, sometimes for opposing aims. If the Soviets harbored ulterior motives, manipulated nationalist forces, or prioritized their own interests, so too did many noncommunist nationalists.[94] In fact, just a few months after the congress, Chiang Kai-shek massacred the communists in China. Hồ Chí Minh barely escaped with his life, fled to Moscow, and then returned to Europe, where he made contact with organizers affiliated with the League against Imperialism.[95]

Despite sharing some similar objectives, borrowing elements from the same model, and collaborating at times, anticolonialists competed bitterly. Every region of the globe witnessed the rise of not one but several anticolonial currents in the 1920s and 1930s, with each struggling to achieve hegemony over the national liberation struggle as a whole.[96] Although the USSR was a source of inspiration, and Leninist ideas were quite popular, communists rarely came out on top in Asia, Africa, and Latin America. In most cases, organized communist parties were simply outclassed by larger nationalist formations such as the Chinese Nationalist Party, Indian National Congress, or Indonesian National Party.

This was also true in Vietnam. The country boasted a rich tradition of dissent, a crowded anticolonial field, and a rising Nationalist Party.[97] By contrast, communism arrived relatively late, individual communists bickered amongst themselves, and a unified party only saw the light of day in 1930. But in that decade a wave of unrest shook Vietnam, taking many anticolonialists by surprise. As it happened, the Indochinese Communist Party (ICP) managed to weather the storm better than its competitors, like the Nationalist Party, which was virtually annihilated by French repression. As historian Pierre Asselin writes, the chaos of these years was "a boon for the ICP, which thereafter dominated the nationalist movement in Vietnam, and for its ideology, Marxism-Leninism, which became the driving force behind Vietnamese anticolonialism and the default creed of patriots hoping to make a difference."[98] Vietnam became something of a historical exception. Unlike many other colonies, where a noncommunist mass nationalist party came to dominate the national liberation struggle, in Vietnam avowed Leninists distinguished themselves in a highly fractured anticolonial field.[99]

Of course, Leninists were themselves far from unified. Many rank-and-file activists were not fluent in Leninism. Those communists who were constantly fought with one another, and their disputes sometimes ended in sectarian warfare, as with the rivalry between the Trotskyists and the ICP. The ICP itself was a site of vicious disagreements. Party leaders offered competing interpretations of Leninism, debated how to adapt it to Vietnamese conditions, and constantly revised their ideas. No position was absolute, the party line went through many twists and turns, and even a figure as central as Hồ Chí Minh could find himself on the defensive, with some of his comrades denouncing him for being insufficiently Leninist. But, at the end of the day, all these leaders thought in Leninist terms, developed their actions with reference to the Leninist problematic, made their course corrections within the framework of Leninism, and publicly affirmed their fidelity to Lenin's thought.[100] Despite these undeniable fissures, Hồ and his comrades were "true Leninists," concludes historian Alec Holcombe.[101]

But the Vietnamese figures who led the revolution were more than just faithful followers of Lenin. They saw themselves as making new contributions to Leninist politics, and they treated Vietnam as a kind of laboratory for Leninism. What is more, they were convinced that the experiment was yielding some promising results. As Hồ attested, the communists have "recorded big results in the creative application of Marxism-Leninism to Vietnamese conditions."[102] The Leninist problematic, they argued, had allowed communists to build a revolutionary force that outmaneuvered their competitors, resisted colonial repression, and fought the Japanese occupation of French Indochina during the Second World War. It was what allowed them to seize control of the postwar tumult, declare independence, and establish the Democratic Republic of Vietnam in 1945. It was what allowed them to organize social life, crush nationalist competitors, and lead a massive struggle against France's bid to recolonize Vietnam with American aid in the 1950s. And it was what allowed them to smash France at Điện Biên Phủ in 1954. These were feats that few liberation movements could match.

To be sure, as scholars have recently argued, communist victory was by no means smooth, inevitable, uncontested, or complete.[103] Even after winning independence in 1954, communists governed only the North, faced stiff internal resistance, and still had to contend with other nationalist forces in the country as a whole. As for their successes, these were the result of many factors, quite a few of which were outside their control and had little to do with Leninist ideas. Nevertheless, it is undeniable that Leninism played a crucial role in building a cohesive, dedicated, popular, and well-supplied revolutionary force that could take advantage of the unexpected opportunities of the time.[104] It is possible, and in fact necessary, to acknowledge the messiness, contingency, and competition that defined the situation in Vietnam while simultaneously accepting the centrality of Leninism in the mental universe of the revolutionaries who played such an important role in shaping this history.

Vietnamese communists believed that, while there were certainly many reasons for their victories, Leninism was one of the most significant factors, if not the most decisive one. As Hồ declared during the fight against France, "We triumph at the present time, we shall triumph in the future, because our path is enlightened by the great Marxist-Leninist doctrine."[105] Even if declarations like these were exaggerations, they confirm the general importance of Leninism to the identity of Vietnamese communists, reveal how communists often sought to create the impression that Leninism was essential to their success, and help explain why so many people, inside and outside the country, would come to see Vietnam as a Leninist proving ground.

Leninist Contradictions

But if Vietnam was to be a test case, as Vietnamese communists contended, the preliminary results were not entirely positive. Even if one were to evaluate the experiment solely on Leninist terms, there were signs of trouble. If anything, the complex reality in Vietnam revealed the fundamental contradictions of the problematic that Vietnamese communists claimed to have adopted as their guide to emancipation.

The communists fought for freedom but repressed individual liberties. They encouraged mass democratic activity but elevated the party-state as the source of all politics.[106] They made concrete efforts to abolish class society but did so by accentuating invented class identities. In their land reform campaign of the 1950s, for example, they sought to identify "class enemies" by using Leninist theory to divide Vietnamese society into class categories. When it became clear that these abstract categories did not apply to Vietnam's distinct social landscape, communists reclassified poor farmers as big landlords to shoehorn reality into their dogmatic schema. The widespread "misclassification" of Vietnamese led to the deaths of innocent peasants, the repression of devoted revolutionaries, and the purge of party activists who protested the campaign. While land reform destroyed the power of landowners and redistributed land, the way the communists went about their project harmed many of the very people the revolution was supposed to emancipate. Faced with growing peasant resistance, the party ended the campaign, and Hồ issued a public apology.[107]

But perhaps the most glaring contradiction of all was Leninism's deep ambiguity as both a project for world communism and a project for national state development. On the one hand, Leninist national liberation was a universalist struggle against imperialism for the emancipation of all people. Vietnamese revolutionaries followed developments across the globe, studied abroad, supported struggles elsewhere, and worked closely with comrades in neighboring countries like China. They resupplied Chinese communists seeking respite in Vietnam, joined their communist comrades in the Chinese Civil War, and fought side by side with them on Vietnamese soil against France.[108] To take just one example of the deep theoretical, political, and affective ties between revolutionaries in Vietnam and China, one of the most important communist leaders in Vietnam adopted the name "Trường Chinh," or "Long March," in honor of the Chinese communists' daring trek.

From this perspective, then, national liberation was less about representing a fixed territory, an essentialized ethnic identity, or a preexisting colonial subject, but more about creating new collective subjects in Vietnam, French Indochina, Southeast Asia, and beyond. The Vietnamese revolution, in other words, was just one part of a single interconnected struggle to create a new world. "A time will come when Chinese and Vietnamese revolutions will merge," Trường Chinh declared during the war against France, to "counter American imperialists and their stooges – French colonialists and Chinese and Vietnamese traitors."[109] On this view, Vietnamese nationalism was about fidelity to the cause of anti-imperialist internationalism, and a traitor was one who sided with imperialism anywhere. This universalism was not lost on other anti-imperialists, which is precisely why so many adopted the Vietnamese liberation struggle as their own. "The great victory of the Vietnamese people at Dien Bien Phu is no longer strictly speaking a Vietnamese victory," Frantz Fanon explained. "From July 1954 onward the colonial peoples have been asking themselves: 'What must we do to achieve a Dien Bien Phu? How should we go about it?'"[110]

On the other hand, the Leninist struggle for national liberation was a nationalist development project. Vietnamese revolutionaries glorified Vietnam's past, mapped out national territory, issued identification cards, recruited labor power, built up industry, fostered a cult of personality, mobilized civil servants from the colonial regime, erected a state atop the old imperialist institutions, cultivated new hierarchical governing structures, and turned Leninism itself into an ideology of governance. From this perspective, then, national liberation was less about international revolution than making a cohesive, independent, modernized nation-state. As the same Trường Chinh explained, it would allow Vietnam to "get rid of its backwardness and become really strong and prosperous."[111] On this view, Vietnamese nationalism was about advancing some essentialized nation, developing an ideology that could create a sense of belonging in service to the government, and constructing a wealthy, hierarchical, territorially bounded state. This vision of nationalism would unify people not as new collective subjects in a universalist struggle against fixed roles, but as atomized members of an ethnic nation organized by a developmentalist party-state.

This tension within Leninist national liberation as simultaneously universal emancipation and nation-building created challenges across the board. When it came to defining the nation, for example, universalism led communists to see it as an inclusive political entity that could bridge all divides, but nation-building led them to treat it as an objective category based in ethnic heritage. Approaching nations in this manner inevitably raised confounding questions. French Indochina had included dozens of self-identified ethnic groups, which meant that "Vietnam" was not necessarily a single nation, but the site of many possible nations. Who counted as a real nation? Who had the power to decide? Who exercised the right to national self-determination? After much waffling, communists redefined the right to self-determination as the right of the dominant nation, that is, the majority Kinh people, to independence. Many communists justified this by imagining the Kinh as first among all the peoples oppressed by the French, in later years going so far as to see minorities as junior cousins in a larger "Vietnamese family." This kind of ethnic chauvinism, coupled with a stagist theory of development, even led some communists to classify other people as stunted in development, and so in need of forced modernization to elevate them to the same level as the Kinh.[112]

This same tension also played out in the realm of internationalism. The universalist aspect of Leninism convinced many Vietnamese communists that their struggle was intimately connected to the emancipation of other people. Because the three zones that comprised Vietnam were not only the largest, most populous, and most developed in what was French Indochina, but also home to the most militant anticolonial movement in the region, Vietnamese communists felt they had a special responsibility to selflessly develop the revolution across Southeast Asia. But the countervailing project of nation-building led quite a few to simultaneously embrace a kind of essentialist national identity, adopt a paternalistic "big brother" attitude, and contemplate the integration of neighboring peoples into an Indochinese Federation to be naturally led by Vietnam. This approach unsurprisingly sparked animosity, particularly from Cambodians, jeopardizing internationalism.[113]

No one personified Leninist anti-imperialism's inherent tensions more poignantly than Hồ Chí Minh himself. He was a cosmopolitan, a ranking Comintern official who knew at least five languages, and a lifelong internationalist who organized revolution in China, defended the struggles of African Americans, and helped found the French, Malay, Thai, Vietnamese, Khmer, and Lao communist parties. He was so deeply attached to the international communist movement, and would become so personally grieved by its growing fragmentation in later years, that one of his final wishes was for Vietnamese to work toward the "restoration of unity among the fraternal parties on the basis of Marxism-Leninism and proletarian internationalism, in a way which conforms to both reason and sentiment."[114]

But at the same time, Hồ began his career as a nationalist, dedicated his life to freeing the "fatherland," and styled himself as the avuncular leader of the grand Vietnamese family. He was so deeply attached to his country that he asked that his ashes be scattered across the north, center, and south of Vietnam.[115] There has been much ink spilled over Hồ's politics, with some scholars asserting he was a communist who used nationalism to conceal his true goal of world revolution and others arguing that he was fundamentally a patriot who used communism as a means to realize his nationalist objectives. The Leninist problematic, however, allowed him to be both at the same time because it treated communism and nationalism as part of the same emancipatory process. For Hồ and his Leninist contemporaries, there was no contradiction between the internationalist project of abolishing the interstate system to make world communism and the nationalist project of constructing a strong, respected, prosperous nation-state.[116]

In practice, however, "communism-building" and "nation-building" were not necessarily the same thing, as the history of Vietnam itself would reveal. Communism, after all, called for the dissolution of all borders, the end of classes, the abolition of work, the withering away of the state, and the proliferation of free activity. But making a modern nation-state meant protecting borders, boosting productivity, expanding the government, creating a bureaucracy, and reducing politics to the state. This contradiction may appear obvious today, but this is largely because the saturation of the Leninist problematic has made it possible to assume such a clear exterior perspective. While it may be difficult to accept, many anti-imperialists at the time did not perceive the inherent ambiguities, if not outright contradictions, in the Leninist problematic. Those few committed anti-imperialists who did see them believed that the positives outweighed the negatives, the problems would resolve themselves, or new solutions could be devised within the terms of the problematic.

This is why so many could treat Leninism as a coherent model of anti-imperialism that harmonized internationalism with nationalism, world communism with nation-building, universal emancipation with national self-determination. Whether they fought in Vietnam or organized solidarity campaigns abroad, many anti-imperialists would continue to see Leninism as the best way to change the world. What is more, the leading role of communists in Vietnam, their open embrace of Leninism as a guide to revolution, and their repeated assertion that Leninism was a major reason for their victories would eventually lead anti-imperialists the world over to treat the long national liberation struggle in Vietnam – including the radical solidarity movements that emerged to support it – as an exemplary test case for the Leninist problematic itself. And Vietnam, they would believe, was proof that it was working.

In the two decades that lay ahead, that faith would face its greatest trial yet.

1   Internationalism

On May 26, 1966, Stephen Smale of the Vietnam Day Committee spoke at the "Six Hours for Vietnam," a colossal teach-in hosted by Parisian antiwar radicals. Smale's friend Laurent Schwartz, one of the event's organizers, hoped the presence of an American at France's most spectacular antiwar action yet could strengthen international solidarity. After surveying the American antiwar movement, Smale stressed the necessity of united action. "People in France have asked me if there is any point in Frenchmen getting involved in the Vietnam protest," he said. "I tell them definitely yes."[1] Because the Vietnam War was an international war, he explained, the antiwar struggle had to be international as well. Only unity between activists in the United States, France, Vietnam, and elsewhere across the globe could halt the war. Powerfully symbolizing this new commitment to antiwar internationalism, Smale concluded his speech by walking across the stage to shake hands with Mai Văn Bộ, North Vietnam's top representative in Paris. The auditorium erupted in wild applause.[2]

Although most Americans initially supported the Vietnam War, some, such as Smale, dissented from the outset. At the forefront of the antiwar struggle were radicals who advanced a systemic critique, arguing that ending the war meant transforming the system that had created it in the first place. Marginalized for decades, these radicals became a significant force in American politics in large part because of the turmoil caused by the war itself. In addition to taking the lead in antiwar organizing at home, some tried to internationalize the struggle, reaching out to antiwar activists across the globe. Radicals in Western Europe proved especially responsive to the call, with the French in particular insisting on the strategic value of international coordination in the North Atlantic.

That night in 1966, they received a tremendous fillip of encouragement from Smale. "What is going on in Vietnam affects the world," he explained. The war was not some isolated American affair, but part of a much broader struggle between the United States and liberation movements fighting for self-determination across the globe. But the

United States could not win this war alone; it needed the support of its "traditional allies," namely, Western European powers such as France.[3] French radicals interpreted this to mean that their activism could play an important role in bringing the American War in Vietnam to an end. Convinced they had a special responsibility to combat the alliance of capitalist governments that sustained US imperialism, French radicals began to cooperate with other European activists to organize their own antiwar alliance. While plenty of tangled transnational connections already wrapped their way across North America and Western Europe in the 1960s, no single issue would bring radicals from so many countries together in such a concrete way as the Vietnam War.

But as they set about organizing international opposition to the war, these radicals soon confronted the limits of the existing left in North America and Western Europe. When the war escalated, much of the established left proved too weak to mount a robust internationalist response, voiced only lukewarm opposition, or simply supported the United States. Disappointed, these activists concluded that they had no choice but to create a new radical international in the North Atlantic.

A New Conjuncture

The Second World War shook the world order, making possible a wave of anticolonial revolts that brought down the old empires. Between 1945 and 1965, the membership of the United Nations increased from 51 to 117 states. Some of these countries triumphed through bloody revolutions, and even those that won independence through relatively peaceful means were in a state of radical ferment. By the early 1960s, much of the planet was caught up in a whirlwind of dramatic social, political, and economic change.[4]

But decolonization did not simply happen "out there" in Asia, Africa, and Latin America. It also shaped the political horizons of countries in North America and Western Europe.[5] These liberation struggles showed that sweeping change was possible, and they radicalized thousands of future activists in the imperialist countries. They generated a wealth of new ideas, with the writings of Frantz Fanon, Che Guevara, Võ Nguyên Giáp, and others spreading across the globe through a transnational network of radical publishing houses.[6] They furnished an army of activists who migrated to the North Atlantic, shared their experiences, organized solidarity campaigns, and injected a kind of radicalism into their new homes.[7] More than anything, they inspired hope in the possibility of a new world.

The ferocious winds from Asia, Africa, and Latin America helped to reveal the cracks in the edifice of the capitalist North Atlantic. Despite an

unprecedented economic boom, relative social stability, and a triumpha-
list rhetoric of progress, these countries were not without their problems.
Stark inequalities persisted under managed capitalism, with entire social
groups excluded from the postwar welfare state. Workers lived a world
apart, viewed as another species, especially in Europe. Racism was prev-
alent, above all in the United States, a land of rampant discrimination,
legal segregation, and lynching. Sexism pervaded nearly every aspect of
everyday life, young women faced sexual assault, and married women
were often forced to leave their jobs to return home. In many countries,
divorce was not considered a basic right, contraceptives were difficult to
access, and abortion illegal.[8]

Even those who could enjoy the fruits of the affluent society were often
left with a bitter taste. While there were more commodities on the shelves
for those who could afford them, the economic boom did not necessarily lead to a more meaningful life. Many people who lived through the
early 1960s recall quotidian life as constricting, conformist, and alienat-
ing. Against this background, the largest cohort of youth yet rejected the
stultifying culture of their parents. Those privileged enough flooded into
overcrowded, inadequate, and authoritarian universities, and while most
students were quiescent, a vocal minority took to politics, redirecting
the critical skills they had learned in the classroom toward not only the
university but also society itself.[9]

Dissatisfaction with the emptiness of everyday life was matched by
disquiet over the political sphere. Not only were young people everywhere denied the franchise, they also saw limited opportunities for formal political change. In Italy, the Christian Democrats had governed
continuously since 1946. In West Germany, the Christian Democratic Union had ruled since the foundation of the country in 1949. In
France, a general came to power through a coup in 1958. Even when
the democratic process seemed relatively open, as in the United States,
mainstream political parties often agreed on core issues, collaborated
to edge out rivals, and pursued some of the same policies, such as
US intervention in Vietnam, which was supported by Democrats and
Republicans alike.[10]

In addition, for those in search of change, inherited radical options
held little attraction. Activists felt betrayed by the leadership of the labor
movement, which fought to maintain the peace at all costs, even if it
meant stifling the demands of the rank and file. They dismissed communist parties, which appeared bureaucratic, undemocratic, overly
dependent on the USSR, and more interested in accumulating votes than
making systemic change. Internationally, they rebuked the Soviet Union,
once the guiding star of revolution, for its dogmatism, authoritarianism,

expansionism, and accommodation to the United States. Seeking alternatives, many budding activists turned to what theorists like Fanon called the "Third World."[11] They studied Cuba, which promised a fresh path, distinct from the Soviet Union.[12] They looked to the new revolutionary government of Algeria, which styled itself as the "mecca of revolution."[13] And they dreamed of the Great Proletarian Cultural Revolution in China, which seemed to breathe new life into the revolutionary project.[14]

Amid decolonization, rapid historical change, and domestic discontent, those looking for change threw themselves into a kaleidoscope of struggles in the early 1960s – rank-and-file labor militancy, countercultural subversion, campaigns for nuclear disarmament, civil rights movements, Black nationalism, student organizing, a nascent women's liberation movement, and dozens of international solidarity campaigns. Although relatively small, and engaging only a minority of the population in any country, these struggles marked a new era of contestation.[15] It was against this backdrop of radicalization that the United States decided to escalate its involvement in Vietnam.

Radicals against the War

US intervention in Vietnam began long before the 1960s. In the 1950s, when Vietnamese struggled against French colonialism, the United States supported France with weapons, supplies, and funds to restore colonial rule.[16] By the end of what came to be known as the First Indochina War, the United States had financed about 80 percent of the French war effort. Although the Vietnamese liberation struggle emerged victorious, the 1954 Geneva Conference temporarily divided the country into two regroupment zones. The accords made clear, however, that the division would not be permanent, and in two years Vietnamese living on both sides would participate in a referendum to determine whether to reunify the country, and if so, under what government.

That vote never took place. As President Dwight Eisenhower himself later confessed, if it had been held possibly 80 percent of the population would have voted for reunification under communism.[17] This could not be allowed to happen. The referendum was postponed indefinitely, and two independent countries emerged. In the North, the Democratic Republic of Vietnam (DRV) set out to build socialism by replicating the Soviet model of development, complete with a party-state, collectivization, and rapid industrialization. In the South, the United States worked to transform the Republic of Vietnam (RVN) into a capitalist democracy in its own image.[18] The Americans helped transport over a million Vietnamese southward to build a support base for the new regime, funneled millions of dollars into South Vietnam's economy, and dispatched hundreds of experts to the RVN to construct everything from irrigation systems to political institutions. For the United States, the best way to beat the communists was not just to kill them but to construct a viable alternative. South Vietnam became the main laboratory of US capitalist nation-building, intended to serve as a model not just for Vietnamese, but for all of Asia, Africa, and Latin America.[19]

The problem, though, was that the RVN soon descended into chaos under the corrupt rule of President Ngô Đình Diệm.[20] Faced with a legitimacy crisis, Diệm repressed dissidents of all kinds, which only heightened discontent across the RVN. Although the communist party, now rebranded as the Vietnamese Workers' Party, had initially instructed revolutionaries in the South to bury their weapons, adhere to the accords, and limit their work to nonviolent opposition, this wave of repression, the ensuing resistance, and the growing impatience of southerners forced Hanoi to reconsider its strategy. Although committed to the southern cause, national unification, and international communism, figures like Hồ Chí Minh urged caution, fearful that openly supporting the revolt might pull the United States deeper into Vietnam. This "North-first" faction argued that the Vietnamese Workers' Party should prioritize rebuilding the North after the devastation of the war with France. They were opposed by a "South-first" faction led by First Secretary Lê Duẩn, who demanded that the party prioritize unification. After much debate, Lê Duẩn's faction prevailed, and Hanoi gave southern rebels the green light. In December 1960, communists in the South joined hands with other dissidents to build a popular front, the National Liberation Front (NLF).[21]

The NLF was one force among many. Across the RVN, students, liberals, Buddhists, Christians, syncretic politico-religious movements like the Cao Đài, and a whole range of noncommunist nationalist organizations competed to shape the destiny of the country. Many of these players hoped to find an independent "third way" between the communists, who were backed by North Vietnam, and the increasingly dictatorial government of South Vietnam, which was backed by the United States. But the NLF quickly distinguished itself as the most organized, dynamic, and militant political force in the South. It soon overshadowed these other groups, co-opted their members, and won millions over to its cause. Its influence climbed to such heights that many contemporaries across the world came to view the NLF as the sole authentic voice of the Vietnamese revolution.[22]

Supervised by Hanoi, which sent supplies, weapons, and operatives down to the South, the NLF waged an implacable guerrilla war against an already unstable RVN state. Recognizing the danger to not only South Vietnam but also its entire Cold War experiment, the United States sent more advisors, sprayed the country with defoliants, dropped napalm on suspected communist strongholds, and forcibly relocated thousands of farmers into camps. Despite substantial US assistance, the Republic of Vietnam slid closer to the edge. Huge swathes of the country fell into the hands of the NLF. In these "liberated zones," the NLF effectively ran a parallel government, building schools, overseeing land reform, and organizing security, tax collection, and food distribution. Socialist countries began to recognize the NLF as the legitimate government of South Vietnam.[23] By late 1964, the future of the RVN looked bleak. If the United States did not escalate its involvement, its grand model of capitalist modernization would very likely fall. In early 1965, President Lyndon Johnson made the fateful decision to bomb the North and deploy combat troops to the South.[24] The United States was at war.[25]

When Johnson escalated American involvement in Vietnam, he could rest easy knowing that public opinion was on his side. According to a 1965 Gallup poll, 64 percent of respondents supported military intervention. Of course, most Americans could not find Vietnam on a map, let alone recount the country's history, but this hardly mattered, as faith in government was at an all-time high and the White House could do no wrong. In the context of the Cold War, with godless communism menacing the free world, most Americans believed it was their duty to back their government, as if replaying the patriotic fervor of the Second World War, whose traces were everywhere, in military parades, television shows, and sermons by veteran priests.

Although a vocal minority of Americans had disapproved of US involvement in Southeast Asia from the beginning, organized mass opposition was rare, largely because of the hazards of protesting during wartime. In the First World War, the federal government arrested antiwar activists under the Espionage Act of 1917, which left some, like socialist leader Eugene V. Debs, languishing in prison. This history, along with the more recent experiences of the House Un-American Activities Committee, the Smith Acts, COINTELPRO, and McCarthyism, continued to cast a long shadow into the 1960s. Publicly challenging the government in its war against professed communists, no matter how peaceful the demonstration or sterling the anticommunist credentials of the organizers, was risky business.

So it should come as little surprise that, when the Students for a Democratic Society (SDS) called for a demonstration on April 17, 1965, they expected no more than a few thousand protesters to show up.[26] To everyone's astonishment, 20,000 gathered in the nation's capital for the single largest antiwar demonstration in American history to that date. After picketing the White House, they marched to the Washington Monument, where they listened to speeches interspersed with performances from musicians such as Joan Baez.[27] In his speech, Senator Ernest Gruening, one of the two members of Congress to vote against the Gulf of Tonkin Resolution, demanded the "immediate cessation of our bombing in North Vietnam."[28] Calling for sustained antiwar action, Staughton Lynd referenced the example of French activists who had opposed the Algerian War.[29] Paul Potter, the 26-year-old president of SDS, headlined the rally with a rousing call to build a mass movement to end the war. "I believe that the administration is serious about expanding the war in Asia," he said. "The question is whether the people who are here are as serious about ending that war." The only way to do that, he explained, was to build a "movement rather than a protest or some series of protests."[30]

Although April 17 promised to inaugurate just such a movement in the United States, the demonstration, much like the antiwar activism that was to follow, was highly fractured, a hodgepodge of isolationists, pacifists, liberals, civil rights activists, Black nationalists, anticommunists, social democrats, communists, antirevisionists, and socialists of various stripes. What is often misremembered as "the antiwar movement" was never a coherent movement, but rather the happenstance coalescence of diverse, and often competing, initiatives, unified only by vague opposition to the Vietnam War. Although they occasionally coordinated their actions, especially for large demonstrations such as the April 17 action, antiwar groups remained independent of one another. They opposed the war for different reasons, pursued different tactics, and proposed wildly different solutions.[31]

Quite a few of the groups protesting that day hailed from the far left of the political spectrum.[32] Contrary to the claims of anticommunist propaganda, the most innocuous of these was the Communist Party USA (CPUSA). Founded in 1919, the CPUSA had emerged from the McCarthyist repression of the 1950s as a shell of its former self. The party had grown so invertebrate that it even opposed immediate withdrawal with the slogan, "Negotiate Now," which infuriated those in groups further to the left, who argued that "negotiations" implied that the United States had a right to be in Southeast Asia in the first place. One of these groups was the Socialist Workers Party (SWP), the largest Trotskyist organization in the United States. Unlike the Communist Party, the SWP demanded the "US Out Now." But despite its intransigent opposition to the war, the SWP consistently opposed overtly confrontational tactics, fearing they would alienate the broader American public, a stance that would later put the party at odds with others on the left.[33]

Another critic of the CPUSA was Progressive Labor (PL). Formed in 1962, PL was firmly anti-imperialist, followed the Chinese line, and organized illegal trips to Cuba. Although mostly composed of older militants, PL's influence over the May Second Movement allowed it to connect with the burgeoning youth movement. The May Second Movement, which had emerged out of coordinated antiwar demonstrations in May 1964 in New York, San Francisco, and several other cities, became one of the first far left youth groups to not only focus on Vietnam, but also openly support the NLF. "We support the National Liberation Front of south Viet-Nam and other revolutionary movements because we realize that their struggle is our struggle, that when we aid our brothers in other countries, we are aiding ourselves, for we are struggling against the same enemy," a 1965 statement explained.[34] After attending the April 17, 1965 demonstration, PL quickly recognized SDS's potential and decided to send its members directly into the larger student organization.

The largest radical formation, and the one that took the initiative to organize the April 17 demonstration, was SDS. Originally founded as the youth affiliate of the League for Industrial Democracy, SDS won its independence in the 1960s, becoming a vessel for a new generation of activists hoping to move beyond what they called the "Old Left." Championing participatory democracy, the struggle for racial equality, and a kind of anti-anticommunism, SDS soon became the premier organization of the white "New Left." Although rather moderate in its early years – at their National Council meeting in December 1964, for example, SDSers voted against two antiwar proposals, one to encourage draft resistance and the other to send medical supplies to Vietnam, for being too radical – SDS would quickly radicalize.[35]

In attendance that day as well was the Student Nonviolent Coordinating Committee (SNCC), one of the leading civil rights organizations of the era. Many SNCC activists immediately connected the antiracist struggle at home with opposition to the war abroad, but while some publicly opposed the war – SNCC leader Bob Moses spoke at the April 17 demonstration – others were reluctant to openly condemn the US government, fearing the loss of funds and the state support that had been decisively leveraged in the Civil Rights Movement. But after much debate, in January 1966 SNCC became the first civil rights group to formally condemn the Vietnam War. Its shift to an open antiwar stance, which soon included draft resistance, marked a general radicalization in the group as a whole, much like its fraternal organization, SDS.[36]

Although these groups, along with others, such as the International Workers of the World, the Spartacist League, or the International Socialist Clubs, all marched side by side against the US government, they were not on the best of terms. They heatedly debated whether to call for US withdrawal or Vietnamese victory; to carry US or NLF flags at demonstrations; to focus exclusively on ending the fighting or connect the war to other domestic issues; to adopt a more centralized structure or remain capillary; to prioritize extraparliamentary organizing or throw their energies into electoral politics; or to organize large actions or promote more local initiatives. They even disagreed over their analysis of the war itself. Was the Vietnamese liberation struggle a single, continuous revolution, or would it follow a two-stage process, first a democratic revolution, then a properly socialist one? Was the Vietnamese Workers' Party an emancipatory international force, or would it degenerate into a Stalinist autocracy once in power?[37]

Yet as serious as these differences were, they belied a deeper unity. Beneath these debates, many of the radicals shared the same general strategic assumption about the antiwar struggle, expressed most eloquently at the Washington, DC protest by Paul Potter. Potter argued that the war was not the product of this or that individual, but rather a much larger system that compelled those individuals to pursue war. "What kind of a system is it that allows good men to make those kinds of decisions?" he asked his audience.[38] Since the Vietnam War was caused by this system, Potter continued, the only way to end the war was to "change the system."[39] Putting a halt to the bombing, pursuing negotiations, or electing a new president, as more moderate antiwar voices suggested, would not stop the Vietnam War. Even if such actions might reduce hostilities in Southeast Asia, if they did not change the system itself then the United States would eventually pursue another "Vietnam" elsewhere. The goal, Potter concluded, was not simply to end this war but to create a new society in which "Vietnams are unthinkable."[40] They might have expressed it differently, but all the radicals present shared this view of the war.

Nevertheless, as the April 17 march revealed, while radicals shared a systemic critique of the war, there was some ambiguity over how to define this "system." Although Potter exhorted his audience to "name it, describe it, analyze it, understand it and change it," he himself did not concretely identify the system that everyone was supposed to overthrow, a conspicuous silence that other radicals could not help but notice.[41] But as Potter later explained,

I did not fail to call the system capitalism because I was a coward or an opportunist. I refused to call it capitalism because capitalism was for me and my generation an inadequate description of the evils of America – a hollow, dead word tied to the thirties and a movement that had used it freely but apparently without comprehending it.[42]

In this way, Potter gave voice to a new generation of radicals who sought to avoid the inherited habits, concepts, debates, and traditions of the old communist left. The desire to rethink radical politics in light of changed conditions was one of the key animating impulses of the "New Left" not only in the United States but also across the North Atlantic. This did not necessarily make their stance any less radical. While New Leftists like Potter may have initially avoided words such as "capitalism" or "imperialism," they still agreed with other radicals about the necessity of changing the system. As we will see, however, over the next few years the radicalization of the New Left, and the concomitant adoption of Marxism as a shared theory, would lead many American radicals, even New Left skeptics, to believe that "imperialism" was in fact the best way to describe the system and Leninist anti-imperialism the best way to change it.[43]

But all that lay in the future. In the early 1960s, the US radical left was still trying to find its way after years in the wilderness. By the start of 1965, for instance, SDS claimed only around 2,500 members in the country, and not all of them even considered themselves to be radicals.[44] But over the next few years, radical networks would find opportunities to grow, consolidate, and escape the political margins. One of the most important of these opportunities was the Vietnam War. First and foremost, it gave them a window. When war broke out, established peace groups, labor unions, and moderate Old Left formations could have taken the lead in antiwar organizing, but years of anticommunism gave them pause.[45] Some, like the National Committee for a Sane Nuclear Policy (known as SANE), spoke out against the war, but stopped short of a full commitment. Others, like the American Federation of Labor and Congress of Industrial Organizations (AFL-CIO), openly supported the Vietnam War, with the federation's leader, George Meany, only coming to oppose it in 1974, after the American withdrawal.[46] Radicals filled this void. Their prior organizing experiences, tireless commitment, and firm convictions compensated for their miniscule size, and they came to play a leading role in early antiwar organizing.[47]

Moreover, as much as anticommunist moderates disliked the radicals, they felt compelled to join them against the common enemy of US militarism. In stark contrast with earlier civil rights and peace demonstrations, where some organizers flatly banned communist participation, SDS activists, even liberal ones, accepted every progressive current in the April 1965 march. Although this infuriated many anticommunist peace activists, they would eventually recognize the importance of organizing mass actions against the war, and they ended up rubbing shoulders with radicals. In this way, the Vietnam War allowed radicals to gain mainstream exposure, a degree of legitimacy, and in time a kind of leadership over the larger antiwar scene.

Lastly, the war itself became the primary, though not the only, "engine" of radicalization in the United States, leading some, especially a younger generation, into the arms of the radicals.[48] When the draft expanded, the death toll soared, and victory continued to elude the United States, the radical left was there, and ready, to propose a coherent political analysis to help Americans articulate their frustrations, push their ideas in more radical directions, and offer concrete ways to translate discontent into action. The Vietnam War, more than anything else, thickened the ranks of the radicals. Lyndon Johnson, some joked, was their best recruiter. His decision to escalate the war gave the radical left a once-in-a-lifetime chance to become a visible force in American political life again.

Internationalizing the Struggle

A little over a month after the Washington, DC demonstration, activists organized the largest teach-in to date in Berkeley, California. On May 21, 1965, Barbara Gullahorn, an antiwar activist at UC Berkeley, Jerry Rubin, a former sociology student who had visited Cuba, organized in the Civil Rights Movement, and had since devoted himself to politics full-time, and Stephen Smale, a famous mathematician with a long history in radical politics, organized what came to be called "Vietnam Day." Drawing nearly 35,000 people, the event rolled a debate, protest, and spectacle into a colossal 36-hour extravaganza. Because of the radical atmosphere of the Bay Area, heightened as it was by the Free Speech Movement of the preceding year, this teach-in was also more militant than previous ones, with nearly all the radical tendencies of the time represented. Paul Potter spoke on behalf of SDS, Bob Moses of SNCC, Mario Savio of the Free Speech Movement, Levi Laub of Progressive Labor, and Jack Barnes of the SWP's youth wing.[49] In addition to creating a space for the most radical perspectives, the organizers sought to foster a sense of unity by hosting a panel called "United Political Action" that featured speakers from rival groups.[50]

After Vietnam Day, Gullahorn, Rubin, Smale, and others decided to continue their efforts as a formal organization, the Vietnam Day Committee (VDC). Less a party than a kind of united front against the war, the VDC welcomed every current of radicalism, from the CPUSA to the SWP, the Independent Socialist Clubs to unaffiliated radicals.[51] This kind of radical inclusivity was one of the VDC's keys to success, and it rapidly, and somewhat unexpectedly, became one of the most prominent antiwar formations in the United States, especially after SDS chose to focus its attention on other projects.[52] For the moment, then, the VDC came to assume leadership over the radical antiwar effort, making several contributions to antiwar organizing in the United States.[53] It served as a model for democratic, grassroots, antiwar organizing. It advocated direct action, such as blocking trains carrying troops through the Bay Area. And, most importantly, it propagated a kind of radical antiwar internationalism.[54]

The radicals who organized the VDC did not just believe that the only way to end the war was to change the system; they were convinced that the best way to transform that system was to amplify their efforts by uniting with other activists across the globe. At the time, this conviction was called "internationalism," and it was central to the VDC. It even preceded the VDC's official founding. In selecting speakers for Vietnam Day, for example, Smale and Rubin reached out to noted antiwar figures abroad. Jean-Paul Sartre, whose opposition to the Algerian War impressed American radicals, refused to visit the United States out of protest, but still promised his support.[55] Bertrand Russell, now in his nineties, could not make the trip but recorded a speech. Iyanaga Shōkichi, a fellow mathematician, organized a solidarity demonstration in Japan to coincide with the event. But the most important international contact was the French mathematician Laurent Schwartz, who took these internationalist ambitions furthest by suggesting a coordinated day of international protest.[56]

On May 14, 1965, about a week before Vietnam Day, Schwartz wrote to Smale about the struggle that lay ahead. Having participated in the opposition to the Algerian War, Schwartz drew parallels between his experiences in France and the nascent American movement against the Vietnam War. You will "know in the following months a situation very similar to ours during the Algerian war," he remarked. "The government will become more and more ferocious and hypocritical; in a general climate of fear throughout the country, you will be rather isolated, calumniated, accused of beeing [sic] enemies of the USA." He then leavened his caution with encouragement: "But your cause is the right one, and is considered as such everywhere in the world." Schwartz wanted Smale to know that he and others like him would do whatever they could to support the American struggle against the war. "You may be sure to receive from your colleagues in France any help you want." He doubted that they could directly assist American activists, but Schwartz wondered if there might be a way to internationalize the movement by inventing ways of ensuring continued support for American efforts: "perhaps we could think of an international Committee against war in Vietnam." And if not that, at the very least, "an international day of protest, say in October; what do you think about it?"[57]

The VDC took up his suggestion. Soon after Vietnam Day, it began preparations for what would be known as the International Days of Protest, the first major, internationally coordinated mass protests against the Vietnam War. As one of the VDC's flyers explained, "People throughout the world must now move beyond single demonstrations and teach-ins to one massive internationally coordinated action." With these global protests, the "full impact of world opinion can be brought to bear against the policy of the American government."[58] In late June 1965, the VDC organized an international committee to contact activists in other countries. Largely composed of international students studying in the United States, the committee issued calls for support in seven languages and, by its own account, sent hundreds of letters to foreign governments, political parties, trade unions, student organizations, and peace groups, asking their support for the October 15–16 International Days of Protest.[59]

The response was "immediate and encouraging."[60] When October 15 arrived, activists protested in dozens of countries, from Mexico to Canada, Senegal to Czechoslovakia, Japan to Australia. In London, Bertrand Russell kicked off a weekend of protest when he "tore up his Labour Party membership card in front of a capacity audience, to show his disgust at the Labour Government's support for US policy."[61] In Italy, activists organized sizeable demonstrations in seven cities.[62] In Brussels, home to a rapidly growing antiwar movement, thousands participated in a weekend of antiwar events. Oddly, the French did not mobilize in great numbers that day, even though the idea for a day of protest in October had come from a Frenchman. Fearing conflicts with the French academic calendar, and thinking they could reach more students another time, French organizers decided to postpone their action until November, which fortuitously coincided with another major American demonstration.[63] Mirroring the November 27, 1965 march on Washington, DC, French student activists organized an international "University Week Against the Vietnam War."[64] They also tried to go beyond the university by using the protests to reach the "wider public," making the Week Against the Vietnam War one of the first big demonstrations in France against the war.[65]

By then, the VDC had joined with radicals from several other antiwar organizations, including SDS, the SWP, the CPUSA, and dozens of smaller antiwar collectives, to form a national organization, the National Coordinating Committee to End the War in Vietnam (NCC). Together with the VDC's international committee, the NCC continued to internationalize the antiwar struggle and made certain that Americans knew just how many people across the world opposed their government's actions. "It is most important," the VDC clarified, "that American citizens be informed about these demonstrations and that the truly worldwide, unified dissatisfaction with current US foreign policy be adequately publicized."[66] Committed to international unity, the NCC called for a Second International Days of Protest for March 1966, which proved even larger than the first.[67]

Although they welcomed international connections of all kinds, those American radicals who advocated some kind of antiwar internationalism tended to prioritize links with other activists in Asia, Africa, and Latin America. Richard Aoki, who worked on the VDC's international committee, spoke for many when he admitted, "I was most interested in Third World people and politics."[68] This was not simply because the "Third World" was where American activists looked for inspiration, but because many radicals believed the "Third World" was the strategic key to the world situation. As Aoki explained in the VDC's newsletter, the Vietnam War was neither an "error" nor an "isolated incident," but a "direct and glaring reflection" of the system's deliberate mission to "crush national liberation movements" fighting for "self-determination" across the "Third World." This made "the war in Vietnam an international war," which meant that "its opposition must be international" as well. But because the fight was primarily between the United States and the "Third World," it followed that internationalism primarily meant coordination with movements in Asia, Africa, and Latin America.[69]

By contrast, American activists did not yet consider Western Europe a decisive battlefield in this international war. While they certainly appreciated the solidarity of Europeans, connections with those movements were secondary. Before 1968 most American antiwar radicals did not pay very close attention to Europe, and especially France, which in any event seemed far more tranquil than its neighbors.[70] They might have admired the French Resistance, or opposition to the Algerian War, but French activism against the Vietnam War did not hold the interest of American radicals.[71] Of course, there were plenty of contacts on an individual basis, but few sustained, formal, international networks linking American radical organizations with those in countries like France. For most Americans in early 1966, building an international coalition between radicals in North America and Western Europe was not a strategic priority.

Nevertheless, these early American initiatives, even if focused on the "Third World," did play a decisive role in fostering a new kind of internationalism between radicals in the North Atlantic. While these connections with Western European activists may not have been important for most Americans, they were vital for Europeans. Although in many respects more radical in their outlook than their American counterparts, most antiwar radicals in European countries like France constantly looked across the Atlantic. They studied the Civil Rights Movement, the Free Speech Movement, and the Vietnam Day Committee. They turned to the Americans for inspiration, strategic guidance, and tactical innovations, such as the teach-in, which spread like wildfire. Many European radicals conceptualized their antiwar internationalism as a way of supporting US activists, whom they saw as the linchpin of global opposition to the war. A group of radical students at the Sorbonne, for example, argued that the rise of a radical antiwar movement in the United States targeting the "system" carried enormous international consequences. "Criticism of the Vietnam War," they optimistically forecasted, "is rapidly transforming into a radical movement of opposition to the Democratic Party and the antidemocratic system that rules the USA." This movement could produce a "real mass political force" in the heart of the United States, which would in turn transform the global balance of power.[72]

By early 1966, then, a genuine sense of antiwar internationalism had taken root, but it was as asymmetrical as it was unidirectional. While US radicals provided the indispensable spark, the heavy task of not only deepening this internationalist feeling but also building a functional international alliance between antiwar radicals in the capitalist world fell to Western Europeans, and especially the French.

French Radicals Answer the Call

Since the Vietnam War was never exclusively an American affair, it is little surprise that European radicals also mobilized against the war. In Belgium, the Young Socialist Guards offered a radical alternative to the existing left. In West Germany, the Socialist German Student League, one of the leading New Left groups in the country, abandoned tepid opposition to the war for militant antiwar engagement.[73] In Britain, radicals dissatisfied with the Communist Party of Great Britain's call for negotiations united in 1966 to form the Vietnam Solidarity Campaign. In France, radicals organized their big debut in May 1966 with the "Six Hours for Vietnam," a gathering of around five thousand French antiwar activists from a variety of otherwise antagonistic political tendencies.[74]

From the very start, French radicals made it their business to unify antiwar activists internationally. The organizers of the "Six Hours," for example, explained that their action aimed to contribute to "the union of all forces who, in France and in the world, notably in the United States, fight against the Vietnam War and support the fight of the South Vietnamese people for their independence, under the direction of the

National Liberation Front."[75] The French, in other words, did not just heed the call to internationalize the struggle; they also worked even harder than their American peers to transform this commitment to internationalism into a robust antiwar international network.

French radicals were admittedly in a better position than Americans to realize such a project. The French were no strangers to Vietnam. Vietnam had been a French colony, and France had already fought a brutal colonial war in Indochina. Although certainly smaller than those that emerged during the subsequent American War, there were plenty of protests against the First Indochina War. Vietnam was therefore very much on the political map for the French, and radicals there had already collaborated with Vietnamese comrades to organize an antiwar movement against imperialist aggression in Southeast Asia years before the Americans arrived on the scene.

Almost immediately after the war's conclusion in 1954, France found itself embroiled in yet another major colonial conflagration. Decolonization in Algeria proved even more transformative, unleashing widespread violence, toppling the government, and creating the conditions for a semi-authoritarian regime under Charles de Gaulle. The fighting in Algeria triggered a kind of civil war that radicalized the political landscape in the hexagon.[76] For the left, the war acted as a crucible. It reactivated older radicals, politicized a generation of youth, and galvanized intellectuals to unify as an engaged force.[77] Some activists formed antiwar committees. Others assisted deserters. Still others helped the Algerian revolution by distributing illegal literature, forging documents, and laundering money.[78] This organized opposition to the Algerian War taught radicals valuable skills, helped turn public opinion against colonialism, and strengthened radical currents that began to challenge the French Communist Party, which adopted a wait-and-see attitude to the war.[79]

In addition to greater familiarity with Vietnam, plenty of recent antiwar experiences, and a highly charged domestic political environment, French activists also benefited from a general anti-American climate. After the Second World War, the United States achieved hegemony over the capitalist world, pressured other capitalist countries to adopt its specific model of development, and exported its mass culture, going so far as to insist that the French screen Hollywood films in exchange for aid. While France's relationship to the United States was of course complex, with some viewing the Americans as liberators, and others happily seduced by American consumerism, many decried what they called "coco-colonization."[80] On the right, de Gaulle countered US influence by rejecting Britain's application to the European Community, recognizing the People's Republic of China, and publicly criticizing the American War in Vietnam.[81] On the left, Jean-Paul Sartre argued that the French were oppressed by "American hegemony," which made them objective allies of other oppressed people like the Vietnamese.[82]

For all these reasons, opposition to the Vietnam War was already more widespread in France than in the United States, and more direct reporting on the war, as opposed to the blatant censorship in the United States, allowed antiwar sentiment to spread more rapidly.[83] Not only was the general public more antiwar, but activists in France were also on the whole more radical than those in the United States. They benefited from a rich revolutionary history, a vibrant Marxist culture, and a greater tolerance of organizing, protesting, and striking. With some exceptions, the French radical groups in the early 1960s generally enjoyed greater numbers, better organization, deeper theoretical sophistication, stronger connections to "Third World" struggles, and more experience with antiwar work than their peers in the United States. In many ways, solidarity with the "Third World" was even more fundamental in shaping the identity of the radical left there than elsewhere in the North Atlantic.[84]

In France, the first national institution to seriously organize against the war was the French Communist Party, particularly through its various front organizations.[85] Unlike the CPUSA, the communists were a major force in French domestic politics, consistently winning more than 20 percent of the vote in legislative elections. The French Communist Party trained generations of activists, organized massive demonstrations, and held out the possibility of another world, even as its practice seemed at times to contradict its vision. Indeed, despite its early adoption of the antiwar cause, the party settled on a rather uninspired approach to the war. It was precisely this lackluster opposition that consummated the split between radicals and the leadership of the French Communist Party, allowing the former to effectively outflank the latter.[86] When the party broadcasted an ambiguous call for "Peace in Vietnam," radicals countered with the intransigent "The NLF will win!" When the party organized only the most moderate actions, radicals called for confrontational struggle. And when the party treated Vietnam as another tragic issue, the radicals argued the war was the center of a global struggle. As in the United States, Vietnam helped radicals come into their own.[87]

But, also like the United States, radicals in France were far from unified, and a number of competing radical antiwar formations rushed to seize the space forced open to the left of the French Communist Party. Many of these grew out of the party itself. The Marxist-Leninist Communist Party of France, for example, split from the official party, and then created its own independent antiwar organization, the Vietnam Information Center.[88] A more consequential initiative came from a group of young Maoists who were expelled from the French Communist Party's youth organization in 1966.[89] They transformed themselves into an independent group, the Union of Communist Youth (Marxist-Leninist), and sponsored the Vietnam Base Committees: flexible, grassroots, anti-war organizations embedded in neighborhoods, schools, and factories.[90]

Another significant push came from other activists who were also forced out of the party's youth wing in 1966. Undaunted, they formed a new organization, the Revolutionary Communist Youth (RCY), which fused Trotskyism with other major currents of the time, above all, Guevarism.[91] Much like these other radical groups, the RCY placed great emphasis on the Vietnam War. As they explained in their inaugural paper, "the struggle against the war in Vietnam will be, in the months to come, one of the essential axes of our fight."[92] But unlike these other formations, the RCY was eager to collaborate with other groups. They cooperated with dissident communists, Christian socialists, activists from the Unified Socialist Party, Trotskyists representing different tendencies, and radical intellectuals like Laurent Schwartz to help launch a new initiative in the fall of 1966: the National Vietnam Committee (NVC). Indeed, the RCY would become a key player in the NVC coalition. It helped organize the grassroots, develop the NVC beyond Paris, and extend the NVC's reach into high schools.[93] One of the RCY's leaders, Alain Krivine, even served on the NVC's National Bureau.

Together, these efforts made the National Vietnam Committee the most successful autonomous radical antiwar initiative in France. Like the Maoist Base Committees, the NVC adopted a radical attitude toward the war, sponsored militant actions, catalyzed grassroots committees across the country, and provided an alternative to the French Communist Party.[94] But the NVC set itself apart from its Maoist rivals in a few ways. First, while the Vietnam Base Committees swore total allegiance to the Democratic Republic of Vietnam, the NVC, though still supporting North Vietnam against US aggression, remained independent of Hanoi, which allowed it to attract more supporters. Second, unlike the Vietnam Base Committees, the much larger NVC took advantage of the star power of celebrities, such as founding member Jean-Paul Sartre, which boosted the group's influence. Third, whereas the Vietnam Base Committees distrusted other groups, the NVC, like the American Vietnam Day Committee, was profoundly inclusive, uniting a number of distinct currents in a way that maximized its popularity.[95] Lastly, the NVC, even more than the Base Committees, cultivated a strong sense of intergenerational solidarity. The NVC sought to unite young high schoolers learning politics for the first time, radicals politicized during the Algerian War, militants who had fought in the French Resistance, and older organizers who had participated in the Spanish Civil War.

The older activists benefited from the uncompromisingly radical energy of the youth while the younger activists benefited from the historical memory, international connections, and organizing experiences of the older generations.[96]

The National Vietnam Committee also took the commitment to anti-war internationalism the furthest, especially with regards to the Americans, the central reference point in the international antiwar struggle in the North Atlantic. NVC organizers sent French activists to the United States to report directly on developments there. They invited US radicals such as David Dellinger and SNCC's Courtland Cox to France to speak about the antiwar struggle in the United States.[97] And they worked with the Paris American Committee to Stopwar (PACS), a group of anti-war American expatriates led by Maria Jolas, to formalize these relationships with their American comrades. "Maria was linked to the American anti-war movement," the NVC's Schwartz recalls, "and was our link with it."[98]

But the NVC did more than just connect with activists in the United States; it consciously sought to expand the transatlantic antiwar network initiated by the Americans. Hoping to further internationalize the anti-war struggle, it built innumerable connections with organizations across Europe. NVC activists were so enthusiastic about internationalism that they chose to turn their first official event, "Six Hours of the World for Vietnam," into a massive international convergence. On November 28, 1966, the NVC gathered thousands of activists from across the world to meet one another, learn about the global nature of the war, and discuss ways to coordinate their efforts. The NVC concluded the event with a symposium on "The Anti-Imperialist Struggle in the World," which showcased talks from an antiwar committee in Italy, the Dutch Provos, and Lawrence Daly from the International War Crimes Tribunal, an international initiative to investigate, and evaluate, US military intervention in Vietnam. By early 1967, the NVC had solidified its place as the nexus of a number of intersecting international antiwar initiatives. But the French activists who came together to make possible the National Vietnam Committee had even greater ambitions; they hoped to move beyond personal contacts, information sharing, or synchronized demonstrations to build a formal "international front."[99]

Building a Radical International

If internationalism referred to the belief that activists had to unite across borders to accomplish their political goals, then radicals defined an "international" as a concrete international organization that could realize such unity. One of the most sustained attempts at building a functional antiwar international in the "heart of imperialism" was led by young radicals in Western Europe.[100] What made their commitment to organized internationalism so intense was not simply the urgency of the war but also their belief that the leaders of the established left in North America and Western Europe had "thrown the principles of proletarian internationalism overboard" precisely when they were needed most.[101]

In their view, the social democratic parties that made up the Socialist International had not just turned their backs on radical internationalism, they had also become accomplices of imperialism. The most egregious example was socialist Prime Minister Guy Mollet's repressive policies in Algeria, but radicals argued that this was not an isolated case, pointing to Vietnam as proof. In France, socialist Léon Blum had declared war on Vietnam back in 1946. In West Germany, Willy Brandt publicly supported the American War in 1965. And in Britain, the governing Labour Party continued to back the United States.

As for the official communist parties, radicals believed they, too, had rejected their internationalist roots. Since at least the Popular Front, many had taken nationalist turns that undermined their anti-imperialist commitments. After the Second World War, quite a few transformed themselves into a kind of loyal opposition that eschewed radical ventures. During decolonization, many of these parties adopted ambiguous positions. All this, radicals believed, was exacerbated by their continued fidelity to the USSR's half-hearted approach to national liberation. Here, again, the long struggle in Vietnam was exemplary. Moscow had displayed little faith in the anticolonial struggle against France, pressed Vietnamese communists to accept the partition of their country, questioned the viability of the Vietnamese revolution, and only reluctantly supported the NLF.[102]

Significantly, radicals felt the problem was less in the founding ideas of the official communist movement than in its contemporary practice. In fact, most radicals would embrace the very same conception of internationalism as the communist movement, that is, the Leninist problematic of national self-determination. They simply believed that the communist parties of the North Atlantic, and the USSR behind them, had betrayed the creative impulses behind this otherwise laudable project. Nowhere was this clearer, radicals thought, than in the policy of peaceful coexistence with the United States, which abandoned the radical internationalism that had been so central to anti-imperialists since Lenin, leaving revolutionaries elsewhere in the lurch. "While the US carried out its imperialist tasks with hypocritical and barbarous cynicism," recalled Henri Weber, a leader of the Revolutionary Community Youth, "the

Soviet bureaucracy didn't hesitate for a moment to sacrifice the Vietnamese on the altar of peaceful coexistence."[103]

It was for this reason that some radicals turned to the People's Republic of China. Blasting the USSR for "revisionism," the PRC argued that the Soviets had renounced world revolution, elevating their own interests over their internationalist duties.[104] As their disputes escalated into an acrimonious split, China maneuvered to become the leader of world revolution.[105] Once more, the Vietnam War played a central role, with Beijing insisting that its generous support of the Vietnamese revolution proved that China had displaced the Soviets as the vanguard of radical internationalism.[106] The PRC even toyed with the idea of creating a new communist international that would include North Vietnam.[107] China's stance convinced many in the North Atlantic, prompting them not merely to create new Maoist groups such as Progressive Labor in the United States or the Union of Communist Youth (Marxist-Leninist) in France but in some cases to construct new international links. Hardial Bains, for instance, hoped to build a network in the Anglophone countries, while Jacques Grippa aimed to do the same in Western Europe.

Despite these efforts, Maoists failed to unite in a new international. The PRC tabled its proposal and was in any case never very interested in overseeing internationalism in the North Atlantic. As for the Maoists in North America and Western Europe, their extreme sectarianism – with multiple groups in the same country viciously denouncing each other for being improperly Maoist – effectively precluded any kind of unity. Although Maoism became politically important in the North Atlantic, as an organized force it could not monopolize the space left open by the perceived betrayal of the official communist movement. Nor did it facilitate the construction of an antiwar international.[108]

The other major radical internationalist current was the reunified Trotskyist Fourth International (FI). For its part, the FI was eager to foster antiwar internationalism. In 1966, the FI leadership declared that the "most urgent immediate task facing revolutionary Marxists on a worldwide scale is to strengthen the struggle against the imperialist aggression in Vietnam and for the Vietnamese Revolution." That meant "tirelessly stressing the need for an anti-imperialist united front on an international scale."[109] But while the FI had the will, theory, and experience, it lacked the capacity. Ernest Tate, an FI international organizer, recalls that in the early 1960s the French section claimed perhaps a hundred members, the Belgian only fifty or sixty, while in Britain the FI did not even have an organized presence.[110] The FI therefore resumed its strategy of "entering" existing leftist organizations to win supporters, especially among "the working and student youth, who stand in the vanguard today in a number of countries."[111]

The FI's efforts proved fruitful. In France, for example, the FI pulled some students in the Sorbonne Letters section of the student wing of the French Communist Party toward Trotskyism, forming the nucleus of what would become the RCY. In this way, the FI not only helped radicalize youth but also provided them with a rudimentary network that made future multilateral conversations possible. That said, some activists in Trotskyist-leaning groups like the RCY wanted to maintain their independence from the Fourth International, and even those young radicals like Alain Krivine who were in the FI came to reject the strategy of entryism, demanding instead the creation of independent radical organizations.[112]

With the forces of the established left now siding with imperialism, disavowing radicalism, struggling through marginalization, suffering from organizational strain, or clinging to increasingly unpopular strategies, the young radicals of the 1960s felt it was up to them to build a radical antiwar international in the North Atlantic. On October 15, 1966, nearly three thousand young radicals representing over a dozen groups some Trotskyist, but others, like the Socialist German Student League, not – held an antiwar convergence in Liège.[113] According to Mary-Alice Waters, a representative of the SWP's youth section, these groups set aside their differences to unite around "support to the Vietnamese Revolution, the demand for immediate withdrawal of American troops from Vietnam, and the demand for European countries to get out of NATO."[114] Together, they adopted a tentative program for future international antiwar coordination.[115]

The RCY, which had brought a contingent of about 220 activists to Liège, enthused: "For the first time, an independent youth organization, attacked by the bureaucratic leadership of the workers' parties, took the initiative of organizing an international gathering against imperialism and capitalist military pacts."[116] When they returned home, the RCY collaborated closely with the Young Socialist Guards to organize an even larger international conference on March 11, 1967, in Brussels.[117] There, delegates representing groups like the Socialist German Student League, the British Vietnam Solidarity Campaign, the French Revolutionary Communist Youth, the youth section of the Italian Socialist Party of Proletarian Unity, and the youth section of the French Unified Socialist Party produced a statement that clearly explained why international unity among antiwar activists in North America and Western Europe was so essential. Whereas most Americans had largely subordinated links with radicals in Western Europe to forging relations with movements in the "Third World," Western European radicals now made the case that a radical international within the advanced capitalist world could be just as important for the antiwar struggle.

They argued that the capitalist countries of North America and Western Europe were bound together in an "international capitalist alliance."[118] That alliance, they continued, was codified through such bodies as the Organization for Economic Cooperation and Development (OECD) and especially the North Atlantic Treaty Organization (NATO), which they interpreted as "the military expression of the solidarity of the principal capitalist countries of Europe and North America."[119] In a certain sense, then, these capitalist countries already had their own "international," with the United States as its "pivot."[120] The existence of such an alliance meant not only that all participating governments were complicit in the actions of the United States, but also that the United States did not act completely alone, even if it doubtlessly played the lead role. Radicals argued that because the US war effort depended on the support of the major Western European countries, they had to form their own international to pressure those allied governments and confront the international organizations that tied them together, particularly NATO.

Although they could not have possibly known all the complexities of the American War in Vietnam, especially since so much remained shrouded in secrecy, these radicals were not that far off the mark. To be sure, European governments did not provide combat troops and offered less support than other capitalist countries such as Japan. When they did ultimately contribute to the war effort, they did so reluctantly.[121] Most European politicians responded to Johnson's pressure to enter the war by dragging their feet. Some thought the war was simply unwinnable. Others were unconvinced that Vietnam posed an immediate threat. Still others feared the war would divert troops from Europe, leaving the region vulnerable to the Soviets. Most simply felt that shipping troops to die in Vietnam would be political suicide.

Nevertheless, whatever their equivocations and evasions, European states did play an important part in the American War.[122] They had no qualms about crushing communists, and quite a few, like France, Britain, and the Netherlands, had already killed many in Southeast Asia. Moreover, while they all dodged Johnson's request for troops, many offered other kinds of assistance. Italy sent aid to South Vietnam. Great Britain offered arms sales, experienced counterinsurgency advisors from Malaysia, and valuable intelligence from its monitoring stations in the region. West Germany provided aid, subsidized US bases, and helped cover the costs of the war by purchasing American weapons. But beyond these contributions, European allies proved most helpful by refusing to openly confront the United States, and in most cases publicly supporting the White House. It was their unwillingness to act in a concrete fashion that ultimately enabled US aggression in Vietnam. In this sense, then, the radicals who gathered in Brussels to hammer out a general strategy for international antiwar activism were right to point to the United States' continued reliance on its European allies.

The major exception to all this was France. In addition to criticizing the war, President Charles de Gaulle withdrew France from NATO's military command structure, much to Johnson's consternation.[123] But French radicals remained undeterred. Despite de Gaulle's rhetoric, they claimed, France continued to support the government of South Vietnam. It also remained a crucial American ally and was still a part of the North Atlantic Alliance. Reminding readers that US aggression in Vietnam was made possible by "an imperialist front" led by the United States, a pamphlet from the NVC in Rennes argued that even if de Gaulle occasionally dissented, "the Gaullist positions differ from the American theses only over the means of containing the peoples' liberation movement: that which JOHNSON attempts to achieve by force, DE GAULLE tries to obtain through the diplomatic route."[124] The headstrong de Gaulle could go his own way on certain matters, but both sides still believed in the same longer term objectives, as could be seen by France's own imperialist maneuvers around the world, especially in Africa. French policy legitimized the broader logic behind American aggression, which meant that the struggle in France was still crucial to breaking the alliance that sustained the Vietnam War. If anything, the French example further invigorated radicals. De Gaulle's behavior, the Brussels statement explained, should be welcomed because it "objectively weakens" NATO.[125] His actions proved that contradictions had appeared within the enemy international, and that US policies were straining the very alliance on which its foreign policy depended. In this context, a radical international in North America and Western Europe could be especially effective.

With their theoretical analysis in place, these radicals set to work. After the conference, they established a secretariat, working groups, a coordinating committee to meet twice a year, and an executive bureau composed of representatives from seven radical organizations, two of which hailed from France, the RCY and the Unified Socialist Students, the youth wing of the Unified Socialist Party. To foster greater coordination, they also published a bimonthly information bulletin with political analysis, updates from the working groups, and reports on actions in Europe. Their first bulletin made clear their goal to "build up the most favourable proportion of strength for the NLF and the government in Hanoi."[126] Concretely, that meant circulating joint propaganda, organizing mass actions such as marches, agitating among US troops stationed in Europe, creating grassroots antiwar committees, collaborating with larger antiwar initiatives like the International War Crimes Tribunal, constructing united fronts in each country, and building ties with Vietnamese representatives. To do that, they vowed to "further the development of national Vietnam committees," and to deepen "their international co-ordination."[127] By early 1967, then, European radicals had developed a formal network, a tactical repertoire, a guiding strategy, and a general framework for doing international solidarity work. In this, they successfully established a sustainable radical international that united radicals from across the North Atlantic with the express aim of changing the world.

Why Vietnam?

In addition to becoming one of the highest priorities for activists across North America and Western Europe, the Vietnamese liberation struggle served as a binding element, allowing radicals to come together. Of course, radicals in the 1960s had already begun to build a number of overlapping transnational networks, quite a few of which were independent of the Vietnam War. But few struggles made possible sustained international coordination on such a mass scale as the Vietnam War. It was Vietnam, more than anything else, that united radicals across borders. But why did Vietnam play this role? The answer lies in the timely and highly contingent encounter between a radicalized international context, nascent domestic ecosystems of struggle, and the unique character of the Vietnamese liberation struggle itself.

The precondition for a reinvented radical international in North America and Western Europe was the unprecedented wave of liberation movements after the Second World War. Not only were more people waging struggles, but they also often saw themselves as part of a global movement and organized regular meetings throughout the 1950s and 1960s to fortify those ties.[128] Bandung in 1955, Belgrade in 1961, and especially Havana in 1966 all laid the groundwork for deeper unity, with each conference growing more radical than the last. At Havana, in particular, radicals established the Organization of Solidarity with the People of Asia, Africa, and Latin America with the unabashed aim of fostering internationalist revolution.[129] This background of decolonization, national liberation, and international coordination provided fertile ground for the international activism of the Vietnam War to take root. To put it differently, radical internationalism in North America and

Western Europe became much easier to operationalize now that radicals in the "Third World" had already shown the way.[130]

The second decisive factor was the reemergence of domestic struggles in the North Atlantic in the late 1950s and early 1960s. These new movements schooled activists, forged an arsenal of tactics, and established new institutions, creating a kind of political ecosystem that made antiwar activism possible later in the decade. In Great Britain, for example, the majority of the Vietnam Solidarity Campaign's rank and file had been active in the earlier Campaign for Nuclear Disarmament.[131] In France, those leading the struggle against the Vietnam War had also protested against the Algerian War.[132] In the United States, many antiwar activists, Black and white, had passed through the Civil Rights Movement before turning to Vietnam.[133] So when the American War in Vietnam began to make headlines, a core of activists in North America and Western Europe were already radicalized, networked, and battle-tested. Vietnam in turn transformed that core, facilitating the formation of a coherent, organized, and alternative radical force.

Without the contingent encounter of domestic ecosystems of struggle on the one hand with a specific international context on the other, the connections that made possible not only a revived radical internationalism in the North Atlantic, but also a functional, independent, radical international, would have never emerged in the 1960s. This is precisely why nothing of the sort took shape during the First Indochina War in the late 1940s and early 1950s. On the one side, an independent radical left was virtually nonexistent in the early 1950s. In the United States, McCarthyism had gutted radicalism as an organized force. In France, the Cold War compelled radicals to choose sides, banishing to the political desert those seeking an autonomous path. While some radical formations survived, and a few even coordinated among themselves, their numbers were too minuscule to form anything like a robust radical international.[134] On the other side, decolonization had only just begun when the First Indochina War exploded in December 1946. Even when Vietnamese revolutionaries smashed the French at Điện Biên Phủ in 1954, nearly all of Africa was still under colonial rule. During the First Indochina War, then, neither element – the domestic ecosystems or the radical international context – existed.[135]

But if the First Indochina War came "too soon," as it were, the Second Indochina War began precisely as domestic struggles in the North Atlantic and international solidarity throughout Asia, Africa, and Latin America were expanding. More than that, the war erupted at a time when both these domestic movements and internationalist efforts were primed for a new internationalist project. In the North Atlantic, the

United States escalated the war in Vietnam not only as the radical left was beginning to reemerge as an organized force, but also when these formative struggles had begun to transition, subside, or collapse, clearing the ground for antiwar activism. In France, the Evian Accords of 1962 precipitated a relative lull in activism. In Britain, the signing of the Test Ban Treaty in 1963 sent the disarmament movement into decline. And in the United States, urban rebellions, civil rights legislation, and political rifts within the broader Black liberation struggle prompted many activists to reassess the movement's trajectory in 1965. In this way, the Vietnam War unfolded at an opportune moment, precisely when activists – hardened by earlier experiences – were searching for a new way forward.

The same can be said about internationalist efforts in Asia, Africa, and Latin America. When the United States deepened its involvement in Vietnam, revolutionary movements in the "Third World" were experiencing setbacks.[136] In 1964, Brazil succumbed to a dictatorship. In 1965, Ben Bella was toppled in a military coup, solidifying authoritarian rule in Algeria. That same year, an anticommunist coalition backed by the United States systematically annihilated the Indonesian left. In this context, the much-anticipated second Asian–African Conference, a sequel to the famous Bandung Conference, was called off. Although the Tricontinental Conference in Havana offered a renewed sense of hope after these defeats, many revolutionaries reassessed the prospects for radical global change. They looked to the Vietnamese revolution as the path forward.

But while the coming together of these domestic ecosystems with a radicalized international context at this unique moment provided the necessary conditions for a renewed radical internationalism, the encounter does not explain why Vietnam, and not some other revolutionary struggle, played the role of binding element. After all, from Palestine to Guinea-Bissau, there was no shortage of movements. In fact, at the same time that the US government intensified its war in Vietnam, it also invaded the Dominican Republic to prevent what the White House feared would be another Cuba. Antiwar activists everywhere rallied in opposition. Quite a few of the French radicals leading the charge against the Vietnam War were simultaneously involved in the Committee for Solidarity with the Dominican People.[137] Vietnam Day in Berkeley was also intended to protest US aggression in the Dominican Republic.[138] The two struggles were often joined in the imagination of many radicals in 1965. But then why was there no Santo Domingo international? Why Vietnam instead?

The answer lies in the specific characteristics of the Vietnamese liberation struggle. To begin with, the sheer immensity of suffering in Vietnam was staggering. The Vietnamese people had toiled under colonial occupation for decades, and hundreds of thousands had died in wars against the Japanese, French, and now the Americans. The United States, together with the Republic of Vietnam, torched villages, decimated acres of jungle, and slaughtered thousands with some of the most lethal weapons.[139] The appalling scale of destruction could not but help motivate activists in the North Atlantic to take action.

In addition, there seemed to be no end in sight. Although the United States deployed troops to the Dominican Republic and Vietnam at roughly the same time, the war in the former effectively ended in late 1965, while the one in the latter not only dragged on, but also grew far more destructive with every passing year. Vietnam became one of the bloodiest active struggles of the period. In other words, unlike other exemplary struggles in China, Cuba, and Algeria, where revolutionaries had already taken power, the Vietnamese revolution was still very much underway, its fate uncertain, the fighting fierce. All this meant that international solidarity with Vietnam could have a real effect, giving it an edge, weight, and exigency that solidarity with many other struggles did not quite have.

But to many activists as well as bystanders in the 1960s, Vietnam was not just any active struggle. It was arguably the most consequential one of the decade. This was largely because activists perceived it to be the place where all the major trends of the postwar era were playing out: decolonization, imperialism, socialist construction, development, nation-building, modernization, self-determination, the Sino-Soviet split, the Cold War. Vietnam "condensed" all the great contradictions of the time: peasants against landlords, the working masses against the comprador bourgeoisie, national liberation against imperialism, antiracism against white supremacy, women's liberation against patriarchy, socialism against capitalism, world revolution against US hegemony, and the promise of a new communism against Soviet revisionism.[140]

It was precisely this confluence that led so many radicals in North America and Western Europe to elevate the Vietnamese struggle over others. "The struggle of the people of South Vietnam against American imperialism and the ruling class of Saigon is not only a struggle of international importance," the Brussels statement explained. "Vietnam is the key to the world situation, a decisive test of strength between American imperialism and the colonial revolution and the whole labour movement. The international capitalist alliance directed by the American government (NATO, SEATO, Treaty of Manila) is locked in combat with the Vietnamese revolution which is an integral part of the worldwide socialist revolution."[141] Vietnam was the "focal point" of the conjuncture. Everything hinged on its outcome.[142]

It is important to note that this interpretation echoed the way Vietnamese revolutionaries themselves framed their project. Nguyễn Khắc Viện – a communist who had organized in France, cultivated strong ties with international antiwar movements, and now managed the DRV's numerous multilingual publishing projects such as the *Vietnam Courier* – publicly argued that the "most important contradictions of our times converge today in Viet Nam."[143] His effective successor in France, Mai Văn Bộ, later argued that the American War was an epochal struggle that "concerns the destiny of all the peoples of the Earth." A US victory

would be not only a defeat for the Vietnamese people but also a setback for the national liberation movement and for world revolution. It would give the United States an excellent opportunity to continue to disrupt liberation struggles in other regions, prevent the trend towards socialism of newly independent and free peoples, and impose America's neo-colonialism everywhere.

If the United States lost, however, it would be not only a triumph for the Vietnamese people in their quest for reunification, independence, and freedom, but also a victory for the worldwide "national liberation movement," the struggle for "joining national independence with socialism," and "world revolution" itself. Vietnam's victory against the United States, he added, would open a new era in the international struggle against imperialism, in the same way that "the Điện Biên Phủ victory that ended Vietnam's resistance war against French colonialism in 1954 has opened the era of the collapse of old colonialism around the world."[144]

On top of these incredibly high stakes, it appeared as if Vietnamese revolutionaries might stand a fighting chance. Somehow, revolutionaries in one of the poorer parts of the world had held their own against the most advanced military in human history. Radicals quickly interpreted the war as a heroic struggle between David and Goliath, a narrative that Vietnamese communists themselves spread. Rejecting surrender, and refusing to show the slightest sign of defeatism, all their public statements reaffirmed the inevitability of their victory. Exclamations such as "Our Unshakeable Will: All the Way to Complete Victory" regularly appeared on the front pages of the *Vietnam Courier*, the primary foreign language publication of the DRV, printed in French and English.[145] This kind of unflappable optimism had a tremendous effect on radicals in North America and Western Europe, captivating them like no other struggle in the 1960s. Vietnam gave them hope, offered them an opportunity to make a meaningful contribution to a live campaign, and allowed them to invest themselves affectively in an ascendant struggle.

Although other liberation movements solicited foreign assistance, Vietnamese revolutionaries were arguably the most committed from the start to orchestrating internationalism. While many of these other movements limited themselves to expelling the foreigner, building a new nation-state, and occasionally gesturing to international cooperation, the communists who led the Vietnamese revolution conceptualized their actions within a fully internationalist framework. As experienced Leninists devoted to anti-imperialist internationalism, they did more than just request support from friendly movements; they saw their own struggle as contributing to those unfolding across the globe. In the South, the NLF's original program from 1960 called for struggle "against all forms of imperialist domination" and support for "the national emancipation movements of the various peoples," as well as solidarity with "all movements of struggle for peace, democracy, and social progress throughout the world."[146] In the North, the communist internationalists governing the DRV aimed not only to unite the country but also to assist in the construction of worldwide communism. "This was one of the things that made the Viet-Nam war very different from the Algerian War: the North Vietnamese government was fully internationalist in the traditionalist Marxist sense of the word," Schwartz explained.[147]

Drawing on the Leninist problematic, the NLF and the DRV repeatedly claimed they were fighting for the liberation of all the people of the world. Vietnam, they argued, stood at the front line of the global struggle for liberation. In April 1966, for example, the National Assembly of North Vietnam declared: "To defeat the American aggressors, the shared enemy of the peoples of the entire world, such is the noble historic mission of our people; all while fighting for the interests of our people, we also fight for those of the peoples of the entire world."[148] In their view, all the struggles were linked, which meant that a victory in Vietnam would help these other liberation movements. By the same token, the victory of these other struggles would assist the Vietnamese people. This explains why Vietnamese revolutionaries placed such great emphasis on internationalism, figuring the success of other struggles into their own strategy.

To that end, the DRV, and especially the NLF, built relations with people in the capitalist core, the socialist bloc, the newly independent countries, and those regions still fighting colonial rule.[149] In 1966, for instance, the NLF participated in approximately 125 conventions across the globe.[150] In 1967, it had more than twenty offices abroad.[151] Vietnamese revolutionaries consciously attempted to fuse heterogeneous struggles into an imagined international unity: struggles still in progress with those emerging victorious, campaigns against formal colonialism with those confronting other forms of imperialism, communist movements with noncommunist struggles, organized labor with new anti-racist, youth, and women's movements. They assumed this unifying role because their struggle stood at the crossroads of these differences: They fought an anticolonial as well as an anti-imperialist war; they were nation-building in the DRV while continuing to fight in the RVN; they were communist in the North while members of a coalition that included noncommunists in the South; they imagined the proletariat as a kind of vanguard but were just as concerned about racism, women's oppression, and the special needs of the youth.[152]

The NLF and DRV consciously propagated the idea that Vietnam served as an international focal point. Every issue of the *Vietnam Courier* featured a section that reported on solidarity struggles across the world. By bringing these distinct antiwar actions – in different countries, by different groups, for different ends – onto the same plane, Vietnamese revolutionaries encouraged the feeling that a unified international movement, centered on Vietnam, already existed.[153] Politically astute, Vietnamese communists strived for maximum inclusivity, carefully promoting and graciously thanking all antiwar forces, whatever their differences.[154] Just as the Vietnamese Workers' Party avoided publicly taking too firm a side during the Sino-Soviet split, recognizing that doing so would weaken the war effort, Vietnamese leaders thanked both the official communist parties and antiwar radicals in groups like the NVC, even though they were perfectly aware of their differences and knew that each "claimed" Vietnam for their own side.

Yet Vietnamese communists did give strong indications to radicals that they supported their efforts. Because of the strategic importance of antiwar opposition in the United States, American radicals frequently received explicit encouragement from both the NLF and the DRV in the form of telegrams, letters, articles, and in person at meetings in Cuba, North Vietnam, or Czechoslovakia. But even the Europeans enjoyed unambiguous support from Vietnamese revolutionaries. In 1966, the DRV applauded in the pages of the *Vietnam Courier* the formation of the NVC, and Hồ Chí Minh wrote a personal message to Schwartz, which NVC activists interpreted as "official recognition" of the National Vietnam Committee's role in the struggle against the war.[155] To the dismay of the French Communist Party, radicals regularly communicated with the DRV delegation in Paris, NLF and DRV representatives spoke at NVC events, and the two sides often collaborated on antiwar actions.[156]

In addition to encouraging radicals in individual countries, the NLF and DRV promoted deeper international coordination between them, largely because they agreed with radical arguments about the strategic value of antiwar struggle in the North Atlantic. During the Brussels conference in March 1967, for example, Mai Văn Bộ sent radicals a letter of appreciation for their international initiative.[157] Radicals across North America and Western Europe viewed this as a ringing endorsement of their new radical international. Linked across borders, armed with a strategy, and now backed by Vietnamese themselves, they prepared to organize a relentless wave of coordinated activism to help make the Vietnamese revolution a definitive triumph.

2 Anti-Imperialism

In 1967, Laurent Schwartz expounded on the significance of the Vietnam War in an editorial for the inaugural issue of *Pour le Viet-Nam*, the official paper of the National Vietnam Committee (NVC). "The American government wants to make an example of Vietnam: by bringing Vietnam to its knees, it wants to show to all people, especially those from underdeveloped countries, but to a certain degree also all the others, that no country can in the future choose a path that does not conform to the wishes of American leaders, or if it harms American capital." It was precisely because the war concerned the fate of people everywhere, Schwartz explained, that "the resistance of the Vietnamese people is that of all free people; their fight is ours."[1]

Vietnamese revolutionaries, along with dissidents inside the United States were the foot soldiers in this global struggle, yet they were not the only ones who "could do something" about the war. The French could, and should, organize "broad international support" for their Vietnamese and American comrades. Internationalism, Schwartz emphasized, was not mere sympathy for a distant struggle, but action. Thankfully, he added optimistically, the French were doing just that. Antiwar activists were writing articles, collecting money, raising awareness about the war, boycotting companies that collaborated with the United States, organizing coordinated demonstrations, helping deserting GIs find safety, shipping antibiotics and typewriters to Vietnam, strengthening ties with Vietnamese revolutionaries, preparing to put the United States on trial for genocide at an International War Crimes Tribunal, and convincing thousands to not only oppose the war but also join the growing antiwar struggle.

This might not seem like much, Schwartz admitted, but he wagered that it still could make a difference. Vietnamese fighters needed not just artillery or planes delivered by the USSR or China but also "moral and political support" from people everywhere. This was the kind of solidarity that activists in the North Atlantic were well positioned to supply, and precisely what Vietnamese officials themselves sought most

from their comrades in this part of the world. Vietnamese revolutionaries believed that the war would be fought not only in the jungles of
Vietnam but also on the terrain of ideas. Marching into the trenches
of the ideological struggle was the best way for antiwar radicals to do
their part.

Schwartz's editorial also signaled the growing popularity of the systemic critique of the war. In their quest to better understand the system
that made the war possible, many antiwar activists turned to Marxism,
defining the system as "imperialism" and the struggle against it as "anti-
imperialism." While there were different ways to combat imperialism,
by the late 1960s most radicals had adopted some version of the Leninist problematic of the right of nations to self-determination, effectively
coupling anti-imperialism with national liberation. Radicals of different stripes debated how anti-imperialist struggles should unfold, how
many stages were necessary, or who should be involved in them, but few
engaged anti-imperialists seriously disputed the central premises of the
problematic. This approach to internationalism became so popular that
even those who did not consider themselves radicals adopted some of its
core elements: they called the enemy "imperialism," advocated "national
liberation," and talked about "changing the system." By the late 1960s,
anti-imperialism was beating out its many internationalist rivals – such
as individualist human rights – to become the dominant way in which
activists in the North Atlantic imagined international change.

The War in Europe

With the US war effort going poorly, opposition in Europe mounting,
and allied governments reluctant to lend further support, Lyndon Johnson dispatched Vice President Hubert Humphrey to Europe in March
1967 to mend fraying relations. Given Charles de Gaulle's criticism
of the war, Humphrey's stay in Paris assumed special importance. In
France, the vice president met de Gaulle, laid a wreath at the Tomb of
the Unknown Soldier, and visited the statue of George Washington on
the Place d'Iéna. Hoping to renew Franco-American bonds, he made a
much-publicized toast to the "friendship that has linked our countries
over so many years and across so many trials."[2]

French antiwar activists organized a welcome committee of their
own. On April 7, 1967, they met Humphrey at the airport with chants
of "US Assassins!" They positioned themselves on the route leading
to the capital, screaming, throwing rotten eggs, and pouring paint on
his motorcade. Once in Paris, they harassed him incessantly, anticipating his every move. They pasted posters that read "Humphrey Go

Home!" at the venues he was scheduled to visit. A thousand protesters broke the police line at the Arc de Triomphe. They threw rocks at the windows of the American Express office. Others attacked the offices of the *New York Times*. Another group tore down the US flag at the American Cathedral in Paris and torched it for the television cameras. Battles raged into the night as protesters and police clashed near the US Embassy.[3]

The French protests were just one act in a coordinated political drama unfolding across Western Europe. Humphrey found little solace as activists waylaid him in nearly every city he visited. In Rome, angry crowds forced the police to rush him to safety; in Florence, an activist pelted him in the face with a lemon; in Brussels, demonstrators showered him with rotten eggs; in West Berlin, thousands of Germans swarmed the vice president with chants of "Vice Killer," and police arrested eleven radical students for an alleged conspiracy to assassinate him; in London, only rain succeeded in thinning the ranks of protesters.[4]

While activists everywhere targeted US symbols, the demonstrations cannot be reduced to a simple expression of anti-Americanism, as many Americans argued at the time.[5] On the contrary, the coordinated actions against Humphrey's European tour represented one of the first achievements of the internationalist strategy that radicals had sketched in Brussels a month earlier. If American power rested in part on support from its European allies, then the best way for Europeans to protest the war would be to attack their own government's implicit or explicit support for US foreign policy. As the NVC explained, in addition to decrying Humphrey's visit, their action sought to "denounce the French Government's complicity in welcoming him."[6] The French heckled not just "The Star-Spangled Banner" but also "The Marseillaise." They followed chants of "Humphrey assassin!" with "De Gaulle complice!" They linked the US military with the French police.[7]

Activists helped make the war so unpopular in Europe that even their own governments began to distance themselves from the United States. As protesters accosted the vice president in the streets, behind closed doors Humphrey's allies raised concerns about the war. In France, de Gaulle remained unmovable. In Great Britain, Prime Minister Harold Wilson suggested a peace settlement, while his foreign secretary criticized US bombing. In the Federal Republic of Germany, the White House's strongest supporter in Europe, West Germans had grown so upset with Chancellor Ludwig Erhardt's close alignment with Johnson that they effectively forced him out of office, leaving his successor wary of increasing support for the war.[8] In Italy, Deputy Prime Minister Pietro Nenni spoke for many when he confided to Humphrey: "Europe does not understand America any longer. America does not understand Europe. The root of the discord is the Vietnam War."[9] Vietnam had strained the postwar alliance between the imperialist powers.[10]

All this had an energizing effect on European radicals. Humphrey's visit seemed to prove that the United States was not only mired in Southeast Asia but also losing decisive international support. "The American troops continue to suffer defeat after defeat," announced a flyer from the Union of Communist Youth (Marxist-Leninist). "That's why the United States Vice President Humphrey, traveling salesman of US imperialism, has come to Europe, and today France, seeking the support of the governments of the so-called 'free' world."[11] But instead of supporting Humphrey, the Union of Communist Youth (Marxist-Leninist) gleefully observed, the "people of the countries of Europe have shown, through particularly dynamic demonstrations, their solidarity with the Vietnamese people and their hatred of American aggression."[12] While these radicals certainly inflated their own importance, the Humphrey protests of early 1967 clearly showed that antiwar opposition was becoming more widespread, more radical, and more coordinated.

Antiwar Soldiers

Hubert Humphrey was not the only American to attract the attention of European activists. In fact, there were hundreds of thousands of Americans working, living, or vacationing throughout Western Europe in the late 1960s. Working closely with American expat groups such as the Paris American Committee to Stopwar (PACS) in France, the Stop It Committee in Britain, and the US Campaign to the End the War in Vietnam in West Germany, activists discussed the war with tourists, convinced eligible men to dodge the draft, and mobilized students studying abroad. But the most important target demographic were the thousands of American troops living in Europe, particularly the 250,000 military personnel stationed in bases across West Germany.

Following the lead of their American peers, activists in the Socialist German Student League began agitating among US soldiers in early 1967.[13] Soliciting desertion was a punishable offense, but this did not stop radicals from inciting soldiers to abandon the military, sheltering GIs in safe houses, and helping deserters flee to neighboring countries.[14] Sweden's progressive policies, general opposition to the war, and refusal to join NATO made it an attractive destination, but quite a few deserters also tried their luck in France, hoping to take advantage of the tense relations between Paris and Washington, DC.

The test came in May 1967, when an American GI named Louis Armsfield was caught in the Latin Quarter. Although technically obliged to return deserters to the United States, the French government unexpectedly allowed Armsfield to legally live and work in the country. By setting such a precedent, France quickly became a popular destination for other deserters, and European radicals pieced together an elaborate network to help them travel safely. West Germans organized the first leg of the journey, passing the Americans to the Provos in the Netherlands, who then sent them off to France.[15] In some cases, deserters would travel directly into France, often meeting with French radicals in cities like Strasbourg before making their way to Paris, where they often connected with NVC activists.[16] By the end of the year, Karl Dietrich Wolff, president of the Socialist German Student League, boasted that they were ferrying nearly 150 soldiers out of Germany a month.[17]

Once in France, a few groups helped deserters find their way.[18] One was colloquially known as "RITA," which was backed by PACS, the NVC, and noted antiwar luminaries such as Jean-Paul Sartre, who allowed the group to use his mailbox.[19] Unveiled at a televised press conference with Student Nonviolent Coordinating Committee (SNCC) leader Stokely Carmichael in late 1967, the new organization aimed to organize not only deserters, but also antiwar soldiers within the military.[20] "A RITA," the group's newsletter put it, "is a Resister inside the Armed Forces, an American Serviceman who resists imperialistic aggression in S.E. Asia."[21] The group's leader, a GI named Dick Perrin, later explained: "We developed a network with soldiers still in the military, guys who wanted to take part but were reluctant to desert. We made a point of saying that was okay. In fact, those antiwar GIs who stayed in became really helpful."[22] Another organization was led by Students for a Democratic Society (SDS) organizer Bo Burlingham, PACS member Larry Cox, and French activists connected to Henri Curiel, some of whom had been involved in the Jeanson network during the Algerian War. Eventually known as the American Deserters Committee, the group organized a number of bold actions, including a public event with the NVC in which American men turned in their draft cards.[23]

In all these efforts, French radicals made a point to cooperate with other activists across borders. They worked with branches of the American Deserters Committee in Sweden and Canada, the primary destination for deserters. They coordinated with Vietnamese revolutionaries, who publicly thanked the efforts of antiwar GIs and regularly urged Europeans to continue helping them.[24] And they collaborated extensively with Americans. Through Carmichael, SNCC partnered with Perrin's group, while SDS reached out to Cox's organization. In July 1967, for example, SDS sent one of its heavies, Greg Calvert, to formalize the link. A former SDS national secretary, Calvert had studied abroad in Paris in the early 1960s, where he was politicized by the Algerian War. "The first anti-war demonstration I was ever in," he recalled, "was a demonstration against the Algerian war, in Paris, France."[25] Impressed by French efforts to organize draft resistance, desertion, and opposition within the military during the Algerian War, Calvert pushed SDS to do the same during the Vietnam War.[26]

While these transnational collaborations deepened radical internationalism, they also illuminated some differences between the Americans and the French. Activists debated whose jurisdiction this work fell under, and by implication, which side should take the lead. They disagreed over tactics, with the Americans eager to use mainstream media to publicize desertion, whereas the French, who had worked with Algerian revolutionaries and in some cases fought in the Resistance, insisted on a more clandestine approach.[27] Most importantly, the budding transatlantic alliance revealed glaring differences in political culture. Although Calvert spoke French, he confronted an almost insurmountable communication barrier. "I was just at my wit's end to even begin to talk in the terms they were talking about," he later exclaimed.[28] The main issue, he realized, was Marxism. In contrast to the United States, Marxism, and by extension Leninism, played an outsized role in France, pervading the general culture, dominating the thought of massive institutions like the French Communist Party, and shaping how radicals organized. As Calvert put it, his sojourn in France was his "first really heavy exposure to people who thought strictly in Leninist terms."[29]

But as frustrating as the encounter may have been, these many transatlantic antiwar connections did facilitate a kind of learning process. The French came to recognize the specificity of the US context, while the Americans were schooled in a different way of thinking. "I came back to the States with a lot more knowledge about something that I really didn't know very much about before," the former SDS national secretary admitted.[30] Indeed, soon after Calvert's visit, American radicals would turn to Marxism en masse, and with it, the Leninist approach to anti-imperialism.

International Brigades

Inspired by the Spanish Civil War, some European antiwar radicals turned to international brigades as yet another form of solidarity.[31] Although it is unclear who proposed the idea first, it was openly promoted by Vietnamese revolutionaries early in the war. In March 1965, just as Johnson escalated the war, the National Liberation Front (NLF) announced that "if the American imperialists continue to engage their combat troops and those of their satellites in southern Vietnam, and to expand the war to North Vietnam and into Laos, the National Liberation Front will call on the peoples of different countries to send young people and soldiers to South Vietnam to join the population in order to annihilate the common enemy."[32]

The call was greeted with great excitement by several antiwar organizations. One of the earliest advocates was a group of Trotskyists led by Michel Pablo, a onetime leader of the Fourth International with plenty of experience with this kind of work. In 1949, the "Pablists" helped organize international work brigades for Yugoslavia, with the French sending over 1,500 volunteers. Later, they threw themselves into solidarity work during the Algerian War, which led to Pablo's own arrest. After the Vietnamese appeal, the Pablists exhorted activists to organize "international brigades to defend, at all costs, heroic Vietnam against the barbarian imperialist oppressor."[33] Following their lead, the Revolutionary Communist Youth (RCY), along with its comrades in the burgeoning radical youth international, also committed to the project. "As soon as the call is launched," they wrote in the first issue of their collective bulletin, "we declare ourselves ready to promote it and organise recruitment on a European scale and even of Americans who would want to fight on the side of North Vietnam."[34]

While the idea of international brigades circulated widely, the French once again took the lead in transforming it into a reality. Encouraged by both the Pablists and the RCY, the National Vietnam Committee formally sponsored the project, with NVC co-founders Jean-Paul Sartre and Laurent Schwartz personally publicizing it. Backed by the NVC, French radicals established a campaign office, published a newsletter, and recruited volunteers. In February 1967, *Le Monde* announced that two hundred French volunteers, including twenty-five women, had signed up. As with all their initiatives, the organizers internationalized the project, claiming they had received applications from such countries as West Germany, Great Britain, Belgium, Italy, Sweden, and Switzerland.[35]

In May 1967, the French contingent met Lê Đình Nhân of the North Vietnamese delegation in Paris to present the first list of 209 volunteers.[36] Publicly, the Vietnamese reaction was exuberant. As Lê Đình Nhân put it, "We thank you most sincerely and appreciate this gesture which demonstrates your militant solidarity with the struggle we are waging against the imperialism of the United States for our national independence and for peace in Southeast Asia."[37] But privately, he rejected it as impractical. As Gilbert Marquis of the NVC recalls: "We were received by the

Vietnamese, who did not discourage us, on the contrary, thanked us, but left us absolutely no hope that they would support this campaign."[38]

NVC activists were not the only European radicals rebuffed in this manner. When Tariq Ali of the British Vietnam Solidarity Campaign visited Vietnam in February 1967, he broached the topic of international volunteers with Phạm Văn Đồng. According to Ali, the prime minister of the Democratic Republic of Vietnam (DRV) raised several objections to the idea, emphasizing its military impracticability in particular. Given the nature of the air war, brigades were of little value in the North. As the prime minister reportedly put it, "this is not Spain in the thirties, where the technological level of combat was primitive. You have seen the scale of the US attacks on us. International brigades are no good against B52 bombers." International brigades would be just as ill-suited to the guerrilla war in the South. "In the South," he explained, "any brigade from abroad would not be able to function at all effectively. Many areas we control by night are overrun by the enemy during the day. We disappear very effectively because, after all, we are Vietnamese. Just imagine trying to hide several thousand European faces in the forests of the South." If anything, volunteers could become a burden. Phạm Văn Đồng explained, "even if we had them to help repair bridges and roads and schools and hospitals we would be more worried about their safety and would have to expend more resources on housing and looking after them." Civil or military, international brigades were off the table.[39]

Why, then, had Vietnamese revolutionaries called for them in the first place? After all, Phạm Văn Đồng himself had publicly promised that Vietnamese revolutionaries would call for "brigades of foreign volunteers in the more or less near future."[40] Even after firmly rejecting these initiatives by North American and Western European antiwar radicals, Vietnamese representatives continued to support the idea. As late as July 1968, for example, the North Vietnamese ambassador to the United Arab Republic announced that he would be "very thankful" to receive applications from Americans willing "to come to fight side by side with the Vietnamese people against the common enemy, that is United States imperialism."[41]

The answer lay in the perceived propaganda value of the endeavor. Though ineffective on the battlefield, international brigades could score a victory in the war of ideas. The fact that North Americans and Western Europeans would consider risking their lives in the jungles of South Vietnam proved that the NLF and DRV enjoyed dedicated international support in their struggle against the United States. If the US government sought to isolate Vietnam, the formation of international brigades, even if only a possibility, dispelled the illusion that Vietnam was alone.

In addition, it could reframe the narrative of the war by drawing positive parallels with Spain, casting Vietnamese revolutionaries as the heroic Spanish Republicans, and the Americans as the rebels, or worse, the Nazis and Fascists who propped up General Francisco Franco's rebellion against the Republic. But most of all, the very idea of international brigades could foster unity. "Sending volunteers can play a political role and create a sentiment of internationalism," the radical youth international explained in its bulletin.[42]

For that reason, Vietnamese continued to endorse the idea of international brigades. As Lê Đình Nhân explained to the organizers of the volunteer corps back in France, the initiative would help develop "active propaganda" in France.[43] The French committee played along.[44] As Marquis put it, "After the meeting with the Vietnamese delegation and Vietnam's response, the volunteer corps became instead a means of propaganda."[45] While the effort to organize international brigades for Vietnam never came to fruition, and would be remembered as a marginal episode in the history of international antiwar activism, it shed light on the kind of solidarity work that Vietnamese revolutionaries expected from activists in the North Atlantic before 1968. For them, the value of internationalism at this time lay in helping to wage the ideological struggle.

The Ideological Front

Vietnamese communists never believed they could defeat the Republic of Vietnam, and its primary backer, the United States, through war alone. So instead they developed a general strategy that combined three different struggles. The first was the military struggle, which was intended to wear down the United States to such a degree that the White House would feel compelled to abandon its ally in the South. The second was political, which aimed to win over as many sectors of South Vietnamese society as possible. If guerrillas were fish, it was the political struggle that made possible the sea of support in which they could swim. According to this framework of "people's war," promoting land reform, mobilizing women, or building schools was just as important as fighting in jungles. The final struggle was diplomatic, which sought not only to secure material aid but also to redirect popular opinion against the United States.[46] This was a lesson they had learned from the war against France. As the DRV's Ministry of Foreign Affairs reflected, "the corrupt colonialists, before losing in the battlefields, had lost in Paris."[47] And it was a lesson confirmed by the recent Algerian War: Even though Algerian revolutionaries had lost to France militarily, they were were still able to wield the weapon of diplomacy to win their independence.[48]

As historian Pierre Asselin has shown, the communists further divided this diplomatic front into three "circles."[49] In the first were the socialist bloc powers of Cuba, China, North Korea, the Soviet Union, and Central and Eastern Europe. The second included the nonaligned, but potentially friendly countries in Asia, Africa, and Latin America. The final circle comprised nonstate actors, especially those in the North Atlantic. There, Vietnamese revolutionaries practiced what was called "people's diplomacy," reaching out to student groups, labor unions, women's organizations, intellectual societies, and above all antiwar movements. The DRV, and especially the NLF, aimed, in the words of Asselin, to "turn Western publics against their own governments supportive of American policy in Vietnam, and against the US government specifically."[50] While they certainly welcomed all kinds of support from activists, Vietnamese strategists made it very clear that they were most interested in international solidarity that could help win the war of ideas.

For their part, most antiwar radicals in 1967, Americans or French, Trotskyist or Maoist, followed suit, prioritizing the ideological front.[51] Collaborating with Vietnamese revolutionaries, they stoked antiwar sentiment, hosted international antiwar conferences, cooperated with friendly journalists to publish sympathetic articles, organized cultural events that humanized the Vietnamese people, and applied pressure on their governments. Since one of the US government's primary objectives was to silence the voices of Vietnamese revolutionaries, a major aspect of this ideological struggle was to propagate Vietnamese ideas through printed materials. This was a huge operation that relied on intricate international networks. In Vietnam, a team around Nguyễn Khắc Viện produced a galaxy of multilingual publications such as the weekly Vietnam Courier, the quarterly Vietnamese Studies, booklets on Vietnamese history and politics, collections of poetry, and specialized magazines about South Vietnam, women, and youth. Outside Vietnam, operatives such as Nguyễn Văn Hiếu of the NLF, press agent Phạm Văn Chương in Eastern Europe, Mai Văn Bộ of the DRV delegation in Paris, and Nguyễn Văn Sao of the weekly Cứu Quốc in London served as intermediaries, organizing travel, translating materials, meeting with the foreign press, coordinating international initiatives, and connecting activists with their counterparts in Southeast Asia. In Europe, sympathetic Vietnamese organizations like the Vietnamese Union in France assisted these officials, offered financial support, and helped pass materials along to the press, antiwar movements, and the general public. And across North America and Western Europe, activists in antiwar organizations such as the National Vietnam Committee or leftist institutions like François Maspero's famous bookstore in Paris discussed these texts, distributed them, and used them as the basis of their own agitational materials.[52] In this way, revolutionary ideas reached diverse audiences in the very heart of the capitalist world.[53]

Unsurprisingly, intellectual celebrities such as Simone de Beauvoir, Jean-Paul Sartre, and Bertrand Russell played an important role in these ideological efforts. In fact, it was Russell, now honorary president of the British Vietnam Solidarity Campaign, who spearheaded what would become the most famous example of internationally coordinated struggle on the ideological front: the International War Crimes Tribunal (IWCT). Wanting to make a greater contribution to the antiwar struggle, Russell proposed a tribunal to investigate whether the United States had committed war crimes, much as the famous Nuremberg trials had done for the Nazis after the Second World War.[54] In the summer and autumn of 1965, he sent one of his representatives, an American named Ralph Schoenman, to meet with Mã Thị Chu, Đinh Bá Thi, and Phạm Văn Chương about the proposal.[55] In February 1966, Schoenman traveled to North Vietnam to speak with Hồ Chí Minh and Phạm Văn Đồng, while Russell Stetler, another American, flew to Paris and Helsinki in the summer to meet with other DRV representatives.[56] Vietnamese officials enthusiastically supported the idea. Speaking for the North, Hồ Chí Minh and Phạm Văn Đồng agreed to donate funds, allow investigators into the DRV, grant the Tribunal access to all facilities, and make available all evidence in their possession. Speaking for the South, Nguyễn Hữu Thọ conveyed to Russell that the "National Liberation Front wishes you to know that we appreciate vividly the War Crimes Tribunal. The National Liberation Front is ready to co-ordinate as actively as possible in all the work of the War Crimes Tribunal. Whatever assistance is required from our Central Committee will be provided concretely and immediately."[57] As historian Harish C. Mehta has shown, Vietnamese were thoroughly involved in the project.[58]

With Vietnamese blessing, Bertrand Russell's Peace Foundation contacted other activists in Europe to expand the Tribunal. As many of Russell's associates were also active in the Vietnam Solidarity Campaign, they easily enlisted the support of other British antiwar radicals. Tasked with contacting the Americans, Schoenman traveled to the United States, where he met with antiwar groups like the May Second Movement, SDS, and SNCC, which agreed to support the Tribunal.[59] Russell personally wrote to Sartre, who happily lent his services, as did many others in the National Vietnam Committee. The French poured considerable energy into the Tribunal. They provided logistical support, prepared to host the Tribunal in Paris, and assumed responsibility for propaganda in France, Italy, Belgium, and West Germany.[60] They also supplied key personnel: Sartre served as executive president, Laurent Schwartz acted as co-president, youth activists like those in the RCY promoted the Tribunal on the ground, and dozens of French doctors, journalists, lawyers, and filmmakers volunteered their services, many traveling to Vietnam as part of the investigative teams.[61]

Tribunal organizers reached out to activists across the world, with Russell even writing a letter of invitation to Che Guevara, who had to decline because he was too busy preparing guerrilla war in Bolivia.[62] Despite these global ties, the Tribunal's organizers decided for strategic reasons to focus their efforts on the imperialist countries of North America and Western Europe. This was reflected in the composition of Tribunal members, the majority of whom were based in the North Atlantic, such as Lelio Basso from Italy; Peter Weiss from Germany; Tariq Ali from Britain; and James Baldwin, Stokely Carmichael, David Dellinger, and Carl Oglesby from the United States. The organizers also strategically sought to unite figures from across the leftist spectrum into a broad coalition, albeit one still explicitly shaped by radical ideas. This sustained commitment to a radical framing in turn convinced the more openly revolutionary militants, such as those in the radical antiwar youth international, to throw their weight behind the IWCT.[63]

During the fall of 1966, activists formalized the Tribunal's procedures, collected documentary material on the war, and deployed a suite of teams to gather firsthand accounts in Vietnam.[64] Despite logistical challenges, the White House's unwillingness to participate, and de Gaulle's refusal to allow the Tribunal to convene in Paris, the IWCT finally met in Stockholm in May 1967 and Copenhagen in December 1967 to review the evidence, hear testimonies, and evaluate US involvement in Vietnam. In deliberating the American War in Vietnam, the Tribunal chose not simply to condemn the United States in abstract terms but instead to determine, in Sartre's words, "whether imperialist policies infringe laws formulated by imperialism itself."[65] The United States, along with all the major powers, had agreed to certain laws governing the conduct of war. But through its investigative missions, the Tribunal amassed a wealth of evidence – villages reduced to rubble, children blown apart, civilians burned alive, temples bombed during worship, rice crops devastated – that suggested the United States was not involved in some peacekeeping mission but instead was trying to break the Vietnamese will to resist in a way that exceeded the parameters of the very laws the US government had itself established.

In addition to the conduct of the war, the Tribunal explored its causes. Lyndon Johnson justified US intervention by arguing that the United States was helping an independent country resist foreign incursion. But

the Tribunal reconstructed the history of the war in a way that demonstrated how the main threat to Vietnam's sovereignty was in fact the
United States. As the lawyer Lelio Basso put it, "not only is there not a
war between the two States of Vietnam, there is not even a civil war in
the South. This war is being fought by the people on one side and by
the American army and mercenary troops on the other."[66] In this way,
activists sought to replace the US government's narrative about the war
with one of their own, reframing the Vietnam War as a grand struggle
between a united Vietnamese people and an invading US military.
Armed with this alternative narrative, and backed by copious evidence
from the field, the Tribunal ultimately found the United States guilty of
all charges, including genocide.[67]

Of course, as many contemporaries noted, the Tribunal could not
possibly enforce this judgment. But that was never the objective. Instead
of meting out punishment, the Tribunal aimed to change opinions.
As French antiwar activists argued, the IWCT "can facilitate rising
consciousness in the western world."[68] Sartre elaborated on this point
in his inaugural statement, explaining that the Tribunal was a jury, but
"the judges are everywhere: they are the peoples of the world, and in
particular the American people. It is for them that we are working."[69]
The primary goal of the Tribunal was to shift the balance of forces on
the ideological terrain.

This was exactly the kind of support Vietnamese revolutionaries
wanted from their North American and Western European comrades. As
Hồ Chí Minh himself put it in his telegram to the preliminary meeting of
the IWCT, "By condemning these crimes the international tribunal will
promote world-wide indignation against the American aggressors and
will intensify the movement of protest among the peoples of all countries
in order to demand the end of this criminal war and the withdrawal of
the troops of the U.S. and their satellites." "It will contribute to the
awakening of the conscience of peoples of the world against American
imperialism," he added.[70] Prime Minister Phạm Văn Đồng underlined
the point: the Tribunal would "have a wide and profound impact on
world opinion, helping to intensify and widen the international movement of solidarity with the Vietnamese people."[71]

Although most accounts assume the Tribunal had little effect, recent
scholarship shows this to have been far from true. The United States saw
the Tribunal as a threat.[72] The undersecretary of state tapped personnel
from the State Department, Department of Defense, US Information
Agency, and the Central Intelligence Agency (CIA) to launch a disinfor-
mation campaign. The task force discussed with the French and British
governments how best to handle the Tribunal, ordered US ambassadors

abroad to convince foreign governments sympathetic to the Bertrand Russell Peace Foundation to withdraw their support, collaborated with the press to present the Tribunal as a communist front, and considered hosting a competing trial – though they ultimately nixed the idea out of fear that it might draw more attention to the Tribunal itself. It was certainly the alliance between the United States and Western European countries that convinced first de Gaulle, then Wilson, to ban the Tribunal from meeting in France and Britain respectively.[73] Far from ignoring the Tribunal, then, the US government worked hard to neutralize it. With worldwide antiwar opposition mounting in 1967, the Johnson administration had reason to worry: A White House study from that year concluded that the DRV's political and psychological campaign in the "free world" was succeeding.[74]

The Tribunal did yield results. In France, activists publicized its findings, the NVC hosted a gargantuan public meeting at the Mutualité to review the evidence, and the mainstream media reported on the proceedings. In this way, the Tribunal contributed to boosting antiwar sentiment in France and Europe more broadly. Given the lengths the White House went to undermine the IWCT, the Tribunal had much less impact in the United States, but even there it still had an effect. Quite a few American activists saw the Tribunal as a valuable resource: It offered a holistic narrative of the war, a set of cutting legal arguments against US aggression, and a mass of damning evidence, much of it quite revelatory, even for engaged activists. It was, for example, the Tribunal that brought to light the use of cluster bombs. As antiwar journalist Karen Wald explained, the evidence, testimonies, and arguments publicized by the proceedings could "be used to recruit and mobilize new people into the anti-war movement."[75]

In his speech at the IWCT's second meeting in December 1967, Carl Oglesby, former president of SDS, confirmed that the Tribunal played an important role among activists in the United States.[76] Echoing Wald, he pointed to three concrete ways it had assisted American antiwar efforts. First, it provided a "clear legal base" for draft resisters since it proved that the United States had itself broken international law.[77] Second, it served as "the clearing-house of information on the war." He explained: "You understand that it is not easy always for us, unless we probe with great care, to get an accurate picture of what actually happens in Vietnam. The Tribunal's capacity for pulling together and then developing in a most public and conspicuous way the elements of the war's reality – this function has been very important to us in the United States." Lastly, Oglesby argued that the Tribunal had contributed to "the building of an internationally solid New-Left movement."[78]

The IWCT formalized ad hoc contacts, forged new ones, and expanded the reach of the network to include representatives from other countries. It was through the IWCT, for example, that the French NVC came to build stronger ties with Black radicals in the United States, a connection that would prove transformative.

But if the IWCT represented one of the high points of antiwar international coordination, it simultaneously revealed the challenges of doing internationalism. Securing adequate resources was an endless battle.[79] Organizing such an involved project was tedious, exhausting, and at times boring.[80] Most of all, harmonizing different interests, personalities, experiences, and objectives across borders, languages, and preexisting organizational divides proved exceedingly difficult. For example, tensions immediately arose between the Russell Peace Foundation and Vietnamese representatives such as Mai Văn Bộ. Vietnamese in London and Paris sought greater influence, insisting, for instance, that they choose the Tribunal's investigative teams to North Vietnam. Russell, by contrast, felt they were imposing too much control, which jeopardized the Tribunal's value.[81] To resolve the issue, Russell went above their heads, writing directly to Hồ Chí Minh. Since the best way Europeans could help the Vietnamese people was to "change opinion in the West," he argued, "our actions and our evidence of the crimes of the United States must be impressive, irrefutable and supported by independent voices drawn widely from sectors of opinion and society."[82] The Tribunal had to appear as neutral as possible.

Hồ Chí Minh agreed, and he took steps to ensure the relative objectivity of the Tribunal. The spat, however, exposed tensions not only between Europeans and Vietnamese, but also within the Vietnamese political hierarchy.[83] Despite projecting a veneer of unity to the world, Vietnamese revolutionaries were themselves embroiled in sharp debates over everything from military strategy to the Sino-Soviet split. At that very moment, Hồ Chí Minh himself was coming under fire in Hanoi. Although radicals in North America and Western Europe continued to celebrate him, as well as the former war hero Võ Nguyên Giáp, as the face of the Vietnamese revolution, complex power struggles at the heart of the Vietnamese Workers' Party were sidelining Hồ, marginalizing figures like Giáp, purging their supporters, and shifting power to Lê Duẩn's faction.[84]

Conflict also raged between Europeans. The organizers fought over who had the right to publish the proceedings. Financial woes turned friends into enemies, with the Russell Peace Foundation censuring the Paris team for never reimbursing Russell.[85] Personalities clashed, with Russell and IWCT Chairman and President of Sessions Vladimir Dedijer conspiring to drive each other from the Tribunal.[86] Tribunal members disagreed over the central question of whether the United States was in fact committing genocide, with some doubting that the US government was killing Vietnamese specifically because they were Vietnamese and others insisting that they all put aside their "intellectual scruples" and denounce the United States in the harshest terms possible as a matter of political principle.[87] They even displayed surprisingly acute political differences, which exploded when some older members backed Israel in the Six-Day War, while some of the younger radicals, such as those in SNCC, took the other side.[88]

Although most of the American, European, and Vietnamese activists involved in organizing the Tribunal saw themselves on the left, shared the radical critique of the war, and had similar ideas about solidarity work, they still found much to disagree about. Internationalism, the whole experience confirmed, provided a general framework for activists across the world to pool their efforts to realize a shared goal, but it could not ensure automatic agreement on all issues. The challenge was to find a way to build unity while working through real, and sometimes irreconcilable, differences over long periods of time. Internationalism was not a single event, fixed once and for all, but a very difficult learning process, full of constant negotiation, adaptation, and revision. And the higher the stakes, the greater the challenges.

Leninist Revival

In his introduction to the published proceedings of the Tribunal, Russell exclaimed, "I hope that the peoples of the Third World will take heart from the example of the Vietnamese and join further in dismantling the American empire."[89] These were fiery words, especially from a nonagenarian pacifist who hoped to preserve at least a semblance of impartiality. Russell was no revolutionary, nor was the Tribunal, and yet the IWCT assumed a strikingly radical antiwar posture. Indeed, between the Tribunal's formation in early 1966 and its second session in December 1967, the radical critique of the war grew considerably more popular across the North Atlantic. More activists than ever now spoke not simply of the draft, the duplicity of the White House, or the unwinnability of the war, but of a larger system that had to be changed.

All this reflected a significant radicalization of leftist activism over the course of 1967. Not only were there more radicals, but the radicals themselves were also becoming more militant. They used more combative rhetoric. They dedicated more of their time to politics. They recovered lost radical histories to guide them in the present. They unearthed, translated, and reissued forgotten radical texts. They turned to anarchism, councilism, socialism, left communism, and various shades of Leninism, especially Maoism, which took the North Atlantic by storm at this time, famously memorialized in Jean-Luc Godard's 1967 film *La Chinoise*. And they adopted Marxism as a kind of universal theoretical language.

These years saw a worldwide Marxist revival. In Asia, Africa, and Latin America, thinkers like Che Guevara, Amílcar Cabral, Mao Zedong, or Nguyễn Khắc Viện breathed new life into Marxism, confirming its role as a living theory of change. At the same time, Europe experienced a genuine renaissance of Marxist theoretical experimentation. Figures such as Louis Althusser, Guy Debord, Henri Lefebvre, and Jean-Paul Sartre in France; Perry Anderson, Stuart Hall, E. P. Thompson, and Raymond Williams in Great Britain; Romano Alquati, Sergio Bologna, Mariarosa Dalla Costa, Antonio Negri, Raniero Panzieri, and Mario Tronti in Italy; and Hans-Georg Backhaus, Frigga Haug, Hans-Jürgen Krahl, and Herbert Marcuse in West Germany all worked to push Marxism in new directions, often in dialogue with one another. Marxism was not simply back; thinkers were reinventing it for a new historical landscape, taking a fresh look at such topics as ideology, organization, class struggle, racism, sexuality, everyday life, capitalist planning, and women's oppression.[90]

Marxism even gained ground in the United States, the most anticommunist country in the history of the planet. There, as opposed to Europe, Marxism had dwelled on the ideological margins after the Second World War, its flickering torch barely kept alive by isolated intellectuals, minuscule organizations, and fading family memories of the 1930s. With the exception of certain Black radicals and red diaper babies, even the new cohort of radicals in the early 1960s generally took their distance from much of Marxism, hoping to create alternatives to what Carl Oglesby called "ancestor-worship politics."[91] Yet the radicalizing political situation in the United States and abroad led many to reassess their earlier assumptions. Even if Marxism remained less popular among American radicals than their peers in Europe, many New Leftists had begun to espouse it by the very end of 1967.[92] A year later, Marxism would become the dominant language of radical change in the United States.[93]

The renewal of Marxism created a kind of lingua franca among radicals in the North Atlantic. While not everyone became a convinced Marxist, many familiarized themselves with core Marxist concepts, even if they could not speak the language fluently. Antiwar activists participating in an international conference may not have understood French, English, or German, but they knew what capitalism, imperialism, class struggle, or the dictatorship of the proletariat were – or at least they thought they did.

The perception of a shared political language – despite various dialects associated with names like Louis Althusser, Antonio Gramsci, Georg Lukács, Rosa Luxemburg, Herbert Marcuse, Leon Trotsky, or Mao Zedong – played a crucial role in not only furthering radical internationalism but also facilitating organized, coordinated, transatlantic strategies.[94]

A major consequence of this sweeping radicalization was a growing tendency to identify the system as "imperialism," even in countries like the United States where many radicals had once shunned such terms. As SDSer David Gilbert explained, "I wanted to understand the economic roots of the power system, and I came to feel that the correct label was – imperialism."[95] As a result, radicals everywhere searched for a working theory of imperialism, which in turn led them to V. I. Lenin, largely because his work had been canonized as the standard Marxist position on the topic.[96] Although Lenin's writings became a kind of touchstone, radicals also drew on other sources, explored new themes such as neocolonialism, and tried to update the Leninist theory to account for recent developments. In line with new theoretical trends, for example, they focused less on the competition between empires than on how those imperialist powers had together "underdeveloped" the "Third World." In so doing, they tended to redefine "imperialism" as the structural dependency of the "Third World" on the capitalistically advanced North Atlantic in a way that redrew the primary line of antagonism between the "core" and the "periphery."[97]

Although the word "imperialism" soared in popularity across the North Atlantic, becoming arguably the most widely used concept in the radical vocabulary, these redefinitions created some semantic ambiguity.[98] Three general uses of the term tended to predominate in the radical milieus of the late 1960s. Imperialism was an act, usually some form of domination, such as military intervention; an agent, usually the United States; or a structure, usually said to be rooted in capitalism. Different radicals emphasized different aspects of the concept, and these overlapping definitions could lead to confusion, especially as radicals fell into the habit of simply calling the United States "imperialism" without any qualifiers. Nevertheless, there was a kind of logical coherency to the schema: Imperialism is a global capitalist structure that needs to be not only protected, but also reproduced and expanded on an international scale; since the end of the Second World War, the United States had assumed primary responsibility for that task; and the United States would accomplish this objective through aggressive actions, like the war in Vietnam. Imperialism was therefore the system created by these three elements of action, agent, and structure, as well as the name given to each of them.

Once they defined the system as "imperialism," many radicals began to call themselves "anti-imperialists." But as with imperialism, it was not entirely clear what anti-imperialism meant. There were, in other words, potentially many different ways to do anti-imperialism. Yet by the end of the decade, the vast majority of anti-imperialist radicals in the North Atlantic came to accept the old Leninist problematic of the right of nations to self-determination as the basis of anti-imperialism. In a way, this was not too surprising. Leninism was already the most widely available way to think anti-imperialism. Instead of having to invent something new from scratch, radicals could simply adopt it as a working framework and tweak it as they saw fit. One of Leninism's strengths was precisely its status as the acknowledged common source of a wide variety of revolutionary discourses such as Maoism, Trotskyism, Stalinism, Titoism, and Guevarism. In some form or another many inspiring revolutionary movements across Asia, Africa, and Latin America had made it their own. What is more, at the time, it appeared to be actually working in places such as Cuba, China, and North Korea.

But a decisive reason why so many anti-imperialist radicals in the North Atlantic turned so completely to Leninism had to do with the Vietnam War itself. Radicals came to believe that the Vietnamese revolutionaries who fought on the frontlines against imperialism – at the very focal point of the world situation – were unabashed Leninists. They were strongly encouraged in this assessment by their study of the Vietnamese revolution, their personal meetings with Vietnamese revolutionaries, and especially the many translated Vietnamese texts they consumed. Indeed, the communists' publishing apparatus unleashed a torrent of jargon-filled articles, essays, speeches, lectures, directives, and booklets that trumpeted an intransigently Leninist viewpoint demanding nothing short of international anti-imperialist revolution. Since Vietnamese communists had a reputation as sophisticated political operators – they were cautious with their limited funds, deliberated at length about their messaging, tailored their materials to appeal to diverse audiences, and often downplayed their communism to secure broader support – the fact that they consistently distributed these blatantly Leninist texts to foreign audiences in the capitalist North Atlantic held great significance to radicals. It seemed to prove that those leading the revolution were fundamentally Leninists, that they were proud of that fact, and that they wanted radicals abroad to know it.[99]

But Vietnamese communists did more than just advertise their Leninism. They repeatedly, and publicly, declared that the Leninist problematic was the key to their success. First Secretary Lê Duẩn, for instance, asserted, "It is because our Party creatively applies Marxism-Leninism to the guidance of the Vietnamese revolution that we have succeeded in our August Revolution of 1945, won the patriotic resistance war, and made tremendous achievements in the socialist construction of the northern part of Viet Nam and in the struggle for the peaceful reunification of our motherland."[100] President Hồ Chí Minh was even more emphatic: "There is a legend, in our country as well as in China, on the miraculous 'Book of the Wise.' When facing great difficulties, one opens it and finds a way out. Leninism is not only a miraculous 'book of the wise,' a compass for us Vietnamese revolutionaries and people: it is also the radiant sun illuminating our path to final victory, to Socialism and Communism."[101] Vietnamese revolutionaries may have overemphasized the centrality of Leninist ideas to the complex struggles in Vietnam, but these oaths of loyalty from such respected authorities could not help but sway radicals abroad into seeing Leninism as the reason for victory.

Lê Duẩn, who effectively became the paramount leader of the DRV during the American War, went so far as to retell the entire history of the Vietnamese revolution as one of Leninism actualized. According to him, in the first stage of the struggle, Vietnamese revolutionaries followed Leninism by assembling a united front to expel the French in a "national democratic" revolution. Despite the setback of 1954, when the Geneva Conference split the country in half, they stuck with the problematic. In the North, where the communists completed the national democratic struggle, the DRV moved to the second stage, abolishing capitalist relations, building productive forces, launching a cultural revolution, and constructing socialism. In the South, where the first stage was left unfinished, and the US government had imposed a "neo-colony" run by traitorous "henchmen," revolutionaries backed by the DRV were working to complete the prerequisite national democratic revolution by redistributing land, combating neocolonialism, and uniting with the North to create an independent socialist nation-state that would make possible the transition to communism.[102]

The Vietnamese revolution not only seemed to validate the Leninist problematic, but its unique development also appeared to justify competing interpretations of Leninism, with both Maoists and Trotskyists paradoxically claiming the revolution as their own. Maoists believed that Vietnamese revolutionaries were correctly applying Mao's two-stage model, especially in the South, by building a cross-class alliance for strictly national democratic goals before fighting for socialism proper.[103] "At this stage of the struggle," the Union of Communist Youth (Marxist-Leninist) argued, "the South Vietnamese working class has been able to keep the task of national liberation front and center."[104] Yet some Trotskyists argued that a weak bourgeoisie, underdeveloped capitalist relations, the decisive leadership of the Vietnamese Workers' Party, and the favorable international context allowed the DRV to skip capitalism to build socialism in the North. After all, the Vietnamese Workers' Party had begun its land reform campaign, one of the pillars of socialist construction, even before fully expelling the French, consolidating an independent state, and completing the first national democratic stage. Trotskyist radicals in groups like the RCY would therefore argue that the Vietnamese revolution represented "the concrete verification of the theory of the permanent revolution."[105] In other words, the same communists who had murdered Vietnamese Trotskyists, and who some Trotskyists continued to denounce as Stalinist, were following Leon Trotsky's path.[106] It is revealing, however, that even when antiwar radicals disagreed over the meaning of the Vietnamese revolution their debates increasingly unfolded within the general parameters established by a shared Leninist source – an index of just how commonsensical the problematic had become by the end of the decade.

That said, in the 1960s some radicals who cared about fighting imperialism did challenge the narrowing of anti-imperialism to the Leninist problematic of self-determination. They warned of the dangers of nationalism; they raised questions about the class composition of these liberation movements; and they voiced concerns about the future of grassroots democracy, political liberties, and self-management in these new nation-states.[107] By this point they could summon several examples that seemed to confirm the limits of Leninist national self-determination: the botched land reform program in North Vietnam, the disaster of the Great Leap Forward in China, the abrogation of civil liberties in Cuba, or the consolidation of dictatorship in North Korea.

But these criticisms went largely unheard. Many of these dissident groups were small. They were comparatively less active in antiwar activism than those supporting national liberation. Their warnings may have been prescient, but they offered no other viable alternatives. Worst of all, some tended to bend the stick too far the other way, promoting a Eurocentrism that devalued struggles in Asia, Africa, and Latin America. In France, the Situationists declared that "state capitalism is the natural tendency of colonized societies."[108] In Italy, the influential theorist Mario Tronti snorted that the "miraculous" struggles of the working class in the capitalist core "have alone made, and are making, more revolutionary history than all the revolutions of all the colonised people put together."[109] In Britain, the International Socialists criticized these national liberation struggles as essentially petty-bourgeois movements destined to end in Stalinism. Unsurprisingly, these kinds of statements could, and often did, discredit these currents in the eyes of other activists. Tariq Ali, for example, admired the International Socialists for being "refreshingly undogmatic," but found them "far too Eurocentric." He contended, moreover, that "Their hostility to the Chinese and Cuban revolutions and the possibility of further outbreaks of a similar sort in the future was, in my eyes, tantamount to writing off a large part of the globe."[110]

Even if they acknowledged mounting evidence against the emancipatory value of the Leninist problematic, many anti-imperialists remained optimistic. Decolonization still felt novel in the 1960s, and everyone knew it would be a rocky process. Given the monumental obstacles people in Cuba, China, or Vietnam had to surmount to win their freedom, radicals were willing to give them a pass. After millions of deaths, decades of colonial rule, and continued harassment from outside powers, it would be foolish to expect, in the words of Simone de Beauvoir, "a miracle that would suddenly bring about the reign of socialism and prosperity."[111] Moreover, while these new regimes did exhibit some worrying trends, such as persistent inequalities, growing repression, and expansionist foreign policies, they also boasted real accomplishments both for their own people and for movements abroad. China, for example, might have been an authoritarian party-state, but many oppressed people still saw it as a lodestar of liberation. And even if they were concerned about these regimes, many radicals felt that there were more promising movements on the horizon, above all, the National Liberation Front in South Vietnam, which many interpreted as a pluralist, grassroots, democratic coalition that fought not for dictatorial rule but an egalitarian Vietnam.[112]

But the most important reason why so many anti-imperialist radicals remained unfazed by these early criticisms of Leninist self-determination is that a few "anomalies" do not generally convince those who believe in a paradigm to jettison it. It takes an accumulation of serious problems, growing incoherency, an overall shift in intellectual climate, subjective transformations in the given community, and a more attractive alternative to reveal the limits of a way of thinking, something that would only happen in the 1970s. In the end, most anti-imperialists dismissed these criticisms of the Leninist problematic. Those who continued to protest the equation of anti-imperialism with national liberation found themselves on the margins of antiwar activism, and the Leninist problematic became the dominant principle of anti-imperialist internationalism across North America and Western Europe in the 1960s.

Competing Internationalisms

Although many activists were turning to anti-imperialism as the best way to change the world, it was never the only internationalist project on offer.

The 1960s was an era of fierce competition between rival progressive internationalisms. Some activists rejected sweeping change in favor of international law, liberal institutions, and capitalist modernization. Others saw women as the ultimate oppressed class, argued that all oppressions stemmed from patriarchy, and grounded their internationalism in a conception of sisterhood. Still others were Black cultural nationalists who viewed internationalism less as the construction of multiracial alliances in an international mass movement for socialist revolution than the elaboration of a transnational Black cultural identity rooted in syncretic African traditions.[113] Many more were Christians who treated international solidarity as an extension of their faith within a religious framework of ecumenism.[114]

But what would ultimately become anti-imperialism's greatest internationalist competitor was a vision of global change anchored not in race, gender, or religion, but human rights. Although in circulation for well over a century, "human rights" were enjoying something of a revival. The Second World War sparked a new round of rights talk.[115] In 1945, the Nuremberg Charter promoted the notion of a "crime against humanity." In 1948, the Universal Declaration of Human Rights proclaimed human rights the "common standard of achievement for all peoples and nations."[116] In 1955, the Final Communiqué of the Bandung Conference made explicit reference to the idea of human rights. And in 1960, the UN Declaration on the Granting of Independence to Colonial Countries and Peoples unequivocally declared that the "subjection of peoples to alien subjugation, domination and exploitation constitutes a denial of fundamental human rights."[117]

As historians have shown, a major force in popularizing human rights were those anticolonial figures in Asia, Africa, and Latin America who struggled to transform the old imperial order.[118] But the concept was often limited to cosmopolitan elites at the United Nations, remained relatively marginal in radical social movements, and lacked any fixed meaning.[119] At the conferences where it was bandied about, delegates used the idea in highly contradictory ways. For some, human rights were a weapon against communism. For others, they meant the civil liberties of individuals. For still others, they were a convenient way to justify the struggle for national sovereignty, often affixing them to the far more popular idea of national self-determination. These competing definitions often prevailed within the same country. Take Iran, which would host the UN's first International Conference on Human Rights in 1968. Some conservatives treated human rights as an anticommunist bludgeon. The Shah claimed them as the basis of the enlightened imperial rule that had allegedly defined Iran since Cyrus the Great was said to have first invented the concept. His twin sister Princess Ashraf interpreted them through a kind of cultural relativist lens that criticized the Universal Declaration itself. And young activists used them not only to draw international attention to repression, but also to make sense of the particular kind of authoritarian capitalism that had taken root there.[120]

Although "human rights" were comparatively less popular in North America and Western Europe, they experienced a minor resurgence there as well. Their appeal was largely limited to affluent liberal elites connected to their respective states, but a handful of leftist social movement organizations occasionally also spoke of human rights, such as the Alabama Christian Movement for Human Rights, the French Committee for Amnesty in Portugal, or the West German Action for Human Rights in Iran.[121] As in Asia, Africa, and Latin America, the concept was unstable, referring to everything from social rights to collective liberation to the protection of individuals from torture. The term's ambiguity often meant it was grafted onto, or more often fused with, the ideas championed by a number of competing political currents. In fact, although the great majority of radicals in the North Atlantic studiously avoided the term "human rights" in the 1960s, there were some notable exceptions, particularly in the United States, where the influence of Marxism was weaker.[122]

The main example was Black radicalism, stretching from W. E. B. Dubois to SNCC. But here, too, the term was extremely polysemic. For example, Malcolm X's famous speech "The Ballot or the Bullet" could appeal to national self-determination, asserting that "black nationalism means that the black man should control the politics and the politicians in his own community," while simultaneously claiming that "human rights are something you were born with. Human rights are your God-given rights. Human rights are the rights that are recognized by all nations of this earth. And any time any one [sic] violates your human rights, you can take them to the world court."[123] Malcolm, then, drew on several competing sources to produce a kind of hybrid discourse based on race, religion, nationalism, collective emancipation, and innate rights.

Because human rights were so ambiguous in the 1960s, it would be a mistake to project a single meaning devised in the twenty-first century backward onto this period.[124] But just as radicals reduced anti-imperialism to the right of nations to self-determination, so too did some activists attempt to reduce the polymorphous idea of human rights to one specific meaning. Over the course of the 1960s, they consciously disentangled human rights from economic rights, social welfare, self-determination, and political struggle, reframing them instead around dignity, morality, individualism, and the market. This was a complex process, spanning several decades, and involving many actors with diverse motivations.[125]

One of the key players in the narrowing of human rights was an organization called Amnesty International (AI). When British lawyer Peter Benenson founded AI in 1961, he aimed to create not only a new international organization to advocate for the rights of those who were unjustly imprisoned but also a distinct vision of progressive internationalism.[126] First, he made human rights synonymous with the rights of the individual against state repression, emptying them of their more expansive connotations. Second, Benenson recast the category of the political prisoner as the "prisoner of conscience," which he defined as "Any person who is physically restrained (by imprisonment or otherwise) from expressing (in any form of words or symbols) any opinion which he honestly holds and which does not advocate or condone personal violence."[127] Third, he attempted to set this new internationalism above politics as such, calling for "a non-political, non-sectarial, international movement."[128] To demonstrate this commitment to transcending politics, AI would select prisoners in sets of three: one from the capitalist "West," another from the communist "East," and the third from the nonaligned "South."

Of course, as important as Benenson was in shaping Amnesty's vision, AI was a heterogeneous organization filled with debate.[129] One of the most explosive issues in its early years was Benenson's refusal to help those political prisoners who advocated violence, a stance that effectively spurned thousands of active fighters across the world, including countless Vietnamese resisting US invasion. Disagreements reached a boiling point in 1964, when Nelson Mandela defended the use of violence to overthrow apartheid at the famous Rivonia Trial. While some felt that he deserved protection anyway, others argued that Mandela had to be excluded from "prisoner of conscience" status since he was effectively a communist terrorist. After much debate, the organization decided not to make an exception for Mandela. While the affair revealed significant disagreements over some of Amnesty's core principles, it nevertheless confirmed that most activists in the new organization adhered to its founder's general approach to internationalism.

Amnesty came to develop an internationalism that was radically different from that of the anti-imperialists. If anti-imperialist internationalism promised to change the world by uniting radicals across the globe in an international political movement that would overthrow the imperialist system in order to build an emancipatory future, this new human rights internationalism promised to change the world by uniting rights activists across the globe in an explicitly apolitical international movement that would save individual victims in order to minimize suffering on the planet. On nearly every major question, from politics to history, the two sides stood apart.

Despite these differences, they did share some surprising similarities, especially when it came to concrete forms of solidarity. Take the International War Crimes Tribunal. Activists might have peppered their speeches with terms like "war crimes," "humanity," and "genocide," but they squarely situated the Tribunal within the anti-imperialist framework of national self-determination. Sartre's inaugural address, for example, argued that the Nuremberg trials, which the IWCT was modeled on, were not about individual rights but condemning the aggression of larger countries against "small, poor countries" and establishing guidelines for trying violations to the rights of nations to self-determination.[130] Echoing the French philosopher, Vietnamese jurists in the DRV similarly saw the Tribunal as unfolding within a framework defined by "national rights."[131] Hồ Chí Minh himself argued that the "Tribunal is an action of world-wide importance for justice and for the right of people to self-determination."[132] Even when the Tribunal investigated the plight of hostages, prisoners, or refugees, these were not coded as violations of the "human rights" of individuals. Thinking in terms of collective rights to national self-determination, anti-imperialists saw these atrocities as attacks on the entire people: a collective subject with a collective right to nationhood. Hence their particular focus on genocide, which they understood not as an attack on individuals, but as violence against a nation.

On the other hand, the Tribunal did bear some affinities with the individualist human rights internationalism of groups like Amnesty.[133] Tribunal members made references to codified international law. They sometimes slid into a kind of moralism, especially in their comparisons between US aggression in Vietnam and Nazi violence. They tended to make the same kind of unnuanced universalist arguments about the rights of nations as Amnesty made about the rights individuals. Their reliance on celebrities who used their positions of privilege to advocate for others bore an eerie resemblance to the kinds of activism that individualist human rights organizations would increasingly pursue. And while many radicals depicted the Vietnamese people as heroic subjects leading the way for the entire world, the proceedings of the Tribunal at times recast them as suffering victims in need of help, another characteristic feature of Amnesty's human rights internationalism. Members of the Tribunal occasionally even used some of the rhetoric that would become fully associated with human rights discourse. At the same time that Russell decried US imperialism, for example, he could tell the Tribunal: "We are not judges. We are witnesses. Our task is to make mankind bear witness to these terrible crimes and to unite humanity on the side of justice in Vietnam."[134]

As these intriguing elective affinities reveal, the many international-isms of the decade certainly differed in crucial respects, but they often overlapped on the ground, even when the projects in question seemed as diametrically opposed as anti-imperialism and human rights. Although very different from individualist human rights, the specific form that anti-imperialism took, that is, the right of nations to self-determination, as well as the repertoire of solidarity that some anti-imperialists at this time adopted, tended to blur the lines between the two sides. This is especially clear if one looks beyond anti-imperialist leaders and dedi-cated human rights activists to the larger progressive milieus whose sup-port they competed over. None of this is to say that the two sides were identical, only that their similarities made them mutually intelligible, which made possible not only future coalitions, but also perhaps one day the movement of activists from the banner of one to the other.

Anti-Imperialism Ascendant

The radicalizing winds of the 1960s convinced tens of thousands to become activists, turned some of those activists into radicals, and trans-formed quite a few of those radicals into anti-imperialists. In their search for a working politics of anti-imperialism, many of these anti-imperialist radicals in turn looked to some kind of Leninism. Although their ranks swelled with every passing year, the actual number of committed anti-imperialist radicals remained quite small across the North Atlantic. They faced bitter competition with other activists, and their correspond-ing project of anti-imperialism continued to struggle against other rival internationalisms.

But by the end of the decade, anti-imperialist internationalism was beating its competitors. There were a few reasons for anti-imperialism's remarkable appeal. It was more successful than many of its rivals in capi-talizing on growing frustration with the status quo. It seemed to offer a more coherent analytical framework for making sense of a world defined by collapsing empires, revolutionary change, successful national libera-tion movements, and the rise of the "Third World" in global politics. And it appeared to provide a more convincing guide to action for all those who did not want just to interpet the world but to change it.

But one major reason for anti-imperialism's increasing success over its internationalist rivals was the Vietnam War. As onetime SDS President Carl Oglesby later explained, there was a kind of inherent logic within the Vietnam War that pushed many of those involved in antiwar work toward some kind of radical anti-imperialism: "(a) because there was no way to resist the truth of the war, no way, that is, to avoid imperialism;

(b) because once the policy critique of the war had been supplanted by the structural critique of the empire, all political therapies short of socialist revolution appeared to become senseless; and (c) because the necessity of a revolutionary strategy was, in effect, the same thing as the necessity of Marxism-Leninism."[135] In other words, the popularity of the systemic critique of the war, the tendency to name that system imperialism, and the resurgence of Leninism as the dominant way to think imperialism all conspired to lead many activists straight into the arms of Leninist anti-imperialist internationalism.

Of course, the American War in Vietnam was a complex issue, antiwar struggles were divided, the antiwar cause was a battlefield of competing internationalisms, and many antiwar activists rejected the anti-imperialist framing. That said, there was an undeniable tide pulling many activists in a radical direction, and this had a great deal to do with the very nature of the war itself. The most powerful capitalist power in the world was slaughtering thousands of people in a poor country that had only recently cast off the colonial yoke. Many Vietnamese who resisted US aggression saw their struggle as a war of national liberation against imperialism. That liberation struggle was led by veteran revolutionaries who explicitly thought in Leninist terms. Their most dynamic supporters abroad were anti-imperialists who were also turning to Leninism. And the entire affair seemed to conform to the imagined Leninist sequence. The Vietnam War seemed almost perfectly engineered for anti-imperialist internationalism. It is little surprise, then, that it became a kind of breeding ground for Leninism.

To be sure, Vietnam was never the only issue on the table. From national liberation in Angola to guerrilla war in Bolivia, the struggle against apartheid in South Africa to campaigns against authoritarianism in Brazil, activists interested in solidarity work had plenty of causes to choose from in the 1960s. Although they overlapped, these movements often differed in goals, composition, organization, and political orientation, with competing internationalisms exercising varying levels of influence in each campaign. For example, the international movement against the Greek junta, which came to power in 1967, included not only anti-imperialist militants but also plenty of liberals receptive to rights talk, giving human rights internationalism an important early foothold.[136] But by the end of the decade, the Vietnam War distinguished itself as the most important issue for internationalist activists looking to change the world. The centrality of the Vietnam War temporarily crowded out solidarity campaigns where other internationalisms enjoyed strong representation and, in so doing, elevated the popularity of the internationalist project with which the Vietnamese liberation struggle increasingly became most closely associated: anti-imperialism.

All this allowed Leninist anti-imperialism to grow immensely popular. In fact, anti-imperialism achieved considerable influence well beyond the small, but growing, circle of committed anti-imperialist radicals. After all, the vast majority of people who began to care about progressive world politics in these years were not hardened radicals. Although they wanted some kind of change, many came to politics only recently, had little experience with activism, were generally unfamiliar with revolutionary theory, did not engage in activism full-time, and paid relatively little attention to organizational feuds. Instead of a fully coherent worldview grounded in theoretical texts, historical references, and rarified debates, they often hybridized all sorts of ideas, frequently drawing on contradictory elements from a wide variety of political projects. But as they grew more political, and more committed to making a difference, hundreds of thousands of people came under the sway of the more radical ideas gaining ground across the North Atlantic. They would never have called themselves Leninists, but many of them came to adopt elements of the Leninist problematic to make sense of the world. They may not have read a word of Lenin, but they used the concept of imperialism to explain what was happening in countries like Vietnam. They may not have wanted violent revolution, but they believed that oppressed nations had the right to self-determination, even if that meant picking up the gun. They may not have been communists, but they began to talk about changing "the system."

So attractive was anti-imperialism's appeal that even those committed activist leaders actively promoting rival internationalisms increasingly came under its influence. They obviously did not all become Leninists, but ideas associated with the Leninist problematic of anti-imperialism shaped their thinking. Progressive Christians, Jewish activists, Black nationalists, social democrats, radical feminists, anarchists, and countless others would talk about class struggle, call the enemy imperialism, advocate national self-determination, support revolutionary struggle, and pay more attention to Marxist theory. Even those most ardently opposed to Leninist anti-imperialism felt compelled to engage with its terms. None other than the US government, for example, found itself speaking of revolution, imperial expansion, international solidarity, national liberation, and especially self-determination. Of course, US politicians gave these concepts a very different meaning than the radicals did. Their version of self-determination, for example, was gradualist, legalistic, and limited to formal independence, excluding collective rights, social transformation, and economic sovereignty. This was an expressly capitalist conception that prioritized self-rule by free individuals over collective emancipation.[137] The United States even came to counterpose self-determination to communism. Since communism equaled totalitarian slavery, the US government argued, it was never freely chosen by individuals, but rather imposed by alien forces who invaded countries, orchestrated internal subversion, or both. Communism, then, was opposed to self-determination, which meant that fighting for self-determination was a way to stop communism.[138]

The debate over the meaning of these terms was especially apparent when it came to Vietnam. The United States saw a free republic in the South, violated by outside agents directed from the North, which was itself under the control of an imperialistic USSR. It was their duty, figures like Lyndon Johnson argued, to answer the Vietnamese people's call for international support, defend South Vietnam's "right to self-determination," and prevent the Republic of Vietnam from being "gobbled up" by the expansionist North Vietnam.[139] By contrast, radicals followed Vietnamese communists in seeing Vietnam as a coherent nation violently broken in half by the United States, which was doing whatever possible to make that artificial division permanent. It was their duty, they argued, to fight the United States, and destroy its puppet government in the South, in order to defend the Vietnamese people's collective right to national self-determination. If the United States thought saving South Vietnam was crucial to repelling communism and keeping the world safe for capitalism, radicals believed that reunifying Vietnam was crucial to overthrowing imperialism and building world communism. Although their positions differed, the fact that the United States had to justify its war with concepts developed by Leninists, and still clearly associated with radical thought, showed just how significant anti-imperialist internationalism had become.

By the same token, those who refused to engage with anti-imperialism found themselves on the defensive. Nowhere was this clearer than with human rights internationalism. In the 1960s, those human rights organizations like Amnesty International that stubbornly swam against the tide found themselves with little influence over leftist social movements. Amnesty's US section, for example, boasted a mere twelve members in 1966, struggled to break into activist circles, and was simply ignored by most progressives. Internationally, the organization fared little better. In 1967, as anti-imperialism was soaring to new heights, AI was mired in crisis.[140] Revelations about Benenson's secret ties to the British government disrupted AI's credibility as an impartial force, exacerbated rivalries within the leadership, and raised questions about organizational structure, professionalization, and goals. Membership growth slackened, financial problems strained the organization, and many sections ran into serious trouble. In the words of historian Jan Eckel, "toward the end of the 1960s Amnesty had reached the lowest ebb in its history."[141] Amnesty's fate was indicative of the relative marginalization of human rights in the activist milieus of those years. Human rights activists were few and far between, social movements in the North Atlantic rarely invoked the concept, and even mainstream liberal outlets such as the *New York Times* made only passing references.[142] By contrast, anti-imperialism was not only winning the hearts of radicals, but also fast becoming the hegemonic common sense among progressives more broadly.

3 Revolution

In the 1967 omnibus film *Far from Vietnam*, Jean-Luc Godard mused aloud about what it meant to support a struggle when one was so far, in every sense of the word, from the scene. He admitted with brutal honesty that he wanted to travel to Vietnam, but the Democratic Republic of Vietnam (DRV) declined his offer. This refusal, he confessed, was for the best. Driven by altruism, yet knowing nothing of the revolutionary struggle abroad, he might have ended up "doing them more harm than good." Vietnam was not his battle; how could he possibly film it? "It is difficult," he explained, "to talk about bombs when they are not falling on your head."[1]

Godard posed one of the most important political questions of the period: How could one most effectively demonstrate solidarity with a struggle that is not one's own? To assist their Vietnamese comrades, antiwar radicals in the North Atlantic experimented with many different solidarity actions in the 1960s, such as marching, organizing teach-ins, and putting the United States on trial for genocide. But over the course of 1967, an escalating war, an increasingly militant global political landscape, and new ideas about anti-imperialist solidarity convinced radicals to expand their antiwar activism beyond the ideological terrain.

The most dynamic partisans of a more aggressive internationalism were Black radicals in the United States. Arguing that African Americans formed an "internal colony," and that they suffered a similar kind of oppression as Vietnamese, they claimed that the best way to support national liberation struggles against the United States was to wage war inside the "belly of the beast." This openly revolutionary strategy received a boost of support from Latin American revolutionaries like Che Guevara, who exhorted radicals across the globe to create "two, three, many Vietnams." As for Vietnamese communists, they publicly welcomed this sharp radicalization of antiwar solidarity work, anticipating a pivotal showdown between the international forces of anti-imperialism and imperialism.

Frustrated with the limits of earlier activism, radicals in France were profoundly inspired by these efforts to rethink anti-imperialist internationalism. "Instead of invading Vietnam with generosity," Godard explained, we must "let Vietnam invade us."[2] In other words, the best way to support the Vietnamese revolution would be to "create a Vietnam" in France. For Godard in 1967, this meant looking to the struggles already unfolding in France, such as the strike at the Rhodiaceta factory in Besançon, which presaged the unprecedented events of the following year. In fact, the directors debuted the film not in a Left Bank theater but at the Rhodiaceta plant. The connection was not lost on the audience. Georges Maurivard, a Rhodiaceta worker, introduced the film by affirming: "It will be about us."[3]

French radicals set about translating the Vietnamese revolution into their own particular context. Their efforts eventually lit the fuse that set off the explosive events of May 1968. Although May '68 grabbed international attention, the radicals who catalyzed the May events did not see themselves at the center of global unrest but as junior partners in a worldwide anti-imperialist struggle. May itself, they thought, was nothing other than another front in a vast revolutionary wave led by the Vietnamese people. In this way, the Vietnam War made May '68 possible.[4]

Just as Vietnamese revolutionaries inspired the French, the events of May '68 inspired radicals elsewhere, who in turn tried to translate May '68 into their own political vernacular. By the end of the year, thousands of radicals across North America and Western Europe had rejected legalistic opposition to war in favor of fomenting domestic revolution. Instead of simply marching to stop the war abroad, they believed it was their internationalist duty to make war at home.

The Internal Vietnam

In the early 1960s, mounting dissatisfaction with the moderation of the mainstream Civil Rights Movement led a cohort of African Americans to found a new group called the Revolutionary Action Movement (RAM). Created in 1962 by several activists who had passed through Students for a Democratic Society (SDS), the Student Nonviolent Coordinating Committee (SNCC), and the Congress of Racial Equality, RAM quickly connected with many of the major Black radical figures of the time. James Boggs served as the group's ideological chairman, Robert F. Williams as its international chairman, and Malcolm X as international spokesman.[5] Despite its relatively small size, RAM soon became the preeminent Black radical organization of the early 1960s.[6]

At the core of RAM's radical politics was the notion that African Americans were an oppressed nation inside the United States. Some version of this idea can be traced at least as far back as the nineteenth century and had formed the basis of numerous back-to-Africa proposals. Although many of the exodus schemes may have seemed far-fetched, they persisted deep into the twentieth century because they testified to an unfulfilled desire for true self-determination.[7] What this meant, exactly, was a point of contention. Some, like Marcus Garvey, defined the fight for self-determination in terms of race, arguing that African Americans constituted an organic racial community, were oppressed by the instinctive prejudice of members of the white race, and could find freedom only through racial separation. Others, like Harry Haywood, recognized the genuine emancipatory longing that buoyed Garvey's project, but criticized its racial framing, arguing that "race" was not some predetermined natural trait that explained the oppression of African Americans, but was instead the very thing that had to be explained.

Hoping to theorize the historical oppression of African Americans without hypostasizing race, Black communists like Haywood instead drew on V. I. Lenin and Joseph Stalin's work on the "national question" to define anti-Black oppression as "national oppression." Working within the Leninist problematic, they argued that the land stretching from Virginia to Mississippi to Tennessee formed the territorial basis of a coherent "Black nation" with an inviolable right to self-determination, a position the Communist International officially adopted as the "Black Belt Thesis" in the 1920s.[8] Haywood insisted that, while the right to self-determination included the possibility of secession, it did not necessarily mean national independence. In the same way that Lenin had argued that the right to secede was the only way to guarantee a truly voluntary international union between oppressor and oppressed nations, Haywood argued that the possibility of independence for African Americans was the only way to ensure genuine equality between Blacks and whites in the United States. In this way, Black radicals like Haywood reimagined the Black nationalist demand for self-determination. Instead of a call for racial separatism, the right to secession became a precondition for deeper unity between all people.[9] As Haywood later emphasized, the "slogan of self-determination is a slogan of unity. Its overriding purpose was and still is to unite the white and Black exploited masses, working and oppressed people of all nationalities."[10]

Although inspired by Lenin's writings on colonialism, the 1928 Comintern Resolution clearly stated that while the national oppression of colonial peoples and African Americans was "of the same character," it was "not correct to consider the Negro zone of the South as a colony of the United States."[11] Even if some communists did use the term "colony" to describe the Black nation, they often placed it in quotation marks, suggesting distance, perhaps even discomfort with the word.[12] But postwar decolonization convinced Black radicals to rethink the history of Black liberation within a fully anticolonial framework. By the early 1960s, a few theorists explicitly reclassified the Black nation as a specifically colonized nation.[13] One of the most important figures in this conceptual shift was another Black radical who had passed through the Communist Party USA: Harold Cruse.[14] "From the beginning," Cruse wrote, "the American Negro has existed as a colonial being. His enslavement coincided with the colonial expansion of European powers and was nothing more or less than a condition of domestic colonialism. Instead of the United States establishing a colonial empire in Africa, it brought the colonial system home and installed it in the Southern states."[15] Since African Americans were a colonized people who happened to live in the continental United States, their struggles had to be understood within the context of "internal colonialism."

The idea of the internal colony not only helped Black radicals clarify their status as oppressed people in the heartland of the oppressors; it also lent their struggles greater legitimacy. With new nations appearing everywhere, and the old colonial powers crumbling one after the other, decolonization appeared to be an unstoppable force. Drawing attention to their own colonized situation allowed the internally colonized to ride the anticolonial wave. As Cruse put it: "Those on the American left who support revolutionary nationalism in Asia, Africa, and Latin America must also accept the validity of Negro nationalism in the United States. Is it not just as valid for Negro nationalists to want to separate from American whites as it is for Cuban nationalists to want to separate economically and politically from the United States?"[16]

This self-identification as a colonized people, as a pocket of the "Third World" inside the "First," made possible a certain kind of internationalism. For Black radicals in groups like RAM, their struggle for national liberation formed an essential part of the "Bandung World." As RAM explained: "we must *all* do what is necessary to gain our rightful freedom; for the world can never be free until Black America is free, and Black America cannot be free until the Bandung world is free."[17] Black radicals could therefore advance a vision of international solidarity with Vietnamese revolutionaries that was unavailable to many other antiwar activists in North America and Western Europe. They could oppose the war not merely on the grounds that African Americans disproportionately suffered, or that the money wasted in Vietnam could be better spent assisting poor Black communities. For Black radicals, the basis of their solidarity with Vietnamese rested primarily in their experience of an analogous form of colonial oppression.

First, they argued, African Americans faced the same kinds of racial discrimination, legal injustice, economic exploitation, and political violence as other colonized peoples. "When a child is murdered by bombs in the Congo, or Vietnam," young Black radicals explained, "it is the same as a child murdered in a church bombing in Alabama or in Harlem."[18] Second, African Americans and Vietnamese shared a special bond; they not only suffered the same colonial violence, but also confronted the same enemy. "The same white man who is killing our brothers in Vietnam," Black Women Enraged, a Black nationalist women's group affiliated with RAM, put it, "is lynching our black brothers here in Mississippi, Los Angeles, and New York."[19] US imperialism, Black nationalists argued, was waging not one war, but two, the first at home against African Americans and the other abroad against Vietnamese. Third, both sides fought for the same project: national liberation. As RAM declared in its open letter of solidarity to the Vietnamese people on Independence Day:

On this Fourth of July 1964 when White America celebrates its Declaration of Independence from foreign domination one hundred and eighty-eight years ago, we of the Revolutionary Action Movement (RAM) congratulate the Vietnamese Front of National Liberation for their inspiring victories against US imperialism in South Vietnam and thereby declare *Our Independence* from the policies of the US government abroad and at home.[20]

Much like Vietnamese revolutionaries, RAM believed that the path to emancipation led through the right to national self-determination. African Americans had to win independence, even if this meant forming a separate Black state.

The strong parallels between African Americans and Vietnamese became a defining trope in the radical discourse of the 1960s. Vietnamese battled the US military abroad; African Americans resisted the police at home. Vietnamese were shot; African Americans lynched. Vietnamese lacked full civil liberties in South Vietnam; African Americans were denied the same freedoms in the American South. Vietnamese were racialized by American troops; African Americans confronted racial discrimination throughout the United States. This kind of analogical thinking occasionally slipped into straightforward identification. As one Black radical publication urged in 1967: "To the Vietnamese people: your confidence and determination lends impetus to our own struggle for national liberation, North America's 'internal Vietnam,' and renews and revitalizes each day our unshakable faith in mankind. SOCK IT TO 'EM!!!"[21]

This imagined unity between African Americans at home and Vietnamese abroad justified different kinds of struggle. If African Americans experienced the same kind of colonial rule, faced the same enemy, and shared the same political objectives as Vietnamese, Black radicals argued, then they could do much more than simply hold rallies, fight the draft, or protest the White House. They could replicate the Vietnamese example within the United States itself. Ridiculing Martin Luther King, Jr.'s promise to help Vietnamese by nonviolently pressuring the US government into negotiations, young Black radicals argued that they should borrow Vietnamese tactics to help African Americans fight their common enemy. "Let us remember, first of all, that the Vietnamese people have already shown that they really know how to handle Charlie. We support the Viet Cong, they are our blood brothers," they declared. "The Viet Cong know how to take care of themselves. It is high time we learned to do the same."[22] To do that, they had to organize their own revolutionary force.[23]

These Black radicals meant what they said. RAM was in fact attempting to levy a Liberation Army capable of organizing revolution inside the United States.[24] Inspired by Robert F. Williams, RAM and other radical organizations experimented with the idea of armed guerrilla warfare, studying military strategy, learning how to shoot, and preparing for the coming insurrection.[25] Some RAM members even participated in the Watts Rebellion in Los Angeles, which they interpreted as "the inauguration of the guerrilla war." Soon after, Williams, RAM's chairman-in-exile, laid out the strategy for fellow Vietnamese communists in person, delivering a speech at the International Conference for Solidarity with the People of Vietnam in Hanoi. "As a representative of the Revolutionary Action Movement, I am here to give support to the Vietnamese people in their struggle against US imperialist aggression," he said. But this was not enough: "Not only do we condemn, protest and raise our fists in indignation at these brutal crimes perpetrated against the noble patriots of this gallant land, but we promise our brothers, and let the whole world bear witness, that we shall intensify our struggle for liberation in the so-called free world of the racist USA. We shall take the torch of freedom and justice into the streets of America and we shall set the last great stronghold of Yankee imperialism ablaze with our battle cry of freedom!"[26]

RAM militants fused Black nationalism with Leninism to create a highly generative iteration of anti-imperialist internationalism. They articulated the fight against racism with the struggle for national self-determination. They also emphatically distinguished their "revolutionary nationalism" from the "bourgeois nationalism" of those African Americans who simply wanted more opportunities, greater representation, and deeper integration into the existing imperialist system. "What Black America needs in the long run, is *not* black businessmen, congressmen, or bourgeois leaders and officials, but militant, revolutionary leadership rooted in the masses of the people, articulating and implanting their highest aspirations."[27] In addition, they situated this revolutionary nationalist struggle within a fully global conflict between "anti-imperialists and capitalist imperialism."[28] On the one side were anti-imperialist revolutionaries in countries like Cuba, China, Algeria, and Vietnam; on the other were NATO, the US government, and all those "bourgeois nationalist" collaborators in Asia, Africa, and the Americas. Lastly, they argued that the best way they could contribute to this international anti-imperialist revolution was to make war at home in America. Recasting their "domestic bondage" in the heart of the United States as an advantage, they argued that they could play a vanguard role in this world revolution by waging revolution inside the "belly" of the greatest imperialist power on the planet.[29]

RAM's pioneering ideas had a profound impact on other organizations. They influenced the trajectory of SNCC, for example, which experienced a sharp turn toward Black radicalism in 1966, transitioning into an all-Black organization, abandoning the principle of nonviolence, adopting the framework of internal colonialism, and embracing the anti-imperialist strategy of waging war at home. "The duty of a revolutionary who finds himself captured in the heart of imperialism is to destroy that imperialism by any means necessary," SNCC activist John Wilson told his Vietnamese counterparts during an American trip to Czechoslovakia in 1967.[30] "We believe this linkage is necessary," he concluded, "because the goals of our struggles are the same and we have the same enemy."[31]

This way of thinking revolutionary internationalism would soon reach its apotheosis in the Black Panther Party. After cutting their teeth in a study circle organized by RAM, Huey Newton and Bobby Seale refined the Revolutionary Action Movement's internationalist project to serve as the basis of what would become the most visible anti-imperialist Black organization in the United States. In the coming years, the Panthers would offer a revolutionary alternative to both the mainstream Civil Rights Movement and the "pork chop nationalism" of those Black groups calling for racial separatism. They espoused Leninist anti-imperialism, established rich coalitions with other anti-imperialist radicals in the United States, constructed a robust internationalist network that included headquarters in several foreign countries, and sought to make war in the heart of America in solidarity with a world revolution increasingly led by Vietnamese communists.[32]

For their part, Vietnamese communists applauded this revolutionary anti-imperialist strategy. As the *Vietnam Courier* explained: "The first front against American imperialism is to be found in Vietnam. The second is in the United States itself. In this country, there are 20 million Blacks oppressed, exploited, despised like slaves." Black Americans, the article went on, "realize that they share a common enemy with the Vietnamese people – American imperialism – and that to win freedom and equality, they must, like the Vietnamese people, oppose anti-revolutionary violence with revolutionary violence." While acknowledging the special bond between Vietnamese and African Americans, the article also broadened the idea of the second front to include the white antiwar movement as well. "These two movements, fusing into an imposing force, constitute the Second Front against American imperialism." The task for the Americans was to overcome their differences to create a unified multiracial revolutionary force behind enemy lines. "Attacked on two fronts," the article concluded, "American imperialism will be defeated by the American and Vietnamese people."[33]

Despite encouragement from Vietnamese fighters, most white radicals did not initially think that they could play such a revolutionary role. The Communist Party USA was happy to link the war to struggles at home, but like much of the official communist movement it opposed revolution, hoping instead to end the war through negotiations.[34] Their rivals in the Socialist Workers Party believed that the best way to end the war was not to bring it home, which sounded adventurist, but to organize a single-issue campaign for immediate withdrawal.[35] The Progressive Labor Party did preach revolution, but was on its way to condemning all national liberation struggles, including those of African Americans at home and Vietnamese abroad, as inherently reactionary.[36] As for SDS, the largest youth formation on the white left, there was a bit more interest now that its members were embracing Marxism, building deeper international ties, and contemplating more aggressive actions. But even there, commitment to domestic revolution was still not a majority position in 1967.

Multiplying the Fronts

If white Americans were reluctant to join this second front, radicals elsewhere were only too eager. In April 1967, Ernesto "Che" Guevara argued that Vietnam had become the "focal point" of the world situation. And yet, he added with sadness, Vietnamese revolutionaries were "tragically alone." It was therefore incumbent on all anti-imperialists to assist their Vietnamese comrades, and the best way to do that would be to intensify struggles wherever else US imperialism was engaged.[37] While in certain respects Che's "Message to the Tricontinental" merely updated an already familiar approach to anti-imperialist internationalism, his contribution nevertheless proved decisive. Not only did he turn a complex strategy into an elegant slogan, but he also found a way to justify the move from the two to the many. While Vietnamese communists often spoke of the "second front," it was after Che's remarks – which one French radical later called the "internationalist manifesto of our generation" – that anti-imperialists across the globe seriously contemplated a plurality of coordinated revolutionary fronts.[38] What is more, Che personally demonstrated how his sensational slogan could be acted upon; he lived his vision of solidarity, setting an example for others to follow.

Che's strategy seemed to prioritize Latin America. Having won their independence long ago, he said, the people of Latin America were the first to feel the brunt of US imperialism, which had now subsumed the colonialism of the old European empires. It was in Latin America, he argued, that the United States had first tested the kind of "neocolonialism" now on display in South Vietnam. The historic staging ground for US imperialism, Latin America therefore offered the most fertile terrain for building new anti-imperialist fronts. "Latin America, a continent forgotten in the recent political struggles for liberation," Che proclaimed, "will have a much more important task: the creation of the world's second or a third Vietnam, or second *and* third Vietnam."[39] He quickly added, however, that imperialism's global nature meant that Latin America was not necessarily the only place where this could happen. Drawing on Lenin's thinking, he argued that, while the United States now served as the "head" of imperialism, anti-imperialists "must definitely keep in mind that imperialism is a world system, the final stage of capitalism, and that it must be beaten in a great worldwide confrontation."[40] What this meant concretely was that anti-imperialists anywhere could make a contribution. The task, then, was to do whatever possible to ensure that "two, three, many Vietnams flowered on the face of the globe."[41]

Vietnamese revolutionaries eagerly gave Che's proposal their stamp of approval at the first meeting of the Organization of Latin American Solidarity (OLAS) in Havana that summer. As a DRV representative there put it: "when, as comrade Ernesto 'Che' Guevara puts it, '2, 3, or many Vietnams' emerge, when in the very heart of the USA the movement of the American people, particularly the black sector, develops with the force of a storm, it is certain that North American imperialism can no longer stay standing."[42] SNCC's Stokely Carmichael spoke at the meeting as well, solidifying the emerging alliance between Vietnamese, Latin Americans, and African Americans.[43] "The struggle we are engaged in is international," he thundered. "We know very well that what happens in Vietnam affects our struggle here and what we do affects the struggle of the Vietnamese people."[44] OLAS's General Declaration echoed the sentiment, formalizing the mutual reciprocity of their struggles: "the heroic struggle of the people of Viet Nam aids all revolutionary peoples fighting against imperialism to an inestimable degree and constitutes an inspiring example for the peoples of Latin America."[45]

All this marked an important change in Vietnamese strategy. Stirred by these autonomous efforts, Vietnamese revolutionaries shifted from their earlier caution. Soon after the OLAS conference, they updated the National Liberation Front (NLF) program to reflect a more aggressive internationalist posture, openly vowing to "actively support the national-liberation movement of the peoples of Asia, Africa and Latin America against imperialism, colonialism, and neo-colonialism," the "just struggle of Afro-Americans for their fundamental national rights," and the "struggle of the American people against the US imperialists' war of aggression in Viet Nam."[46] In a passage read by radicals the world over, the 1967 program urged antiwar forces to consolidate their efforts into a "world peoples' front in support of Viet Nam against the US imperialist aggressors."[47] In late 1967, Lê Duẩn, the first secretary of the Vietnamese Workers' Party, went further by publicly arguing that the radicalizing international situation had made revolution the order of the day. The goal was to unite all revolutionary forces across the planet into a "united front" to not only fight US imperialism but also overthrow the entire "imperialist system."[48] In this, the "anti-war movement" in the advanced capitalist world could play a "new, really revolutionary and offensive significance."[49] By the very end of 1967, then, Vietnamese revolutionaries were radicalizing their own approach to anti-imperialist internationalism. Where they once sought assistance primarily on the ideological terrain, they now spoke of active revolutionary struggle in the imperialist centers.

French anti-imperialists followed these developments with great interest, and some felt inspired to consider the possibility of opening new fronts inside Western Europe. This idea was not new to radicals. As early as 1965, for example, the Revolutionary Communist Youth (RCY) drew on Lenin to argue that the "best way to help the Vietnamese revolution is to weaken global imperialism by actually threatening the capitalist order in one's own country."[50] This idea also found some echoes in texts like the Brussels Statement of 1967. But most radicals believed that such notions, however rhetorically persuasive or intellectually seductive, were simply unrealistic as strategy. Radical groups were far too marginal, they had no examples to follow, and struggles at home never approached the level of mass militancy needed to transform "bringing the war home" from rhetoric to action. For most of the 1960s, then, radicals tabled the idea, focusing instead on winning the ideological war, which was, after all, what Vietnamese revolutionaries had formally requested.

But over the course of 1967 the political conjuncture shifted in a way that convinced many French anti-imperialists to adopt the idea of waging war at home as the most effective form of solidarity. Despite coordinated international opposition, the United States continued to escalate its war. In December 1967, the number of military personnel on the ground reached over 480,000. By the end of the year, the United States had dropped over 1 million tons of bombs on all of Vietnam – compared with 635,000 tons during the Korean War and 503,000 tons in the Pacific theater during the Second World War.[51] In the face of such mounting carnage, radicals began to argue that the kind of intellectual condemnation exemplified by the International War Crimes Tribunal was inadequate. It was time to move beyond the ideological terrain to make a more direct contribution to the Vietnamese revolution.

At the same time, a new wave of worker struggles broke out across France. Workers struck at a textile factory in Besançon in February 1967, with demonstrations rapidly spreading to neighboring plants.[52] Hailing the action, which was one of the most militant in over a decade, radicals claimed it signaled the definitive return of "class struggle."[53] As the RCY put it: "the length, scale, and violence of the movement undercuts the many neo-capitalist 'theories' about the deep complacency of a sated and bourgeoisified working class."[54] The strike inspired many others, opening a long cycle of what historian Xavier Vigna has called "worker insubordination."[55] This noticeable uptick in domestic struggle suggested to many radicals that the "objective conditions" for mass disruption at home were riper than ever.

Lastly, struggles in the United States seemed to indicate that the idea of opening new fronts might actually work. In the late 1960s, the United States was rocked by a wave of urban rebellions, which climaxed in over 150 riots during the summer of 1967. Many radicals abroad viewed these uprisings as proof that Black struggles were ripping the world's capitalist superpower apart from the inside. Radicals from the Union of Communist Youth (Marxist-Leninist), for example, triumphantly announced that the "resolute struggle of the African American people of the United States is a blow against American imperialism, it forms an integral part of the revolutionary struggles of the oppressed peoples and nations of the world." They assured their supporters that "each battle fought by Black Americans weakens imperialism and supports the revolutionary struggles of people elsewhere in the world."[56] Although bitter rivals of the Maoists, the RCY felt similarly. For Pierre Rousset, these events confirmed that African Americans were emerging as the "vanguard" of an American struggle increasingly linked to revolutionary movements across the world.[57] Quite a few radicals no doubt projected their desires onto the rebellions, seeing each uprising as a new front in a civil war, and every African American activist as a Black anti-imperialist guerrilla committed to revolution. Although not the most accurate picture of what was happening abroad, the misreading was nevertheless a highly productive one for the French. The thought of an organized revolutionary force struggling inside the United States gave substance to the idea of multiple fronts, galvanizing the French to undertake bolder actions themselves.

Some Black anti-imperialists deliberately encouraged this interpretation of events in the United States. In December 1967, for example, the National Vietnam Committee (NVC) invited Stokely Carmichael to Paris to discuss Black politics, the Vietnam War, and the international situation.[58] Speaking at the NVC's "Che Guevara Week," Carmichael launched into a militant critique of the war, urging a shift from protest to active resistance. The crowd of more than 4,000 listened in rapture as Carmichael preached: "We don't want peace in Vietnam. What we want is the victory of the Vietnamese people over the United States. In spilling our blood to help this victory, we feel that we are not paying too high a price, even if it means we have to destroy the structures of the United States."[59] At a later press conference, he was even more direct:

The war in Vietnam must be brought to the United States of America. If Ho Chi Minh cannot sleep, Lyndon Johnson shall not sleep. The babies in Vietnam are in threat of their lives, and people in the United States must be in threat of their lives. If fire is raging in Vietnam, then fire must rage in the United States. And as long as the United States oppresses black people inside the United States and oppresses Vietnamese in Vietnam, we have a common bond against a common enemy.[60]

By all accounts, Carmichael's speech had an electrifying effect, further convincing young French anti-imperialists that the United States was on the verge of revolution and that they should push their own activism in a more revolutionary direction.[61]

By the end of 1967, many radicals no longer felt that opening a new front of the war in Europe was a pipe dream. Given the course of the war, they now believed they had no choice but to change their approach. It was at this point that Che's call to create "two, three, many Vietnams" became, in the words of RCY activist Daniel Bensaïd, "the categorical imperative of solidarity."[62] Of course, French radicals knew full well that they could not justify this revolutionary turn by following those African

Americans, Vietnamese, and Latin Americans who claimed that they struggled against the same direct oppressor: US imperialism. Instead, they rationalized their inclusion in this growing anti-imperialist front by arguing that, while the United States had certainly become the most aggressive imperialist force in the world, it was only acting as the representative of a broader imperialist system. Since imperialism was not just an agent, but also an entire global system, it could, and should, be challenged from anywhere, even Europe. This was, radicals believed, what Lenin had suggested long ago, what Che had recently pointed out, and what Vietnamese communists like Lê Duẩn were now insisting. European radicals had a real part to play in this growing international revolution.

These ideas were codified in the antiwar youth international's official announcement for their next conference in Berlin. The statement, released by the executive bureau in December 1967, claimed that imperialism's "goal is to terminate the development of the global revolution," wherever it may be. While Vietnam was certainly the flashpoint of the struggle – "a decisive confrontation between the international revolution and the counterrevolution" – that struggle extended globally. For that reason, the statement continued, Europe could also serve as "a decisive battlefield in the anti-capitalist and anti-imperialist struggle." The duty of revolutionaries in Europe was therefore to open another front against the imperialist counterrevolution. "This strategy finds its expression in Guevara's words, 'create two, three, many Vietnams!'" In this way, the young radicals promised, they would revive the "proletarian internationalism" that the Old Left had allegedly abandoned.[63]

If the early 1960s saw many antiwar activists transform into radicals, the late 1960s witnessed the subsequent transformation of many radicals into revolutionaries. Instead of just hoping to change some larger system, they now actively organized for that system's immediate overthrow. By the start of 1968, many anti-imperialist radicals came to believe that dramatic change was not only desirable but also necessary, possible, and imminent. This marked a significant shift in what it even meant to be "antiwar." Antiwar radicals were making it very clear that they were not pacifists who opposed war as such.[64] Although they stood against imperialist wars of aggression, they not only supported the right of oppressed nations to wage wars of national liberation, but were now also proclaiming their own right to wage revolutionary wars at home in the name of internationalist solidarity against the common enemy of imperialism. Working across borders, they began to seriously contemplate making some kind of revolutionary change in the North Atlantic. With this, the radical antiwar international that took shape just a few years ago became a revolutionary anti-imperialist international.

Bringing the War Home

The decision to host the next radical antiwar youth convergence in West Berlin was no coincidence. To many observers, the city was a tinderbox. On the one hand, it was the capital of one of the most conservative bulwarks against revolution. West Germany was the strongest US ally on the continent, the most robust capitalist economy in Europe, and the forward post of the Cold War. The government had banned the Communist Party of Germany, the mainstream press demonized antiwar activists as terrorists, and the two leading parties – the Christian Democratic Union and the Social Democratic Party – joined hands in a grand coalition that assured them firm control over the Bundestag, effectively eliminating all formal political alternatives. The coalition was in turn working to ram through new Emergency Acts, which evoked bad memories of the 1930s, especially since West Germany had never completely de-Nazified. As activists regularly emphasized, some former Nazis still taught in universities, the leader of the country's most powerful employers' association had served in the SS, and even the chancellor had once been a card-carrying Nazi.[65]

On the other hand, West Germany's activist movements were some of the most radical in Europe. Activists were notoriously pugnacious, their rhetoric was inflammatory, and their actions captured international attention. They condemned the older generations for their complicity with the Third Reich, insisting that the same attitudes that made possible Adolf Hitler's rise to power still pervaded West German society. Just as Germans did nothing to prevent the Holocaust, they argued, so too were they doing nothing to stop the Vietnam War, another genocide in which they were complicit.[66] This allegation, along with activists' relative isolation, radicalized them even further, with some radical youths making a virtue out of their isolation, casting themselves as heroic resisters in a society of collaborators. Unsurprisingly, the combination of a militant youth movement and a hostile general public proved especially explosive, producing some of the most violent clashes in Western Europe.[67]

It was against this charged backdrop that thousands of activists from across North America and Western Europe filed into trains, boarded planes, and packed into automobiles to participate in the International Vietnam Congress on February 17, 1968.[68] If in 1884 the leaders of the most powerful empires on the globe gathered in Berlin to better organize imperialist wars of conquest, in 1968 antiwar activists returned to that city to organize the war against imperialism. The only way to do that, many of them now believed, was to build a new front inside the advanced capitalist world. Dale Smith of SNCC spoke of the need to wage revolution in the United States. "As long as parents in Vietnam are crying about their children," Smith exclaimed, "parents in the USA should also cry about their children."[69] Peter Weiss declared that the "National Liberation Front of South Vietnam – the sole and victorious representative of the revolutionary people – has given us the task of organizing the resistance in the metropoles."[70] Socialist German Student League leader Rudi Dutschke dramatized the need to internationalize the revolution: "Unless the Viet Cong is joined by an American, a European, and an Asian Cong, the Vietnamese revolution will fail like others before it."[71]

At the same time that these radical anti-imperialists strategized revolution, Vietnamese communists unleashed a devastating new offensive. Beginning on January 31, 1968, tens of thousands of Vietnamese insurgents rose across South Vietnam, overrunning villages, seizing provincial cities, and even attacking the US Embassy in Saigon. The "Tet Offensive" exposed the US military's vulnerabilities, demonstrated the weaknesses of the South Vietnamese government, and showed that the revolutionaries could win. Its effect on young radicals was immeasurable. To anti-imperialists, the worldwide anti-imperialist front was no longer rhetoric; revolution seemed to have become a reality. Tariq Ali, one of the leaders of the Vietnam Solidarity Campaign in Great Britain, later recalled:

The Tet offensive had begun even while we were preparing to open the Congress. Every fresh victory was reported to the Congress amidst louder and louder applause. The Vietnamese were demonstrating in the most concrete fashion imaginable that it was possible to fight and win. This fact was critical in shaping the consciousness of our generation. We believed that change was not only necessary, but possible.[72]

Following the offensive as it unfolded, radicals felt that they were fighting alongside the NLF. "This was a time," Ali continued, "when it really seemed as if our actions in the West were co-ordinated with what was happening on the actual battlefields of Vietnam."[73] Vietnamese revolutionaries were beating imperialism in Southeast Asia; it was time for radicals to do their part in the heart of imperialism. Tet united different national radical lefts. It accelerated political time. It made victory seem possible.

Eager for action, the International Vietnam Congress ended with more than 10,000 activists marching side by side, waving red flags, singing revolutionary songs in different languages, and raising portraits of revolutionaries like Che, Lenin, Luxemburg, and Hồ Chí Minh. When radicals left Berlin they took with them a feeling of unity, optimism, and urgency.[74] The approximately 500 anti-imperialists who made up the

French contingent returned home with a variety of confrontational street tactics, the fast-march chant "Ho, Ho, Ho Chi Minh," and a commitment to escalating the struggle in France, a country which seemed, for all intents and purposes, far too placid.[75] Losing no time, they prepared to "inaugurate a new type of political demonstration" on February 21, 1968 to "break decidedly with the routine of nonchalant processions."[76] That day, radicals from groups like the National Vietnam Committee, the Revolutionary Communist Youth, the Unified Socialist Party, and the National Union of Students of France did not simply protest the war but vowed to remake the "Latin Quarter" into the "Heroic Vietnam Quarter."[77] As the NVC put it, the task at hand was to ensure that this "European Front" could become more than just words on paper and grow into a real force in "the war against imperialism in the metropoles."[78]

On February 21, radicals from the Vietnam Base Committees hung the NLF flag on the Embassy of the Republic of Vietnam, a team from the NVC did the same for the Sorbonne, and hundreds of others changed street signs, renamed buildings, passed out copies of the *Vietnam Courier* to everyone in sight, and covered the walls of the Latin Quarter with posters celebrating the recent victories of the NLF.[79] Boulevard Saint-Michel became boulevard du Vietnam Héroïque; the lycée Saint-Louis became the lycée Nguyễn Văn Trỗi, after the young revolutionary executed in 1964 for attempting to assassinate US Secretary of Defense Robert McNamara and Ambassador Henry Cabot Lodge, Jr.; an effigy of Lyndon Johnson was hung in the Fontaine St. Michel, just over the subdued devil, and set ablaze; and the words "NLF Will Win" appeared in burning letters above the gates of the Jardin du Luxembourg. In arguably their most militant antiwar action yet, a coalition of radicals took Che's idea of "creating two, three, many Vietnams" literally, bringing Vietnam to Paris by altering its very landscape.[80]

The campaign continued into the following months. On March 18, 1968, antiwar radicals bombed the offices of three US businesses. Two days later, several hundred demonstrators smashed the windows of the American Express offices. The police arrested six activists, including Nicolas Boulte, one of the leaders of the NVC, and Xavier Langlade of the RCY. Radicals saw the arrests as part of a state campaign to repress antiwar demonstrations, and the NVC issued a communiqué calling on all activists to mobilize.[81] The need to defend antiwar activists brought rival factions closer together. On March 22, 1968, students occupied an administrative building on the Nanterre campus, forming the March 22 Movement, a coalition that included activists from a variety of radical groups like the RCY.[82] The actions of the March 22 Movement soon snowballed, prompting the closure of Nanterre and the Sorbonne and ultimately eliciting the police repression that kicked off the events of May '68.[83] That month, mass student unrest combined with a general strike of about ten million workers to paralyze the country.[84] For a moment, it seemed as if France was sliding into revolution.

There were of course many factors that made May '68 possible, but the transformative struggles in Asia, Africa, and Latin America played a decisive, though sometimes forgotten, role. Of these, Vietnam was particularly significant, so much so that Jean-Paul Sartre later suggested that "the origins of May lie in the Vietnamese Revolution."[85] As French radicals themselves admitted, the "Vietnamese revolution played a determinant role in radicalizing the youth."[86] It allowed young radicals to become an independent force, gain organizational experiences, and invent new political forms. In some cases, especially at the high school level, antiwar organizations formed the basis of the action committees of May.[87] In this way, historian Laurent Jalabert argues, antiwar activism provided radicals with a veritable political education.[88]

But Sartre had something more profound in mind. The Vietnamese revolution lay at the origins of May '68 because it expanded "the field of the possible."[89] If an army of poor rice farmers could defeat the United States, radicals thought, then anything was possible. They believed that Vietnam expanded horizons precisely by putting the idea of revolution squarely on the agenda. The Vietnamese struggle ruptured the reigning logic of peaceful coexistence by showing that imperialism could be confronted instead of accommodated. For radicals like Herta Alvarez, Alain Geismar, Evelyne July, and Serge July, members of the March 22 Movement who were all deeply involved in the May events, "the Vietnamese people are opening a new historical period," one of "generalized offensive," where people everywhere could finally reclaim the "right to make Revolution."[90] This in turn made Vietnam the single most important revolutionary catalyst in the contemporary world: "whether it is the Great Proletarian Cultural Revolution, the Latin American guerrillas, the North American urban guerrillas, or the mass strike of May–June '68 in France, we are all indebted to our Vietnamese comrades."[91] The following year, some radicals went so far as to declare that "All militants know that the ideas they had in their heads during the May struggles came for the most part from the practice of the Vietnamese people."[92]

One of the most important ideas in the minds of those radicals who detonated the May events was to follow the example of Vietnamese revolutionaries by making revolution at home. On May 9, for example, the Revolutionary Communist Youth held a massive meeting at the Mutualité to discuss the possibility of domestic revolution: "Can the struggles waged up to now, the struggles in support of the Vietnamese revolution, be coordinated and radicalized? Can they be the beginning of revolutionary struggles against imperialism (highest stage of capitalism) in the advanced capitalist countries? Can they organize themselves in such a way as to form the revolutionary vanguard of tomorrow?"[93] The very next day, on May 10, these same radicals raised the stakes in a dramatic showdown with the police known as the "Night of the Barricades." On May 13, workers went on strike in solidarity. Within a week, the revolt had spread to the entire country.

The Vietnamese revolution played an "exemplary" role by inspiring French activists to make revolution against all the odds.[94] Vietnam, in other words, set in motion the defining characteristic of this period, what might be called a "chain of exemplarity." "As the Vietnamese successes inspired the students," Ali reflected on May '68, "so now the triumph of the students inspired the workers."[95] To this sequence of resonating examples – which was by no means unidirectional, as militant worker struggles worked back on the students – one could easily add how the workers' rebellion in France in turn inspired radicals across the North Atlantic.

In addition to training radicals, expanding the field of the possible, signaling the actuality of revolution, and setting in motion a chain of inspiring examples, anti-imperialist struggles like those in Vietnam redefined the very project of changing the world: The best way to make the world a better place was to synchronize multiple coordinated fronts across the globe into a unified international revolution against imperialism. All the struggles act "reciprocally," the RCY explained in June: Struggles in France could help the world revolution, while "the victory of the Vietnamese revolutionaries reinforces our own fight."[96] For many radicals, May '68 was not a singular French event; it was merely one front in that worldwide anti-imperialist revolution, with Vietnamese at the head. As the RCY argued, the "French revolution," by which they meant the events of May '68, was just "one of the 'many' Vietnams that Che advocated." For groups like the March 22 Movement, the National Vietnam Committee, and the Revolutionary Communist Youth, opening this new revolutionary front was made possible by translating Vietnamese struggles into the French context, that is, making "Vietnam" their own.

While many of the radicals who helped prepare, trigger, and sustain the May events saw things this way, not everyone who participated in them did, not even other radical anti-imperialists.[97] The Union of Communist Youth (Marxist-Leninist), for example, argued that this idea of translating Vietnam only instrumentalized the struggles of the Vietnamese people, doing violence to the particularity of the Vietnamese revolution.

Their alternative was a very literal form of solidarity: convincing everyone to read the *Vietnam Courier*, for them the first and last word on anything that had to do with Vietnam. Echoing every position of the DRV, the Union of Communist Youth (Marxist-Leninist) served as a mouthpiece. While it made for effective propaganda, this stance ultimately rendered the group's solidarity work inflexible, preventing it from taking the creative leaps that other radicals did. It is no coincidence that it was caught completely off guard when events rapidly escalated in France.[98]

Content to simply present what it assumed to be the authentic voice of the revolution abroad, unwilling to interpret Vietnamese struggles for their own conditions, and unable to see how deeply Vietnam resonated with issues at home, the Union of Communist Youth (Marxist-Leninist) missed the events of May '68.[99] Instead of joining thousands on the barricades, the group's leadership convinced its members that marching to the Hôtel Lutetia, where the North Vietnamese delegation was staying, was the best way to show their "support and total solidarity" for North Vietnam, at that moment engaged in negotiations with the United States in Paris.[100] After the May events, the RCY admonished the Union of Communist Youth (Marxist-Leninist), explaining that remaining loyal to the Vietnamese people did not mean mechanically echoing Hanoi's line but activating the essence of the Vietnamese revolution's example. As the RCY put it: "it was stupid to put ourselves at the service of the Vietnamese because the Vietnamese cannot judge for us the possibilities of our actions."[101] In the same way that French radicals could not determine from afar the exact steps Vietnamese revolutionaries had to take in order to bring their revolution to victory in the unique conditions of Southeast Asia, Vietnamese communists could not decide what their French comrades had to do in order to make revolution a reality in the unique conditions of France. That was something only French revolutionaries could do for themselves.

Their literal vision of solidarity, which prevented them from playing a part in a potential revolutionary opening, was one major reason why the Union of Communist Youth (Marxist-Leninist) dissolved itself. After their organization's collapse, some former members decided to take a different approach. In June, for instance, they conceded that "The Vietnamese example is universal."[102] These radicals – many of whom later formed the Proletarian Left, the most dynamic of the Maoist groups in France after 1968 – developed the new direction in their paper *La Cause du peuple*. "The mass movement of May–June in France," explained a lengthy article announcing their adherence to the worldwide anti-imperialist front, "is a link in a long chain that encircles imperialism before strangling it. The revolutionary flames spread from one end of the world to the other."[103]

May '68 prompted radicals to confront the challenges of "creating many Vietnams." On the one hand, as the Union of Communist Youth (Marxist-Leninist) pointed out, this way of thinking internationalism risked speaking for the oppressed with an orientalist, even imperialist, perspective. By ignoring difference, radicals risked decontextualizing struggles abroad, privileging their own idealist projections over Vietnamese voices, and substituting themselves for Vietnamese people, turning solidarity into its opposite. Others like the RCY, however, argued that bending the stick too far the other way by insisting on absolute difference risked foreclosing all creative resonance with Vietnamese struggles, reducing internationalism to either hero worship or an imperative to police others. In these years, radicals struggled to find the best way to approach this field of differences to make generative solidarity possible. Without difference there could be no repetition, only imitation; but too much difference would occlude all resonance, as well as solidarity itself. Both ignoring difference and fetishizing it, radicals soon learned, could undermine radical politics.[104]

Resonating Revolutions

The exhilarating events of May 1968 convinced radicals across North America and Western Europe that the strategy of building multiple fronts against imperialism could succeed. In retrospect, it seems unsurprising that the breakthrough would come in France, a country known for its vibrant revolutionary past, but nothing seemed more unlikely at the time. Luigi Bobbio, a leader of Continuous Struggle, one of the largest extraparliamentary groups in Italy, spoke for many when he recalled how most radicals initially saw not the French but the American and German movements as vanguards.[105] As RCY leader Alain Krivine explained in an interview with US radical Mary-Alice Waters: "We worked here month after month to organize demonstration after demonstration in support of the students' struggle in Germany and Italy. We never thought that our turn would come so soon."[106]

If Tet showed that the Vietnamese people could defeat the United States, the surprise of May '68 seemed to show young activists that revolution was possible in the advanced capitalist world. The May events transformed the political horizon by giving substance to the idea of creating "two, three, many Vietnams." As the new slogan went, create "two, three, many Parises."[107] May '68 and Vietnam coalesced in the minds of many radicals. "The world had to be changed and France and Vietnam proved that it is possible to move forward," recalled Ali.[108] For this reason, radicals from neighboring countries flooded into the

French capital soon after the events. Krivine explained, "They want to discuss with us, they want to learn from our experience, they want to aid us financially."[109] As the Italian revolutionary Sergio Bologna recalled, "The French May changed everything"; it was "a watershed in the collective imagination."[110]

Radicals interpreted May in light of their own national contexts. The Italians in particular had reason to pay attention; similar conditions – a rich Marxist culture, a militant working class, a long history of revolutionary struggle, and a massive mainstream communist party – suggested that Italy could be next. In fact, May '68 erupted at the height of the Italian student movement, and hundreds of activists traveled to Paris to experience the revolt firsthand. Awed by the power of workers' struggles, they threw themselves into the world of the factory upon returning home, hoping to build a worker–student alliance. As activist Elsa Gili recalled, "We went to the factory gates for every change of shift. The workers told us what had happened. Then we went to the local cafés with them and wrote leaflets based on what they were telling us."[111] The alliance bore fruit the following autumn, when nearly a quarter of the Italian workforce went on strike, triggering Italy's own decades-long wave of struggles, sometimes called the "Creeping May."[112]

The May events even had an effect in countries such as Great Britain where revolution seemed extremely unlikely. "France shook the ruling classes throughout Europe," Ali later put it, "and the British decided to take no chances that the disease would spread."[113] In an almost farcical rerun of 1789, the British state prepared for the worst, with the authorities fearing that the Vietnam Solidarity Campaign's upcoming antiwar demonstration in October 1968 would devolve into "a French-style insurrection."[114] The media ran inflammatory stories about the coming "October Revolution," and police raided the offices of the *Black Dwarf*, a prominent radical paper with ties to the Vietnam Solidarity Campaign.

While a few radicals were also whipped up in the excitement, hoping Britain would be next, the majority took a more sober attitude. As Ali put it, "none of us ever believed that anything remotely resembling France could happen in Britain that year."[115] That said, British radicals still thought that the May events could be translated into the British context, but this did not mean simply mimicking the sequence that played out in France. "What is required is not the heroic gesture or the symbolic confrontation (any more than the perfect resolution); nor is it vicarious participation in the self-activity of others (whether they be in Hanoi or Paris)," the International Socialists explained.[116] Revolution in Britain would have to assume a different form, one that involved a much longer, less glamorous struggle. But even while recognizing those differences, the International Socialists could still declare: "France today, Britain tomorrow!"[117]

The May events also commanded attention outside Europe. In the United States, they impacted activists like no other European event. May '68 exercised a tremendous influence on the New Left in general and SDS in particular, accelerating several transformations in the premier organization of white leftist youth. First came a reassessment of the "working class." Aside from a few important exceptions, many of the activists who formed the core institutions of the New Left tended to discount workers. "Simply stated," historian Peter Levy summarizes, "the New Left inherited an anticlass perspective; it assumed that class struggle and class structure were essentially irrelevant to the modern American experience."[118] Convinced that white workers were racist, conservative, or bought off by capitalism, many activists turned to other subjects, ignoring the militant workers' struggles slowly reemerging across the country.

The May events helped change that view, something observed by Jean Dube of the RCY during his speaking tour of North America in August 1968:

On almost every campus the students asked how we in the student struggle in France had managed to achieve a link with the working class, how we had been able to involve the working class and work together. I think the fact that this question was asked is extremely important, because it shows that a lot of people here have understood the main lessons and drawn the most important conclusion from the May and June struggle in France: the main task of the student struggle in any country, if you want to carry it to a higher state, is to involve the young workers in the struggle.[119]

The image of nearly ten million workers grinding a capitalist country to a standstill compelled many radicals to reconsider their relationship to workers' struggles in the United States.

Second, May '68 helped shift the New Left's approach to internationalism. For most of the 1960s, the majority of radicals in the United States prioritized ties with the "Third World," not Western Europe. The transatlantic connections that did exist were often ad hoc, isolated, or limited to personal ties. The United States was far more important for Europeans than Europe was for Americans.[120] But 1968 changed all that. As historian Kirkpatrick Sale notes, the events of that year – from the International Vietnam Congress in February to the assassination attempt on Rudi Dutschke in April to the French events in May – led to a "growing international consciousness for the American Movement."[121] Reflecting on these developments immediately after May '68, Carl Davidson, SDS inter-organizational secretary, argued in *New Left Notes*, "Our struggles, however isolated they may seem, are part of this single revolutionary process within a multi-national imperialism."[122] For that reason, American radicals had to deepen international ties with activists abroad, and he proposed developing coordinated "international actions around Draft-resistance, desertion, or attacks on the CIA, NATO, and other military alliances."[123] He added: "Hopefully, the recent dramatic struggles of the European New Left students will change some of our isolationist attitudes."[124]

At the next national interim committee meeting in June, much of the SDS leadership had come around to the view that it was time to reorient toward Europe. "On the whole," the meeting minutes made clear, "the consensus was that European travel is to be stressed at this time. Everybody shouldn't go to Hanoi as we have been doing; the struggle in the advanced capitalist countries has been ignored by SDS."[125] While some had suggested the best way to build ties with Europe was to invite leaders like Daniel Cohn-Bendit or Tariq Ali to the United States, others countered that focusing on celebrities would defeat the purpose of understanding the real movements developing on the ground. In the end, it would only reinforce "the inexcusable provincialism of American SDS." Instead, Americans had to personally travel to Europe, ideally for a period of several months.[126]

Barbara and John Ehrenreich did precisely that, embarking on an SDS-sponsored tour of Europe in the summer of 1968. "We wanted to import whatever European movement ideas looked useful to us," they reported to SDS. "But it became clear to us that if ideas, tactics, strategies, et cetera are something more than fads, they cannot be transferred at random from country to country." Before translating these ideas, American anti-imperialists had to first "understand the setting in which they were developed and the context in which they were applied," which necessarily meant studying Europe more closely.[127] In an interesting reversal of early trends, Americans now looked to Europe as a crucial fount of radical ideas. The transatlantic polarities had reversed.

Third, the May events helped push American radicals – especially those in the white New Left – even further toward revolution. A series of dramatic domestic events such as Johnson's decision not to seek reelection at the end of March, Martin Luther King, Jr.'s assassination just days later, the urban rebellions that immediately followed, and the occupation of Columbia University a few weeks after that had already conspired to radicalize many activists in the New Left. It was in the midst of this turmoil that the May events exploded in France. "May '68 in Paris," former SDS President Carl Oglesby recalls, "made people think that it wasn't at all so crazy to think there could be a revolution in a modern developed industrial country." At the very moment the United States appeared to be coming apart at the seams, a mass uprising had erupted in another developed capitalist country. "Who was to say that if events kept developing as they were in 1968 that the same thing couldn't happen here?"[128]

A few days after Robert Kennedy's assassination in June, SDSers gathered at Michigan State University for their annual National Convention. In stark contrast to previous years, hammer and sickle emblems made an appearance, portraits of Lenin festooned the walls of the Student Union, and SDSers donned red armbands. Tom Bell, Bernardine Dohrn, and Steve Halliwell submitted a proposal to develop SDS into a "professional revolutionary organization."[129] Dohrn, the new inter-organizational secretary, proudly called herself a "revolutionary communist."[130] Many SDSers now made the leap to revolution, and they imagined their struggle as a front in the worldwide revolutionary movement. The struggles of French activists against President Charles de Gaulle, Japanese radicals against Prime Minister Satō Eisaku, Iranian militants against the Shah, or the Socialist German Student League against Chancellor Kurt Georg Kiesinger, SDS now declared, "are a few of the current fronts of a single war. We are your allies and brothers."[131]

Within the span of a single year radicals had witnessed the Tet Offensive in Vietnam, a general strike in France, the Tlatelolco massacre in Mexico, a wave of student occupations in Japan, the rise and fall of the Prague Spring in Czechoslovakia, violence outside the Democratic National Convention in the United States, and countless other political explosions across the world. As 1968 came to a close, radicals everywhere believed they were on the verge of something truly historic, and that they had to get ready. It was in this febrile context that tens of thousands of anti-imperialist radicals began to insist that the heterodox New Leftist experiments of the 1960s might not be up to the tasks ahead.

After 1968, numerous radicals dismissed the New Left as too disorganized, politically undisciplined, and theoretically unsophisticated to successfully channel this mass upsurge in a revolutionary direction.[132] It is little coincidence that this was when many of the classic New Left organizations that had once tried to chart a new course beyond the inherited categories of the traditional communist left began to fold. SDS's revolutionary turn contributed directly to its implosion in 1969, SNCC was effectively dead by the end of the year, and the Socialist German Student League limped to its dissolution in 1970.

In their place, many radicals across the North Atlantic turned to some version of the Leninist problematic.[133] "Lenin," Daniel Bensaïd recalls, "was all the rage."[134] Quite simply, Leninism promised a comprehensive model of revolution at a time when ambitious radicals needed it most.

Even a vocal critic of Lenin like Carl Oglesby felt obliged to admit that in the wake of the New Left's failure to invent a robust radical internationalist alternative, Leninism remained the only revolutionary path available: *"There was – and is – no other coherent, integrative, and explicit philosophy of revolution."*[135]

Vietnam Is Everywhere

After 1968, Vietnam become more important than ever for radicals. And yet it paradoxically seemed to fade as a particular issue. Although radicals still talked about Vietnam, organized events, and responded to new developments such as the US invasion of Cambodia, radical antiwar activism as such experienced a relative decline throughout much of the North Atlantic. Anti-imperialists appeared to withdraw from specifically antiwar solidarity work to refocus their energies on new struggles at home.

This dynamic was even apparent in the exceptional case of the United States, where the draft, death toll, and domestic political ramifications made certain that Vietnam remained a palpable issue. Although mass antiwar actions there certainly continued, and in fact grew even larger, the anti-imperialist radicals who had once so prominently assumed leadership of antiwar struggles tended to shift their attention to other matters such as organizing industrial workers, constructing new feminist movements, or building revolutionary parties.

The change was especially pronounced in France.[136] Having just experienced an unprecedented upheaval, anti-imperialists suddenly went from organizing solidarity campaigns for movements abroad to keeping the fires of May burning at home.[137] Attempting to explain this turn of events, some historians have argued that radicals "returned to the hexagon" because domestic events overtook international ones. Others have argued that radicals no longer had any use for Vietnam now that they had secured autonomy from the French Communist Party. Still others have suggested that when the United States finally agreed to peace talks with North Vietnam in 1968 radicals saw their antiwar demands fulfilled.[138]

But radicals were well aware that the war was far from over, and they remained convinced that Vietnam was a decisive front in the world revolution. If explicitly antiwar activity declined, then this was not because radicals somehow stopped caring about Vietnam. Quite the contrary: they now came to believe that the best way to aid Vietnamese revolutionaries was not simply to rally around Vietnam as just another cause but to integrate it as thoroughly as possible into their everyday lived reality. Anti-imperialists never abandoned Vietnam; they assimilated Vietnam so thoroughly it seemed to disappear as a separate issue. As Fredy Perlman, an American radical active in the May events, reported on French radicals in 1968, "The war in Vietnam ceased to be an 'issue' and became a part of their own daily lives."[139] For them, the goal was to liberate Vietnam from the news cycle by translating it into a domestic idiom.[140]

By the turn of the decade, tens of thousands of radicals came to see anti-imperialist internationalism as a process of translating the exemplary struggles in Vietnam into their own contexts. Most understood that this did not just mean automatically copying them. Translation was not mimicry; it required creative experimentation that took account of historical differences. But even with this widely acknowledged proviso, the idea of translating Vietnam left considerable room for interpretation. The Vietnamese revolution was a complex phenomenon, leaving many radicals wondering exactly what they were supposed to translate.

"Vietnam" was such a rich laboratory of struggle that it could potentially serve as a model for many different movements. It might mean occupying universities to create self-administered "liberated zones," waging urban guerrilla warfare, or organizing workers at the point of production. For some, it meant patient collective struggle, lasting years, through many ups and downs. For others, it meant glorifying subjective will against all the objective obstacles in a spectacular moment of voluntaristic revolt. In the very late 1960s and early 1970s, feminists claimed it meant nothing short of women's liberation, queer radicals interpreted it as gay liberation, and a number of indigenous activists thought it meant the right to national sovereignty at home. There were, in other words, many ways to interpret Vietnamese struggles in the context of domestic conditions, a process that anti-imperialists tried to capture through such paradoxical expressions as "Vietnam is in our factories" and the "University is our Vietnam," slogans such as "The struggle at FIAT must become the Vietnam of the bosses of Italy," or even portmanteaus like "FIAT-NAM."[141]

Although there was no such thing as a "correct" translation, this did not prevent different groups from quarreling over who had the right one. In France, for example, an important battle for women's liberation played out precisely over how to interpret Vietnam. During the war the French Communist Party tried to bolster its antiwar message of charity and goodwill by inviting women to express their antiwar politics through their "natural" maternal instincts. "Today we address ourselves in particular," one flyer read, "to all the women, to you mothers, and to you whose profession it is to care for, heal, and teach children."[142] In contrast to this victim-centered approach to solidarity that forced women back into traditional roles, revolutionary feminists pointed to Vietnam, insisting that women there were obliterating these very roles in the act of revolutionary struggle. As a flyer from the Women's Liberation Movement explained:

In Vietnam, women have not remained confined to their maternal and domestic role, expressing the pain of the country through their tears. They take on, in their own right, constant reconstruction, the defense of villages, or they enlist in the liberation army. *They therefore wholeheartedly take part in the fight*, whether that means picking up the rifle or taking on responsibilities.

In actively struggling, in the same way as the men, for the liberation of the Vietnamese people, they move toward their own liberation, breaking with the image and the role that until now has been assigned to them: passivity, domestic tasks, the exclusive functions of mother and spouse.

"There is ruin, death, suffering in Vietnam," feminists concluded, but also the seeds of something new: "*the laying of the groundwork of a new world, liberating women and men.*"[143]

The two sides could adopt these views precisely because the ambiguous role of women in the Vietnamese revolution lent itself to such different readings. On the one hand, many Vietnamese women did believe in the centrality of the family, interpreting the war as a life or death battle to defend it. As historian Helen E. Anderson explains, "Although Vietnamese culture defined women's roles in terms of bearing children and taking care of their homes and family, resistance of invaders who threatened the village's safety was indeed part of the struggle to protect and save the family. Hence, the war against the Americans in Vietnam, a continuation of the war against the French, became a struggle to preserve the most important Vietnamese institution – the family."[144] Many Vietnamese women were not simply driven by a sense of family, motherhood, and traditional roles; in their international antiwar efforts they often made strategic appeals to some imagined sense of universal motherhood to win the support of other women across the world. As one statement put it, "Whatever continent we may live in, and whatever the colour of our skin and our political convictions, our motherly feelings bring us very close to one another: We all love our children, are deeply attached to national independence and peace, and stand ready to defend the lives of our dear little ones."[145] In this regard, the French Communist Party was not necessarily wrong to interpret the role of women in the revolution in the way that it did.

On the other hand, some version of women's liberation figured as a cornerstone of the Vietnamese revolution from the start. In the 1950s, women challenged traditional gender relations in the North by finding work outside the home, participating in political life, and winning legal equality with men. North Vietnam notably promised women paid maternity leave, access to childcare, the right to divorce, and equal rights of use, ownership, and disposal of property acquired before and during marriage. During the American War, revolutionary women in both the North and the South continued to push gender boundaries. They played an indispensable role in the war, carrying supplies, building infrastructure, managing the village economy, organizing political opposition, taking up arms, and at times assuming leadership positions in the revolution.[146] In the North, it is estimated that some 1.5 million women served in the army, militia, or local forces; in the South, a million women joined the resistance as part of the NLF, making up around one third of active guerrilla forces.[147]

While important barriers to full gender equity continued to exist, the strong presence of women in the revolution led many North American and Western European feminists to feel quite justified in upholding Vietnam as a model for women's liberation in their own countries.[148] They took inspiration from these struggles, celebrated such personalities as the beloved diplomat Nguyễn Thị Bình on the political front and the revered commander Nguyễn Thị Định on the military front, and even learned directly from Vietnamese women themselves. At an antiwar meeting with Americans in Czechoslovakia, for example, a team of Vietnam revolutionaries led by Madame Bình organized a separate meeting for women. Activist Vivian Rothstein recalls her surprise: "'What? Meet separately with women?' The whole concept was unfamiliar. I really had no feminist consciousness at all. But Vietnamese revolutionaries felt there were special concerns women shared, things they cared about that no one else did, and it was very important to meet separately."[149]

Rothstein took these lessons back home, where she participated in a new wave of feminist activism in the United States, building one of the first independent women's organizations in Chicago. "For me, there was a direct relationship between the Vietnam War and the women's movement. This whole concept of building a political base with women as the constituency was something I brought back from Vietnam. I talked to my colleagues in Chicago about the Women's Union in Vietnam and how it had chapters in every little village and built institutions for women with political power. So we sort of modeled our organization along those lines."[150] Rothstein's experience was by no means unique – many feminists shared the view that the struggles of Vietnamese women could help build a new women's liberation movement in the North Atlantic. "Our Vietnamese sisters hold out their hand," the first issue of the French feminist paper Le Torchon brûle explained. "They show us the example."[151]

For their part, Vietnamese revolutionaries were well aware of the role they played, invited feminists to emulate their struggles, and were fully cognizant that activists abroad were translating their example in competing ways.[152] In fact, they encouraged these different readings.[153] Activists in the Vietnamese Women's Union, for example, deliberately calibrated their message to appeal to diverse audiences. To older peace activists, they emphasized the maternal role of women in protecting the family. To more liberal feminists, they pointed to the many legal victories that women were winning in Vietnam. To radical feminists, they talked about how women were breaking traditional gender roles. To women of color, they offered personal examples of how to combine the struggles against racism, sexism, and imperialism. To socialist feminists, they emphasized the ways women were contributing to the construction of socialism. Vietnamese revolutionaries, in other words, strove to make their example translatable for different contexts.[154]

It was not uncommon for this process of translation to assume a life of its own. In some cases, activists interpreted Vietnamese struggles in ways that were far beyond what Vietnamese revolutionaries themselves imagined. In other cases, translations gave way to projections as some radicals tried to make "Vietnam" a model for what they wished to see, ignoring the concrete realities of the struggle. In still other cases, radicals detached "Vietnam" from its particular context – a divided country in Southeast Asia – and turned it into a universal symbol. In the words of the workers who self-managed the Lip watch factory in Besançon for several months in 1973: "VIETNAM: is not the endowment of the Vietnamese. In Franc-Comtoise, you say 'Lip.'"[155] "Vietnam" ceased to belong to Vietnamese; it became a kind of global tendency that assumed different forms. Just as some anti-imperialists redefined the relationship between imperialism and the United States as one of synecdoche, they did the same with "Vietnam" and the country of Vietnam, positioning them as opposites in a Manichaean struggle. Imperialism was reaction, repression, counterrevolution; Vietnam was revolution, autonomy, and heroism. Vietnam became everything as everything became Vietnam.

While it is certainly true that radicals in the North Atlantic at times appropriated Vietnamese struggles, treated Vietnam as a projection screen, and abstracted the Vietnamese revolution into a kind of master symbol in ways that were sometimes orientalist, it must be emphasized that Vietnamese actors were active participants in this process. First, Vietnamese communists also projected their desires abroad. Quite a few believed, for example, that American movements were pushing the United States to the brink of socialist revolution.[156] Second, they encouraged others to use, adopt, and translate Vietnamese struggles in ways that could enliven their own struggles.[157] In their view, this was the very meaning of internationalism. As DRV Prime Minister Phạm Văn Đồng explained in a letter to the National Vietnam Committee, "our struggle is also yours, dear friends, let's move forward to victory!"[158] Lastly, they reframed their struggles, messages, and ambitions to appeal to as many parties as possible. While this was no doubt tactical, many

Vietnamese communists did believe that their struggles possessed a kind of universalist appeal that could overcome all divides.[159] At one point, for instance, they even thought their revolution could reunite the USSR and the People's Republic of China.[160]

There were, however, some challenges in this approach. First, consciously playing to different imagined identities could lead to essentializing the very divisions that Vietnamese communists sought to transcend. Second, downplaying their communist ties in order win wider support could lead to duplicitous shortcuts that might ultimately undermine the stated long-term goal of building a truly emancipatory future. While it made tactical sense for communists to make the National Liberation Front appear autonomous from Hanoi, for example, this often meant misleading not only supporters abroad but also sympathetic Vietnamese in the South, which would inevitably lead to problems in the future.[161] Third, allowing their revolution to take on so many diverse meanings might give rise to troubling contradictions. When speaking to sympathetic audiences in the North Atlantic, for example, Vietnamese communists could at one moment wear an áo dài, put on traditional dances, and present themselves as peaceful patriots who only wanted to defend their family, culture, and nation and at another wear military fatigues, equate nationalism with internationalist communist revolution, and present themselves as seasoned revolutionaries leading just one front in a global struggle to abolish imperialism. As Leninists, they saw no theoretical conflict between fostering national identity and fighting for world communism, but this was not necessarily true in practice: Cultivating national identity could encourage a kind of essentializing self-orientalism that would derail the struggle for universal emancipation, while insisting on an undifferentiated universalism could lead to a homogenization that blurred important differences.[162] The internationalist project of "translating Vietnam," then, was a profoundly messy process for everyone involved, Vietnamese revolutionaries included.

That said, it concentrated many burning questions about internationalism in those years. It is therefore no surprise that so many radicals interested in changing the world found themselves obsessed with the meaning of Vietnam in these years. "Vietnam" was not just a tragedy, a bloodbath, a fateful struggle, a showdown with enormous stakes. For activists in France, the United States, Vietnam, and across the world, it became a semantic tapestry; a captivating riddle; an immense storehouse of revolutionary symbols, ideas, experiences, and feelings; and a condensation of intractable problems inherent to the very project of changing the world. As one American anti-imperialist later recalled, "There were layers upon layers in Viet Nam, meanings within meanings, wheels within wheels."[163]

Figure 1 Far from being an isolated US affair, opposition to the Vietnam War was widespread, with antiwar demonstrations taking place across the globe, such as this one in Paris organized by the National Vietnam Committee in 1966. (Getty)

Figure 2 The escalation of US involvement in Vietnam radicalized international antiwar opposition, turning many to Leninist anti-imperialism. (La contemporaine, Mémoires de 68)

Figure 3 In February 1968, anti-imperialist radicals from across the North Atlantic met in Berlin, where they resolved to support the Vietnamese revolution by opening new fronts at home.

Figure 4 The events of May '68 in France seemed to prove that revolution was possible in the capitalist North Atlantic, energizing radicals everywhere. (Tamiment Library and Robert F. Wagner Labor Archives, Black Dwarf)

Figure 5 In their campaign to bring Vietnam home, radicals in Paris planted the flag of the National Liberation Front on the spire of Notre-Dame Cathedral. (Tamiment Library and Robert F. Wagner Labor Archives, Liberation News Service)

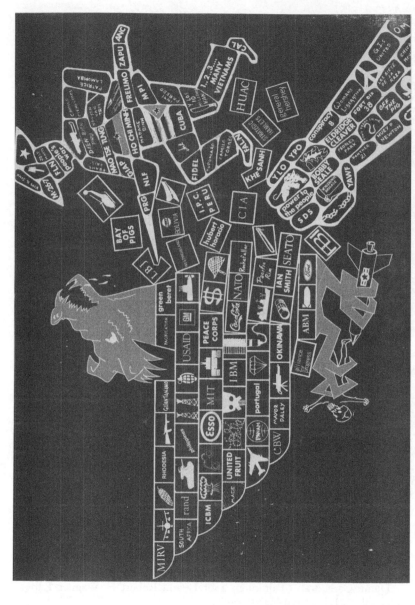

Figure 6 US radicals imagined themselves as fighting alongside revolutionaries in what was then called the "Third World." (Temple University Special Collections, Liberation News Service)

Figure 7 Similarly, French radicals envisioned their efforts as just one front in a united international movement against imperialism. (La contemporaine, Vive la révolution)

Figure 8 Like many anti-imperialists, the Black Panther Party believed that the best way to change the world was to unite diverse struggles across the globe against US imperialism. (Tamiment Library and Robert F. Wagner Labor Archives, Black Panther)

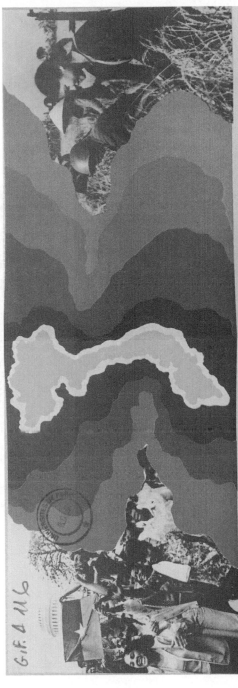

The Vietnamese people, like all people, like ourselves, simply want to govern their want to live. They want to live. They want to survive. They want peace with freedom. We territory themselves. We have opposed this war not only for it basic evil, but because we want peace with freedom. The U.S. government opposes and oppresses them. The U.S. know that the struggle of the Vietnamese people is all our struggle. They want to live. We government opposes and oppresses us. They are winning, we, too will win.

Figure 9 Radicals in the North Atlantic tried to translate "Vietnam" into a domestic idiom, drawing parallels between struggles at home, such as those led by women of color, with Vietnamese struggles abroad. (La contemporaine, États-Unis, New Left, Mouvements de résistance à la guerre du Vietnam)

Figure 10 North American and Western European anti-imperialists and Vietnamese revolutionaries forged durable relationships through meetings such as this one in Cuba. (Tamiment Library and Robert F. Wagner Labor Archives, Liberation News Service)

Figure 11 When the turn to revolution sparked widespread state repression, groups like the Proletarian Left embarked on a "democratic turn," building a united front with famous intellectuals such as Simone de Beauvoir and Jean-Paul Sartre, who exposed the French government's selective repression of radicals by illegally selling copies of the banned paper *La Cause du peuple*. (Getty)

Figure 12 In the early 1970s, antiwar activists connected their experiences with incarceration to state repression abroad, working with human rights activists to organize demonstrations such as this one in Paris, which drew attention to the many political prisoners tortured in "tiger cages" in South Vietnam. (Tamiment Library and Robert F. Wagner Labor Archives, Liberation News Service)

Figure 13 Antiwar activism continued even after the United States withdrew from Vietnam in 1973, with radicals organizing a massive international convergence in Milan to protest repression in South Vietnam. (La contemporaine, Solidarité Indochine)

Figure 14 The communist seizure of Saigon in April 1975 electrified anti-imperialists everywhere, including many Vietnamese living in Paris, who celebrated the victory on May Day. (Tamiment Library and Robert F. Wagner Labor Archives, Liberation News Service)

Figure 15 In the 1970s, anti-imperialists believed that the many diverse struggles in Southeast Asia were part of a single united international force against US imperialism. (Archives nationales, Pierrefitte-sur-Sein, Collectif intersyndical universitaire d'Action Vietnam Laos Cambodge)

Figure 16 Despite a veneer of unity, China, Cambodia, and Vietnam went to war in 1979, shattering faith in anti-imperialist internationalism. (La contemporaine, Rouge)

MEETING DE SOLIDARITE AVEC LE PEUPLE DU KAMPUCHEA DEMOCRATIQUE EN LUTTE CONTRE L'AGRESSION DU VIETNAM SOUTENUE PAR L'UNION SOVIETIQUE

VENDREDI 2 FEVRIER 1979 A 20 h 30

Organisé par le Comité des patriotes du Kampuchéa démocratique en France

Salle de la Mutualité 24 rue St Victor Paris 5e Métro Maubert Mutualité

Soutenu par plus de 20 organisations françaises et étrangères

Figure 17 The chaos of the Third Indochina War led some anti-imperialists not only to defend the deposed Khmer Rouge but also to ally with the United States in a campaign against the Socialist Republic of Vietnam. (La contemporaine, Marnix Dressen)

Figure 18 The refugee crisis in Southeast Asia created an opportunity for the partisans of individualist human rights to fill the void left by the collapse of anti-imperialism, with some erstwhile radicals such as Bernard Kouchner taking it upon themselves to intervene directly to save victims abroad. (Getty)

4   Repression

In June 1970, Simone de Beauvoir defied the French government's new censorship laws, promenading down the avenue du Général-Leclerc in Paris with other intellectuals in tow, hawking a stack of political newspapers. "Read *La Cause du peuple!*" "Support the freedom of the press!" she shouted, distributing copies of the recently banned radical paper. Six days later, she did it again. This time, the police detained de Beauvoir and her coterie, shoved them into a police van, and drove them to the station for questioning. Once there, however, the police decided to release everyone, sparing them the prison sentence that less famous activists faced for the same crime. As one of France's most accomplished philosophers, de Beauvoir expected as much. As it was, the whole point of the action was not simply to protest the government's flagrant violation of civil liberties but to lay bare for the French public the hypocrisy of the state's selective repression of the radical left. "What we wanted was not," she explained, "to get ourselves arrested but to put the government in a state of self-contradiction by reason of its failure to arrest us."[1] By releasing famous intellectuals but imprisoning radicals, the state revealed how its new repressive laws were designed with no other aim than to crush organized revolutionary movements.[2]

In response to the turn to revolution in the late 1960s, many governments in North America and Western Europe turned to vicious repression. With so many of their comrades ending up behind bars, radicals in the United States and France, from the Black Panther Party to the Proletarian Left, were forced to reevaluate their strategies: How could they continue the revolutionary project in the face of such harsh repression? Their answer was to pay closer attention to civil rights, build alliances with progressives, and rebrand themselves as defenders of liberty. Having only recently shunned talk of reform in favor of violent revolution, they now demanded rights from the very states they sought to abolish.

At the same time, experiences of incarceration pushed many radicals to reconsider the status, rights, and struggles of prisoners. While many activists had initially overlooked the prisons, internalizing commonplace assumptions about criminality, they soon turned their attention to organizing prisoners, learning from one another in an intricate transnational network. This organizing in turn prompted a substantial reconsideration of the repressive role of the law, the struggle for reform, and the rights of the individual in general. Radicals now saw struggles for what they called "democratic rights" as not only a legitimate form of activism but also a strategically necessary phase of the revolutionary process.

At the same time that activists were reconsidering their revolutionary priorities, the United States reoriented its war in Vietnam. Just as radicals made the political prisoner the focal point of their new strategy, so too did the Nixon administration transform the prisoner of war into the centerpiece of its own new strategy. With the war going poorly, the White House struggled to revive flagging support. Backed by a coalition of conservatives, President Richard Nixon gambled that he could use the plight of the POWs to do just that. While the POWs had always been a topic of concern, Nixon used the issue to justify the extension of the war, reframe US intervention as a fight for humanitarian principles, and transform the entire discourse around Vietnam into one about the repression of POWs.

The response of antiwar radicals in the United States and France was to draw attention to the tens of thousands of political dissidents imprisoned, tortured, or disappeared by the repressive government of South Vietnam. Drawing on their experiences with prison organizing, they connected their newfound appreciation of civil liberties to antiwar activism, calling for the liberation of political prisoners in South Vietnam. After the United States withdrew from Vietnam in January 1973, depriving anti-imperialist movements of their main target, antiwar radicals across Europe made the liberation of the political prisoners in South Vietnam one of their primary concerns, demanding that the Republic of Vietnam free its dissidents, restore civil liberties, and adhere to the Paris Peace Accords.

Despite their reassessment of civil rights, both at home and abroad, anti-imperialist radicals still thought in Leninist terms, framing their internationalism around the right of nations to self-determination. Yet in arguing that South Vietnam violated civil rights, anti-imperialist solidarity increasingly took the form of criticizing the internal affairs of a sovereign state, which brought radicals quite close to competing visions of internationalism like human rights. While most radicals never agreed on a single radical rights discourse, and did not convert to human rights in the early 1970s, their new collective attention to rights in general, along with alliances with rival groups such as Amnesty International (AI), shifted the political terrain in a way that allowed a rival approach to global change to attract new audiences. In so doing, anti-imperialists lent legitimacy to a competing idiom of internationalism that shared the progressive aspirations of anti-imperialism but rejected nationalism in favor of human rights.

The Leninist Offensive

Although committed radicals were always a minority in North America and Western Europe, their numbers surged in the very late 1960s and early 1970s. West Germany saw the rise of numerous militant organizations.[3] In the United States, Students for a Democratic Society may have succumbed to a frenzy of factional fighting, but there were now more radical groups than ever before. While some were quite small, groups like the Revolutionary Union, the October League, the Socialist Workers Party, or the Black Panther Party would all claim over a thousand members each.[4]

In France after May '68, a hundred organizations blossomed. Groups like the pro-Chinese Marxist-Leninist Communist Party of France, the Trotskyist Communist League (successor to the Revolutionary Communist Youth), and the Maoist Proletarian Left (successor to the Union of Communist Youth (Marxist-Leninist)) each counted several thousand members, an army of sympathizers, and a robust international network. Meanwhile in Italy, radicals turned their country into the revolutionary center of the continent, with organizations growing larger than anywhere else. Continuous Struggle, for instance, claimed possibly 30,000 members by 1971, and even then, represented only one pole in a radical universe that included other hefty groups such as Workers' Power.[5]

Not only were there more radicals, but they also enjoyed more favorable conditions. The swinging Sixties may have been spectacular, but the Seventies were more radical. Confrontations were more frequent, actions larger, radical ideas more popular, and struggles more consequential. Students agitated in high schools, workers fought in factories, and women organized a new feminist wave. Gay liberationists, people of color, immigrants, and indigenous activists led new social movements that broadened the very meaning of politics. This dense ecosystem of movements in turn allowed radicals, and especially Leninists, to exercise influence far beyond their numbers. These were the years of Leninism's peak popularity.

Although there were now more political currents, Leninism's hegemony over the wider leftist scene reached unparalleled heights. To be sure, some radicals did reject Leninist anti-imperialism, but in these years many accepted it as a general framework. Even those who promoted competing political projects nevertheless retained key Leninist concepts.[6]

They came to see imperialism as the system that bound together sexism, racism, poverty, and everything else they fought against. They made national liberation the template for a variety of different struggles, an emancipatory motif that could be linked to women's liberation, gay liberation, and more. They increasingly embraced some version of world socialism. And they often adopted Leninism as a working model that could be expanded to tackle many different forms of oppression.

Take, for example, the Third World Women's Alliance, a pioneering organization of women of color in the United States. In the inaugural issue of their journal, they explicitly encouraged their readers to study Lenin. They cited Cuba, China, Vietnam, North Korea, and the USSR as inspirational examples of liberation. And they drew on Leninist language to explore the relationships between different oppressions in order to develop a more expansive, multilayered, and emancipatory conception of revolutionary change. "As a socialist organization, the Third World Women's Alliance recognizes the fact that our primary fight at this stage is the overthrow of imperialism. Nevertheless, out of imperialism has grown two destructive forces which we, as third world women must contend with – racism and male chauvinism. In this context, an alliance of third world women has a specific role to play."[7] Leninism, in other words, became the basis of a remarkable process of political discovery, innovation, and pluralization across the North Atlantic. As historian Gerd-Rainer Horn points out, far left political spaces inspired by Leninism could be extraordinarily creative, flexible, fulfilling, and democratic. They offered tens of thousands of activists a home to forge durable relationships and build a meaningful life. They facilitated sophisticated debates about changing the world. And they made possible countless experiments with new ideas about tactics, organization, and political struggle.[8]

But while this engagement with Leninism helped make possible many new emancipatory political inventions, it also led to a kind of ossification.[9] Many radical anti-imperialists interpreted the recent political crises, the rise of mass movements, and the surging popularity of Leninism as proof that revolution was around the corner. In France, for example, Alain Geismar and his comrades famously predicted an imminent revolutionary situation.[10] Thousands of radicals responded by constructing militant organizations that could channel the political unrest of the time in a focused revolutionary direction. With so much on the line, the very Leninist ecosystem that made possible pluralistic discovery could at the same time transform into a rigid space characterized by guilt, sectarianism, dogmatism, denunciations, ruthless discipline, fierce hierarchy, personality cults, and the glorification of revolutionary violence as an end in itself.[11] Instead of thinking the new, some Leninist radicals became obsessed with parroting the classics, overloading shaky concepts, rehashing unproductive debates, and drawing inappropriate historical analogies with events like the October Revolution. All this could lead radicals to misperceive the specific conditions of the capitalist North Atlantic, foreclose potentially more generative strategies for this unique moment, and lose touch with reality.[12] If these were the glory days of "creative Leninism," then this was paradoxically also an era of what Daniel Bensaïd later called "hasty Leninism."[13]

Radicals under Attack

But it was not just radicals who imagined imminent revolution. While historians can now safely argue that governments had little to fear, contemporaries were not so confident. The political atmosphere terrified rulers to such a degree that they cracked down on social movements as if their lives depended on it. In West Germany, the state increased surveillance and modernized its police forces. In Italy, state repression and fascist terror precipitated a period of violence known as the "years of lead." In France, the police augmented their characteristic brutality with an array of punitive legal measures.[14] Convinced an international conspiracy was afoot, the French minister of the interior responded to the May events by outlawing demonstrations, arresting radicals like Alain Krivine, and banning around a dozen organizations, including the Revolutionary Communist Youth, the Union of Communist Youth (Marxist-Leninist), and the Paris American Committee to Stopwar.[15] He then tightened censorship laws, harassed publishers like François Maspero, and banned radical publications. In March 1970, Jean-Pierre Le Dantec, the editor of the Proletarian Left's paper, *La Cause du peuple*, was arrested. In April 1970, the state issued the "Anti-Casseurs" law, which stated that anyone associated with a demonstration in which persons were harmed, property damaged, or police injured could be arrested for those crimes, no matter how tenuous the connection.[16]

In the United States, a moment of interparty, interagency, and interstate collaboration unleashed a similar wave of repression. Under J. Edgar Hoover, the Federal Bureau of Investigation (FBI) continued to harass activists. Richard Nixon's administration expanded attacks on social movements. The Democratic majority in both chambers of Congress passed new legislation that meted out harsher sentences, expanded the FBI, strengthened local police departments, and funded weapons research. Meanwhile, the Vietnam War served as a laboratory for new forms of repression. Private counterinsurgency consultants offered advice gleaned from the field, officials studied guerrilla warfare in Vietnam to counter urban rebellions at home, veterans serving in police forces drew on their combat experience, and local police departments integrated weaponry developed in Vietnam – such as sensors, tear gas, and helicopters – into police operations in the United States. In the same way that radicals believed their struggles at home were linked to those in Vietnam, the forces of order also saw a clear connection between pacification in Southeast Asia and repression in the United States.[17]

While repression smothered nearly everyone, the state bore down hardest on those involved in antiwar activism. The Vietnam Day Committee (VDC) is a case in point. The FBI monitored all phases of its activity, tracked its leaders, burglarized the VDC office, collaborated with local police to harass activists, jammed radios during marches, tampered with mail to cancel or change the dates of proposed actions, coordinated with right-wing groups such as the Young Republicans to plan counterdemonstrations, and kept tabs on Stephen Smale when he visited Paris to meet with antiwar comrades.[18] Against this backdrop of repression, a bomb mysteriously blew apart the VDC headquarters.[19] But the VDC's experience was not unique; a Senate select committee later confirmed that the FBI had targeted almost every antiwar group.[20] In a few cases, state repression of antiwar activism led to deaths, as in May 1970 when National Guardsmen murdered four antiwar students on the campus of Kent State University in Ohio and killed two and injured eleven at Jackson State College in Mississippi.

There were a few reasons why the state acted with such extreme hostility toward antiwar activists, but one crucial factor had to do with their deep international ties. Many ranking politicians interpreted the internationalism of antiwar protesters, and radical anti-imperialists in particular, as proof that the entire antiwar cause was a Soviet conspiracy.[21] Lyndon Johnson was convinced that "the communist way of thinking had infected everyone around him," and ordered the CIA to prepare an investigation into the movement's international connections.[22] Richard Nixon harbored the same suspicions, no doubt encouraged by Hoover's continuous stream of memos alleging communist infiltration.[23] For Democrats and Republicans alike, antiwar activism was international subversion.

The antiwar activists who suffered the most in the United States were Black anti-imperialists.[24] Police repression had put enormous strain on the Student Nonviolent Coordinating Committee, forced the Revolutionary Action Movement to dissolve, and virtually beheaded the Black Panther Party (BPP). The Panthers in particular became the state's primary target, with Hoover labeling them the "greatest threat to the internal security of the country."[25] Police smeared the BPP, raided offices, and arrested activists. Huey Newton was in prison. Eldridge Cleaver fled the country. Fred Hampton, leader of the Illinois chapter, was murdered in December 1969. Bobby Seale, already sentenced to four years imprisonment, was put on trial again, this time for a murder he did not commit, in 1970. Faced with this kind of repression, radicals everywhere realized that they had to rethink their strategy.

The United Front

Although destructive, state repression was never total. As much as the forces of order wanted to obliterate these movements, they could only afford to go so far. After all, these countries were nominally representative democracies, and their governments went to great lengths to present themselves as standard bearers of liberty during the Cold War contest against "totalitarianism." While states bent the rule of law, the objective of smashing the radical left never authorized a transition to dictatorship in North America and Western Europe. As a result, state repression certainly weakened oppositional movements, but could not annihilate them. What it could do, and what it did do quite well, was to not only increase pressure on these movements but also substantially alter the political terrain on which they operated, effectively throwing activists off balance. It was not necessarily repression as such that threatened to kill movements, but rather activists' failure to adapt to changing circumstances.

While a minority of radicals responded with their own counterviolence, many tried to take advantage of the reigning ideology of liberty to turn the tables on the state. The Panthers, for example, used repression to generate sympathy, presenting themselves as victims. While repression weakened the Black Panther Party, the repeated trials of Black radicals, often over fabricated charges, before white juries, and in the courts of racist judges did win many Americans over to the cause. Arguing that the justice system was broken, the Panthers convinced even those who disagreed with their revolutionary politics that they were being unfairly targeted and that Black activists could never receive fair trials. The key to the Panther strategy was to transform this sympathy into formal alliances with progressive, but by no means revolutionary, groups, such as the American Civil Liberties Union, and then use those alliances as protection from the state.[26]

The Panthers also drew international awareness to their cause by building solidarity committees in Europe, sending members on speaking tours, and convincing comrades abroad to speak on their behalf.[27] One of these was famed writer Jean Genet, who was approached by Connie Matthews, the BPP's international coordinator, to put his talents to the service of Black liberation. As Angela Davis recalls, "We thought Genet could help us create a multi-racial audience."[28] Genet enthusiastically agreed, slipping into the United States in early 1970. For two months he traveled across the country to rally support for the BPP and Black political prisoners in general.[29] His tour culminated on May 1, 1970 at Yale University, where he addressed a crowd of some 25,000 about Seale's pending murder trial.[30] "For Bobby Seale, I repeat, there must not be another Dreyfus affair," he said, referencing his country's own racist history. Calling on the audience to "speak out across America" on behalf of the Panthers, he declared, "Bobby Seale's life depends on you. Your real life depends on the Black Panther Party."[31]

Genet returned to France as embattled activists began to experiment with their own united front. The French state continued to ratchet up its activities against radicals, targeting in particular the Proletarian Left. As the most dynamic Maoist group of the time, the Proletarian Left had made a name for itself through a string of assaults against the police, factory security forces, and even the French Communist Party. In May 1970, the minister of the interior arrested hundreds of radicals, banned the Proletarian Left, and imprisoned one of its most visible leaders: Alain Geismar. Outlawed, the "ex-Proletarian Left," as it was now called, reconsidered its approach: It would attempt to complement its commitment to violent revolution with a new focus on nonviolent struggles for democratic unity. If in the heady days of the 1960s the goal had been to break with the Old Left to forge a new revolutionary direction, they explained, then the shifting balance of forces in the 1970s compelled them to replace their "habit of dividing" with a new "habit of uniting." Now the objective was to "conquer the center" with a style of work that emphasized unity, democracy, and reaching the majority.[32] If the Proletarian Left had once rejected reforms, legalistic campaigns, and alliances with moderates in favor revolutionary confrontation, the ex-Proletarian Left now called for a united "democratic front" with all progressive forces to strengthen the legal opposition to the state's repressive turn.[33]

Concretely, this meant de-escalating rivalries with other radical organizations, collaborating with intellectuals, and cooperating with diverse political forces. To hold this potential bloc together, the front would fight for civil liberties such as the freedom of assembly, speech, or the press. This "democratic front," radicals argued, would serve several functions. It could offer protection.[34] It could help the underground ex-Proletarian Left stay connected to ongoing movements. And it could elevate their cause in the eyes of a public that had been told that radicals were terrorists. Instead of symbolizing the enemy of democracy, radicals could become its greatest champion. By uniting radicals with more moderate sympathizers, this democratic front, the ex-Proletarian Left declared, "is perfectly capable of taking back from the bourgeoisie that which it has stolen: liberties."[35]

The ex-Proletarian Left took this new role seriously. After a mining disaster at Lens left sixteen dead, they partnered with Jean-Paul Sartre to organize a popular tribunal that found the state-owned mining company guilty of murder for neglecting the safety of the workers.[36] In the factories, they defended workers who kidnapped their bosses, arguing that these "sequestrations" were forms of popular justice.[37] At the same time, they advocated for the rights of immigrants, organizing antiracist campaigns.[38] They even extended an olive branch to small shopkeepers who were sympathetic to the xenophobic populism of Pierre Poujade.[39]

Not all radicals shared this perspective. The Communist League disagreed with the ex-Proletarian Left's claim that France was undergoing "fascistization," cautioned that widening the "democratic front" to include potentially reactionary forces would dilute unity, and criticized the Maoists for confusing "popular justice" with "revolutionary justice."[40] The philosopher Michel Foucault, who collaborated closely with the ex-Proletarian Left, also raised concerns about the group's approach, in particular its advocacy of the popular tribunal or court as the vehicle of justice: "my hypothesis is not so much that the court is the natural expression of popular justice, but rather that its historical function is to ensnare it, to control it and to strangle it, by reinscribing it within institutions which are typical of a state apparatus."[41] But since state repression affected everyone, the various players saw little choice but to temporarily set aside their differences. As early as May 1970, a panoply of otherwise fratricidal groups — including the Proletarian Left, Red Line, Workers' Struggle, Long Live the Revolution!, the Communist League, and the Unified Socialist Party — gathered to discuss their future in this changed environment.[42] While relations were tense, and disagreements widespread, many of these radical groups ultimately embarked on their own "democratic turns."

This consensus made possible a number of collaborations, the most important of which was a revived Red Aid.[43] Formed in June 1970, Red Aid brought together lawyers, academics, Christian socialists, former WWII resistance fighters, intellectual celebrities like Sartre, and radicals from groups like the ex-Proletarian Left, the Unified Socialist Party, and the Communist League into what promised to be a nonsectarian "democratic association" that aimed to "assure the political and legal defense of victims of repression and to give them and their families material and moral support with no exceptions."[44] Advocating for immigrants, activists, revolutionaries, workers, prisoners, and really anyone suffering repression, Red Aid became one of the leading organizations in the fight against state violence not just in France but across Western Europe. As Red Aid explained, "Repression is, like imperialism and reaction, international." Since so many European countries were experiencing similar repressive turns, this new democratic strategy, radicals argued, had to assume a transnational dimension. Radicals set to work establishing branches of Red Aid in countries like Belgium, Italy, and West Germany, laying the scaffolding for an international movement for democratic rights.[45]

The fact that Red Aid described its mission as fighting to defend "fundamental freedoms" and "rights" signaled an important shift in the trajectory of radicals in North America and Western Europe.[46] Immediately after 1968, many radicals equated the struggle for rights as mere reformism and called for worldwide revolution instead. But, by the early 1970s, state repression compelled them not only to reassess campaigns for civil rights but also to prioritize them. Unlike the wild days of 1968, they attempted to find ways to couple the goal of violent anti-imperialist revolution with the struggle for "democratic rights."

Political Prisoners

For most of the 1960s, French radicals tended to pay relatively less attention to the prison than other institutions. An ex-Proletarian Left circular, for example, complained that "aside from some rare exceptions, concern for the prisoners *does not exist*," and many act as if "an imprisoned militant is a dead militant."[47] But with the state now throwing thousands of anti-imperialists behind bars, many revolutionary groups began to identify the prison as a political space, committing themselves to prison organizing. Facing the brunt of state repression, the ex-Proletarian Left quickly distinguished itself as one of the most significant representatives of this realignment. Soon after the state banned their organization, ex-Proletarian Left radicals established the Organization for Political Prisoners (OPP) to advocate for imprisoned militants. In September 1970, they worked with Red Aid on their first campaign: a coordinated hunger strike in six prisons, including one for women.[48] The results were mixed. Although the Supreme Court of Appeals granted "political regime" status to Alain Geismar, which accorded him certain privileges, the strike had little effect on the overall political situation.[49]

Convinced that the action's limited results stemmed from the isolation of the strikers from those on the outside, OPP militants such as Jacques Rancière and Daniel Defert sought a new direction. To widen the struggle, and link prisoners to the democratic front outside, Defert proposed "the formation of a commission of inquiry to look into the general situation of prisons, an inquiry to be conducted by experts and directed by Michel Foucault."[50] Foucault agreed, and along with other intellectuals – such as Jean Genet, philosopher Gilles Deleuze, editor Jean-Marie Domenach, and historian Pierre Vidal-Naquet – helped build a coalition.[51] On February 8, 1971, Foucault unveiled the Prisons Information Group: "Little information is published on prisons; it is one of the hidden regions of our social system, one of the black boxes of our life. We have the right to know. We want to know."[52] Drawing on the "workers' inquiry" model proposed by Karl Marx in 1880, and later adopted by Maoists in the 1960s, the Prisons Information Group drafted a questionnaire.[53] With the help of doctors, lawyers, and families, activists smuggled inquiries into the prisons to gain valuable information, give voice to silenced prisoners, and guide future organizing efforts.

These experiences were transformative for radicals, forcing them to change how they understood the law, imprisonment, subjectivation, and revolutionary politics.[54] When French anti-imperialists, and especially Maoists in the Proletarian Left, first entered prison, they tended to draw a line between the "political" prisoners and the "common law" inmates, insisting that they alone deserved the "political regime" status. "The campaign to win the 'political regime' status aims to force the enemy to recognize us as a political force and not as a band of criminals, as communists and not as thieves," they explained. "The car thief, the common law criminal, reflects society; the communist transforms it."[55] As Michel Foucault later put it:

When Maoists were put in prison, they began, it must be said, by reacting a little like the traditional political groups, that is to say: "We do not want to be assimilated with the criminals of common law, we do not want our image to be mixed with theirs in the opinion of people, and we ask to be treated like political prisoners with the rights of political prisoners."[56]

This was, after all, the objective of the first strike in September 1970. But that strike's limited gains, the subsequent prison inquiries, collaboration with "common law" prisoners, and engagement with Foucault's ideas about prisons all pushed radicals to question this narrow conception.[57]

Another major factor in this rethinking had to do with transnational connections to prisoner movements in other countries.[58] After reading Continuous Struggle's coverage of prisoner rebellions in Italy, Daniel Defert and Jacques Donzelot traveled south in 1971 to study Italian prison organizing firsthand. More than a simple tactical response to repression, the Italian turn to prisons belonged to a broader shift in strategy. After the wave of workers' strikes in 1969 won pay raises, better benefits, and greater say in the factory, business owners counterattacked by attempting, among other things, to increase the cost of living.[59] "In view of this," Italo Sbrogiò, a factory worker at the Porto Marghera petrochemical plant, recalled, "we put our back into it and said that the intervention inside the factories would have to be carried to the outside, to the 'social,' as well, broaching the issue of the rise of living costs."[60]

Radicals adopted a new strategy of surrounding the factory with struggles on what they called the terrain of "social reproduction," that is, streets, schools, civic centers, and neighborhoods.[61] Housewives, for instance, launched a movement of "autoreduction" to unilaterally reduce bus fares, electricity bills, or rents.[62] Continuous Struggle, one of the strongest advocates of this strategy, approached the prisons from this perspective. Prisons, they argued, were sites of social reproduction, and prisoners' struggles were linked to the fight for lower rents, affordable food, and accessible transportation.[63] The French Prisons Information Group was intrigued by this approach and in the report on their meeting with Continuous Struggle reflected that "the struggle of the detainees is taken up in a strategy of struggle in the neighborhoods."[64] This perspective inspired many French radicals, and groups like Red Aid launched new campaigns over issues like housing, following the lead of tenant struggles organized by Continuous Struggle.[65]

But an even more important transnational influence was Black prison organizing in the United States, and particularly the reflections of George Jackson, which prompted French radicals to further reassess their work. To begin with, they stopped treating the prison as a kind of political black hole. They took to heart Jackson's argument that prisons, like schools or factories, could be sites of politicization. As Jackson's own life seemed to demonstrate, prisons were places where many people learned politics for the first time. "He is one of the first revolutionary leaders to acquire his political education entirely in prison," the Prisons Information Group reported, "but he is also the first whose political action has been wholly framed by the prison."[66] In a reversal of its earlier position, the ex-Proletarian Left now argued that prisons should be treated as "Marxist universities."[67]

In addition, Jackson, and the Panthers more broadly, helped French radicals overcome their scorn for the "lumpenproletariat" – the underclass of criminals, vagabonds, and other marginalized figures allegedly hostile to revolution. This bias had prevented them from recognizing the class dimensions of the prison, leading anti-imperialist radicals to separate themselves from "common law" prisoners. Jackson, now seen as "the first to make a class-based analysis of prisoners," changed their view.[68] In an interview translated by the Prisons Information Group, Jackson admitted,

"All these cats in here are lumpen, that's all I've ever been." But, he continued, "You would be very surprised to see how these particular lumpen in here accept class war and revolutionary scientific socialism." Jackson argued that lumpen prisoners were not selfishly individualistic, as previous Marxist theory seemed to suggest. Quite the contrary: Their isolation generated an intense "longing for community, commune-ity." And that, Jackson said, is "what helps define us as a class."[69]

Lastly, Jackson helped demonstrate that concepts like the "lumpen-proletariat" were constructed by "bourgeois law" itself. In 1971, for example, *La Cause du peuple* translated Jackson's arguments about how released prisoners still carried a record, were forever branded as dangerous, and were effectively destined to be rearrested.[70] Learning from Black prisoners, French radicals began to see how the justice system defined certain people as always-already guilty. As Genet wrote in his introduction to Jackson's *Soledad Brother*, "the black man is, from the start, natively, the guilty man."[71] In other words, the law itself had created an entire category of largely racialized people designated as criminal, expendable, surplus, unemployable, or fit for only the most exploitative and precarious jobs.[72] The history of Black prison struggles, the Prisons Information Group later wrote, "upsets many commonly accepted ideas, in the history of the labor movement, about the prison population."[73] These experiences in the United States, insights from Italy, and their own discoveries in French prisons led many radicals to seriously rethink prison organizing. Instead of separating themselves from the petty criminals, whose existence they once deemed nonpolitical, radicals now demanded the special "political regime for all."[74]

Reflecting on this change, an article in *La Cause du peuple* argued that "the struggle of prisoners is no different, at its core, from those that are waged in the society from which they are 'excluded.'"[75] The new political project, therefore, was to overcome these artificially imposed divisions. Commenting on the Prisons Information Group's discovery, Alberto Toscano notes that radicals increasingly saw unity as "breaking a division" that "was both imposed upon and eventually affirmed by the workers' movement, with its debilitating introjection of a bourgeois morality itself reproduced by legal and penal institutions: the division between the proletariat and the 'non-proletarianized plebs.'"[76] The struggles of the mythical vanguard, the male wage worker in the factory, had to be reintegrated with those of forgotten, invisible, so-called "backwards" subjects, shifting the focus away from independent class figures to the relationships between different political forces, a task all the more pressing given the proliferation of new social movements at this time.

This reconsideration demanded a more nuanced engagement with the law. Through their experiences with prisons, some radicals began to see the law as a more subtle form of power, rather than a blunt instrument. Foucault again summarized the new thinking:

If one makes the distinction, if one accepts the difference between political law and common law, that means that fundamentally one recognizes bourgeois morality and law as far as respect for the property of others, respect for traditional moral values, etc., are concerned. The cultural revolution in its widest sense implies that, at least in a society like ours, you no longer make the division between criminals of common law and political criminals. Common law is politics, it is, after all, the bourgeois class that, for political reasons and on a basis of its political power, defined what is called common law.[77]

As they began to understand the law as a creative political force, activists called for the formation of study groups to investigate legal matters, the publication of accessible brochures to help militants familiarize themselves with the function of the law, and the mobilization of sympathetic lawyers. Through this transnational experience of prison organizing, radicals began to see the ways in which politics were at work in those places they once wrote off as "nonpolitical."

French radicals initially pursued a "democratic turn" as an immediate strategic response to changed conditions. But as they followed this turn, they began to rethink many of their assumptions. The democratic turn did not just buy radicals time, space, and allies, leaving the core of their project unchanged; it transformed the way many radicals imagined revolution as well. An openly radical organization like the Prisons Information Group, for example, now argued that experiences in the prisons showed that thinking about rights should not be denounced as simple reformism, a stopgap measure, or a temporary detour. Engaging with rights was a fundamental aspect of any revolutionary project that seriously aimed to unite different people in the complex and shifting terrain of modern representative democracies. And since the very boundary between the legal and illegal was constantly changing, with rights won one day taken away the next, and their meanings always challenged, the struggle for rights would not be finished once and for all, a mere step on the way to revolution. Rights and revolution, they argued, were deeply intertwined in a single process from beginning to end.[78]

Although radicals increasingly adopted new discourses about rights, they did not take up the notion of individual human rights; instead, they continued to place their advocacy of "democratic rights" within the framework of Leninism. But attempting to reconcile a commitment to democratic rights with the overall struggle for violent international communist revolution was bound to raise some serious questions about the meaning of both rights and revolution. This tension risked rendering the politics of some of these groups – especially the ex-Proletarian Left – incoherent: At the same time that the ex-Proletarian Left talked about democratic rights and assured the French public of its commitment to civil liberties, its militants violently attacked so-called enemies of the revolution and plotted to overthrow the French state.[79] While anti-imperialists may not have recognized it yet, their concrete practice increasingly revealed the limits of the Leninist problematic in the unique conditions of representative capitalist democracies in the 1970s. In the coming years, inherited ideas about democracy, the vanguard party, and the classical insurrectionary sequence would all come into question.

Prisoners of War

At the same moment that radicals began to concentrate on political prisoners, the White House looked to another kind of prisoner: the American POW. Over the course of the war, Vietnamese revolutionaries had captured several hundred US military personnel, the vast majority of them pilots shot down over the Democratic Republic of Vietnam (DRV). Although Vietnamese communists had long politicized American POWs as part of their overall strategy, the White House remained relatively silent about the issue, practicing instead what was called "quiet diplomacy" to secure their freedom.[80] But by the end of the decade, a new set of forces compelled the United States to change its approach.

In the late 1960s, dissenting voices in the military began to urge the White House to mobilize the POW issue for "counter-propaganda." The Marine Corps insisted on countering North Vietnam's claims to treating American POWs humanely, believing the United States could influence "world public opinion" on the matter. The Army suggested that the US government needed "a strategy which aggressively grasps the initiative for us and keeps the other side reacting in the desired direction." The Air Force exhorted the White House to seize this opportunity to influence both domestic and foreign audiences by targeting major institutions, national media, social clubs, and Congress. By the late 1960s, a joint working group recommended that the White House go on the offensive.[81]

These initiatives from within the state were matched by grassroots pressure outside. Frustrated families of prisoners of war and combatants missing in action launched an aggressive campaign to publicize the POW/MIA issue. Led by Sybil Stockdale, wife of the highest-ranking naval officer imprisoned in North Vietnam, they eventually created a new organization called the National League of Families of American Prisoners and

Missing in Southeast Asia. They published stories in newspapers across the country, appeared on television shows, and cultivated close ties with major Republican politicians, including Secretary of Defense Melvin Laird, California Governor Ronald Reagan, Senator Bob Dole, and President Nixon himself.[82]

Most importantly, a new administration had moved into the White House. Although Nixon promised to end the war, he wished to do so on his terms, extricating the United States through an honorable settlement that left South Vietnam's government intact, North Vietnam's ambitions contained, and America's reputation untarnished. To do that, Nixon had to buy time, which meant prolonging the war. There were, however, a few obstacles in his way. A pesky peace process had already begun in Paris, antiwar movements were biting at his heels, the majority of Americans now saw the war as a mistake, and even some conservatives began to express doubts about the war. Nixon gambled that he could work with the military, veteran associations, the League of Families, conservative politicians, wealthy philanthropists, and mainstream news media to use the POW issue as a way to counter antiwar activists, rebuild a prowar coalition, revive support for the war, and reframe US imperialism.[83]

On May 19, 1969, the last birthday Hồ Chí Minh would live to celebrate, Secretary of Defense Melvin Laird unveiled the Go Public campaign by demanding the "prompt release of all American prisoners."[84] In July 1969, prowar groups printed 5,000 bumper stickers with the words, "Don't let them be forgotten: POWs, MIAs." In October, POW/MIA families flew to Paris to accost the "enemy face-to-face."[85] The following month, Congress unanimously declared November 9 a National Day of Prayer for US POWs in Vietnam, and the House Subcommittee on National Security Policy condemned "the ruthlessness and cruelty of North Vietnam."[86] In late 1969, billionaire Ross Perot ran full-page advertisements in major newspapers and purchased airtime on television stations in more than fifty cities to run a propaganda film. On May 1, 1970, International Workers' Day, Bob Dole teamed up with the League of Families to organize a rally called the "Appeal for International Justice" that featured a thousand POW/MIA families. Around the same time, activists began selling bracelets engraved with the names of POWs and MIAs. By the time the United States formally withdrew from Vietnam, over four million Americans wore them.[87]

Although the hackneyed refrain about defending South Vietnamese self-determination from global communist subversion had not disappeared, Nixon increasingly sold the war by focusing on individual American POWs. He inflated the number of POWs and MIAs. He deliberately showcased white, middle-class, highly educated, prowar career officers.[88] He exaggerated their conditions, manipulated their motivations, and erased the voices of numerous antiwar, dissenting POWs.[89] He made their release an official priority of the US government.[90] He authorized a military raid on the Sơn Tây prison camp outside Hanoi to prove his commitment to the cause. He even suggested that the future of US involvement in Vietnam depended on the status of the POWs. In April 1971, he threatened, "as long as there is one American being held prisoner in North Vietnam," he would have no choice but to "retain" a military force in Vietnam.[91] By this time, most prowar Americans had effectively made the war about freeing the POWs. "The issue of prisoners," Reagan proclaimed in June 1971, "is the single most important issue involved in this long and savage war and we want them back *now*."[92] The United States, these figures implied, had to stay in Vietnam precisely to free the prisoners of war.

The logic was fuzzy – the US War in Vietnam had created the very thing it was now allegedly being waged to end. But the prowar campaign appealed to emotions, not reason, with Nixon himself taking every opportunity to paint the DRV as a land of savages. The "North Vietnamese," he declared, "have, without question, been the most barbaric in their handling of prisoners of any nation in modern history."[93] Classifying the POWs as victims and Vietnamese revolutionaries as torturers enabled the United States to enact a series of reversals. At the very same time that the US government violated civil liberties at home, it could arraign the DRV for infringing on "basic rights." At the same time that prowar Americans disregarded the Geneva Accords of 1954 on Vietnamese self-determination, they could fulminate against Vietnamese for breaking the Geneva Convention of 1929 on prisoners of war. And, at the same time that the United States murdered hundreds of thousands of Vietnamese, American hawks could divert attention to a tiny group of handpicked prowar POWs. In this way, the prowar alliance used the POWs to rewrite the narrative of the war. As writer Jonathan Schell observed, "many people were persuaded that the United States was fighting in order to get its prisoners back." He continued: "Following the President's lead, people began to speak as though the North Vietnamese had kidnapped four hundred Americans and the United States had gone to war to retrieve them."[94]

If anti-imperialist radicals reconceptualized revolution for a changed conjuncture, prowar Americans did the same for imperialism. Neither side gave up on their respective projects, they just tried to update them by shifting tactics, rhetoric, and intermediate objectives, with both making the figure of the prisoner – the political prisoner in one case and the prisoner of war in the other – the emblem of their transformation.

But they did so in different ways. While radicals aimed to repoliticize seemingly nonpolitical experiences, such as "common law" imprisonment, the United States tried to depoliticize the emphatically political experiences of the POWs. The Nixon administration redefined the plight of the POWs as a purely humanitarian affair to be treated independently of all political concerns. Invoking a "moral plane," the president argued that "all civilized peoples are subject to the basic humanitarian standards long established in international law and custom."[95] Releasing the POWs, he said, "would be a simple act of humanity."[96]

The prowar bloc hoped to move the war beyond its specific historical origins, turning it into a moral affair about individual suffering. The conflict in Vietnam was a hostage situation, US involvement a humanitarian intervention, and the goal to save innocent individuals from mistreatment. This reframing became immensely popular: Just as many Americans were repudiating the war, growing tired of hoary ideas like self-determination, and even questioning US imperialism itself, they found a new issue that kindled their imagination like nothing else during the Vietnam War.[97] To be sure, the POW issue did not renew support for the war, caused new problems for the White House, and was appropriated for different ends. But this remarkably widespread obsession with helping the suffering individuals whose names were worn by millions on their wrists allowed US leaders to weather a potentially devastating crisis by moralizing, personalizing, and depoliticizing imperialism. In so doing, they shifted the discourse onto a new terrain: morality instead of politics, absolutes instead of historical contingency, and individual rights instead of collective rights to self-determination.

The Other POWs

Since Nixon made the POWs the kernel of his new approach to the war, antiwar forces poured considerable energy into challenging the administration on the issue. Some anti-imperialists simply exposed the POW campaign as a cynical ploy. In this, they echoed the assessment of DRV Prime Minister Phạm Văn Đồng, who claimed that this fixation on POWs was merely a way for the White House to "cover up its odious crimes against the Vietnamese people, its war acts against the Democratic Republic of Viet Nam, and its schemes to prolong and extend the war of aggression."[98]

Others, such as the Black Panther Party, pointed to political prisoners in the United States. In November 1969, for example, the Panthers proposed that North Vietnam would release American POWs in exchange for freeing Bobby Seale and Huey Newton, both incarcerated as "political prisoners here in 'fascist Babylon.'"[99] "If you have sons, husbands or friends who are prisoners of war in Vietnam," their paper enjoined readers, "send us their name, rank and serial numbers."[100] The US government's unsurprising refusal to consider trading political prisoners at home for the liberation of prisoners of war abroad, the Panthers argued, revealed its hypocrisy on the issue.

Still others responded by claiming that antiwar forces could do more for the POWs than Nixon. As proof, they pointed to how North Vietnam had already been releasing POWs not to the US government but antiwar activists.[101] Just months after the White House fired the opening salvos of its Go Public campaign, the DRV released three more POWs to activists, bypassing the Nixon administration. They followed this up by working with a contingent of American antiwar activists led by Cora Weiss and David Dellinger to form the Committee of Liaison with Families of Servicemen Detained in North Vietnam (COLIAFAM) in late 1969. Tackling the issue from a resolutely antiwar perspective, COLIAFAM announced from the very beginning that "the safe return of American pilots held in North Vietnam can only come with a decision on the part of the US government to withdraw from Vietnam."[102] Until then, it would cooperate with the DRV to improve the situation as best as possible. The Committee produced a list of American POWs, convinced the DRV to allow prisoners to receive heavier packages, and provided a functional channel for relaying mail to them. COLIAFAM was so successful that even Nixon's ally, the League of Families, voted down a proposal to boycott its work.[103] This of course did not stop the White House from sabotaging the Committee, with the US government going so far as to seize hundreds of letters from POWs sent to COLIAFAM.[104]

While pursuing these other paths, antiwar radicals eventually directed much of their energy to one approach in particular – publicizing repression in the United States' great ally in the fight for democracy: South Vietnam. Although a stunning political victory, the Tet Offensive came at a high price. Southern forces were decimated, local party organs fell into disarray, and the NLF lost control of strongholds in the countryside.[105] With the communists on the defensive, South Vietnamese President Nguyễn Văn Thiệu declared martial law. Working closely with the United States, the Republic of Vietnam (RVN) unleashed a massive counterinsurgency program called Phoenix to dismantle the communist infrastructure in the South. In 1968 alone the government detained 16,000 suspects.[106] The most politically active were shipped to Côn Sơn island, home to the RVN's largest civilian prison, where they were beaten, starved, electrocuted, blinded by caustic lime, kept awake for weeks, and crammed into "tiger cages."

Many communist fighters would remember the period from late 1968 to 1970 as one of the most "difficult" of the war.[107] In response to this repression, they embarked on their own democratic turn. They encouraged the creation of an Alliance of National, Democratic, and Peace Forces to build wider support; announced a new Provisional Revolutionary Government (PRG) to consolidate diplomatic relations; and cooperated more closely with the "Third Force," that is, South Vietnamese activists who were critical of both Thiệu in the South and the DRV in the North, but urged both sides to bring the war to a peaceful end through negotiations.[108] In fact, the tumultuous events of those years prompted millions of people across the South to become more politically engaged. The earthquake of Tet showed that the cities could not avoid the conflict. The government's increased repression raised concerns about the future of the country. The horrors of pacification unsettled countless lives. And the Nixon administration's new policy of "Vietnamization" dragged even more people into the vortex of war: As a concession to antiwar sentiment, Nixon began to gradually withdraw US military personnel from Vietnam while transferring greater responsibilities to the RVN; but since the Republic of Vietnam was not strong enough to survive on its own, Vietnamization ultimately meant press-ganging millions of Vietnamese into a ballooning RVN army to compensate for the departing American troops. With the war now touching more lives than ever before, workers, students, intellectuals, professionals, government officials, Buddhists, and Catholics took a stand. After 1969, nearly a hundred different Third Force groups protested such issues as repression, the ongoing war, the desultory peace process, rampant government corruption, and the expansion of the draft.[109]

An enraged Thiệu responded with more repression. "We will beat to death the people who are demanding immediate peace," he promised in 1970.[110] Communists and noncommunists alike were imprisoned without trial. This only further radicalized Third Force activists, drawing them closer to the communists. In this way, communists came to play important roles in a number of Third Force groups, some of which were effectively communist front organizations.[111] Together, these activists made the struggle against repression a top priority. In 1970, the peak year of student activism in South Vietnam, university unions demanded everything from the release of arrested students to the end of military programs on campus.[112] Catholics, once a pillar of the regime, spoke out against repression, with Father Chân Tín launching a Committee to Reform the Prison System.[113] That same year, Ngô Bá Thành, anti-war activist, former political prisoner, mother of four, and international lawyer with advanced degrees from universities in both Europe and the

United States, launched the Women's Movement for the Right to Live, mobilizing Vietnamese women in defense of the political prisoners.[114]

As one of its first actions, the Movement delivered a letter to Vice President Spiro Agnew during his visit to South Vietnam in August 1970. Although opposed to the US presence in Vietnam, and making a point to remind Agnew that Americans had trained the local police, supplied them equipment, and funded the carceral system in the RVN, the women adopted a rhetorical strategy that played to Agnew's conservatism. They interpolated him as "a father, the head of a family," themselves as "Mothers," and the political prisoners as "our children," framing their appeal around the gendered ideals of paternal leadership, maternal care, and the integrity of the family. "As a father, you have deep love towards your children and you have experienced moments of anxiety when your children are in danger," the women wrote.[115] Adopting this discourse allowed them to assuage suspicions that they were communists, potentially giving themselves greater credibility. Despite their careful messaging, Agnew would not even read the letter.

When the White House refused to acknowledge the existence of political prisoners, Vietnamese activists went to work drawing international attention to the issue. They relied heavily on antiwar movements in the North Atlantic, which they still fondly called the "second front." They suspected that American accounts in particular would add credibility to their case, and it was an American named Don Luce who helped furnish indisputable proof of imprisonment. In Vietnam, former prisoners informed Luce of the deplorable conditions in Côn Sơn, with one drawing him a map to the tiger cages. Armed with this information, in the summer of 1970 Luce accompanied a US congressional delegation to the island, where he led them to the mysterious cages. Luce later recounted: "The faces of the prisoners in the cages below are still etched indelibly in my mind: the man with three fingers cut off; the man (soon to die) from Quang Tri province whose skull was split open; and the Buddhist monk from Hue who spoke intensely about the repression of the Buddhists. I remember clearly the terrible stench from diarrhea and the open sores where shackles cut into the prisoners' ankles."[116] The story broke in *Life* magazine.

Through overlapping transnational networks, antiwar activists of all political backgrounds united to keep the issue of political imprisonment, and repression more generally, in the news. Quakers and Vietnamese abroad circulated prison letters smuggled out by Father Chân Tín.[117] Feminists met with Vietnamese women to publicize the specific condition of women prisoners.[118] Academics mobilized on behalf of intellectuals such as Ngô Bá Thành, who was rearrested in 1971.[119]

In February 1972, a group of antiwar Vietnamese students living in the United States occupied the South Vietnamese consulate in New York City to protest Thiệu's repressive policies.[120] By May 1972, when Thiệu declared martial law, repression in South Vietnam had become mainstream American news.[121]

While the Americans took the lead, European activists also helped make the political prisoners a central international issue. Two French antiwar activists, Jean-Pierre Debris and André Menras, provided what was widely regarded as the most authentic non-Vietnamese eyewitness evidence about the treatment of political prisoners. Working as schoolteachers in South Vietnam, Debris and Menras were arrested in the summer of 1970 for speaking out against Thiệu, imprisoned alongside other dissidents, and finally released in December 1972. Immediately upon returning to Paris, they gave a press conference at the offices of Red Aid, which had helped free them. From there, they spoke at a mass meeting organized by Vietnamese living in France, embarked on an international speaking tour, and worked closely with American activists such as Maria Jolas and Don Luce to translate their testimonies.[122] Together, they supplied the factual basis for much of the antiwar literature – and even mainstream media coverage – about the issue in North America and Western Europe.[123]

Focusing on South Vietnamese political prisoners became the most effective way for antiwar activists to challenge the US government's new focus on POWs. "For years Americans have worn name bracelets symbolizing their deep concern for the release of American POWs," one activist group wrote. "But a tragedy of a far larger scale continues for 200,000 Vietnamese. These are the *civilian* POWs in the prisons of South Vietnam."[124] How could the US government, antiwar radicals everywhere asked, criticize the DRV for its treatment of a few hundred POWs when it supported a brutal dictatorship that tortured tens of thousands, if not hundreds of thousands, of prisoners in the South? Drawing on Debris and Menras's testimony, the Black Panther Party asked, "What about the Other POWs?"[125]

Reorienting the Antiwar Struggle

Paris was drizzly and gray when Americans and Vietnamese met at the Hotel Majestic to sign the Paris Peace Accords on January 27, 1973.[126] With the United States withdrawing from Vietnam, America's longest war yet came to a close. The Nixon administration touted the Accords as an unimpeachable triumph. As Nixon boasted to a room of returned POWs, they ensured "the return of all Americans from Vietnam, all of our combat forces, the return of all of our prisoners of war, the end of the American involvement in Vietnam, a peace agreement which, if adhered to, will mean peace for Vietnam and Southeast Asia."[127] Mission accomplished.

But, of course, the war was not over. Vietnam remained divided, with each side refusing to accept the other's legitimacy and both immediately violating the terms of the treaty. Even the full withdrawal of the United States remained uncertain. Military aid cascaded into the region, advisors freely operated on the ground, and some officials, such as Secretary of Defense James Schlesinger, threatened to bomb North Vietnam again if necessary. This was no idle threat: Even after the signing of the Accords the United States continued to bomb both Cambodia – dropping a whopping 250,000 tons of ordinance in 1973 alone, more than the tonnage dropped on Japan during the entirety of the Second World War – and Laos, which became the most heavily bombed country per capita in human history.

In retrospect, it may seem that with the departure of US troops, communist victory in Vietnam was a foregone conclusion. Nothing could be further from the truth. Years of bombing left the North devastated, the failed Spring Offensive of 1972 exhausted communist forces, Thiệu's regime hardened into a police state, and the United States left South Vietnam's military with a bonanza of equipment. In the spring of 1974, the RVN mobilized over a million soldiers, four times the number of communist forces in the South. The RVN had far more tanks than the DRV, twice as many aircraft, and received more aid from the United States than North Vietnam did from the Soviet Union and China combined. Militarily, the RVN had the upper hand, and the communists knew it.[128] The struggle for a unified, socialist Vietnam was not going to be easy.

With such high stakes, veteran anti-imperialists vowed to continue fighting. But 1973 was not 1968. The antiwar struggle had been steadily diminishing everywhere. Already tormented by fatigue, repression, and sectarianism, organized antiwar activism in the United States slid into terminal decline after the Accords.[129] Activism had been dwindling in Europe as well, but there the Accords actually had the opposite effect, sparking a new round of engagement, especially in France.[130] "We must not demobilize," André Menras announced to thousands in January.[131] The Indochina Solidarity Front (ISF), successor to the old National Vietnam Committee in spirit, outlook, and composition, led the way.[132] Having spent the last couple of years protesting the bombardment of the North, the wartime collaboration of American and French companies, and the extension of the war into neighboring Cambodia, the ISF redoubled its efforts after January 1973, boldly announcing that "Nothing is decided! Nothing is finished." As the new slogan put it, "Total support until the final victory!"[133]

But the Accords presented activists with a strategic dilemma. With the withdrawal of US combat forces, anti-imperialists had to find other targets, raise new demands, and rethink their internationalism. For Vietnamese revolutionaries, who counted on the continued support of antiwar movements abroad, the answer was clear: Antiwar radicals should work for full democratic freedoms in South Vietnam and draw more attention to Thiệu's treatment of political dissenters. As early as October 1972, they told radicals abroad that, while the upcoming Accords were a boon, there was still much to be done about Thiệu's regime. Isolated internationally, unpopular at home, and indignant about US withdrawal, Thiệu was growing even more dictatorial in the months leading up to the Accords. In this context, Nguyễn Ngọc Dung of the PRG delegation in France confided to Madeleine Rebérioux of the ISF that Vietnamese fighters were most worried about "the imminent possibility of generalized massacres in the prisons of the South." Thiệu's regime, she continued, aimed to "decapitate" the struggle by eliminating its most experienced cadres.[134]

Such fears only grew after the signing of the Accords. Although all sides were required to free their political prisoners, Thiệu now declared that the RVN had none, only common law criminals and communists, who were illegal according to the constitution. To force reality to fit his story, his regime either tortured prisoners to confess to communism or reclassified political prisoners like Ngô Bá Thành as common law criminals. With the lives of some 100,000 to 200,000 prisoners at risk, revolutionaries unable to liberate them militarily, and the war likely to last longer than expected, Vietnamese revolutionaries turned to the "indispensable" internationalism of their comrades abroad: "We ask you to focus your support on the following themes: the prisons of South Vietnam; obtaining and respecting democratic freedoms; denouncing Thiệu's regime, regime of the dollar and corruption."[135]

With Laurent Schwartz at the helm, the ISF led the way. "Nothing is more urgent right now than freeing them," the ISF wrote of the prisoners in February 1973. "The Vietnamese revolution needs them. It is up to us to make sure that they are returned to it."[136] Although continuing to champion other demands – such as cutting aid to Thiệu, withdrawing military advisors, or ending the bombardment of Cambodia – the ISF made the liberation of the political prisoners in South Vietnam a priority for anti-imperialists engaged in Vietnam solidarity work. The ISF wrote about the prisoners in its paper, circulated brochures across radical milieus, and organized meetings throughout the country, often in close collaboration with Vietnamese living in France. After one demonstration in February 1973, the PRG delegation formally thanked their ISF "friends" for prioritizing the struggle to "improve the living conditions of the population, realize democratic freedoms in the occupied zones, and demand the liberation of all patriots detained by the Saigon regime."[137]

Others followed suit. Ex-Proletarian Left radicals participated in ISF actions against repression in the South. The Unified Socialist Party lent a big hand. François Maspero published ISF materials.[138] The Communist League collaborated especially closely, sharing resources, printing the ISF's paper on its presses, allowing the ISF to use its offices, and co-organizing a day of solidarity with the prisoners in South Vietnam on February 26, 1973.[139] Even those groups that opposed the ISF pursued the same goals. Pro-Chinese radicals, for example, created their own anti-imperialist formation known as the National Movement of Support for the People of Indochina and urged radicals everywhere to "*actively* contribute" to the ongoing international struggle for the liberation of the political prisoners in South Vietnam.[140] Despite sharp animosities, these anti-imperialist groups made the struggle for democratic rights the primary axis of solidarity with Vietnam.

As in the 1960s, the French internationalized the campaign, sparking a new round of international antiwar activism across Europe in 1973. In early March, the ISF united antiwar groups from such countries as Italy, West Germany, Great Britain, Denmark, Sweden, and Belgium to discuss the possibility of restarting a coordinated antiwar campaign.[141] ISF radicals then organized an even larger gathering of a dozen European antiwar organizations in Paris, which included their rivals, the National Movement of Support for the People of Indochina. Later that month, they kicked off a week of organizing for "*the liberation of all of Saigon's prisoners*," and "the immediate establishment of *democratic freedoms* in South Vietnam," hoping to reactivate the international antiwar movement.[142]

Together they approved a collective statement to guide their struggles against the "neo-colonial presence" of the United States in Southeast Asia. They issued a broad range of demands that included the withdrawal of the US military from the region, cessation of all bombing in Southeast Asia, full amnesty for deserting GIs, and condemnation of all companies supporting the United States and its allies, but paid special attention to repression in South Vietnam. While the DRV had already freed American POWs, they argued, Thiệu was violating the Paris Peace Accords, imprisoning more dissidents, and crushing all opposition. In this context, their statement declared, Vietnamese revolutionaries still had a long struggle ahead, and it was the duty of anti-imperialists to do everything possible to defend the "democratic rights" of the people of South Vietnam, force Thiệu and the United States to "scrupulously respect the clauses of the signed accords," and, of course, ensure the "immediate liberation of all prisoners."[143] To that end, delegates agreed to organize "a European campaign for the liberation of the political prisoners," which would culminate in an international event in Milan on May 12, 1973.[144]

In anticipation, radicals organized demonstrations in France on April 12, Italy the day after, and Belgium on May 5.[145] In France, the ISF, Red Line, Revolution!, the ex-Proletarian Left, the Unified Socialist Party, Christian Fraternity for Vietnam, the Communist League, and the National Movement of Support for the People of Indochina all signed their names to a joint appeal for the grand event in Milan.[146] The Communist League billed it as the successor to the famous International Vietnam Congress back in 1968. "For the first time since the Berlin demonstration, in February 68," they wrote, "anti-imperialist Europe will gather in one single city, *en masse* in the streets."[147] All told, tens of thousands of radicals from across Europe descended on Milan to demonstrate their solidarity with the unfinished Vietnamese revolution.[148] Even some Americans attended, such as Vernon Bellecourt, an indigenous activist from the American Indian Movement who had participated briefly in the recent occupation of Wounded Knee. Others, such as Angela Davis, delivered letters of support, which were read aloud.[149]

The event began with a march, and radicals consciously invoked their earlier antiwar activism with such slogans as "Berlin 68, Milan 73, our support continues!"[150] They demanded that the United States cut aid to Thiệu, halt the bombardment of Cambodia, and end its involvement in Laos.[151] But again the struggle to win democratic liberties in South Vietnam took center stage. And once again, radicals were strongly encouraged in this direction by the Provisional Revolutionary Government of South Vietnam, which reminded anti-imperialists in Milan that the three major issues in this new stage were "respect for the ceasefire," "the liberation of all political prisoners," and "the guarantee of democratic freedoms" in the South. As always, Vietnamese revolutionaries made sure to express their deep appreciation for this solidarity. As PRG representative Phạm Văn Ba told radicals: "We sincerely thank you for organizing this European demonstration and for your support in the past as well as in this new stage of our struggle."[152]

Of course, many radicals refused to attend the demonstration, and even those who did participate remained divided, with Italian radicals from a pro-Chinese group physically attacking the "Trotskyist fascists" of the Fourth International contingent.[153] But while the radical left was as disputatious as ever, the majority of anti-imperialist radicals committed to solidarity with Vietnam nevertheless came to adopt a shared focus.

In the same way that in the early years of the war many radicals thought that the best way to assist their Vietnamese comrades was to win the ideological war, and in the late 1960s came to believe that the most effective way to support the Vietnamese revolution was to bring the war home, in the changed conjuncture of the early 1970s radicals reached a new consensus that the most important kind of solidarity that they could provide was to fight for the liberation of the prisoners, the restoration of democratic rights, and the observance of the Paris Accords.

This shift was noticeable even beyond the campaigns that focused on Vietnam. Whatever the specific figures, struggles, or countries in question, progressive activists of all stripes began to equate internationalism as such with the issues of repression, incarceration, and civil liberties. This remarkable convergence stemmed from at least three factors. First, the continued centrality of Vietnam in the radical imagination. As one of the most important issues of the time, and the revolution that had radicalized so many of these internationalists in the first place, Vietnam served as a kind of pacesetter for international solidarity. It was only natural, then, that the ideas developed around this revolution would influence solidarity work more generally. Here, again, Vietnamese figures played a leading role by using their stature – and their sophisticated public relations apparatus – to urge radicals in the North Atlantic to prioritize rights, prisoners, democracy, and repression. In those years, for example, virtually every issue of *South Viet Nam in Struggle*, the foreign language publication of the National Liberation Front, ran an article on these topics. In fact, the Vietnamese revolutionaries so many radicals looked to for inspiration often made the struggle against repression the center of their own solidarity work with other movements in the world. They helped their comrades in North America and Western Europe by shining a spotlight on state violence, condemning the violation of civil liberties, and drawing worldwide attention to political prisoners in the North Atlantic. In the early 1970s, for example, the *Vietnam Courier* could in the very same issue thank activists in the North Atlantic for helping political prisoners in South Vietnam while at the same time promising to fight for imprisoned radicals like Angela Davis.[154]

Second, a changed international conjuncture. Although Vietnam played a special role in radical politics, it never exhausted anti-imperialist internationalism. Just as the earlier turn to revolution was inspired not simply by the Vietnam War, but also by events across the globe, so too did other international developments inspire this turn to civil liberties. The early 1970s witnessed a frightening spike in repression, state terror, and outright authoritarianism across the planet, forcing many radicals in the North Atlantic to increase their involvement in campaigns for civil liberties abroad. Africa, Southern Europe, and especially Latin America became a major focus.[155] In fact, many antiwar activists also participated in other solidarity campaigns. To take just one example, French anti-imperialists such as Alain Krivine, Daniel Bensaïd, Simone de Beauvoir, François Maspero, Jean-Paul Sartre, and Laurent Schwartz participated in groups like the Committee for the Defense of Argentine Political Prisoners, making links with Italians like Rossana Rossanda and Pier Paolo Pasolini, British activists affiliated with the Russell Peace Foundation, as well as radicals in the United States.[156] If in 1968 radicals saw a world on the verge of revolution, in 1973 they saw struggles everywhere hammered by state repression.

But a final reason for this general reorientation had to do with domestic developments. Internationalism was always the product of encounters between events abroad and those at home. Just as important political shifts in the imperialist centers in the late 1960s made it possible for the international call for revolution to resonate in the first place, so too did their experiences struggling against repression at home allow radicals to refocus their attention onto repression, imprisonment, and civil liberties in places like South Vietnam. In so doing, radicals drew on insights gleaned from domestic prison organizing to nuance their antiwar work. At a press conference on South Vietnamese prisoners in early 1973, for instance, Madeleine Rebérioux of the ISF argued that antiwar activists had to demand "*the liberation of all the detainees* and not only the 'political' prisoners" since "the label 'common law' is stuck to all those who oppose the regime, whoever they may be."[157] In this, she drew directly on the lessons radicals learned about how the law itself creates divisions within those it oppresses, deciding what counts as political and what does not.

It is essential to emphasize, however, that while radicals prioritized combating repression at this time, few would have been satisfied if Thiệu somehow relaxed his rule, reestablished civil liberties, and freed the dissidents. Most anti-imperialists fought not for a more democratic regime in the South but the overthrow of the Republic of Vietnam as such. Their goal was a united, independent, socialist Vietnam.[158] Far from a single humanitarian "issue," freeing the political prisoners was an intermediate demand in a longer international revolutionary process. Speaking on behalf of those at the Milan convergence, the Italian Vietnam Committee put it best when it declared:

The struggle for the liberation of the political prisoners in southern Vietnam cannot and must not be considered a purely "humanitarian" battle to be entrusted to some "charitable" organization devoid of political connotations and based on choices or characteristics that have nothing to do with the class struggle: it is a first-order struggle of great importance for both the context of all the work of supporting the Indochinese peoples in struggle and for the future development of the situation in Vietnam.[159]

This did not mean that radicals lacked genuine concern for the prisoners, only that they believed the new balance of forces meant the route to victory had to pass through the liberation of the prisoners. Under the current regime, with democratic freedoms routinely violated, political organizing in the South had become arduous. If radicals in North America and Western Europe could contribute to freeing the prisoners, they might help their Vietnamese comrades come one step closer to overthrowing the RVN. In the same way that the shift to revolution did not mean abandoning the ideological struggle, the turn to civil liberties did not entail the rejection of revolution. The call to free the prisoners was not a retreat from anti-imperialist internationalism, but a strategic readjustment in response to changed historical circumstances. Radicals remained committed to Leninist anti-imperialism.

That said, just as the shift toward civil liberties had unintended effects on revolutionary strategy, this new perspective on political prisoners also affected the way that activists thought about anti-imperialist internationalism. In their quest to save the prisoners, a few hardened radicals, and especially many of the progressives who had only recently gravitated toward Leninist anti-imperialism, came dangerously close to replicating the kind of humanitarian, moralistic, depoliticized approach to victimization that they denounced. In a bizarre mirroring of Nixon's Go Public campaign, they sold buttons, bumper stickers, and plastic bracelets with the names of individual Vietnamese political prisoners.[160] Instead of the POW days of prayer, they organized the "International Days of Concern with Saigon's Political Prisoners."[161] And where some prowar activists sat in bamboo cages to dramatize the plight of the POWs, antiwar activists now built their own model tiger cages.[162] These antiwar activists began appealing to moral conscience, invoking humanitarian standards, and personalizing repression through lachrymose testimonies of suffering. Instead of heroic subjects fighting for their collective liberation, the Vietnamese people were increasingly recast as a lot of miserable victims in need of saving. As one American antiwar flyer put it, "their lives are in *our* hands."[163]

Convergences

On April 12, 1973, Vietnamese in Paris brought together nearly 100 local, national, and international organizations for an International Conference for the Liberation of the Political Prisoners of South Vietnam.[164]

As the conference made clear, while the anti-imperialists may have been some of the most ardent supporters of the struggle to restore democratic freedoms in South Vietnam, they by no means monopolized the issue.[165]

Alongside the radicals, Christians played a particularly active role. While publications like *Témoignage chrétien* had already run articles documenting the tiger cages, the Accords transformed the political prisoners into the primary issue for antiwar Christian groups in France. These groups successfully mobilized preexisting religious links to build an international movement in support of the prisoners. In November 1973, delegates from twenty countries – including the DRV and territories under the control of the PRG in the South – gathered in Turin, Italy to discuss reconstruction, national reconciliation, and the future of the political prisoners. For these activists, the question of the prisoners was fully tied to the fate of the neutralist Third Force, which they viewed as an interfaith religious force, and therefore the only hope for unity. Since the Third Force was under attack, internationalism meant getting Thiệu to respect civil liberties so that this Third Force could begin the process of peaceful reconciliation.[166]

The rising stars of this new round of antiwar engagement were the human rights groups, with Amnesty International leading the way. Formally established only in 1971, the French section leapt into action, publishing pamphlets, hosting conferences, and co-organizing a silent march of around 200, with each activist wearing a placard inscribed with the name of a different political prisoner, and a few demonstrators carrying models tiger cages.[167] Like the radicals and Christians, the French section tapped into a larger international network to amplify its efforts. AI activists from across the world wrote standardized letters to comfort adopted prisoners, explain to Thiệu that the detention of said prisoner violated the Universal Declaration of Human Rights, and ask the RVN to release the prisoner in question.[168] At the national level, Amnesty wrote detailed reports on the prisoners, made efforts to negotiate with the RVN, composed a Draft Protocol that called for all civilian prisoners to be placed under UN protection, and dispatched Chairman Sean McBride to North Vietnam.

Amnesty inscribed this work within its signature worldwide campaign against torture, launched in December 1972. Amnesty had come to see torture, and specifically its use by states, as the defining issue of the age. According to AI, "what for the last two or three hundred years has been no more than an historical curiosity, has suddenly developed a life of its own and become a social cancer."[169] Torture was "a malignant growth on the body politic," a disease that had reached "epidemic proportions," infecting radically diverse countries with no regard for ideology, political system, mode of production, or Cold War allegiance.[170] Instead of interpreting the world as a struggle between, say, national liberation and imperialism, communism and capitalism, or democracy and dictatorship, Amnesty International saw an epochal conflict between what it called "torture states" and individual citizens.[171]

Amnesty approached repression in South Vietnam from a very different perspective than other activist groups. First, instead of seeing repression as the product of specific historical trajectories, and therefore inscribed in specific social relations, connected to specific political projects, Amnesty tended to flatten societies, which allowed it to equate dissimilar countries, such as capitalist South Vietnam and communist Cuba, subsuming both under the ahistorical category of "torture states." Second, and relatedly, AI tried to bracket all politics. "Please take special care NOT to advance political or religious positions," Amnesty instructed its letter writers in the campaign to save the South Vietnamese political prisoners.[172] "Your mission is purely humanitarian. It is not to criticise or reform the government but to *Protect* and *Help* the individual person."[173] More than a tactical attempt to appear neutral, Amnesty strove to transcend politics as such. Instead of asking whether Thiệu's regime should exist to begin with, Amnesty only aimed to alleviate misery in the RVN, a position it claimed was beyond politics, but was of itself political. Third, AI imagined internationalism in a way that centered the individual above all else. Individual members wrote to other individuals, adopted specific prisoners, and scrawled their names on placards at marches. Lastly, Amnesty shifted agency from Vietnamese prisoners to their advocates abroad. Letter writers, for example, were instructed to reassure adopted Vietnamese prisoners that "there are people all over the world working for 'human rights' who think of you, and hope for your early release."[174] Salvation, AI suggested, would not come through mass agitation on the part of political prisoners themselves, but from the fact that other individuals, primarily in North America and Western Europe, believed in human rights.

Despite such fundamental differences in the ways these competing currents conceptualized internationalism, activists united on the issue of the political prisoners. Of course, localized collaborations were by no means new, and there had always been similarities, elective affinities, and overlaps between these competing approaches, but the changed global conjuncture made possible an unprecedented degree of convergence in the early 1970s. The inescapable context of international repression led these different currents to adopt a shared focus on rights, with the figure of the prisoner as a central point of reference. Consequently, activists found themselves pursuing some of the same projects, such as the campaign to free the political prisoners in South Vietnam. While their methods, approaches, and ultimate goals no doubt differed, they shared the same immediate objective of fighting repression in South Vietnam. Given the gravity of the situation, the challenges of making change from so far away, and the fact that Vietnamese themselves constantly urged unity, these different activists often cooperated. Liberals, pacifists, women's groups, human rights activists, religious institutions, anti-imperialist radicals, and many others attended the same conferences, participated in each other's events, and promoted each other's work. Even their tactics began to converge, and the gap that separated anti-imperialist activism from the others – perhaps at its greatest in 1968 – considerably narrowed, with all sides often doing some of the same things.

This context of convergence brought together the two great competing internationalisms of the era: individualist human rights and nationalist anti-imperialism. Transposing their domestic experiments with united fronts to the international arena, some radicals put aside their confrontational stance to collaborate with groups like AI. Quite a few anti-imperialists believed that Amnesty's approach to political prisoners, although opposed to their own, held great value. Since AI presented itself as nonpolitical, and based its authority on an illusion of objectivity, some radicals felt that Amnesty's data, testimonies, and reports would have more authority in the eyes of the public than information produced by radical groups.[175] From the French Indochina Solidarity Front to the Italian Vietnam Committee, anti-imperialist radicals drew on Amnesty's efforts to give their own work an air of legitimacy.[176] But a few radical groups went further, going out of their way to promote human rights groups as partners in a common struggle. In March 1973, for example, the ISF praised Amnesty's contributions to the campaign, arguing that, "Any joint initiative that can contribute today to solving this essential problem must benefit from our full support."[177] A united front was taking shape.

But this convergence had another – albeit unexpected – effect: It contributed to the reconfiguration of the balance of forces within this tenuous front. After all, not every current was of equal strength. Although dominant today, human rights internationalism was relatively marginal in many activist milieus in those years. In 1969, its leading international proponent, Amnesty International, counted no more than 15,000 members internationally, most of them concentrated in Northwest Europe.[178] In 1973, the French section reported a few thousand paper members at best. Not only were there more anti-imperialists than human rights advocates, but their vision of changing the world also enjoyed greater popularity in most activist circles. Even those who did not consider themselves anti-imperialist revolutionaries – like many pacifists, progressives, social democrats, and religious figures – still thought in terms of the ideas so central to Leninism, such as imperialism, national liberation, self-determination, and revolution.

This was true not only in the North Atlantic but also in Vietnam itself, where many neutralist Third Force activists conceptualized their activism within the framework of anti-imperialist internationalism instead of human rights. In 1973, Father Nguyễn Ngọc Lan, a member of the Committee to Reform the Prison System, used the twenty-fifth anniversary of the Universal Declaration of Human Rights to mock human rights as little more than the empty right "to live in misery":

Whereas the problem that ought to be set – if it has not already been set – is a whole social system that ought to be changed from top to bottom. A social system encouraged and protected by imperialism can only enslave a population to the profit of that imperialism. A social system created for a minority can only serve the interests of that minority, can only reserve to itself the right to oppress [and] exploit the majority.

The Rights of Man will be more than a useless word only when the day comes that the boots of imperialism are not treading the soil of our country, when the hand of imperialism no longer interferes in our affairs, and when our people succeed in their efforts to change the present social relationships.[179]

Despite new interest in prisoners, civil liberties, and rights talk, anti-imperialism retained its hegemony among activists in the early 1970s.

But human rights were gaining ground rapidly. In these years, activists, journalists, politicians, intellectuals, and exiles were all starting to turn to the kind of human rights discourse championed by groups like Amnesty International. There were of course many reasons for this relative surge in popularity, but one often overlooked factor had to do with the radicals.[180] Through alliances on campaigns like the one to free the political prisoners in South Vietnam, radicals unknowingly boosted Amnesty in particular and human rights internationalism in general. Collaboration brought groups like Amnesty greater visibility, drawing them closer to progressive audiences. It also gave them much needed political credibility in the eyes of these progressives. Until this point, even if progressives knew of AI, many did not consider it a legitimate fighting force. Amnesty's unwillingness to defend arrested radicals, like Alain Geismar, did not win it many friends, and it is little surprise that AI did poorly in countries like France where levels of militancy were high. As for the US section, it was particularly conservative, going so far as to oppose two German groups who wanted to adopt Angela Davis as a prisoner of conscience.[181] Yet the decision by some radicals to not only collaborate with AI on symbolically charged campaigns like repression in Vietnam, but also advocate for the organization, helped change Amnesty's image. As the ISF assured its radical audience,

"At the international level, Amnesty International was one of the first movements to condemn, with supporting evidence, the fate meted out to the detainees and the threats hanging over them."[182] The ISF even promoted AI's Amsterdam conference on political prisoners in October 1973.[183] Amnesty was becoming a potentially trustworthy ally.

Most importantly, radicals shifted the terrain of struggle in a way that was more favorable for human rights. Although they had initially rejected rights talk, the need to respond to state repression convinced many activists to turn to rights in the early 1970s. While radicals developed competing ideas, and never formulated a single radical rights discourse that they could all agree on, their combined attention to rights helped make them a central focus. When anti-imperialists transferred this concern with rights to their international solidarity work, they began to parallel other visions of internationalism. With Vietnam, for example, anti-imperialists now devoted much of their energy to criticizing the international affairs of a sovereign state. Fighting imperialism increasingly took the form of denouncing the government of South Vietnam for violating civil rights, mistreating political dissidents, and failing to adhere to the Paris Accords. While few radical anti-imperialists became advocates of human rights at this time, and most still adhered to some kind of Leninism, the shift unwittingly developed the intellectual terrain on which a properly human rights discourse could thrive. In the process, radicals in the early 1970s rendered Amnesty's vision more comprehensible – and attractive – to activists more broadly.

For their part, human rights activists displayed a remarkable ability to take advantage of this opportunity. Amnesty again led the way, introducing a series of innovations that turned it into a model for other groups. AI offered a tight organizational structure, semiprofessional staff, effective division of labor, and a functional fundraising apparatus. At a time when people craved reliable information about what was happening, Amnesty went beyond synthesizing data to producing original research, earning political capital and making itself an indispensable resource. Amnesty also improved its profile by organizing large international campaigns, coordinating with the media, winning friends in the United Nations, applying pressure on governments, and building alliances with unions, doctors, lawyers, intellectuals, religious institutions, and activists of all kinds. Human rights became not merely an appealing idea, but the guiding thread of an effective international force promising to make the world a better place.

As historian Jan Eckel has argued, the key to Amnesty's success was that it could channel activist energies but also present a new path, offering both continuity and departure. Instead of the violent sectarian warfare that characterized the radical left, AI provided a more civil space for doing activism.[184] Instead of a maximalist vision to overthrow the system through world revolution, which seemed increasingly unlikely, Amnesty planned its campaigns around measurable goals, which gave activists a sense of accomplishment, encouraging them to continue the fight. Instead of demanding a total commitment to the cause, AI welcomed activists with varying levels of engagement, allowing it to build a broader base among those who just wanted to do good. Instead of facing brutal state repression, Amnesty's moderate approach allowed it to operate in peace. In contrast to the besieged radicals of 1973, Amnesty enjoyed an enviable upward momentum. AI seemed to present a viable alternative to anti-imperialism.[185]

For these reasons, many progressives in North America and Western Europe began to gravitate toward Amnesty in the 1970s. In the United States, for example, AI's ranks swelled with young antiwar activists.[186] Antiwar religious organizations began to directly engage with human rights, increasingly forming a core constituency of the human rights movement led by groups like Amnesty.[187] Even those antiwar organizations like the Indochina Peace Campaign that did not adopt the language of human rights mimicked Amnesty by zeroing in on torture, circulating personal narratives about repression, and instructing supporters to "adopt" a prisoner, write them a message, and copy a sample letter to Congress.[188]

The same thing happened across the Atlantic. In France, for example, Christian antiwar activists went from participating in Amnesty events to emulating AI's model altogether, transforming their antiwar work into a campaign against torture that involved adopting individual dissidents, publishing testimonies of suffering, and promoting human rights. In this way, argues historian Sabine Rousseau, Christian antiwar internationalism experienced a kind of "mutation" from a conception of collective emancipation to one of individual human rights.[189] Groups like Amnesty, then, were not just pulling more people into the orbit of rights internationalism; they were beginning to convince them to embrace a similarly narrow definition of human rights. Amnesty's success in the 1970s helped transform human rights from a highly amorphous field of competing interpretations to a single idea. Human rights would increasingly become synonymous with individual freedom from state violence, making possible a new kind of dehistoricized, depoliticized, and decollectivized internationalism.

Although rights activists worked hard to distinguish human rights as a new alternative to anti-imperialist internationalism, they realized that marketing human rights as completely different risked losing many activists who would turn to more robust competitors like anti-imperialism. The challenge for human rights activists was to find a way to somehow maintain the uniqueness of their project while presenting human rights as a similar kind of progressive internationalism, that is, with the same general aspirations as anti-imperialism, so that it could resonate with the needs of a new generation of activists. They found their solution in those collaborative projects of the early 1970s.

In this respect, the effort to free South Vietnamese prisoners was a pivotal but forgotten early episode, providing a model of collaborative action that activists from competing internationalist projects would replicate in later campaigns, the most famous of which were the movements against the dictatorship in Chile after September 1973.[190] Many radical anti-imperialists drew directly on their experiences fighting repression in South Vietnam to organize campaigns against repression in Chile, with Vietnam solidarity groups such as the Indochina Solidarity Front effectively converting to Chile solidarity. Many of those human rights groups that turned to Chile, and Latin America more broadly, explicitly referred to the legacy of the Vietnam War.[191] Both sides remembered their earlier collaborative efforts on behalf of political prisoners in South Vietnam and significantly expanded on them in the even wider campaign against repression in Chile. Through these struggles, and many others in Argentina, South Africa, and beyond, the complex overlaps between anti-imperialism and human rights deepened throughout the 1970s.[192]

All these entangled collaborations would allow human rights groups like AI to blaze a new path while simultaneously presenting themselves as allies, and perhaps even credible successors, to other internationalist projects, capable of winning over all those who still cared about transforming the world. And Amnesty knew it. As Peter Benenson once explained, speaking privately of Amnesty's ambitions, "The underlying purpose of this campaign – which I hope those who are closely connected with it will remember, but never publish – is to find a common base upon which the idealists of the world can co-operate. It is designed in particular to absorb the latent enthusiasm of great numbers of such idealists who have, since the eclipse of Socialism, become increasingly frustrated; similarly it is geared to appeal to the young searching for an ideal ...." And to further underline the scope of his project, he admitted, "If this underlying aim is borne in mind, it will be seen that, à la longue, it matters more to harness the enthusiasm of the helpers than to bring people out of prison."[193]

5   Crisis

On April 30, 1975, a tank flying the flag of the National Liberation Front (NLF) rammed through the metal gates of the Independence Palace in Saigon. As troops poured into the country's capital, an advance unit stormed the Palace itself, where they found South Vietnam's leaders dressed in their finest suits, sitting around a giant table, prepared to surrender power. A veteran of the famous battle of Điện Biên Phủ, and now the most senior communist officer on the scene, Colonel Bùi Tín is said to have replied: "Your power has crumbled. You cannot give up what you do not have." But he assured them that they had nothing to fear. "If you are patriots, consider this a moment of joy. The war for our country is over."[1]

After nearly a century of combat, the struggle for a united Vietnam free from imperial rule had finally come to an end. Although their ranks had thinned, anti-imperialists across the North Atlantic rejoiced. Vietnamese living in Paris poured into the streets, waving portraits of Hồ Chí Minh. Millions across the globe gaped at images of Americans shoving helicopters off the deck of aircraft carriers to make room for the incoming evacuees. The White House struggled to explain how the strongest military power in the world had been defeated in Vietnam. There was no greater symbol of the weakness of the United States and the triumph of anti-imperialism.

To make matters worse, the communists captured Saigon at an especially bad time for the United States, compounding the domestic crisis gripping the country in the 1970s. The new social movements severely challenged assumptions about race, gender, sexuality, and the family. Though liberating for some, the counterculture's glorification of drugs, free love, and nonconformity left many Americans apprehensive. A skyrocketing crime rate triggered panic about social decay. A stupefying recession terminated the unprecedented economic boom, dealing a psychological blow to millions who had believed postwar prosperity might last forever. Richard Nixon became the only president in history to resign the office, kicking distrust in the government to an all-time high. By the latter half of the decade, political scandals, gas rationing, rising divorce rates, and Cold War anxieties led many Americans to believe the world was coming to an end, a sentiment captured by the spate of disaster films that hit theaters in those years.[2]

But the United States was far from alone in its troubles. Because of structural commonalities, a similar historical trajectory, a shared model of postwar development, and deep transatlantic connections, the entire capitalist North Atlantic was plunged into crisis. What made the crisis so severe was not simply the presence of fractures in every sphere of life – the family, economy, culture, international relations – but their vertiginous fusion. The crisis of masculinity, to take just one example, intersected with the recession, as resentful male breadwinners with once steady factory jobs found themselves unemployed just as their working wives were taking charge. Although these fractures all had their own origins, rhythms, and stakes, their articulation made them all the more severe.[3]

Theorists like Stuart Hall called this generalized breakdown an "organic crisis" because it revealed the limits of the existing hegemonic order, shook inherited assumptions, and challenged ways of life that many once took as immutable truths. The world was burst open, creating opportunities for new alternatives. Of course, this crisis, like all crises, did not mean that the forces of order were necessarily defeated, only that, if they wished to restore their leadership, they would have to reinvent the existing world. The crisis, Hall quickly added, was not some terminal collapse that would lead inevitably to apocalypse or the long-awaited revolution, but instead a window of opportunity, which any political force could conceivably turn to its advantage.[4]

For the radicals, the opening was precisely what they had been waiting for. Throughout the 1960s and early 1970s, they had fought for an opportunity to change the system, and now, in part through their own efforts, their chance had come. But, ironically, these radicals found themselves mired in a crisis of their own. Anti-imperialists everywhere were in disarray – their groups folded, their ideas came under attack, and their former comrades abandoned activism, rejoined mainstream politics, or even pole-vaulted to the other end of the political spectrum. In France, to a degree unparalleled elsewhere, prominent former radicals did not merely disavow anti-imperialist internationalism; they rallied behind a rival human rights internationalism. In so doing, they brought with them a set of experiences, which strengthened human rights activism. There is no better example than Doctors Without Borders, a radical humanitarian organization with roots in anti-imperialism that served as a kind of relay station, not only facilitating the transfer from anti-imperialism to human rights but also helping to transform human rights into a vigorous internationalist project with some progressive credibility. In this way, anti-imperialism found itself disoriented by crisis as well as faced with an insurgent challenger in the high-stakes competition between different visions of global change.

Despite their fading fortunes, radicals tried to reinvent anti-imperialist internationalism. But they found themselves stuck in an uphill battle facing one obstacle after another. One of the most devastating blows came from none other than Southeast Asia. In December 1978, the Socialist Republic of Vietnam (SRV) shocked the world by invading Cambodia. Within a week, the omnipresent Bùi Tín accompanied the vanguard of the Vietnamese military as it marched into Phnom Penh, overthrew the Khmer Rouge, and installed a new pro-Vietnamese government backed by an occupation force. A few weeks later, China entered the fray, assisting its Khmer Rouge allies by invading Vietnam from the north. All three states had come to power through national liberation struggles, all of them had developed a revolutionary strategy based in Leninism, all of them had once joined hands in the struggle against imperialism, and all of them claimed they were transitioning to communism together. Now they slaughtered each other in the name of national self-determination. Anti-imperialist internationalism had become fratricidal war. Nothing like this had happened before.

In an article published in the radical paper *Lotta Continua*, Marco Boato captured the gravity of the crisis. He began by recalling how the radicals of the 1960s and 1970s were so thoroughly inspired by Vietnam that they had been called "generation Vietnam." "We accepted this moniker with pride and satisfaction, because it was truly with Vietnam that we had experienced a new form of revolutionary internationalism," he wrote. "In 1967, we took to the streets with Vietnam; in '68, we said 'Vietnam is here,'" he reminded readers. Precisely because of this profound political, intellectual, and psychological connection to Vietnam, the internecine war in Southeast Asia could only have catastrophic consequences. While developments there had once put wind in the sails of radicals, thrusting anti-imperialist internationalism forward, the storms raging in the late 1970s were now pushing them back. "In light of the events of these days," Boato wrote, "it must again be exclaimed, though now with much bitterness, that 'Vietnam is here.'"[5]

Although the Third Indochina War did not single-handedly destroy radicalism, it severely destabilized radical politics. The war turned radicals against one another, exacerbated an identity crisis, and deepened creeping doubts about anti-imperialist internationalism. After all, radicals had long viewed Vietnam as a proving ground for the Leninism they believed would help them change the world, a belief regularly confirmed by Vietnamese revolutionaries themselves. Their fight for national self-determination, Vietnamese communists claimed, could help lead the broader international struggle for universal emancipation. But the Third Indochina War suggested that the opposite might be true. Their anti-imperialist revolution had led not to a unified struggle for a new world but instead to war, autocracy, and virulent nationalism.

Although much of this failure can be traced to longer histories of colonialism, imperialism, and intervention in the region, revolutionaries, and the ideas that guided them, played a role as well. When the Vietnamese revolution fell short of expectations, then, its animating ideas – such as the right of nations to self-determination specifically, and the Leninist problematic more generally – came under heavy fire. The contemporary "crisis of Marxism and Leninism," Boato explained, was to be measured not simply by theoretical debates in the North Atlantic, "but by what is happening in Cambodia and Vietnam."[6] The horrific events in Southeast Asia heightened the gnawing crisis of Leninism, which would in turn bring down anti-imperialist internationalism as such, creating a perfect opportunity for human rights internationalism to seize the stage.

Radicalism in Crisis

From the mid-1970s onward, the radical left declined as a meaningful organized force nearly everywhere in the North Atlantic. While the proximate causes were manifold, and varied from country to country, the general crisis stemmed from the radical left's inability to reinvent its politics in the face of a changed conjuncture. To begin with, the state's multipronged counteroffensive proved difficult to handle. Governments continued to arrest activists, dissolve organizations, and restrict civil liberties, which kept radicals off balance, sapped their resources, and limited their room for maneuver. Yet states defused dissent not simply through repression but with sweeping reforms that included everything from lowering the voting age to increasing wages. In some cases, like France, states co-opted movements by granting workers greater decision-making powers, promoting experimental universities, and integrating oppositional forces into the formal political system.

The forces of order often went further by fundamentally restructuring the conditions that made mass rebellion possible in the first place. The militant workers' struggles of the 1970s, for instance, convinced many capitalists that concentrating thousands of workers in giant factories had unwittingly put them in control of the levers of economic power. They responded by decentralizing firms, relocating plants, replacing restive workers with robots, and turning long-term contracts into precarious jobs.[7] The factory universe – which had been the condition of possibility for the historical workers' movement, the basis of its political culture since at least the early twentieth century, and the very horizon of revolutionary politics in much of the North Atlantic – was painstakingly dismantled.[8]

These sweeping changes aggravated problems within radical circles. Radicals had trouble sustaining movements over the long run. They found it increasingly difficult to maintain the delicate strategy of combining civil reforms with violent confrontation. Above all, they struggled to bring together a diversity of voices into an inclusive unity with a common theoretical language, a general program of change, and a shared set of interconnected organizations. In many cases, their failures to build a more inclusive unity produced the opposite, as intense frustration, coupled with combative rhetoric, ideological rigidity, and moralistic sectarianism led to factionalization. Movements divided like cells, with some embracing essentialist conceptions of identity, others turning into dogmatic sects, and still others converting to armed struggle, which in nearly every case isolated, delegitimized, and ultimately weakened radicals in the North Atlantic. In this climate of disappointment, acrimony, and division, many began to lose hope. The revolution everyone thought was just around the corner drifted further away. While some vowed to keep the flame of revolt burning, many others burned out, grew disillusioned, or decided to get on with their lives, which they had put on hold for a revolution that never came.

These major shifts provoked a crisis in the guiding theory of Marxism. Once viewed as a skeleton key powerful enough to open all doors, versatile enough to unlock all the secrets of history, Marxism's major limitations were becoming more apparent. One theorist after another declared the "crisis of Marxism."[9] As Ernesto Laclau and Chantal Mouffe later put it: "In the mid-1970s, Marxist theorization had clearly reached an impasse."[10] This did not mean that radicals suddenly abandoned Marxism, only that they began to more accurately identify its blind spots, challenge its major assumptions, and question some of its core concepts, such as class, the party, and the state. Some radicals hoped that the crisis could have a salutary aspect, spurring a renewal of Marxism. But with movements in decline and the radical left losing popularity, this was no easy task. In the end, the crisis of Marxism accelerated the decomposition of movements, and the decomposition of movements deepened the crisis of Marxism.

Another decisive, though sometimes forgotten, factor in the decline of radicalism in the North Atlantic had to do with the fate of national liberation struggles in what was called the "Third World."[11] Since the trajectory of radicalism was not shaped exclusively by domestic events but through complex encounters between developments at home and those abroad, major transformations in national liberation movements contributed to the radical left's decomposition in the 1970s. At the very same moment that radicals confronted a strange new political conjuncture at home, the "Third World" descended into crisis. While anti-imperialists scored a few wins, they suffered more defeats. By the mid-1970s, countless movements had been crushed, some with extreme violence, as in Chile. But even those that ended in some kind of victory found themselves in a predicament. Many newly liberated countries discovered not only that political sovereignty did not guarantee economic independence but also that delinking from the capitalist system was easier said than done. Years of imperialist domination left behind undeveloped industries, weak infrastructures, and dependent economies. Attempts to break out of cycles of dependency led to borrowing, which indebted many of these new countries to their former imperial masters, who would demand "structural adjustments." Despite coordinated efforts to alter the international system through initiatives like the New International Economic Order, imperialist reaction proved too powerful.[12]

Not only were many liberation struggles unable to live up to their great promises, but quite a few also betrayed their stated emancipatory goals. In its desire to counter the USSR, the People's Republic of China, for example, did the unthinkable – seeking rapprochement with the United States. To the chagrin of many radicals, this new relationship soon surpassed mere friendship, as the PRC began to back the White House abroad. In 1973, when General Augusto Pinochet seized power in Chile, the PRC followed the White House's lead, becoming one of the first countries to recognize the new regime. China, a country that only a few years ago had called for world revolution against the United States and had been upheld by many as the epitome of internationalism, now supported a pro-US capitalist dictatorship that had just destroyed a democratically elected socialist government. In the years that followed, China continued its retreat from anti-imperialist internationalism, supporting the anticommunist regime in Pakistan, taking the side of the United States against communist movements in Angola, and later backing the mujahideen against the communist government in Afghanistan.[13]

What radicals found most disheartening was the persistent authoritarianism of these new regimes. Revolutionary movements founded states that repressed their own citizens, curtailed civil liberties, abolished democratic politics, and refused to recognize the self-determination of minority peoples. In Cuba, communists continued to harass dissidents. In North Korea, they bolstered a hereditary dictatorship. In Vietnam, they forced hundreds of thousands of people into reeducation camps. In Cambodia, they committed mass murder. News of these disturbing developments entered North America and Western Europe through a series of highly publicized "revelations," a phenomenon that was especially pronounced in France.[14] In 1973, journalist Olivier Todd announced that Vietnamese revolutionaries had tricked leftists like himself into believing that Hanoi was the leader of some democratic revolution when it was in reality the capital of a despotic state that combined Stalinism with Confucianism.[15] In 1976, Gérard Chaliand, a former member of the National Vietnam Committee, published a rich survey of the "Third World" that deflated many of the myths held so dearly by the radical left.[16] In 1977, erstwhile Maoists Claudie Broyelle, Jacques Broyelle, and Evelyne Tschirhart claimed that their recent trips abroad showed that China was not a model revolutionary society as they had once believed but a land of repression no different from the USSR.[17] That same year a progressive missionary working in Southeast Asia named François Ponchaud detailed the horrors unfolding in Cambodia in *Cambodia: Year Zero*.[18]

In some cases, such as Cambodia, these reports came as a genuine surprise. Rony Brauman, for instance, described Ponchaud's book as a "shock." A onetime anti-imperialist revolutionary who had been politicized by the Vietnam War, joined the Proletarian Left, and proudly celebrated the communist seizure of Saigon in 1975, he later recalled how Ponchaud's accounts convinced him to "break definitively with political radicalism."[19] But in many other cases, these "revelations" were far from new. Radicals already suspected there was an unsavory side to some liberation struggles, just as they had all been aware of Soviet crimes before the publication of Aleksandr Solzhenitsyn's *The Gulag Archipelago* in 1974.[20] Yet these "revelations" had such an enormous impact in the mid-1970s because they found fertile ground at home in the North Atlantic. Disorientation, exhaustion, bitterness, and disillusionment in France, as elsewhere, amplified the resonance of these reports. If in the 1960s radicals already aware of these unpalatable developments chose to give national liberation struggles the benefit of the doubt, hoping they would eventually overcome their growing pains, by the mid-1970s many began to classify them as structural problems inherent to anti-imperialism itself. Just as the encounter of the domestic and the international had helped galvanize the radicals in the 1960s, the same confluence in the 1970s now worked against them.

The effects of all this were profoundly unsettling. The struggles that once inspired radicals did not just fall short of expectations: Instead of making the world a better place, they seemed to be making it worse; instead of liberation, they brought disaster. Since radicals had devoted so much of their lives to defending these liberation struggles, this real-ization took an incalculable political, intellectual, and emotional toll. Many radicals felt angry, confused, dismayed, and personally respon-sible. This is precisely why these "revelations" were so important. They often doubled as collective self-criticisms, allowing radicals to work through their disappointments, clear their conscience, settle accounts with their past, and find a way to move forward.[21]

Against the "Third World"

Radicals responded to the impasse in different ways. After years of frenetic activity fueled by messianic faith in the coming revolution, some dropped out of politics altogether. Others returned to the land, looked to countercultural experiments, or immersed themselves in the autonomist scenes that dotted Europe like an archipelago. Still others tried to find some kind of salvation in mysticism, spirituality, or even organized religion. As former Proletarian Left radical Nadia Lacroix recalled:

I felt I'd given my life for a cause that no longer had any point. I was still on the left, but I couldn't see any longer where Marxism, Maoism could lead. Everything was so black that I wanted to kill myself. If I hadn't returned to the Catholicism in which I was brought up, I would have committed suicide because everything that had made my life worthwhile had collapsed.[22]

One of the most common responses was to refocus one's political energy on contesting elections. Battered by repression, weary of subsist-ing on the margins, and desperate to take advantage of new reforms, many radicals set their sights on the ballot box. In Britain, some radicals took another look at the Labour Party. In the United States, quite a few rejoined the Democratic Party. In West Germany, many former activ-ists founded new electoral parties like the Greens. In France, a growing number of anti-imperialists became so seduced by the growing possibil-ity of a leftist electoral victory that they backed François Mitterrand's newly reformed Socialist Party.

During the May 1974 elections, large swathes of the French radical left supported Mitterrand instead of abstaining, as many had done in the past. When some diehards still refused to vote, a number of prominent intellec-tuals, including Simone de Beauvoir, Michel Foucault, and the anarchist Daniel Guérin, issued a manifesto exhorting radicals to participate.[23] In an act that spoke volumes about how deeply the left had changed, Daniel Cohn-Bendit, renowned student leader of the May events, replaced the famous '68 slogan, "Elections: a trap for idiots," with "Abstention: a trap for idiots."[24] Although Mitterrand lost the presidential elections to Valéry Giscard d'Estaing, the razor-thin margin seemed to justify the electoral turn. For its part, Mitterrand's Socialist Party sought to absorb these radicals by inviting representatives from practically the entire leftist spectrum to a major national conference in October 1974. Enticed, many radicals abandoned their revolutionary organizations to join the Socialist Party outright. It was at this time, for example, that Michel Rocard, a leader of the radical Unified Socialist Party, formally joined the Socialists, bringing a sizable contingent with him. Even some radicals from openly revolutionary Leninist groups such as the Revolutionary Communist League (successor to the banned Communist League) soon followed.[25]

If many radical activists reacted to the crisis by rejoining the political mainstream, others went a step further to wage war on the far left itself. In the mid-1970s, a number of former radicals began to publish vituperative public attacks on their former politics, with some, such as André Glucksmann, going so far as to equate Marxism with the gulag. In this context, Maurice Clavel, a journalist, philosopher, and onetime ally of radicals after May '68, gathered many of these figures – quite a few of whom were former Proletarian Left militants such as Glucksmann, Alain Geismar, and Jean-Pierre Le Dantec – to discuss their shared disillusionment with radicalism.[26] This convergence, which became the first of many regular meetings, contributed to the bizarre rise of the "New Philosophers." A mass media phenomenon, the New Philosophers were a farraginous group of intellectuals whose only real point of commonality was that they traded on their radical past to justify a denunciation of the far left in the present. In a barrage of popular books – including Glucksmann's *La Cuisinière et le mangeur d'hommes* (1975), Christian Jambet and Guy Lardreau's *L'Ange* (1976), and Bernard-Henri Lévy's *La Barbarie à visage humain* (1977) – the New Philosophers abandoned Marxism, repudiated anti-imperialism, and argued that all leftist attempts to radically change the world would inevitably result in "totalitarianism." The most visible symptom of radicalism's disarray, the New Philosophers represented new trends in French political life – a turn to ethics, a rehabilitation of the individual, an obsession with totalitarianism, and a sweeping rejection of the radical project of systemic change.[27]

Because the radical left was so thoroughly shaped by national liberation struggles abroad, this disavowal of radicalism inevitably took the form of a furious assault on anti-imperialist internationalism.[28] In June 1978, Jacques Julliard fired the first shots with an incendiary article, "The Third World and the Left," which excoriated radicals for not just projecting their desires abroad, but also exporting their "ideologies" – in particular the old European idea of national self-determination – to the "Third World."[29] Those dreams had led to unmitigated calamity. Instead of freedom, self-determination brought tyranny. Instead of harmony between equal nation-states, it produced only interstate conflict. Instead of independence, it had subjected the people of the "Third World" to Cold War spheres of influence. Pointing to places like Cambodia, Vietnam, and Guinea, Julliard concluded that the "Western" idea of making radical change through the right of self-determination was doomed to fail everywhere in the "Third World." Socialism in Africa – in fact anywhere in the "Third World" – could never be anything other than "totalitarian."[30]

Julliard's criticism was not limited to national self-determination or anti-imperialist internationalism more broadly. The assault that he initiated aimed to obliterate any political project that advocated collective emancipation. This is precisely why the offensive took as its object not anti-imperialism but rather the more expansive, and deliberately vague, notion of "Third Worldism." In fact, "Third Worldism," the alleged cause of all that was bad in the world, was an invention of these renegade leftists themselves, created by the very onslaught against it in the late 1970s. Although the concept of the "Third World" had been ubiquitous for decades, "Third Worldism" was almost nowhere to be found in the radical literature of the 1960s. It only really appeared in the early 1970s, but even then carried little meaning for Americans and was not in wide circulation among French radicals. When describing their politics, most French radicals spoke not of "tiers-mondisme" but rather "anti-impérialisme."[31]

If "Third Worldism" held any coherent meaning for radicals in the 1970s, it referred to the extreme position that revolution would only happen in the "Third World," and would arrive in North America and Western Europe from the outside through encirclement, in the same way that some claimed that national liberation was said to happen in the countryside, and only later enter into the cities after revolutionaries had surrounded them in a protracted struggle. Since this specific political strategy effectively wrote off the possibility of radical change in the capitalist core, undermining one of the central tenets of anti-imperialism itself, it is little surprise that it remained quite marginal among radicals not only in the North Atlantic but also in much of the rest of the world. As Samir Amin, a participant in these French debates, explained at the time: "Its proponents seize on literary expressions, such as 'the East wind will prevail over the West wind' or 'the storm centers,' to illustrate the impossibility of struggle for socialism in the West, rather than grasping the fact that the necessary struggle for socialism passes, in the West, also by way of anti-imperialist struggle in Western society itself."[32]

This "Third Worldism," for lack of a better term, amounted to reducing politics to moralism, substituting internationalist unity for orientalism, essentializing the "Third World" into some holy force that would save the world, and centering the guilt of those in the North Atlantic instead of the liberation movements they claimed to support. While it is certainly true that not everyone was immune to moralism, orientalism, or hero worship, the great majority of anti-imperialists in the North Atlantic nevertheless vehemently denounced this kind of "Third Worldist" politics as an obstacle to winning an egalitarian future for all.

Yet the term was immensely useful for renegade leftists, such as Julliard, Jean-Pierre le Dantec, and Bernard Kouchner, who helped popularize it in the late 1970s. It allowed these figures to reduce the concrete politics of anti-imperialism to a mere sensibility based on some of the most extreme features of the "Third Worldist" approach roundly rejected by most anti-imperialists. André Burguière's commentary on the debate around Julliard's essay, for instance, asserted that "Third Worldism" was "the mix of retrospective guilty conscience and messianism by proxy that for the last fifteen to twenty years has characterized the left's attitude towards political events in the third world."[33] Rich debates over strategy, diverse solidarity campaigns, dense transnational networks that tied together activists from across the globe – all these were reduced to illusions, fantasies, and feelings of guilt. From there, these critics of anti-imperialism could peremptorily lump into a single group anyone who cared about oppressed peoples fighting for their liberation, discrediting them all through association with this absurd caricature. All of them could now be condemned as naïve fools irresponsibly abetting mass murder abroad.[34]

The concept of "Third Worldism" allowed these renegades to castigate not just the anti-imperialist left at home but the people of Asia, Africa, and Latin America as well. The ritualistic critique of "Third Worldism" inflated the negative aspects of liberation struggles, recoded victorious movements as symbols of absolute evil, and dismissed all radical struggles for emancipation as totalitarianism in embryo. In so doing, critics of "Third Worldism" denied the self-activity of oppressed peoples, washed away any of their positive gains, and erased the fundamental role that these liberation struggles played in catalyzing change in North America and Western Europe. In this way, Kristin Ross argues, critics of "Third Worldism" used language that almost exactly mimicked old colonial rhetoric to recast the "Third World" as a miserable death camp in need of saving by the civilized "West."[35]

The "debate" over "Third Worldism" played yet another function. As Ross notes, it served as a kind of cathartic performance that sanctified the conversion of a number of former radicals to a different way of imagining internationalism.[36] Attacking such a bloated and conceptually meaningless target as "Third Worldism" allowed these figures to distance themselves not only from the anti-imperialism of the radicals but also from the imperialism of their own government. As Paige Arthur points out, at the same time that these renegade leftists were turning on the radicals, the French government intervened in Zaire to prop up the ruthless dictator Mobutu Sese Seko.[37] This is precisely why Julliard insisted that while he defended the plight of individuals suffering from totalitarian autocracies in the "Third World," he also opposed state interference: "A French government, no matter its politics, can do practically nothing for the Czechs. Nor for the Cambodians nor the Vietnamese nor the Argentines. Nor for the Ethiopians nor the people of Zaire."[38] What figures like Julliard wanted, then, was an internationalism grounded in neither revolutionary collective liberation nor interventionist states, but rather individualist human rights. In the very article that sparked the debate, Julliard echoed Amnesty International's discourse by explaining that while the "Third World" was certainly divided into two camps, these were not the capitalist and communist, "the American and the Soviet," but "torturing States and the martyred peoples."[39] Claiming that the *"right of peoples has become the principal instrument for strangling the rights of man,"* Julliard made an explicit appeal to build a new kind of internationalism based on human rights.[40]

Radical Humanitarianism

A peculiarity of the French scene in the 1970s was that a significant number of former anti-imperialists not only broke with their radical past but also consciously threw their weight behind human rights. There were, again, many reasons for this reversal, but developments in Asia, Africa, and Latin America played a critical role, with the civil war in Nigeria acting as a particularly important catalyst.

Soon after securing independence from Britain, Nigeria sucumbed to a military government that repressed ethnic Igbos. In 1967, the predominantly Christian Igbo leaders of the country's oil-rich Eastern Region declared independence as the Republic of Biafra. In addition to sending troops to quash the rebellion, Nigeria's military government blockaded the region, threatening to starve the Biafran people. The Biafran Republic charged genocide and called for international assistance, wagering that framing the conflict as a humanitarian crisis might legitimate its political claims. Britain backed the federal government in order to preserve its ties with what was now Africa's most populous country. France sided with Biafra, figuring that secession would weaken Nigeria's influence in the region. To make matters more complicated, the Soviet Union found itself on Britain's side, while apartheid South Africa joined France in supporting the fledgling Biafran Republic. The whole affair was a political hornets' nest.[41]

Confused, preoccupied with making domestic revolution, or transfixed by other struggles like those in Vietnam, many radicals in France and abroad tried to avoid the issue. After all, it revealed disconcerting contradictions within the very framework of anti-imperialism. Both sides in the war justified their actions through the language of self-determination. Biafrans claimed they were an oppressed nation with a right to self-determination; the Nigerian government claimed that Biafra was not a nation, secession jeopardized the viability of postcolonial nation-states, and self-determination meant defending the right to territorial integrity. Anti-imperialists abroad found themselves in a quandary. Should they defend the federal government's right not only to administer its own affairs but also to protect the integrity of a united Nigeria against its fragmentation? Or should they defend the Biafran struggle against national oppression by supporting their right to self-determination?

A few French activists defended the Biafran people, arguing that they were a nation with an irrevocable right to self-determination. Leading the charge was a young doctor named Bernard Kouchner.[42] A committed anti-imperialist, he had protested the Algerian War, traveled to Cuba to meet Fidel Castro, and joined the National Vietnam Committee. As a doctor, he was particularly drawn to Che Guevara, to whom he dedicated his medical thesis. Much like his hero, Kouchner's brand of anti-imperialism glorified humanism, daring action, voluntaristic will, and individual initiative. In September 1968, he volunteered with the International Committee of the Red Cross to serve in Biafra. When he returned to France, he recounted his experiences in *Le Monde*, helped organize a solidarity committee, and reproached other anti-imperialists for not mobilizing to save Biafra as they had with Vietnam.[43] Although the Biafran Republic collapsed in 1970, Kouchner's resolve did not. France was the one place where the pro-Biafran campaign did not dissolve but survived to contribute to a new kind of activism.[44]

Hoping to continue the struggle, Kouchner and his comrades helped create a new humanitarian group called Doctors Without Borders (known internationally as "MSF," after its French name, "Médecins Sans Frontières") in December 1971. But disagreements soon erupted. One side insisted that MSF not interfere politically in the affairs of other countries, while Kouchner's wing advocated emergency actions, media publicity, and overt political engagement. Tensions came to a head in

September 1974, when Kouchner and two other veterans of the Biafra campaign traveled to Iraq to meet with Kurdish rebels fighting for self-determination against the Iraqi government. His call to lend MSF's support to the guerrillas precipitated a power struggle that left Kouchner's wing triumphant.[45] Under his leadership, MSF would channel the anti-imperialism of many of its members into a new kind of radical humanitarianism.[46]

MSF took a keen interest in the plight of oppressed minorities. In this, its activists sought to expose what they perceived as the contradictions inherent to the idea of national self-determination. Kouchner and his allies criticized the left for selectively supporting struggles based on preconceived ideological criteria. As he put it in 1976: "if the struggle is said to be progressive (Cambodia), the progressives will take notice, if not, peoples can very well die (Kurdistan)."[47] By the end of the decade, he had elevated this argument into an internationalist principle: Ideological criteria should not favor the suffering of one oppressed group over another. There are, he said, "no good or bad dead."[48] One effect of this claim was to equalize all oppressed people. With historical context and larger structural dynamics erased, what they all had in common was their suffering.

MSF also began to move beyond the traditional humanitarian principle of neutrality by promoting the practice of "témoignage." Kouchner and his allies believed that keeping silent made them accomplices of suffering, oppression, or genocide. It was imperative that they share what they had seen, and that meant making full use of the media. Of course, humanitarians had long used vivid images, emotional appeals, and riveting news stories in their campaigns, but Kouchner went further, combining the old '68er emphasis on attention-grabbing spectacle with the New Philosopher's mastery over the newly emerging mediasphere. In his view, orchestrating a media uproar, or a "tapage médiatique," to dominate airtime, coax celebrity endorsements, and stir the emotions of viewers was just as vital to the success of a humanitarian campaign as the actual relief work. Historian Michael Barnett argues that Kouchner believed "a primary purpose of relief was to generate publicity and international action; that is, MSF's relief operations might save some lives directly, but the real value in the operations was their ability to attract concerted action."[49]

Lastly, Kouchner increasingly insisted on a right to intervene. While this impulse was also not entirely new, Kouchner once again tested its limits by linking the idea of intervention to other related concepts, such as "engagement," so dear to French intellectuals; "militantisme," a term borrowed from the radical lexicon; and "urgence," which framed humanitarian intervention as a kind of state of emergency in which the swift need for medical attention to save lives could justify the suspension of official rules. For Kouchner, it was up to individuals to take urgent action to save those in need, wherever they may be and whoever they may be, even if that meant interfering in the internal affairs of another country. In later years, Kouchner would develop this approach into the "droit d'ingérence."[50]

The consolidation of this new kind of radicalized humanitarianism ran parallel with the spectacular rise of human rights in the same decade. "The revelations of Alexander Solzhenitsyn, the Helsinki conference, the proliferation of dictatorships in Latin America, the crisis in revolutionary ideologies after the failure of the socialist experiments in the Third World, and the 1977 award of the Nobel Peace Prize to Amnesty International," Rony Brauman later explained, "all created a widespread agreement in French society on the primacy of human rights."[51] As historian Eleanor Davey has noted, despite their differences, the strain of radical humanitarianism represented by MSF and the kind of individualist human rights represented by Amnesty began to converge in the final years of the decade.[52]

Human rights allowed MSF to ground humanitarian practice in a coherent conception of internationalism. Kouchner's wing of MSF began in part as an internal critique of anti-imperialist self-determination. Dissatisfied, Kouchner and his colleagues began by exposing its contradictions, then pushing the idea to its limits. When their project mutated into something else, they cast about for an alternative way of thinking internationalism. Human rights provided just such a vision. "The questions of human rights, freedom, and dignity are the motifs of the end of this century," the former anti-imperialist and MSF co-founder Xavier Emmanuelli explained, "and we are speaking today of orienting Méde cins Sans Frontières' action towards this field of morality and justice."[53]

At the same time, MSF's radical pedigree helped to further confirm human rights as a legitimate successor to the progressive aspirations of the 1960s and early 1970s. Kouchner repeatedly branded MSF as an heir to 1968, a number of MSF members had espoused some kind of radicalism in their youth, and several of its most visible leaders – such as Kouchner, Brauman, and Emmanuelli – were once committed anti-imperialists. Despite MSF's political ambiguities, Kouchner's wing managed to preserve its radical credentials by aligning itself with some of the same struggles – especially in places like Palestine or Nicaragua – that many anti-imperialists supported in the 1970s.[54]

In addition to investing human rights with a more radical aura, MSF expanded the appeal of human rights internationalism by deepening its activist repertoire. While the moderate forms of activism promoted by most human rights groups were well suited for those seeking to change the world without the maximalist commitments of radicalism, this tepid approach did little to attract others looking for an alternative to anti-imperialism without having to replace a high level of militant engagement with letter-writing campaigns. MSF helped fill the gap. Its partial origins within the anti-imperialist left allowed MSF to funnel some of the bold, confrontational, and personally transformative activism of the anti-imperialists into the camp of human rights, and in the process recruited those who hungered for militant action. Just as Che Guevara offered the model of the selfless radical guerrilla hopping around the globe to advance the world revolution under the banner of anti-imperialism, MSF helped fashion the model of the selfless radical humanitarian racing across the planet to save victims under the banner of human rights.[55] MSF, in other words, could be especially appealing to those restless anti-imperialists most enamored with the voluntarist currents of the time, taking advantage of some of the intriguing overlaps between the individualistic adventurism of some radicals in the 1960s and the kind of individualism so central to human rights in the 1970s.

While the astonishing success of human rights among activists in the late 1970s had many causes, the defection of so many former radicals, particularly in France, was crucial in tipping the scales. These figures brought with them ideas, contacts, networks, resources, experiences, and styles of activism that allowed human rights to channel some of what had once made anti-imperialism so appealing. In this way, they helped human rights become the basis of a robust activist internationalism in its own right. The only answer to the "International of States," Julliard declared in 1978, was to create an "International of Human Rights."[56]

The Third Indochina War

In the final few years of the 1970s, radicalism found itself in serious trouble. Against the backdrop of defeat, hemorrhaging support, and a changed political landscape, most of the older groups had collapsed, and those that survived shrank in influence. The radical ideas that many once took for granted came under merciless bombardment. The hegemony that radicals had won over the broader left was in doubt, as anti-imperialism slowly lost the support of a shrinking pool of progressives, who now began looking for alternatives. To make matters worse, some former radicals were jumping ship, turning their guns on their erstwhile comrades, and strengthening a competing vision of internationalism that posed a grave challenge to anti-imperialism.

The crisis of radical anti-imperialism did not spell its end, however. Crisis is not death, but rather the destabilization of the old order in a way that creates opportunities. As a few optimistic radicals pointed out, this was a chance for anti-imperialists to reinvent themselves into a more effective, inclusive, and sophisticated force. Although reduced to a small core, those anti-imperialists who remained true to their convictions fought to regain their lost influence. They exposed the New Philosophers as sound-bite charlatans, slammed Julliard's scurrilous article as a species of neocolonial apologism, and tried their best to enrich radical politics in the late 1970s.[57] But defeat after defeat, at home as well as abroad, kept setting them back, making it extremely difficult to reinvent anti-imperialist internationalism for this new conjuncture. In the midst of this rearguard struggle, something inconceivable was brewing in Southeast Asia, the so-called "cradle of revolutions."[58]

Although radicals tried to stay as informed as possible about the struggles in Southeast Asia, there was much they did not know, and could not know – especially given how much the United States and Southeast Asian communists deliberately obscured. For instance, many radicals assumed that the Khmer Rouge were the Cambodian equivalent of the National Liberation Front, and that the two were harmoniously united in the same struggle for emancipation, a belief encouraged by the communist leaders of these very movements. The reality, however, was much more complex. While the Khmer Rouge did claim Leninism as a shared source, and also allied with Vietnamese communists, their leaders developed a ferociously nationalist variant of communism that complicated their internationalism.[59] Nowhere was this more apparent than in the Khmer Rouge's frosty relations with Vietnam. From the start some Cambodian communists distrusted their Vietnamese neighbors. They denounced the Vietnamese people for annexing ancient Khmer territory in their southward push in the seventeenth century. They recalled with bitterness how the French had elevated Vietnamese above Khmers during the colonial period, leaving Cambodia not simply undeveloped but administered by many Vietnamese civil servants. They despised the paternalistic attitude of those Vietnamese who fashioned themselves as the vanguards of the "Indochinese revolution." And they criticized the Vietnamese communists for collaborating with the neutralist Prince Sihanouk, who allowed them to use base areas in Cambodia, instead of supporting the Khmer Rouge.[60]

This tense relationship worsened after Sihanouk's ouster in 1970 motivated Vietnamese communists to play a direct role in Cambodian affairs. Infuriated, the fanatically nationalist Khmer Rouge leaders suspected a Vietnamese takeover.[61] Although ostensibly allies, the Khmer Rouge became openly anti-Vietnamese, and they attacked, and even killed, Vietnamese communists in the early 1970s. Relations degraded further when the Khmer Rouge seized power in 1975. Almost immediately after Vietnamese communists took Saigon, Khmer Rouge forces invaded Phú Quốc, Vietnam's largest island, claiming it as Cambodian territory. In retaliation, the Vietnamese military recaptured the seized territory, but then attacked one of Cambodia's own islands. In the years that followed, the Khmer Rouge not only slaughtered Vietnamese villagers in former Khmer territory but also systematically repressed ethnic Vietnamese in Cambodia. The Khmer Rouge's aggressive irredentist foreign policies were directly linked to their domestic project of purification. Under Pol Pot's leadership, the Khmer Rouge created a new government called Democratic Kampuchea (DK), which emptied the cities, militarized the economy, herded people into camps, and targeted hundreds of thousands for extermination. In the end, nearly a quarter of Cambodia's population died of disease, overwork, starvation, and execution, including much of the ethnic Vietnamese community.[62] Although most radicals in the North Atlantic suspected things had gone awry, many believed that the reports of genocide in DK exaggerated the violence, overemphasized communist savagery, and downplayed the role of the United States in disrupting the region.[63] After all, so many of the official claims made about Southeast Asia over the previous decade turned out to be outright lies. In this context, quite a few radicals hoped that communists abroad might find a peaceful solution to the crisis in Cambodia, the conflict between DK and Vietnam, and the brewing tensions between all the revolutionary governments in the region.

But as it turned out, the situation was only growing worse, not just in Cambodia, but also in Vietnam and China. Although Vietnamese and Chinese communists were once firm allies, the friendship between the Socialist Republic of Vietnam and the People's Republic of China began to sour. A major factor was the split between the USSR and the PRC, which turned Vietnam into a battleground in the competition for international influence. In the late 1960s, for instance, the USSR urged Vietnamese to negotiate with the United States in the Paris peace talks, but Chinese fears of growing Soviet influence over Hanoi led the former to protest vigorously.[64] In the early 1970s, China's rapprochement with the United States annoyed Vietnamese communists.[65] In the mid-1970s, Vietnamese revolutionaries grew more critical, marginalized pro-Chinese elements in the Vietnamese Workers' Party, and censured China for betraying internationalist unity. For its part, China now saw Vietnam as firmly in the pocket of the USSR. After the communist victory of 1975, fears of encirclement led Beijing to counterbalance growing Vietnamese power by fortifying relations with DK, which was only too happy to find an ally in its struggle against Vietnam.[66] This, in turn, prompted a war-torn Vietnam desperate for aid to align itself even more closely with the USSR. In November 1978, the SRV signed a treaty of friendship and cooperation with the Soviets that promised not only economic support but also Soviet backing in the event of Chinese aggression.

Disturbed by the Khmer Rouge's domestic policies, border incursions into Vietnam, and deepening alliance with China, the Socialist Republic of Vietnam decided to put an end to Pol Pot's regime once and for all by invading Democratic Kampuchea in December 1978. Two weeks later, the Khmer Rouge were on the run, and Vietnam established a friendly provisional government staffed by Khmer communists who had turned against Pol Pot's regime. But the fighting continued, and the PRC rushed to the aid of its Khmer allies. After informing US President Jimmy Carter of its intention to "teach Vietnam a lesson," Beijing invaded Vietnam on February 11, 1979.[67] The Soviets deployed forces on the Sino-Soviet border.[68] The United States moved an aircraft carrier into the South China Sea, and Carter's National Security Advisor Zbigniew Brzezinski gave the Chinese ambassador regular intelligence reports on Soviet troop movements.[69] World war appeared imminent. Only a few years after winning peace, Southeast Asia had once more become a geopolitical powder keg, though this time between countries all governed by Leninists preaching internationalism. Although the PRC withdrew after three weeks, tens of thousands perished, northern Vietnam was ravaged, and China continued to arm Pol Pot's guerrilla war against Vietnamese forces in Cambodia. At the same time, the United States convinced other countries to impose an embargo that reduced the SRV to a kind of pariah state. And for the next decade Vietnam would occupy Cambodia under the leadership of none other than Lê Đức Thọ, chief negotiator of the Paris Peace Accords and recipient of the Nobel Peace Prize.[70]

Since anti-imperialists in the North Atlantic had invested so much affective energy into this region, projected so many of their desires onto the revolutions there, and based so much of their identity on the fate of national liberation in Southeast Asia, the Third Indochina War devastated radicals like few other events. It complicated the story that many had told themselves about the region, shattered their illusions about the revolutions they had long defended, shook their political identity to its core, and left thousands of radicals baffled. The fact that the war involved the very Leninist movements that radicals had long considered the paragons of anti-imperialist internationalism could not help but sow disappointment, demoralization, and disillusionment. As Daniel Bensaïd of the Revolutionary Communist League explained: If the first fall of Phnom Penh in 1975 – followed just weeks later by the fall of Saigon – was the "highest symbol of the struggle against imperialism and the rallying point of militant internationalism across the world," then this "second" fall of Phnom Penh, now at the hands of Vietnam, "concentrates to the point of tragedy this 'illogical moment' in the history of humanity."[71]

The confounding nature of the war led those anti-imperialist radicals with fight still left in them to declare war on one another. Although they always had something to disagree about, radicals knew to put aside their differences when it came to choosing between US intervention and the Vietnamese revolution. The Third Indochina War, however, disrupted alliances, scrambled the old political coordinates, and blurred lines that were once so clear. To be sure, a few radicals tried to take a balanced approach. José Sanchez of the Unified Socialist Party, for instance, welcomed the fall of Pol Pot's genocidal regime but objected to Vietnam "deliberately violating the sovereignty of an independent State," which opened Hanoi up to charges of "imperialism."[72] Daniel Bensaïd, to take another example, argued that, while China and Cambodia's hostile actions compelled Vietnam to act, radicals everywhere had to condemn the SRV for violating the core principles of internationalism and demand the "immediate withdrawal" of Vietnamese troops from Cambodia.[73]

But many others took a side. A few publicly defended the Khmer Rouge as victims of Vietnamese aggression.[74] Others supported Vietnam. One radical, for instance, argued that "there is nothing questionable" about Vietnamese "lending a helping hand to the struggle of the real Khmer communists" in their war against Pol Pot's regime.[75] Citing France's shameful nonintervention policy during the Spanish Civil War, he argued that the duty of real internationalists was precisely to involve themselves in civil wars of this kind. Overthrowing Pol Pot, then, was proof that Vietnamese communists remained true to their internationalist bona fides. Still others sided with China. Maoist groups such as the Revolutionary Communist Party argued that Vietnam's expansionism left Beijing with no choice but to launch a "defensive action" against Vietnamese "aggressions." China was not merely defending its right to national sovereignty, the Revolutionary Communist Party continued, its swift action was "helping to reduce the danger of world war," and in this sense was in full accord with "the interests of the peoples of the world." China's invasion, then, was the high point of internationalism.[76]

This was of course not the first time that radicals had split so sharply over a thorny international issue, but their discord now assumed a different magnitude. Constant attacks at home left radicals pricklier than usual. The unexpectedness of the war gave their responses a frantic tone. The emotional ties that so many radicals had forged with the revolutionary movements now at war made their polemics all the more heated.

Most importantly, the incomprehensible toll of the long struggles in China, Vietnam, and Cambodia raised the stakes to unimaginable heights. The Vietnamese revolution, the Chinese Civil War, the First Indochina War, the Great Leap Forward, the Second Indochina War, the Cultural Revolution, the Cambodian Civil War, the Khmer Rouge's murderous regime, and the Third Indochina War had caused untold death, destruction, and devastation. This was no mere academic debate, but a visceral crisis in which one's political position was directly connected to millions of deaths. At the very moment when the beleaguered radical left most needed unity, the shrinking radical ecosystem grew even more disoriented, fissiparous, and combative – so much so that one current of anti-imperialists turned on the others with such vehemence that it found itself allied with the United States against Vietnam.

The Anti-Vietnam International

Over the course of the 1970s, the People's Republic of China pursued a new direction. Although Mao Zedong still considered himself a communist internationalist, and the PRC continued to project itself as a radical anti-imperialist force, the Chinese Communist Party stepped up its opposition to those countries aligned with the USSR, attacked revolutionary movements backed by the Soviets, decreased aid to liberation struggles such as those in Vietnam, drew much closer to the United States, normalized relations with the United Nations, imported new technology from capitalist countries abroad, and gradually opened China to capitalist world markets.[77] To justify this bewildering shift, and guide the PRC's foreign policy in the years to come, Mao adumbrated a new theory of the world situation, later codified as the "Three Worlds Theory," which Deng Xiaoping officially presented to the world at the United Nations General Assembly in New York on April 10, 1974.[78]

The theory divided the globe into three worlds based less on political orientation than on economic and military power. The "First" was composed of the two superpowers, the United States and the Soviet Union; the "Second" included all the developed countries, primarily the advanced capitalist powers of Western Europe; and the "Third" comprised the developing world. According to the theory, the competition between the two superpowers for global hegemony would lead to instability, even world war. It was therefore up to the "Third World" to build the largest possible international front to repel the "imperialism, colonialism and hegemonism" of these two superpowers, especially the Soviet Union, which Beijing identified as the main threat to world peace.[79] While the "Third World," naturally led by China, constituted the core of this front, it needed to win the help of countries in the "Second World," especially Europe, now deemed a strategic focal point of the world situation. Faced with the growing threat of war, and needing to defend their "national independence" from the encroachment of the superpowers, it was in the best interest of "Second World" countries like France to join this international front.[80]

The theory stretched the Leninist problematic of the right of nations to self-determination to its limits.[81] It elevated national sovereignty as the end goal of politics, championed the widest national fronts possible, and completely substituted the contradiction between nations for those between classes. Those Maoist radicals who adopted this iteration of anti-imperialism followed China's lead by downplaying all domestic struggles in favor of building national unity to fight the "hegemonism" of the two superpowers. Across Western Europe they promoted the most extreme nationalism in the hopes of pushing their respective countries into an alliance with the "Third World" against the superpowers. In France, for example, the Marxist-Leninist Communist Party (successor to the Marxist-Leninist Communist Party of France) allied with Gaullists, monarchists, and even elements of the extreme right to defend French national sovereignty against the United States and the Soviet Union.[82] Internationalism had become national chauvinism.

The PRC did more than just urge loyal Maoists to foster national unity at home. Beijing encouraged them to create a kind of coordinated pro-Chinese international that stretched from Argentina to France to East Germany to Cambodia. In contrast to the 1960s, China now took special interest in cultivating ties in North America, and especially Western Europe, the core of the "Second World" and – it hoped – a key ally in the fight against the superpowers. For their part, devoted parties in the North Atlantic were only too eager to contribute. In 1976, for example, the October League – a Maoist formation that attracted many activists from the dissolved Students for a Democratic Society (SDS), as well as some older communists like Harry Haywood – ran a series of articles introducing American readers to the fraternal parties in Western Europe, the prime battleground in the fight against "hegemonism."[83] "US Marxist-Leninists have a lot to learn from the communist movement in the countries of the second world," the League explained. "In many cases, they have longer and broader experience in both the class struggle and the struggle against modern revisionism. The workers in all countries have always learned and supported each other, and it is in this proletarian internationalist spirit that this series is written."[84] In December, they published a lengthy interview with Jacques Jurquet, leader of the Marxist-Leninist Communist Party (MLCP). In June 1977, when Maoists reorganized the October League as a formal vanguard party with Beijing's blessing, the French MLCP saluted them on the front page of its paper: "The creation of your Party, in the very heart of one of the two most aggressive imperialisms of the present epoch, is a harsh blow to the international bourgeoisie."[85]

In addition to binding these parties closer together, these rituals harmonized them behind the PRC. What held this international together was unanimity on the correct ideological line broadcast from Beijing. Its organizing principle was the People's Republic of China, its theoretical core the Three Worlds Theory. Whatever the issue, the PRC could expect a united chorus to echo its line throughout the world. In this way, the international's tight coordination compensated for its numerical weaknesses. Indeed, with the exception of Norway, which boasted a Maoist party with about 5,000 members, most pro-Chinese parties never claimed more than 1,000 members at their height. But they amplified their power by working in unison, trumpeting the same line at the same time in every major country in the North Atlantic. It was precisely this machine that sprang into action when Vietnam invaded Cambodia in December 1978.

Since the Khmer Rouge were China's closest allies in Southeast Asia, these pro-Chinese parties immediately turned against Vietnam. They excoriated the SRV for violating Cambodia's national sovereignty. They compared the SRV's offensive to US intervention in Vietnam. They even blamed Vietnam for the misery in Cambodia, falsely stating that the SRV, not the Khmer Rouge, had perpetrated genocide. In the United States, former 3D3 leader Carl Davidson called the invasion a "war of extermination."[86] In France, the MLCP – whose leader, Jacques Jurquet, had visited Pol Pot in September 1978 – claimed that Vietnam had knowingly unleashed a "holocaust" in Cambodia.[87] Some French radicals suggested that Vietnam was planning to colonize the occupied territories after eradicating the Cambodian people, just as the Nazis had tried to do in Eastern Europe. The MLCP saw the invasion as blatant "settler colonialism."[88] The Revolutionary Communist Party added that Vietnam would not stop with Cambodia but planned to colonize all of Southeast Asia.[89]

While one might dismiss these accusations as the ravings of marginal extremists, in countries like France pro-Chinese radicals played a surprising role in shaping the broader discourse surrounding the crisis in Southeast Asia. They did this by downplaying their radical views, in particular their support of Pol Pot, and building as wide a united front as possible. They began by linking with other pro-Chinese radicals, then built solidarity with Cambodians living in France, and finally reached out to unions, universities, and religious institutions. In January 1979, the MLCP gathered signatures for a call to solidarity with the Cambodian people, which they published in *Le Monde*. "We who once supported the struggles of the Vietnamese, Laotian, and Cambodian peoples against American aggression," the statement read, "condemn the occupation of this country by the Vietnamese army and denounce it as an infringement of the independence of a State and of a people."[90] In addition to confirming their radical credentials, recalling the Vietnam War in this manner allowed these activists to legitimate their campaign by grounding it in the same principle of national self-determination that had guided the anti-imperialist struggle against the United States.

These radicals also looked to the old antiwar struggles for organizational models. The MLCP founded a Kampuchea Committee, modeled on the National Vietnam Committee and the Vietnam Base Committees, in which some of these activists had once participated.[91] As in the Vietnam War, these anti-Vietnam radicals internationalized their campaign. After a preparatory meeting held in Paris over the summer of 1979, they drew on the networks of the pro-Chinese international to unite over 250 delegates from over 30 countries – including Khmer Rouge militants such as Minister of Social Affairs Ieng Thirith – at the International Conference of Solidarity with Kampuchea in Stockholm on November 17, 1979.[92] To reach the widest audience possible, organizers encouraged sympathetic journalists, artists, scientists, academics, priests, and politicians to endorse the event. They secured the support of such luminaries as philosopher Alain Badiou, filmmaker Joris Ivens, and writer Albert Memmi.[93] Folk singer Joan Baez sent a message of support and the Swedish writer Jan Myrdal delivered a rousing speech.[94] "Our work of solidarity," he said, could "mean the life or death of an entire generation in Kampuchea, maybe even for the Khmers as a nation and people as well."[95]

These activists formed an international movement, the Cambodian Solidarity Movement, and organized a series of other events, including two more international conferences in Tokyo and Paris.[96] Echoing the language of the old antiwar struggles, this new movement's platform condemned Vietnam for violating Cambodian national sovereignty, demanded the withdrawal of Vietnamese troops, and insisted on the Cambodian people's inviolable right to self-determination. In the fight for the "liberation and independence of Cambodia," it also called on activists to support all Cambodian struggles without exclusion – which really meant supporting the Khmer Rouge. Significantly, the Cambodian Solidarity Movement tried to bolster its demands by appealing to the principle of nonintervention enshrined in the United Nations Charter. All these efforts helped the pro-Chinese activists become a part of the mainstream discussion.[97]

Pro-Chinese parties also found allies in nongovernmental organizations such as MSF, the International Committee of the Red Cross (ICRC), and the United Nations Children's Fund (UNICEF), which were also turning their attention to the humanitarian disaster in Southeast Asia. The Vietnamese invasion, which aggravated years of social dislocation under the Khmer Rouge, triggered a demographic catastrophe. Cambodians freed from the work camps rushed to escape, while others fled in panic, spurred on by Khmer Rouge propaganda, which claimed that Vietnamese troops would slaughter everyone in their path. The retreating Khmer Rouge abducted thousands more at gunpoint, driving them into crowded camps on the Thai border to serve as slave laborers, human shields, or soldiers for the resistance. In this context, humanitarian organizations like MSF soon made the Cambodian border a priority.[98]

But the situation inside Cambodia appeared even worse. As they retreated from the Vietnamese military, the Khmer Rouge appropriated, and in some cases destroyed, significant amounts of rice. When Vietnamese troops closed the collective farms, hundreds of thousands of Cambodians abandoned the recently planted crop to return to their home villages. Against the backdrop of ongoing war, many more harvests were lost in the fighting, and the main 1979 crop went largely unplanted, virtually ensuring a famine.[99] Humanitarian organizations begged the new People's Republic of Kampuchea and its Vietnamese benefactors to allow them into the country. Although they needed the assistance, the authorities downplayed the magnitude of the crisis. When they finally agreed, they imposed strict requirements. Fearing infiltration, foreign intervention, and the possibility of aid falling into the hands of Khmer Rouge forces amassing in the border camps, they forbade humanitarian organizations from entering Cambodia unless they surrendered control of distribution to the new government and promised to abandon the refugee camps on the border. Their fears were not entirely unjustified: The Khmer Rouge had appropriated large quantities of medical supplies, organizations like the ICRC and UNICEF were knowingly working in camps controlled by the Khmer Rouge, and the White House was well aware that these relief operations were helping Cambodian guerrillas fight Vietnamese forces. This aid was keeping Pol Pot's ousted regime alive.[100]

That said, Vietnam's stance aggravated the crisis, which infuriated the humanitarians.[101] This in turn led the pro-Chinese international to see them as potential allies against Vietnam. Recognizing the growing attention to the humanitarian crisis, the international Cambodian Solidarity Movement made the call for immediate medical relief the central pillar of its program.[102] In France, the MLCP hosted public events to explain how Vietnam blocked humanitarian groups such as MSF, the ICRC, and UNICEF from entering Cambodia, calling on activists to put pressure on Vietnam, support humanitarian efforts, and donate to groups like the ICRC and UNICEF.[103] Since these latter two organizations were working in camps with the Khmer Rouge, the MLCP signaled them out in particular, praising their work as "positive" for the struggle.[104]

Some humanitarians agreed to collaborate with the pro-Chinese. In November 1979, an MSF worker who had just returned from refugee camps on the Thai border accepted an interview with *L'Humanité rouge*, the Marxist-Leninist Communist Party's newspaper. Choosing to remain anonymous, the MSF activist made damning remarks about the Vietnamese-installed government in Phnom Penh. "There is a paradox we have to emphasize: there are volunteers, there are people, there is money, there are donations, in short, all the means are in place to offer massive assistance, which, probably, would be extremely effective in Cambodia. And all that is blocked."[105] The situation grew so intolerable that a month later MSF as a whole decided to intervene in Cambodian affairs. "Today, in Cambodia, children starve to death in front of tons of rice," began their call to action, published in the major newspapers. "But the hundreds of doctors, surgeons, and nurses whom we are holding ready have for months found themselves forbidden from entering the country."[106] Tired of waiting on the Vietnamese authorities, MSF took matters into its own hands, organizing a campaign, the "March for Survival," to forcibly enter Cambodia to save the dying. The MLCP quickly endorsed MSF's call, pleased with the growing front against Vietnam.

By late 1979 many activists, lawyers, humanitarians, intellectuals, and politicians were coming to agree that something akin to genocide was happening in Cambodia – not the prior genocide committed by the Khmer Rouge, but an allegedly new one under the Vietnamese occupation. Aid agencies blasted the airwaves with advertisements warning of two million dead by Christmas.[107] François Bugnion of the ICRC compared Cambodia to Buchenwald. Claude Malhuret, who had been active on the Thai border since 1976 before becoming MSF's president, spoke to the rightwing *Le Figaro* about an impending "massacre" in Cambodia, comparing the Vietnamese invasion to the Armenian genocide.[108] Kouchner spoke of the "extinction of Cambodian children," proclaiming that "Genocide is happening every evening, over supper."[109] The New Philosophers also chimed in, with Bernard-Henri Lévy speaking of a "new look final solution."[110] Even mainstream French politicians joined the chorus, with Foreign Minister Jean François-Poncet warning that Cambodians were "on the edge of extinction."[111]

Nearly identical statements were heard across North America and Western Europe. They reached a fever pitch in the United States. *Time Magazine* called Cambodia the "Auschwitz of Asia," First Lady Rosalyn Carter visited a refugee camp to raise awareness about the new holocaust, and the president himself spoke of genocide.[112] Smarting from its defeat in Vietnam, the United States relished in Vietnam's discomfiture, accusing the Vietnamese military of looting peasants, destroying food stocks, hoarding outside aid, and murdering Cambodians. The Carter administration not only condemned Vietnam, but also tacitly backed the ongoing guerrilla war against Vietnamese forces. The United States provided the Khmer resistance with humanitarian aid, US representatives nixed a proposal from the Association of Southeast Asian Nations to disarm the Cambodian guerrillas, and the White House secretly supported Chinese efforts to arm the Khmer Rouge.[113] For all his talk of a new direction after years of deception and war, the liberal Carter was now effectively on the same side as mass murderers. While the White House kept much of this under wraps, it did express public support for Pol Pot's deposed DK government. In September 1979, the United States voted with the majority at the UN General Assembly to formally recognize Democratic Kampuchea – a regime responsible for the deaths of millions – as the rightful voice of the Cambodian people.

More than simply drawing attention to a humanitarian crisis, then, the language of genocide served a clear political function. Genocide does not just happen on its own – someone is responsible. It could not be the Khmer Rouge because they had been ousted nearly a year ago. Nor the new People's Republic of Kampuchea, since this government was widely seen as a mere puppet of the occupying Vietnamese forces. The only possible answer was Vietnam itself. While some politicians left this conclusion implicit, many others tried to draw it into the open. Brzezinski, for instance, pushed state agencies to unambiguously name Vietnam as the perpetrator of genocide, thereby downplaying the actual mass murder perpetrated by the Khmer Rouge.[114] In this way, the unlikely alliance between Maoists, humanitarian organizations, the mainstream media, and both liberal and conservative politicians created the widespread impression that Vietnamese were deliberately committing genocide in Cambodia, just as the Nazis had done only a few decades before in Europe.

This was how the fanatical ravings of a tiny group of pro-Chinese radicals on the political margins helped shape mainstream discourse.

Although their concrete influence on the postwar settlement in Southeast Asia was limited, and the campaign did little to reverse their declining fortunes, they could take pride in having played a part in this outcome. Still, the whole affair left them in an awkward position: They were now on the same side as the United States, a country they had once denounced as the number one enemy of all the peoples of the world. There was perhaps no clearer symbol of how far anti-imperialist internationalism had fallen. In less than a decade, these radicals went from fighting US imperialism in Vietnam to joining hands with conservatives, siding with renegades like Bernard-Henri Lévy, and becoming objective allies of the United States against what they now called Vietnamese imperialism. In responding to the crisis of anti-imperialism by doubling down on the idea of the right of nations to self-determination, these pro-Chinese radicals made possible a kind of monstrous internationalism. Changing the world in an emancipatory direction now meant extolling national identity, unquestioningly defending nation-states abroad, and allying with the most ruthless imperialist governments to advance the narrow interests of nationalist regimes. If Leninism's promise was to harmonize communism-building and nation-building, the pro-Chinese replaced the former with the latter.

Meltdown

Perhaps the greatest effect of the Third Indochina War on radicals in the North Atlantic was to challenge the core assumptions of the Leninist problematic. This was in large part because radicals had long regarded the Vietnamese revolution as the prime test case for Leninist anti-imperialism and for a few years convinced themselves that it had passed with flying colors. Armed with the problematic as their guide, Vietnamese communists not only destroyed French colonial rule, defeated US intervention, overthrew the Republic of Vietnam, unified their divided country, and began the process of building socialism, but also galvanized countless other struggles, united diverse political forces across borders, shook the entire imperialist system, and popularized a politics of universal emancipation. Vietnam showed that Leninism worked.

Yet by the end of the decade the Vietnamese revolution had clearly run into problems. The economy was in crisis, depoliticization set in, people fled their homes, and the new state waged war against its neighbors. Of course, much of this can be traced back to decades of imperial domination, and Vietnamese revolutionaries could hardly be faulted for not having built a flawless society in a few years. Given the enormous challenges that Vietnamese communists faced after seizing power, most

radicals believed that many of the unsavory features of Vietnam's postwar communist government were justified. In their view, for example, it
was perfectly reasonable for communists to want to punish those leaders of the Republic of Vietnam who had allied with the United States to
exterminate countless revolutionaries fighting for a freer, more egalitarian world. If anything, the fact that the communists scheduled them for
reeducation instead of annihilation showed that the SRV was heading in
an emancipatory direction. But even many of these sympathetic radicals
had to admit that Vietnamese communists had made a few questionable decisions. The communists canceled promised elections, relocated
hundreds of thousands of people to special economic zones, abolished
regional automony for Vietnam's many ethnic minorities, subordinated
independent democratic politics to state supremacy, turned the party
into a kind of oligarchic ruling body, and abrogated the very civil liberties they had once claimed to champion in the South. The party-state
even turned on loyal revolutionaries, which led to widespread feelings of
betrayal, demoralization, and disillusionment, especially among southern militants.[115] In August 1978, a figure as dedicated as Trương Như
Tảng, one of the founders of the National Liberation Front and later the
Provisional Revolutionary Government's minister of justice, decided to
flee the country.[116] He would eventually be joined by hundreds of thousands of others, including communists such as Bùi Tín.

While it is true that these mistakes stemmed in part from unfavorable
conditions, improper execution, unexpected challenges, internal divisions,
uneven leadership, and institutional inertia, part of the blame rests on the
Leninist ideas that were so central for those revolutionaries like Lê Duẩn
who called the shots. This is not at all to say that everything that happened
in Vietnam was the direct outcome of problems inherent to Leninism.
There was, after all, a very high degree of contingency in postwar Vietnam. Nonetheless, the problematic undeniably informed how revolutionaries responded to those contingent challenges: It fixed their assumptions,
filtered their options, determined the field of the possible, and foreclosed
other routes. The culpability of Leninism becomes even clearer when one
considers the fact that other revolutionaries who followed the problematic
ended up facing many of the same difficulties. One need look no further
than Vietnam's Leninist neighbors.

Although the three liberation struggles that found themselves at the
heart of the Third Indochina War involved different people with different personalities in different countries facing different situations, they all
encountered a similar set of problems linked to Leninism. In all three
cases the Leninist problematic's promise to eliminate national oppression
through nation-building led to a kind of primordialist nationalism that

sanctioned the oppression of national minorities, encouraged chauvinism at home, and fueled expansionist tendencies abroad. In all three cases the problematic's promise to win freedom from the state through the construction of a new kind of state led to the consolidation of hypertrophic party-states that repressed civil liberties, demolished autonomous politics, and redefined universal emancipation as statist development. In all three cases, the problematic's promise to mobilize national liberation as the basis of an internationalist struggle to build a world beyond capitalist imperialism led to border skirmishes, territorial annexation, geopolitical maneuvering, and war. It was in the Third Indochina War, in other words, that the internal contradictions at the heart of the Leninist problematic exploded most poignantly.[117]

As if that were not bad enough, all sides in the Third Indochina War justified their actions with recourse to Leninism. Democratic Kampuchea rationalized its incursions into Vietnam by claiming it was exercising its right to self-determination by reclaiming stolen national territory. The SRV justified its invasion of Cambodia by asserting that the Cambodian people asked for Vietnam's internationalist assistance to help fight for their right to self-determination from the hated Khmer Rouge oppressors. The People's Republic of China claimed that its counterattack was a preemptive operation to protect its national sovereignty from an expansionist neighbor that had already violated the Cambodian nation's right to self-determination.

And yet their attempts to marshal Leninist concepts to explain why things had turned out the way they had all fell flat. Drawing on elements of Lenin's theory, China argued that Soviet leaders had turned the USSR's socialist economy into a "state monopoly capitalist economy," a kind of capitalism in which banks, finance, and monopolistic firms had fused with the state apparatus.[118] At the same time, Soviet leaders had turned the Soviet socialist state into a "fascist dictatorship."[119] And this in turn had made possible what Chinese communists called "social imperialism," which they claimed was very similar to capitalist imperialism, except that it masqueraded under the flag of revolution, which made it more dangerous.[120] Capitalist, fascist, and imperialist, the Soviet Union now pursued "hegemonism," that is, the expansion of its hegemony across the world. In its quest to conquer the globe, the USSR's "big" or "world" hegemonism had enlisted Vietnam's "little" or "regional" hegemonism. A "pawn" of the USSR's grand schemes, Vietnam carried out incursions into neighboring countries, encroached on Chinese territory, and invaded Cambodia to exert its hegemony over the region. Upholding "proletarian internationalism," the PRC was duty-bound to come to Cambodia's aid.[121]

The Vietnamese take was little better. In their view, "great-nation chauvinistic forces" had seized control of China in the 1950s, betrayed socialism, and embarked on Chinese hegemonism.[122] This expansionist turn, some Vietnamese thinkers argued, was actually a continuation of China's ancient imperial history. As the SRV's vice minister of foreign affairs explained to the UN General Assembly, China's "behaviours are but the revival of the Chinese emperors' concept, who considered the people around their 'Heavenly Empire' as barbarians or at best as vassals who had to be placed under domination."[123] Recognizing the value of China's "hegemonist" turn, imperialist powers led by the United States hoped to use the Chinese people as "the shock troops for international imperialism against Vietnam."[124] Goaded in this way, the PRC was extending its hegemony by fighting border wars, using ethnic Chinese minorities as "fifth columns," turning Pol Pot's Cambodia into a "Chinese neo-colony," and abetting the Khmer Rouge's irredentism. But, Vietnamese theorists explained, "the Kampuchean people could not sit idly by to let the Pol Pot clique sell out their fatherland and to await systematic massacre; consequently, they rose up in an effort to stay the hand of the Beijing agents."[125] In their fight for self-determination, the Cambodian people asked Vietnam for help. Justifying their government's actions, Vietnamese communists argued that it "is our national mission and internationalist obligation" to "oppose the expansionism and hegemonism of the Beijing reactionaries."[126]

The Khmer Rouge's explanation of the war was even more teleological. In a speech to the United Nations after the Vietnamese invasion, for example, Ieng Sary, co-founder of the Khmer Rouge, and now the public face of the deposed Democratic Kampuchea, argued that the root of the problem lay in the incorrigible expansionism of the Vietnamese people. "Already in the seventeenth century, the Vietnamese, coming down from Tonkin, which is present-day North Viet Nam, annexed and completely absorbed the Islamic Kingdom of Champa, which is now central Viet Nam, so that at present there is no longer any Cham citizen." Afterwards, the Vietnamese people pushed "even farther south and, up to very recently, annexed 65,000 square kilometers of Kampuchean territory," which has now become "present-day South Vietnam." Today, under the guise of an "Indochina Federation," Vietnam sought nothing less than "the total absorption of Kampuchea and Laos," which would in turn "serve as a spring-board for the expansion of Viet Nam throughout South-East Asia." Vietnam's "hegemonist" invasion of Cambodia, in other words, was simply the realization of ancient expansionist impulses.[127]

Although they claimed their positions were drawn from Leninist principles, not one party could offer a meaningful political assessment of the crisis within the terms of the theory developed by Lenin.[128] In the end, their answers were unconvincing, their descriptions did not align with the reality on the ground, and their theories failed to explain anything. How was capitalism restored? Why did nationalist elements seize control? Where does hegemonism come from? Why did national self-determination lead so quickly to expansionism? Why did anticapitalist revolutions end up establishing regimes that acted in ways that Marxists had long associated with capitalism? What was the relationship between socialist construction and imperialism? Why did these regimes fail to build world communism together? The very theoretical language that could formulate these problems, explain them, and evaluate them was itself now in question. The impasse, to borrow a formulation from Alessandro Russo, remained inexplicable within the horizon of the problematic in which it had taken place.[129]

In this way, the war only deepened the doubts that so many radicals were starting to express about the concepts that they had held so dear for nearly a century. The repression in Southeast Asia further discredited the idea of the vanguard party. The militant statism of the three countries dealt another blow to the increasingly untenable idea that the state could be a vehicle for emancipation. And the aggressive nationalism of the belligerents further convinced radicals that they had misunderstood the historical role of nations. Explicitly referencing the Third Indochina War in the introduction to what would become the most famous book on nationalism, Benedict Anderson admitted that "nationalism has proven an uncomfortable *anomaly* for Marxist theory and, precisely for that reason, has been largely elided, rather than confronted."[130] One theorist after another turned their attention to the topic.

Most of all, the war raised doubts about the concept of imperialism itself. According to the inherited theories, imperialism is an extension of capitalism. But the Third Indochina War saw three countries that had abolished many recognizable features of capitalism locked in a war defined by border disputes, retaliatory incursions, annexationist impulses, military occupation, and economic restructuring – in short, everything one would expect from capitalist imperialism. One way to explain the paradox while saving the theory might be to declare that the Third Indochina War was not imperialist; but that only evades the original question of what it was, how it happened, and why it looked so similar to capitalist imperialism. Another approach could be to claim that the war was ultimately caused by US imperialism; but any cursory study would show that, while the legacy of American intervention played a role, the war's causes are to be found squarely with the belligerents. One might even be tempted to argue that these actions happened because those involved were all capitalist in some way; but this runs against reality. While one could argue that China was transitioning to capitalism, it would be more difficult to say the same about Vietnam in the 1970s, and it would be a real stretch to designate as capitalist a country like Democratic Kampuchea, which at times lacked currency, markets, and financial institutions of any kind.

By revealing the limits of the Leninist problematic in so sharp a way, the Third Indochina War suggested the limits of anti-imperialist struggle as such. If the whole point of the Leninist problematic was to find a way for diverse forces to unite across borders to change the world by destroying imperialism, what did it mean for anti-imperialist politics now that revolutionaries had mobilized the same problematic to build nation-states that acted in ways that were disturbingly similar to the imperialism they had set out to abolish? What did it mean for Leninism now that the internationalism it made possible had become something very close to imperialism itself?

6   Human Rights

In 1981, just a few years before his death, Michel Foucault lent his voice to yet another cause. Flanked by photographs of suffering refugees, he spoke of the disaster in Southeast Asia.[1] In the late 1970s, hundreds of thousands of people fled communist governments in Laos, Cambodia, and Vietnam. Over the next quarter century, their numbers would swell to several million. While some left by land, many took to the seas in decrepit, teeming boats. Those fortunate enough to survive the perilous journey to neighboring Southeast Asian countries found themselves thrown into overcrowded camps. Under considerable strain, and unwilling to host any more refugees, some of these countries began to push incoming boats back to sea. By 1979, all of Southeast Asia was gripped by a humanitarian crisis of calamitous proportions.

In Geneva, Foucault promoted an International Committee of Piracy headed by Bernard Kouchner. While Foucault's support for a people in need was unsurprising, the way he chose to theorize international solidarity certainly was. Instead of drawing on the ideas that marked his earlier activism with the Maoists – such as revolution, class struggle, or the dictatorship of the proletariat – Foucault now grounded his internationalism in the notion of the "private individual." He gestured to a new "international citizenship," whose duty it was to "always bring the testimony of people's suffering to the eyes and ears of governments," to "speak out against every abuse of power, whoever its author, whoever its victims." He called for a new right, "that of private individuals to effectively intervene in the sphere of international policy and strategy."[2] He concluded his speech, subsequently published as "Confronting Governments: Human Rights," with glowing praise for the work of organizations such as Amnesty International and Doctors of the World, Kouchner's new humanitarian organization.[3]

If the Vietnamese invasion of Cambodia helped to shatter an already ailing anti-imperialist internationalism, the concomitant refugee crisis offered human rights internationalism an exceptional opportunity to fill the void. What remained of the anti-imperialist left contributed little to resolving the disaster, yet the human rights internationalists stepped into the breach. Former French radicals turned humanitarians such as Alain Geismar, André Glucksmann, Bernard Kouchner, and Claudie and Jacques Broyelle worked with Vietnamese refugees, Eastern European dissidents, and human rights groups such as Doctors Without Borders to organize a campaign against what they called "human rights violations" in Vietnam. Channeling the social movement strategies of the 1960s, they formed a committee to save the "boat people," won over intellectuals such as Michel Foucault, and chartered a hospital ship to rescue the refugees. Their campaign, which amounted to interfering in the internal affairs of a sovereign nation-state, showcased a new kind of humanitarian interventionism that promised to surpass Cold War ideological divisions.

The campaign spread internationally, entering the United States through the efforts of Joan Baez and Ginetta Sagan, leaders of the West Coast branch of Amnesty International (AI), and now directors of a new human rights organization called Humanitas. In addition to popularizing the struggle against human rights violations in Vietnam for American audiences, they worked with the Carter administration, underscoring how closely imbricated this new human rights internationalism was with statecraft, despite claims to the contrary. For his part, Jimmy Carter had already made human rights a cornerstone of his administration, though they played an ambiguous role in US foreign policy. Some used the new rights discourse to criticize pro-US dictatorships, while others wielded human rights to lambast communists in countries like Vietnam. In Southeast Asia, where the latter approach tended to predominate, politicians jumped at the "refugee issue," sensing a perfect opportunity to divert attention away from the ignoble end of the Vietnam War, make Americans feel good again, and restore US leadership in the "international community." The United States found that with human rights it could accomplish in Southeast Asia what a decade of war had failed to do.

Not even five years after the "fall of Saigon" the United States would successfully deploy human rights to rebrand itself as the moral leader of the new age. Meanwhile, the Socialist Republic of Vietnam (SRV) languished in isolation, devastated by war, weakened by sanctions, abandoned by other governments, and condemned by international public opinion. "For 10 years no people had shed as much blood as the Vietnamese to defend their independence and freedom," and yet "the press, radio, and television, in general the mass media of Western countries raced to condemn Vietnam for 'violating human rights,'" recalled Mai Văn Bộ, the Vietnamese representative who had spent most of the war years in France fighting on the diplomatic front. This "malicious" campaign, centered in the United States and France, had "caused Vietnam extremely heavy political losses."[4] Despite numerous efforts to deflect these charges of human rights violations, the SRV could do little to explain itself in the face of undeniable evidence of internal repression. By the end of the decade, Vietnamese revolutionaries had lost the ideological war they had worked so hard to win. If anti-imperialism helped secure their international victory in the 1960s, human rights sealed their defeat a decade later. Having won the war, Vietnamese communists lost the peace.

The remaining radicals in France, and especially in the United States, where human rights became state policy, fought back by exposing the White House's instrumentalist use of human rights while trying to distance themselves from an authoritarian regime they once dedicated their lives to supporting. But, however accurate their criticisms of human rights may have been, anti-imperialists had little to offer as an alternative. Mass murder in Cambodia, a refugee crisis in Vietnam, and an internecine war between China, Cambodia, and Vietnam had largely discredited the far left's project not just in Southeast Asia, but internationally. With the core notions of the Leninist problematic in question, the radical left's vision of internationalism lost its appeal, particularly among a new generation of activists looking for a way to do good in the world. And with anti-imperialism's influence over the wider progressive milieu slipping fast, human rights internationalism made a giant leap in consolidating its hegemony, so much so that even some committed anti-imperialists ended up accepting its terms as the least bad option.

Humanitarian Intervention

On the night of November 9, 1978, a rusty freighter crawled into Port Klang, Malaysia. Its cargo: around 2,500 Vietnamese refugees. Unwilling to accept more refugees, the Malaysian authorities ordered the vessel to turn back. For several weeks, the ship remained anchored beyond the port limits. Trapped at sea, the refugees struggled to survive as food, water, and medicine dwindled, while disease and misery engulfed the ship. The suffering aboard the *Hai Hong* was promptly televised to anguished audiences across the world.

After an initial round of departures in 1975, several factors converged to create a second wave of refugees in the late 1970s. Resentful anticommunist Vietnamese recently released from reeducation camps searched for ways out. The state's attempts to revive the postwar economy failed, prompting others to consider emigration. A disastrous drought, followed by devastating floods, pushed still others to flee. Most importantly of all, the communists decided to formally integrate the hitherto capitalist

South into a single socialist economy through an aggressive campaign of expropriations, nationalizations, forced collectivization, and harsh punishments.

Overrepresented in commerce, and in general wealthier than many other Vietnamese, the 1.5 million ethnic Chinese suffered perhaps the worst. The communists saw Cholon, the bustling Chinatown of Ho Chi Minh City, as not only a "strong capitalist heart beating inside the Socialist body of Vietnam" but also a den of subversion.[5] Collapsing relations with the People's Republic of China prompted many Vietnamese to view ethnic Chinese throughout Southeast Asia as a dangerous "fifth column" in the service of Beijing. Party officials ransacked homes, confiscated money, shuttered businesses, and targeted Chinese institutions.[6] Many fled, sometimes by land into China, but also by boat into the South China Sea, accounting for the vast majority of those who would soon be known as the "boat people." Escape was no easy matter. In many cases, smugglers, criminal organizations, and corrupt Vietnamese officials forced refugees to pay exorbitant prices for a place on crowded boats. Those who took to the sea risked starvation, drowning, or pirate attacks. The ones who survived were herded into deplorable camps, waiting for neighboring Southeast Asian countries to determine what to do with them. By the end of 1978, these camps housed more than 61,700 refugees, and Southeast Asian governments refused to take any more.[7]

Mounting evidence of political repression and mass exodus reached North America and Western Europe in 1978. The issue was taken up especially forcefully in France. This was in part because the country was home to a vibrant Vietnamese community, which had long played a crucial role in circulating information about Vietnam. Although most politically engaged Vietnamese remained loyal to the Socialist Republic of Vietnam, newly arrived anticommunist immigrants relied on a dense network of social groups, political organizations, journals, religious institutions, and conservative politicians like the Mayor of Paris Jacques Chirac to organize opposition to the SRV.[8] Vocal figures such as Đoàn Văn Toại eagerly shared their firsthand experiences. A former activist imprisoned by both Nguyễn Văn Thiệu and the communists, he fled Vietnam in 1978, alleging that the communists had detained some 800,000 political prisoners. Soon after arriving in Paris, he organized a campaign on their behalf. In this, he joined many other Vietnamese refugees in taking inspiration from the human rights campaigns already waged by dissidents from the Soviet Bloc.[9] "Our goal," he explained, "is to launch a campaign like those organized in the West in support of Soviet prisoners."[10] Võ Văn Ái, who founded the journal Quê Mẹ in Paris, recalls that the earliest supporters of the campaign against what were now being called human rights violations in Vietnam were the many Eastern European dissidents taking refuge in Paris.[11]

Đoàn Văn Toại formed a solidarity committee for political prisoners in Vietnam, gave numerous interviews for publications across North America and Western Europe, wrote a book documenting his experiences, and organized events with French intellectuals and Eastern European dissidents.[12] French journalists added to these revelations by producing a stream of reports condemning developments abroad. These articles were not limited to those rightwing papers like Le Figaro seeking to shame the left but could even be found in the pages of leftist publications such as Jean-Paul Sartre's Les Temps modernes. On October 5, 1978, Le Monde went so far as to link repression in Vietnam to genocide in Cambodia in an editorial titled "Peace Crimes." "Between the Cambodian genocide and the Vietnamese repression there is, of course, an enormous difference of degree. But the inspiration, alas, is of the same kind. In both cases it is to level, to eliminate, all differences that exist."[13] The editorial sparked a public discussion over the refugee crisis that involved many activists from the old antiwar campaigns.

Some of the journalists reporting on repression in the SRV were former critics of the war who had spent time in Vietnam. Writing for Le Monde, Roland-Pierre Paringaux, once a fierce critic of Thiệu's regime in the South, now turned his pen against the new communist regime. In a detailed article about human rights violations in Vietnam he asked: "Do the circumstances justify how the communist regime of Hanoi today – just like the anticommunist regime of Saigon yesterday – systematically resorts to repression and preventative detention on the basis of mere suspicion or denunciation – which it has elevated to a civic duty – and leaves to rot in camps all those who do not conform to the new model, thereby aggravating their hatred and desperation?" Recalling the explosive issue of political imprisonment in the early 1970s, he lamented how those involved in the massive international campaign to defend political prisoners in South Vietnam had gone silent.[14]

In fact, some former antiwar radicals in France were about to act. They were just waiting for a dramatic symbol. When news of the Hai Hong broke, they found their "opportunity" to get the campaign underway.[15] That very night, Claudie and Jacques Broyelle called Bernard Kouchner to organize a strategy session. Meeting in the offices of Continent, a publication by Soviet dissidents in Paris, Võ Văn Ái, the Broyelles, Kouchner, Alain Geismar, André Glucksmann, Bernard-Henri Lévy and others discussed ideas. A former member of the March 22 Movement, and later a leader of the Proletarian Left, Geismar insisted that they had a special responsibility to act since they had once supported the very revolutionaries who were now causing so much suffering in Vietnam.[16] Channeling the antiwar tactics of the 1960s, Lévy suggested they attack the Vietnamese Embassy.[17] The group rejected the proposal, but agreed with its spirit by taking another page from the 1960s radical playbook – sending a boat to Vietnam.[18]

In 1967, over thirty French antiwar organizations, including various Christian groups, the Unified Socialist Party, French Communist Party, the National Vietnam Committee, and the Franco-Vietnamese Medical Association – of which Kouchner had been a member – organized a campaign to help the Vietnamese people by sending a boat filled with medical equipment, bicycles, motors, and other supplies.[19] Just over a decade later, these erstwhile radicals decided to reprise the action. But instead of delivering supplies to Vietnamese guerrillas fighting US imperialism, they would rescue Vietnamese refugees fleeing from those very guerrillas. They created a new committee, "A Boat for Vietnam," with Claudie Broyelle as president; Olivier Todd, the former antiwar journalist, in charge of public relations; and Françoise Gautier, a former Amnesty International activist with ties to Vietnamese living in France, as treasurer.[20] Kouchner was tasked with gaining the support of MSF. Indeed, the radical humanitarians of MSF had by then grown very close to the rights activists spearheading the campaign. As MSF President Claude Malhuret reflected, "In Paris, we were all acquainted, Bernard-Henri Lévy, Glucksmann and many others. We used to meet, we held frequent discussions and we evolved in the same way. Our friends backed up their reflections, [and] unveiled books that they prepared from the facts, the analyses which we brought back from Vietnam and Cambodia."[21]

On November 22, 1978, they published their appeal in Le Monde: "Let us do more: let us go find these fugitives. A boat in the China Sea must permanently be able to seek and recover the Vietnamese who have taken the risk of leaving their country."[22] Leaning on their experiences in the antiwar movement, the committee raised funds, circulated petitions, held public meetings, published articles in newspapers, appeared on television, and connected with famous intellectuals. Their efforts proved remarkably successful, and they convinced over 150 figures to sign their names to their call to action, including politicians like Michel Rocard, former anti-imperialist militants like Jean-Pierre Le Dantec and Christian Jambet, intellectuals like Simone de Beauvoir, Michel Foucault, Jean-Paul Sartre, and Raymond Aron, and, for good measure, the movie star Brigitte Bardot.[23] The committee also garnered international assistance, enlisting Irving Brown, head of the European office of the AFL-CIO. The radical humanitarians scored another coup when they acquired a ship, the *Île de Lumière*, or "Isle of Light," a name that perfectly captured their ambitions.[24]

But they risked running aground on difficult questions. Chartering a ship to rescue Vietnamese nationals at sea, possibly even in Vietnamese waters, meant interfering in the internal affairs of a sovereign country. What jurisdiction did these activists have in Southeast Asia? Who could they claim to represent? Could international law justify an action of this kind? What would be the legal status of those refugees rescued in this manner? What political message would such an action send? All this unsurprisingly triggered sharp debates.[25] Internally, the committee deliberated such issues as the political framing of the action, with some hoping to stay politically neutral, while others like Jacques Broyelle – a former member of the Union of Communist Youth (Marxist-Leninist) who now believed that "we would have been better off on the side of the Americans in the Vietnam War than on the side of the North" – wanting to give the project a more unequivocally anticommunist direction.[26] Externally, the group's allies worried about the legal ramifications of the action, with the United Nations High Commissioner for Refugees refusing to support the expedition.[27] Disagreements even consumed MSF as some activists criticized the campaign's interventionism, excessive reliance on the media, and alliance with national governments, with Kouchner's megalomania only adding fuel to the fire. After an acrimonious break, Kouchner left to create his own rival organization, Doctors of the World.[28]

Despite these setbacks, the committee successfully launched the *Île de Lumière* in April 1979. The campaign marked a decisive moment in the development of human rights internationalism. First, it helped legitimate the idea of interventionism in the name of human rights. The impact was so profound that even some of the committee's detractors eventually followed suit. Those MSF leaders who had criticized the decision to send a boat to save refugees, for example, nevertheless embraced the general approach. MSF effectively replicated the model in its next campaign when it ignored the conventions of interstate law to organize a march straight to Cambodia to provide direct relief to refugees.[29] Just as the Leninist problematic had united otherwise hostile groups of radicals in the 1960s, so too did this individualist human rights problematic bring together rival humanitarians in the late 1970s. Although they may have competed with one another, they all began to accept the same general assumption about internationalism: Individuals had the right, in fact the duty, to intervene in the internal affairs of sovereign states to stop human rights abuses against individual victims.

Second, the campaign further codified the centrality of refugees in human rights discourse. If the preeminent figure of anti-imperialist internationalism was the "heroic guerrilla," the preeminent figure of human rights internationalism was fast becoming the "refugee." Where anti-imperialists imagined the guerrilla as fighting for collective liberation, human rights activists imagined the refugee as fighting for individual survival. Where the guerrilla drew power from an intimate knowledge of the home terrain, the refugee was one who no longer had a home. Whereas the guerrilla hoped to build a new polity, the refugee hoped to escape from one. In this way, the imagined figure of the refugee resonated perfectly with the declared antistatism of human rights internationalism. As a stateless person excluded from the rights granted by governments, the refugee exceeded the boundaries of the nation-state, and thereby raised questions about the entire logic of the state system. The direct international links that human rights activists could forge with the individual refugee, unmediated by states, pointed to a different kind of world order.[30]

Lastly, the campaign confirmed the human rights ambition to bypass not only nation-states but also entrenched political divisions. Ilios Yannakakis, a member of the Boat for Vietnam committee, recalled that the initiative aimed to "break the distinction between Left and Right."[31] This is why the organizers deliberately invited figures from across the political spectrum to participate. "People of the right, people of the left, former revolutionaries," Jacques Broyelle remembered, "everyone was there."[32] Nothing captured the sense of an imagined new beginning more powerfully than the campaign's successful bid to reunite Jean-Paul Sartre and Raymond Aron at a grand event on June 20, 1979. After refusing to speak to each other for decades, Sartre and Aron, schoolmates who had subsequently come to represent two competing strands of French political thought, finally came together to save the "boat people." Sartre, once one of the most visible defenders of Vietnamese national liberation, now spoke of a "moral" duty beyond politics to "save lives."[33] In the face of such human suffering, he said, political questions had to be put aside. Glucksmann reportedly described the event as "the end of the Cold War in our heads."[34]

Despite the self-congratulatory fanfare, the encounter brought not rapprochement but defeat, something poignantly captured in Aron's rather patronizing greeting, "Bonjour, mon petit camarade," to an infirm Sartre, so shriveled and blind he had to be ferried around by Glucksmann. After years of relative marginalization in progressive circles, the anticommunist liberalism that Aron represented reinvented itself, while the anti-imperialist radicalism of Sartre had withered, barely outliving the old philosopher, who died the following year. As Jacques Broyelle admitted years later, the meeting was not actually "a convergence, a consensus, a symbol of rapprochement" as so many were claiming, but rather the "victory of Aron's thought. Period."[35] And this was precisely the power of the new rights discourse – it disguised a decisive victory as apolitical reconciliation. It advanced its own partisan ideology as the supersession of ideology itself. Human rights were, in other words, on their way to achieving hegemony.

Internationalizing the Campaign

In the same way that anti-imperialist radicals envisioned their actions as part of a larger international struggle, so too did the human rights activists behind the Boat for Vietnam campaign try to internationalize their efforts. As Kouchner put it, self-consciously inverting the famous slogan of anti-imperialist internationalism, the goal was to "create one, two, or three boats."[36] And just as the French anti-imperialists who triggered the events of May '68 inspired radicals abroad, so too did the French human rights activists who organized the committee to save the "boat people" help catalyze an international grassroots campaign against human rights violations in Vietnam.

While visiting Paris in February 1979, German journalist Rupert Neudeck met Glucksmann, who in turn introduced him to the Boat for Vietnam committee. Inspired, he and his wife Christel launched a similar campaign in neighboring West Germany. Emulating the French strategy, they established a committee, courted intellectuals, won over former radicals such as Rudi Dutschke, and secured their own ship – *Cap Anamur* – to save thousands of Vietnamese refugees in the South China Sea. Neudeck remained in contact with the French throughout this time and attempted to introduce some of their ideas about humanitarian interventionism into Germany.[37]

Although the campaign against human rights violations in Vietnam spread widely, it achieved its greatest success in the United States, in large part through the efforts of two veteran antiwar activists, Joan Baez and Ginetta Sagan. Though never a committed radical herself, Baez was one of thousands of progressives who briefly drifted into the orbit of anti-imperialism during the Vietnam War. She protested the war, got arrested at the Stop the Draft Week demonstrations in 1967, and traveled to Hanoi with the Committee of Liaison with Families of Servicemen Detained in North Vietnam (COLIAFAM) to deliver mail to POWs. But as the radical left's grip over the larger progressive ecosystem began to falter in the 1970s, she found herself rethinking her internationalist politics. At that moment, Sagan appeared at her doorstep with "a big messy bundle of documents" under her arm and told her "about something called Amnesty International and its work on behalf of all political prisoners, regardless of ideology, race, or religion."[38]

A political prisoner tortured under Italian fascism, Sagan immigrated to the United States, where she joined Amnesty International. Soon after she founded its West Coast branch, which first met at her home. In the early 1970s, Sagan joined the national board of directors of Amnesty International USA, and with Baez developed the West Coast branch, which eventually came to boast more than half of the organization's total membership.[39] Sagan supported many causes, including the long struggle to end US intervention in Vietnam. "The Vietnam war was paramount," she later recalled.[40] A powerful organizer, Sagan was one of many human rights activists who helped make possible the convergence between different internationalist currents through her work on campaigns like the one to liberate the South Vietnamese political prisoners. In 1973, for example, she organized a three-week speaking tour in the United States for Jean-Pierre Debris and André Menras that reached a broad audience.[41]

But after the communist victory in 1975, both Baez and Sagan began to cast a more critical eye on Vietnam. In 1976, Baez admonished the Vietnamese government to improve its human rights record, but her efforts gained little traction on the left since few people were ready to criticize a struggle they had spent so long supporting, and because they felt the evidence of rights violations was too thin. All that would change in 1978, with the start of the campaign in France and the efforts of Vietnamese refugees like Đoàn Văn Toại, who toured North America in late 1978.[42] As it happened, a representative from Amnesty International attended one of his talks at Berkeley and put him in contact with Baez.[43] She immediately set to work, forming "a research group of five people, including Ginetta."[44] Sagan recalls how the team relied, in particular, on the invaluable help of "European journalists, scientists, refugees, and intellectuals," some of whom they had befriended through the international campaign to liberate the political prisoners under Thieu's government.[45]

Of all their European contacts, the French proved the most valuable, so much so that the research group effectively headquartered itself in Paris. Baez recalls "seeking out well-known French journalists of the left who as early as 1976 had begun to realize and denounce Hanoi's policies."[46] Sagan, who had studied in Paris, devoured all the French literature she could find on the subject. Baez paid equally close attention to the French scene. According to historian Paul Berman, she avidly followed "the French debate over Communism, Marxism, New Philosophy, Indochina, and all the rest."[47] Baez and Sagan would develop ties with the French intellectual community, meet Vietnamese living in France, build links with MSF, connect with French humanitarian activists, talk with journalists like Olivier Todd, and team up with French comrades to throw benefit concerts.[48]

Their research left them so convinced of human rights violations in Vietnam that Baez and Sagan decided to extend the campaign unfolding in France to the United States. Drawing on accounts from Vietnamese activists like Đoàn Văn Toại, reports from journalists like Paringaux, and the human rights debates of French activists, Baez and Sagan penned an open letter condemning the government of Vietnam. Along with a packet of supporting materials, they circulated the letter among noted American antiwar activists for signatures, winning the support of such figures as Alice and Staughton Lynd, Cesar Chavez, Daniel Berrigan, and Allen Ginsberg. Before publishing the letter, Sagan and Baez gave Vietnamese officials an ultimatum: "Either Hanoi make [*sic*] a written promise that Amnesty International representatives would be allowed into Vietnam within six months, with free access to go where they chose, or we would print our full-page letter."[49] The SRV rejected the proposal, and on May 30, 1979 Baez published the letter in the *Washington Post, New York Times, Los Angeles Times,* and *San Francisco Chronicle.* A copy was also sent to the UN High Commissioner for Refugees (UNHCR) with a long, unpublished, handwritten list of Vietnamese American signatories.[50]

In her letter, Baez anachronistically depicted the new human rights campaign against Vietnam as a natural extension of the earlier antiwar movements, with the former faithfully upholding the commitments, aspirations, and guiding ideas of the latter:

It was an abiding commitment to fundamental principles of human dignity, freedom and self-determination that motivated so many Americans to oppose the government of South Vietnam and our country's participation in the war. It is that same commitment that compels us to speak out against your brutal disregard for human rights.[51]

In writing history this way, Baez hoped not only to legitimize her campaign against the SRV in the eyes of activists who had once fought against the American War in Vietnam, but also to naturalize human rights as the pivot of both the antiwar struggles of the past and the rights movements of the present. Yet the old antiwar activism and the new human rights campaign against Vietnam differed in several key respects. First, although the antiwar movements were certainly heterogeneous, their dominant ideological pole was based not in individual human rights but rather anti-imperialism, national self-determination, and collective liberation, ideas shared even by those who did not consider themselves radicals. Second, they had radically different conceptions of agency. The human rights activists of the 1970s thought it was up to them to save victims in countries like Vietnam. As Baez put it in her letter, "we raise our voices now so that your people may live." By contrast, many antiwar activists in the 1960s believed that the struggles of revolutionaries in Asia, Africa, and Latin America would help free the people of the North Atlantic. As Jean-Paul Sartre had explained back in 1966, "The defeat of the Vietnamese people would politically be our defeat, the defeat of all free people. Because Vietnam is fighting for us."[52]

Lastly, they articulated very different approaches to politics. The earlier struggles were emphatically political. Sartre had again spoken for many when he declared, "We want peace in Vietnam, but not just any peace." He clarified, "we don't want this peace for simply moral reasons. Morality is not a sufficient motive. Our motive, the motive of our struggle, must be political."[53] But if the anti-imperialists of the 1960s saw their work as part of a life-and-death struggle between competing political visions of the future, the human rights activists of the 1970s believed that their movement stood above politics, partisanship, and ideological divisions. As Baez explained in the *Washington Post*, "It is a time to put conscience before ideology."[54] In their communications, Baez and Sagan often characterized their efforts as "non-partisan, non-political, non-governmental."[55] The goal of these human rights activists in the late 1970s was not simply to scramble established political lines, but to develop a new project that appeared to transcend politics itself.

In this, the human rights campaign against Vietnam offered a radically depoliticizing brand of internationalism. These activists saw a planet filled not with political subjects autonomously thinking about the future, experimenting with new kinds of politics, and striving to create a more egalitarian world, but only suffering victims who wanted nothing to do with politics, had no real political ambitions of their own, and only wanted to eke out a living. They claimed the reason why these poor people suffered was not oppressive global systems, but the political schemes of revolutionaries deluded by ideas of radical change such as anti-imperialism. And they argued that after years of fierce political struggle and sharp polarization, the only way to improve the world was to escape politics forever.

In reality, however, these rights activists had a clear agenda. They advocated a set of actionable policies, promoted a vision of what they wanted the world to look like, and cooperated closely with career politicians to realize their goals. In the United States, Baez and Sagan personally collaborated with the president himself. In fact, it seems Sagan was one of the first to speak with Jimmy Carter about adopting human rights as state policy. While on the campaign trail in 1975, the Democratic candidate stayed at the California home of Sagan's Amnesty International colleague, Rodney Kennedy-Minott, whom Carter would later appoint as ambassador to Sweden.[56] There, he met with Sagan. "Carter then told me," Sagan later explained, "that he admired Amnesty's work and promised that if he were elected, he would make human rights and decency in foreign policy a priority."[57] Soon after his visit, Carter wrote to Sagan, affirming their partnership, "I enjoyed being with you, & really admire the work you are doing. During the campaign ahead your advice & active support will be very valuable to me."[58] Despite its claim to operate independently of national governments, Amnesty, along with other human rights organizations, substantially benefited from ties to the Carter administration. As Sagan put it, "Carter's initiatives mean a great deal," especially in terms of "AI access to governments."[59]

Their campaign against human rights violations in Vietnam further deepened this alliance between human rights internationalism and the US government. Baez and Sagan's new human rights organization, Humanitas, directly appealed to the president to help further their cause. On July 19, 1979, for example, Baez hosted a concert at the Lincoln Memorial with 10,000 supporters, then led a march to the White House carrying lit candles. Baez wrote to the president before the event, assuring him that "the march was not in any way a protest, but rather a show of support from the American people who would back him in any humanitarian effort he made on behalf of the boat people." In particular, she suggested sending the Navy into the South China Sea on a rescue mission. Although Carter declined the invitation to attend the concert, later in the evening, as marchers chanted "save the boat people" outside the White House, he surprised everyone by walking across the White House lawn and announcing that he had decided to send the Seventh Fleet to rescue Vietnamese refugees. The next morning Carter personally called Baez and they "exchanged mutual congratulations."[60]

What began as an activist campaign organized by Vietnamese exiles, French journalists, and former radicals had become a massive international movement composed of not merely other humanitarian organizations but even national governments, many of which took an active role in rescuing, transporting, and adopting refugees. The surprising collaboration with these nation-states exposed an ambiguity at the very heart of human rights internationalism. Although its proponents dreamed of a kind of solidarity that superseded not only regimes established by revolutionary movements in the "Third World," but also the powerful governments of the North Atlantic, human rights activists soon discovered that they still had to operate in a world of nation-states. Some of them went a step further by seeking out alliances with those states, entranced by their resources, legitimacy, logistical capacities, and sheer might. For their part, a few governments saw the alliance as a unique opportunity to remake themselves during a time of crisis. One of the most eager was the US government. Desperate to rethink US foreign policy after

Vietnam, the Carter administration became the loudest advocate of the "boat people," leading the charge against violations of human rights in Vietnam. The very state those onetime anti-imperialist radicals had protested against so vehemently only a decade earlier would now become their most important ally in the fight for human rights.

Winning the Peace

In the mid-1970s, millions of Americans were gripped by a sense of malaise, pessimism, and distrust. Carter hoped to change all that. Campaigning on a politics of morality, he aimed not only to restore faith in government but also to heal the guilt, shame, despair, and division that many Americans felt after the trauma of the Vietnam War. He began his inaugural speech with a call for unity. "For myself and for our Nation," he began, "I want to thank my predecessor for all he has done to heal our land."[61] In contradistinction to the corruption, deception, and outright immorality of past administrations, he spoke of compassion, transparency, leading by example. A core idea of his presidency would be human rights, which he took to mean not just a new foreign policy program but a new age for humanity. "The world itself is now dominated by a new spirit. Peoples more numerous and more politically aware are craving, and now demanding, their place in the sun," he continued, "not just for the benefit of their own physical condition, but for basic human rights."[62]

The Carter administration had somewhat unexpectedly discovered that human rights could serve as a cure for the malaise that characterized American politics in the 1970s. As historian Barbara Keys argues, human rights could restore American virtue, manage the legacy of Vietnam by redirecting everyone's attention away from the horrors of the war, and redefine the US government's role in the world in the wake of Richard Nixon's *Realpolitik*. Yet the diverse currents that coalesced to make Carter's presidency possible voiced competing ideas about how championing human rights could achieve those ends. On the one side were those who thought human rights could offer the United States a way to recover the country's honor after a period of Cold War immorality that included not only the Vietnam War but also continued US support of dictatorships. On the other were people like Democratic Senator Henry Jackson, a Cold War zealot who thought human rights could help reestablish the legitimacy of the US government's war on international communism, providing the perfect way to circumvent a politics of isolationism, guilt, and compromise after the debacle of Vietnam.[63]

Because of these competing impulses, human rights came to play a highly ambiguous role in the Carter administration's foreign policy.

Figures like Patricia Derian, head of the State Department's Bureau of Human Rights, rebuked pro-US dictatorships for human rights violations. But others, like Richard Holbrooke, assistant secretary of state for East Asian and Pacific affairs, resisted openly criticizing allies. The tension produced contradictory policies, as when Derian pushed to ban the sale of tear gas to the Shah of Iran, while Holbrooke personally deleted criticism of the Shah from one of Carter's speeches.[64] These conflicts played out over different areas of foreign policy, with partisans of each approach winning the upper hand in different parts of the world. In some regions, especially Latin America, officials like Derian scored important victories. In Argentina, for example, the Carter administration reduced aid and military assistance and generated public pressure against the dictatorship. But in Vietnam, those who saw in human rights a weapon against communism successfully turned the country into a prime testing ground for their anticommunist strategy.[65]

When Carter assumed office, "Vietnam" was synonymous with American dishonor, cruelty, and failure. By the late 1970s, the vast majority of Americans believed that sending troops to fight in Vietnam had been a mistake. In the eyes of millions across the globe, the United States had committed egregious crimes. A stain on America's virtue, the Vietnam War had severely weakened the US government's image as the benevolent leader of the free world. Since Vietnam lay at the heart of the United States' predicament, Carter's ambition to restore the country's reputation depended on changing the way the world thought about the United States in that highly symbolic part of the globe. With this priority in mind, Carter broached the question of normalizing relations with the SRV just weeks after his inauguration.[66]

The SRV was eager to cooperate and talks began in May 1977. Discussions, which involved several congressional visits to Vietnam, culminated in September 1978 when Holbrooke secretly met with Deputy Foreign Minister Nguyễn Cơ Thạch. Both men agreed to normalize relations without preconditions.[67] But not everyone close to Carter assented. Henry Jackson, for example, voiced his opposition.[68] National Security Advisor Zbigniew Brzezinski, a hardline anticommunist and onetime member of Amnesty International's board of directors, was even more blunt: The goal was to counter the Soviet Union, which meant prioritizing relations with the USSR's enemy, China, and not its ally, Vietnam.[69] With people like Jackson and Brzezinski in mind, Carter turned against normalization two weeks after Holbrooke's meeting. Feeling betrayed, isolated, and anxious about China's designs on the region, the SRV turned completely to the Soviet Union in November.[70]

Despite all the talk of morality, new directions, and human rights, the Carter administration's lofty visions ultimately came second to geopolitical concerns. Nowhere was this clearer than in Southeast Asia, one of the historic hotspots of the Cold War, and a region of continuing importance. In the Philippines, Carter went easy on Ferdinand Marcos's corrupt and repressive regime.[71] In China, the Carter administration's commitment to securing such a prized ally against the USSR muted its rhetoric of human rights violations. In Cambodia, Carter went from decrying Democratic Kampuchea as "the worst violator of human rights in the world today" to resuscitating Pol Pot's murderous regime.[72] In Vietnam, the United States denounced the one country that had done the most to free the Cambodian people from the Khmer Rouge as an enemy of human rights on par with the Nazis. This hypocritical approach was not lost on the public, which criticized the administration's machinations.

But the "boat people" offered the United States the perfect opportunity to reconcile human rights with those overriding strategic interests. Here was a way to erase the memory of the war, make Americans feel good about themselves, restore the government's global credibility, take attention away from its other unsavory policies in the region, and win the support of an increasingly vocal Vietnamese diasporic community – itself rallying behind the language of human rights – without compromising the White House's imperialist ambitions. The campaign to save the Vietnamese migrants was one of the few cases in Asia, Africa, and Latin America where singing the praises of human rights could be the best way to further US geopolitical interests.[73]

Even still, some protested throwing the state's weight behind the issue. The Pentagon felt the matter was out of its jurisdiction, some in the National Security Council worried about finances, and others in the State Department argued that taking action would be tantamount to interfering in the affairs of a sovereign state. Yet the strategy found a strong advocate in Vice President Walter F. Mondale, who had visited a refugee camp in Thailand in the spring of 1978, and fully believed that Vietnam's approach to refugees was "a sinister and largely racist policy, putting people to sea in something that approached genocide and a form of revenge for their support of the United States during the Vietnam War."[74] Mondale argued that the crisis offered the United States a kind of win-win because it allowed the administration to appear completely genuine in its commitment to human rights while simultaneously advancing US political objectives. "Quite apart from the humanitarian case, I saw an important foreign policy argument," Mondale explained.[75] That proved enough to convince the skeptics.

Beginning in early 1979, the United States took a series of well-publicized steps to alleviate the refugee crisis. In February, Carter created the position of coordinator for refugee affairs. In March, a team led by Senator Ted Kennedy introduced the Refugee Act to Congress. In June, Carter pledged to double the number of Southeast Asian refugees admitted to the United States from 7,000 to 14,000 a month. "We can and will work together," he promised, "to find homes and jobs for the Indochinese."[76] By the end of September, the United States boasted that it had admitted a total of 248,436 refugees since the end of the Vietnam War.[77] People everywhere took notice. The United States had found a way to restore its name in the very part of the world where it had so recently been associated with dishonor.

This stunning transformation was best captured at the UN's International Meeting on Refugees and Displaced Persons in Southeast Asia in July 1979.[78] To prove its commitment, the United States sent a "high-level delegation" to the conference, which included Mondale, the attorney general, the coordinator for refugee affairs, congressional representatives, and Elie Wiesel, the Holocaust survivor, author, and humanitarian. Mondale's speech in Geneva was a coup. With rhetorical subtlety, he reminded his audience that "Forty-one years ago this very week, another international conference on Lake Geneva concluded its deliberations."[79] He spoke of the Evian conference, where delegates from thirty-two countries gathered to find a solution to the plight of Jews fleeing the Third Reich. "At Evian, they began with high hopes. But they failed the test of civilization."[80] He then transitioned to the refugee crisis in Southeast Asia, "Let us not re-enact their error. Let us not be the heirs to their shame."[81]

After implying that Vietnam had behaved like the Third Reich, and that the exodus of the "boat people" was similar to the Holocaust, Mondale went on the attack, slamming Vietnam for "failing to ensure the human rights of its people."[82] He then cast the Americans as the heroes of the story: "The United States is committed [to] doing its share, just as we have done for generations. 'Mother of exiles' it says on the pedestal of the Statue of Liberty at the port of New York. The American people have already welcomed over 200,000 Indochinese."[83] By not only welcoming the refugees but also dispatching "our Navy to help the drowning and the desperate," the United States was leading by example, retaking its rightful place as the leader of the free world.[84] Instead of the unilateral actions of his government during the Vietnam War, Mondale now called for a united multilateral effort. He ended his sermon to the sound of loud applause.

Tellingly, Mondale did not make a single mention of the US War in Vietnam. He left out the history of free-fire zones, strategic hamlets, deforestation, pacification, and forced relocation. He erased the fact that the United States had dropped around 7 million tons of ordinance, sprayed millions of gallons of herbicides, and littered the country with tens of thousands of unexploded bombs. He ignored how the war had orphaned 800,000 children, killed over a million Vietnamese, directly exposed around 4 million people to toxic chemicals, scarred the landscape with bomb craters, obliterated countless villages, and scorched acres of jungle. He said not one word about how the US government leveled the majority of the North's industrial capacity while dislocating the economy in the South, which collapsed once the United States withdrew, leaving behind perhaps 300,000 vulnerable sex workers and an estimated 8 million unemployed people in the urban regions. He skipped over how the United States not only refused to pay promised reparations but also slammed Vietnam with a trade embargo, forcing the country into dependence on the USSR. Most of all, he refused to admit that this sordid history had in any way contributed to the refugee crisis.[85]

The United States successfully recast the refugee as a purely postwar phenomenon. Rewriting history in this way obscured the complex factors that led to the crisis at hand, allowing the Carter administration to define all refugees as anticommunist defectors fleeing from inevitable totalitarian rule. The postwar mass exodus, the White House suggested, proved that communism was an unpopular imposition, that the United States had good intentions when it intervened in Vietnam, and that the war itself had only been a friendly humanitarian mission to rescue those in need. By manipulating the figure of the refugee, Yến Lê Espiritu has argued, the United States rebranded itself as the paramount land of refuge, "a refuge-providing rather than refugee-producing nation."[86] As Secretary of State Cyrus Vance put it, "We are a nation of refugees."[87]

Years later, Mondale recalled that the campaign "changed the way the world looked at America – after some pretty difficult years for us abroad – and I'm proud of it."[88] Remarkably, when it came to Southeast Asia, the United States redeemed itself not by making a meaningful peace with Vietnam, or even by taking responsibility for its actions in Southeast Asia, but by using the peace to launch another offensive. Instead of making amends, paying the promised reparations, or normalizing relations with the people it had devastated, the United States used the figure of the refugee, the international issue of the "boat people," and the language of human rights to turn Vietnam into an oppressor and the United States into a liberator.

Responding to Human Rights

Vietnam raced to defend itself. Since the flashpoint of the controversy was the refugee crisis, the SRV tried to offer an explanation. A common approach was to argue that the whole affair had nothing to do with repression but rather conditions beyond the control of the government. Officials claimed that those who chose to flee were economic refugees weary of hardship, ethnic Chinese deceived by PRC propaganda, foreign agents tasked with fomenting chaos, or wartime collaborators who had until recently been unable to escape. Vietnam's foreign-language publications, from the *Vietnam Courier* to *Vietnamese Studies*, echoed these explanations, sometimes supplementing them with greater historical background, colorful anecdotes, or interviews with ethnic Chinese who claimed they had been treated well.[89]

Another strategy was to shift the blame by historicizing the crisis. Far from some isolated postwar development, Vietnamese writers argued, the refugee crisis had to be situated in the context of "multiple problems left by several decades of war and more than a century of colonialism."[90] Between 1954 and 1973, the combined effects of colonial rule, civil strife, imperialist wars, and forced relocation had displaced about ten million people in South Vietnam alone. According to one estimate, by the time the communists seized Saigon in April 1975, approximately half the population of South Vietnam had been displaced at least once in the last two decades.[91] The unprecedented dislocation destroyed life in countless villages, threw agricultural production into disarray, and turned the cities into overcrowded slums. When the communists won the war, they inherited a colossal demographic crisis. In this way, the SRV charged, the refugee crisis had really begun with the United States.

But the most convincing response was to take concrete steps to alleviate the crisis itself. In addition to welcoming more than 150,000 Cambodians freed from Pol Pot's camps, Vietnam did try to find collective solutions for those Vietnamese nationals trying to flee. Hanoi welcomed a delegation commissioned by Senator Ted Kennedy, agreed to collaborate with the United Nations, and promised to begin granting exit visas to those who wished to leave.[92] In May, about a month and half before Mondale compared Vietnam to the Third Reich, the SRV and UNHCR signed a Memorandum of Understanding on Orderly Departure to establish a program for safe, legal, and orderly emigration from Vietnam.[93]

At Geneva in July 1979, the SRV delegation worked with other countries to develop a new set of measures, which included resettlement, regional processing centers, and an agreement to promote orderly departures. After the conference, the UN secretary general announced that

Hanoi had promised to "make every effort to stop illegal departures."[94] According to W. Courtland Robinson's study, the number of Vietnamese boat arrivals in the region dropped from 56,941 in June to 17,839 in July to 9,734 in August.[95] By the end of the year the number of arrivals averaged only 2,600 per month.[96] As for resettlement, UNHCR, Vietnam, and other countries led by the United States implemented the Orderly Departure Program, which allowed for a direct transfer of refugees from Vietnam to countries of resettlement.

While these efforts helped contain the flow of refugees, they did little to exonerate Vietnam in the eyes of its critics. Some argued that Vietnam deserved no credit because Hanoi had been forced to agree to these measures. Others pointed out that Vietnam's solution of halting illegal departures was itself a violation of human rights because it denied the freedom of movement, a right expressly proclaimed in the Universal Declaration. But most argued that while Vietnam may have attenuated the crisis, the fact remained that the SRV had created it in the first place through massive state repression, which had not been resolved at all. The root of the problem, in other words, had not changed: Vietnam was still violating human rights. In this context, the SRV came to believe that the problem was not the refugee crisis as such but the general framework of human rights, which could make a moral weapon out of any issue. Today, it was the refugees; tomorrow it would be something else. To win the ideological war, Vietnam had to do much more than address the crisis; it had to respond to the notion of human rights itself.[97]

Vietnamese representatives mobilized a series of related, though at times contradictory, arguments about human rights. One was to unmask them as a cover for aggression. Drawing on her extensive legal training and international reputation as a famous political prisoner committed to fighting repression, the tenacious Ngô Bá Thành came to the SRV's defense. She argued that the combined effects of domestic strife, economic recession, Watergate, and the American War had created a profound crisis in the United States that called "into question US leadership of the modern world."[98] Fearing a loss of hegemony, the United States "decided to take defence of 'human rights' as the starting point for 'regaining' this leadership."[99] The new doctrine of human rights, Ngô Bá Thành continued, allowed countries like the United States to assume the moral high ground and "set themselves up as international judges empowered to hand down judgments on the conduct of other countries, on their internal affairs."[100] A *Vietnam Courier* booklet on the Vietnamese refugees was even more blunt:

This campaign is no novelty. It has indeed started in Washington where the American leaders, unable to use Vietnam's tribulations to erase from people's minds the immense responsibilities of their government and stubbornly refusing to honour their aid pledge, seek to give a good conscience to the American people. Jimmy Carter has found the method: human rights. Vietnam, the victim of American barbarity, will thus find itself in the dock while the USA will smartly join the ranks of the defenders of law and justice. There have been former friends of Vietnam who have lent a hand to this legerdemain trick; some in good faith and without being aware that they are being manipulated; others knowingly.[101]

Human rights, then, were a sophisticated weapon used by countries like the United States to renew their imperialist ambitions.

A second line of reasoning aimed to relativize human rights. Human rights did not have a single, universal definition, Vietnamese revolutionaries argued, but meant different things in different contexts. Just as anti-imperialist revolution had to unfold differently in North America or Western Europe than in Vietnam, so too did human rights. For a society freeing itself from the ravages of colonialism, occupation, and imperialist war, human rights meant building a functional society. They meant combating illiteracy, repairing communication lines, establishing healthcare, finding work for hundreds of thousands of unemployed people. It was therefore absurd to hold war-torn Vietnam to the standards of a developed country like the United States. When viewed in this properly historical lens, the SRV claimed, Vietnam was not a violator of human rights, but their greatest upholder.

The third strategy was to contend that human rights were not so much a thing as a terrain of struggle between different political forces. There were, according to this view, two distinct interpretations of human rights: the bourgeois and the proletarian, the capitalist and the socialist, the individualist and the collectivist, the narrowly civil and the broadly socioeconomic. As Ngô Bá Thành argued, the new champions of human rights only wanted the rights of the abstract individual, and above all, the right to private property. As she put it, "the 'free world' calls 'free' one who is without a job, does not have enough to eat, lives in poverty, is constantly threatened by unemployment, is deprived of the most elementary medical assistance, or sleeps in a hovel."[102] Vietnam, on the other hand, advocated a view of human rights that placed primacy on more "fundamental" rights such as education, employment, universal healthcare, and self-determination. These competing interpretations were locked in a fierce "ideological struggle." Although the advocates of the collectivist interpretation of rights had scored a tremendous initial victory when they demanded both "civic and political rights" and "socio-economic rights" in the Universal Declaration, the partisans of the individualist conception had since tried to narrow the definition of human rights while hoping to turn the Declaration "into a purely formal legal document with no concrete provisions to guarantee the effective exercise of human rights."[103]

Vietnam, then, promoted not simply a different idea of human rights, but one that was more expansive and therefore qualitatively better. If taken to its logical conclusion, this line of argument suggested that by emphasizing foundational socioeconomic rights, Vietnam was providing the best guarantee for the kind of individualist civil rights that so obsessed the United States. The rights of the individual could never guarantee the rights of the collective, but a collectivist emphasis on socialist socioeconomic rights ensured the growth of the rights of the individual. "History has shown," Ngô Bá Thành argued, "that by freeing the workers from exploitation and the oppressed peoples from arbitrary rule on the national and social levels, socialism has effectively ensured genuine freedom and democratic rights for the individual."[104]

While theoretically clever, this rebuttal was contradicted in practice. Vietnam not only failed to safeguard the rights of the individual but also appeared to fall short on collective rights. In addition to censoring papers, arresting dissidents, and abolishing competing parties, the newly renamed Vietnamese Communist Party tried to solve many of the country's problems through centralized coercion in a way that often backfired. A particularly tragic example was the SRV's decision to rely on forced relocation to address the massive demographic dislocations caused by the war.[105] The SRV resettled hundreds of thousands of Vietnamese in what were called "new economic zones." Many of these collectivization experiments failed, and the reduced agricultural output further weakened the national economy, with per capita income actually declining in these years.[106] Although partly due to terrible weather, and the absence of promised foreign aid, blame also fell to the aggressive statism of the project, which eschewed dynamic grassroots democratic participation in favor of inflexible directives from above. In the end, Vietnamese were not only denied their promised civil liberties, they also appeared to be getting poorer, undermining the government's claim that guaranteeing socioeconomic rights would ensure individual freedoms. It seemed the SRV could do neither.

What is most significant about this entire debate was not simply the SRV's inability to parry the human rights assault, but that in their efforts to do so Vietnamese representatives often found themselves accepting the very terms of their enemies. They variously argued that Vietnam did support human rights, that Vietnam's conception of human rights was better than that of the United States, or that the earlier struggle for national self-determination had been a kind of human rights struggle all along, even though Vietnamese revolutionaries rarely made reference to the concept in the 1960s. The idea of human rights had become so commonsensical, upheld so universally as an unqualified good, that everyone felt compelled to present their arguments within its framework.

This was a dramatic reversal. For most of the Vietnam War, the United States had to compete on a relatively disadvantageous ideological terrain shaped by such ideas as anti-imperialism, self-determination, and collective liberation. While Vietnamese revolutionaries could easily project themselves as exemplars of these ideas, US politicians struggled to prove to the rest of the world that their government truly cared. It was very hard to believe, for instance, that the United States murdered hundreds of thousands of Vietnamese people in order to defend their right to national self-determination. While US officials might find a way to explain away a foreign intervention here or there, the ideological deck was decidedly stacked against the United States. This in turn presented a major obstacle to the successful realization of US foreign policy objectives. Policymakers were well aware of this difficulty, but they had no choice but to continue playing the game.

A decade later, however, the US government finally gained the ideological advantage over its Vietnamese rivals. It did this not by demonstrating that the United States was a better proponent of national self-determination than the Socialist Republic of Vietnam, but by taking advantage of the ascendant human rights discourse to displace the struggle onto a far more favorable ideological terrain. Shifting the battlefield from self-determination to human rights allowed the United States to win the initiative. Instead of having to constantly justify its brutal interventions in Asia, Africa, and Latin America, the United States could now focus attention on human rights violations in unfriendly regimes like the SRV, hitting Hanoi precisely where it was most vulnerable, while forcing Vietnamese revolutionaries to defend themselves in an unfavorable language.

Activist Impasse

Anti-imperialists across the North Atlantic also struggled to counter the human rights offensive against Vietnam. Some maintained that the campaign was based on shaky evidence.[107] Others contended that the human rights framing conveniently erased US complicity in creating the refugee problem in the first place.[108] Still others suggested that many of those leading the human rights campaign against Vietnam were really just acting out their disillusionment with the national liberation struggle they had once worshipped.[109]

While criticizing the rights campaign against Vietnam was one thing, proposing a concrete alternative to the refugee crisis was another. Internationalism was not just about condemning the enemy but taking positive action. And here, the anti-imperialists often missed the mark. For instance, the Revolutionary Communist League, the largest Trotskyist organization in France, did not run an article on the refugees until the end of June 1979 – in fact was effectively pressured to do so by irritated readers – and predictably laid all the blame on the United States. Content to simply denounce the campaign to save refugees as nothing but "a large-scale anticommunist political operation," the article's author, Michel Thomas, said little about the situation in Vietnam, and even less about what actions radicals could take, besides a vague call for Carter to organize an airlift.[110]

This left many anti-imperialists dissatisfied. One radical argued that it had become very difficult, not to say impossible, to think politics in 1979 without confronting the plight of the refugees, in the same way that it was impossible to have thought politics in the 1960s without confronting the Vietnam War.[111] For this reason, it was inexcusable that the Revolutionary Communist League had not simply ignored such an important issue, but that when it finally addressed the suffering of the Vietnamese refugees, it did so with platitudes. The leadership's answer, it seemed, just boiled down to exclaiming that it was all "imperialism's fault."[112] But what was imperialism today? How should radicals respond? And, most of all, what was the responsibility of a generation of activists who were radicalized by the Vietnamese revolution itself?

Another member of the League emphasized the criticism by arguing that Michel Thomas's "attitude is a bit like someone who passes by a woman getting raped, explains that her rapist is only a product of society, and then takes off."[113] In the face of a crisis, one that demanded some kind of concrete internationalist response, all that anti-imperialists had to offer were rote criticisms of imperialism, calls for capitalist countries to pay reparations to Vietnam, and nebulous statements about the degeneration of the Vietnamese revolution. While these positions were not necessarily wrong, they did not amount to an actionable response to a calamity that spoke directly to the very basis of their political project.

After all, the whole point of anti-imperialist internationalism in the 1960s had been to invent new solutions to major international issues precisely at a time when the ossified "Old Left" seemed out of touch. Radicals, in other words, promised not only to revive the Leninist project that their forebears had abandoned but also to update it for changed conditions so that it could act as a living guide to concrete action. But in the late 1970s these same radicals appeared to have grown just as sclerotic as the Old Left they had once criticized. The Revolutionary Communist League's response to the refugee crisis, some radicals observed with a note of self-criticism, was basically identical to that of the French Communist Party and, by extension, the Soviet Union.[114] Criticizing human rights without offering any alternative action made the radical left appear petty, impotent, and exhausted.

To be sure, some radicals did try to act on the issue from an explicitly anti-imperialist point of view. One of the most important figures in this respect was Laurent Schwartz, a leader of the old National Vietnam Committee in the 1960s, the founder of the Indochina Solidarity Front in the 1970s, and now one of Vietnam's most visible public advocates in France. As someone who supported the Vietnamese revolution but opposed the SRV's repressive policies, he considered the refugee crisis particularly vexing. He found himself in the unenviable position of simultaneously challenging those unapologetic radicals who refused to believe the SRV had done any wrong while confronting those renegades "who now hated the same Viet-Nam which they had adored and idealized before."[115] Fighting on two fronts, Schwartz tried to find a way to defend the SRV while at the same time taking positive action to curb state repression. He helped refugees in Paris, advocated for prisoners in the SRV, and exhorted his old contacts in Hanoi to withdraw from Cambodia, release political prisoners, and find a permanent solution to the refugee crisis.

But even as he criticized the campaign against rights violations in Vietnam as an anticommunist assault, Schwartz and figures like him could not help but accept its terms. Schwartz signed his name to the Boat for Vietnam operation. He also championed Amnesty International as an "apolitical and neutral" organization that could help set the SRV on the right track.[116] Effectively echoing Baez's proposal, he traveled to Vietnam to convince his personal friend, SRV Prime Minister Phạm Văn Đồng, to allow an AI delegation into the country in December 1979.[117] He even tried to somehow combine anti-imperialism with human rights by arguing that radicals had to demonstrate their "solidarity" with the Socialist Republic of Vietnam while simultaneously also defending "victims" of human rights violations.[118] Of course, Schwartz could have criticized Vietnam's repression without supporting the humanitarians, relying on groups like AI, or turning to the language of human rights, but it is significant that he did. Although they had worked together for over a decade organizing anti-imperialist solidarity with Vietnam, the divergent responses of the Trotskyist leaders of the Revolutionary Communist League on the one hand and Schwartz on the other spoke volumes: denounce human rights but take no real action on a serious issue that cut to the heart of anti-imperialist internationalism's future or try to take concrete action but reluctantly accept the discourse of human rights. The fact that the anti-imperialists could not find a third way – organizing robust, meaningful, emancipatory, international solidarity within the terms of their own anti-imperialist framework – revealed the gravity of their project's impasse at the start of the new decade.

The Ends of Anti-Imperialism

Despite these challenges, anti-imperialists did not suddenly vanish from the North Atlantic in the 1980s. They organized solidarity campaigns in support of movements in Poland, South Africa, and especially Guatemala, El Salvador, and Nicaragua. They tried to expand the meaning of anti-imperialism to include new movements such as gay liberation.[119] They continued to challenge rival internationalisms such as human rights, especially in places like the United States, where rights discourse had become a part of the government's imperialist repertoire.

In the United States, anti-imperialism continued to capture some attention in mainstream politics, especially when many radicals entered the Jesse Jackson campaign in the Democratic primaries of 1984. While the favorite Walter Mondale continued to defend the White House's aggressive foreign policies, such as the US military presence in Honduras, Jackson united anti-imperialists, activists of color, the peace movement, and the Christian left into a new "Rainbow Coalition" that articulated a foreign policy emphasizing disarmament, nonintervention, and support for liberation movements. Jackson himself participated in leftist demonstrations against Ronald Reagan's invasion of Grenada, spoke against US involvement in Central America, and even met with Fidel Castro. Far from passively accepting defeat, anti-imperialists continued to organize deep into the 1980s and 1990s.[120]

But it was clear the heyday of anti-imperialist organizing was over. Conditions in North America and Western Europe were much less hospitable to radical politics. There were far fewer committed anti-imperialists left, and they had lost their hegemony over the wider progressive scene, which now rallied to all sorts of other politics. What is more, with conservatives gaining power everywhere, organized labor on the defensive, leftist institutions collapsing, and radical ideas falling out of fashion, the general pool of potentially sympathetic activists had itself shrunk. In this context, it is little surprise that the anti-imperialist solidarity movements that did continue fighting in the 1980s looked very different from those that defined the 1960s and early 1970s. In most cases, these newer solidarity movements were much smaller – the US campaigns in support of Central American movements, for instance, likely counted fewer than 20,000 individuals at any one time.[121] They were also generally more politically fragmented. The old antiwar struggles were certainly heterogeneous, but the campaigns in support of Solidarity in Poland, for example, took this to a new level by including not just anti-imperialists but many zealous anticommunists as well.

Most importantly, their aims could not help but be less revolutionary. A prominent US activist in the Central American solidarity movements could admit, for example, that "this was never a movement with any deep concern for whether or not it would or could change the United States."[122] This was a striking departure from the high point of anti-imperialist internationalism in the 1960s and 1970s, when activists in the North Atlantic understood solidarity as not just calling for nonintervention, or even aiding struggles on the ground in other parts of the world, but seeing those struggles abroad as intimately connected to radically transforming politics at home in one massive internationalist revolution. It is telling that in many of those cases where anti-imperialist activists did aim to make radical political change at home, as with Jackson's campaign, they now often did so by trying to work "within the system," so to speak.

In spite of all this, the true believers did not lose hope. Politics, they insisted, comes in ebbs and flows. As bad as the situation seemed, things would eventually turn around. After all, this was not the first time the radical left had experienced crisis. Since the early twentieth century, several generations of radicals had seen friends imprisoned, movements end in defeat, comrades disavow emancipatory politics, vanguard parties transform into authoritarian organizations, revolutions culminate in repressive states, and ostensibly internationalist regimes invade neighbors. And some of these remaining anti-imperialists had already successfully modified anti-imperialist internationalism in response to challenges at home and abroad in the 1960s and early 1970s. But this new crisis was of a different order. As Daniel Bensaïd recalled, "something cracked and broke."[123] The issue was not a defeat here or there, but the generalized collapse of the very problematic that had allowed anti-imperialists to overcome such defeats in the first place. Leninism – the basis of so many radical attempts to transform the world – had reached its limits.

The Leninist problematic had always presented itself as the unification of a theory of Marxism and a practice of communism into a harmonious whole that could lean on historical reality as its ultimate verification. As a theory, the Leninist variant of Marxism promised to answer all questions. As a practice, the Leninist mode of communism promised to win in all conditions. If Lenin had once declared that "Marxism is omnipotent because it is true," hundreds of thousands of radicals across the world came to believe the same about Leninism.[124] With empires imploding, imperialist powers retreating, national liberation movements winning, and over a third of humanity eventually coming to live under regimes that claimed they were transitioning to communism, it seemed, for a moment, that they were right. History itself, they claimed, was confirmation.

But beginning in the late 1970s the Leninist problematic succumbed to catastrophic crisis as the internal coherency of its theory came undone while the external proof of its practice collapsed. On the one side, Leninism's inherent theoretical contradictions became unavoidable, the problematic's core concepts unraveled, and its endless epicycles lost the ability to convince. The language of Marxism began to disintegrate. On the other side, Leninism's external practical references crumbled. In the USSR, the Soviet regime's trajectory raised serious doubts about whether the Soviet model of development could guarantee the transition from socialism to full communism. In China, the aftermath of the Cultural Revolution prompted many to question the role of the vanguard party in the struggle for universal emancipation. In Vietnam, Hanoi's war with its Leninist neighbors shattered the belief that national liberation necessarily facilitated international communism. In Poland, the emergence of an organized labor movement that took direct aim at Leninism challenged the conviction that the proletariat was the natural social subject of communism. In Iran, the transformation of a seemingly classical revolutionary sequence into an Islamic regime led by a self-described anti-imperialist cleric who lambasted both capitalism and communism confounded inherited assumptions about stages, linearity, historical time, and universal models. The breakdown of the theory made visible the failures of the practice, and the breakdown of the practice made visible the failures of the theory.[125]

In the 1980s, the radical left had been beaten so badly, anti-imperialism had failed so spectacularly, the general intellectual terrain had shifted so dramatically, internationalist alternatives had become so attractive, and the incoherency of the problematic had grown so pronounced that it was no longer possible to simply brush Leninism's problems under the rug. The general meltdown had become so clear that Leninism in all its forms began to rapidly fall out of favor across the planet. In the context of the Soviet invasion of Afghanistan, the economic stagnation of the Soviet bloc, the defeats of national liberation movements, revived US power, a sweeping neoliberal offensive, and a destabilizing debt crisis in what was once called the "Third World," millions of people living in Asia, Africa, and Latin America disavowed the Leninist problematic.[126] Figures who once tilted toward Leninism as a guide to emancipation now turned to other internationalisms like radical Islam. Countless more embraced privatization, foreign investment, and market capitalism. Instead of looking to Cuba, China, or Vietnam as the leader of a new world, they now bestowed that honor on Hong Kong, Singapore, or Taiwan.[127]

Even committed Leninists began to jump ship. The most shocking case was Vietnam, once the perceived focal point of the Cold War, the primary battlefield in the struggle between communism and capitalism. When postwar recovery fell short of expectations in the late 1970s, reformers attempted to stabilize the planned economy through a series of tactical adjustments.[128] But in the 1980s, none other than Trường Chinh – one of the most ardent Leninists in the history of Vietnamese communism – encouraged reformers to move from piecemeal reforms to the construction of a market economy. The Vietnamese Communist Party began to decollectivize the countryside, legalize private enterprise, develop economic incentives to spur growth, solicit foreign direct investment, and reintegrate Vietnam into the capitalist world market. Although the process would take years, and was by no means smooth, the trend toward capitalism was clear.[129] For those who had lived through the Cold War, the reversal was astonishing. After fighting one of the most destructive wars of the era, the communist revolutionaries who millions of people across the world once looked up to as vanguards in the internationalist struggle against capitalist imperialism were now themselves going capitalist.[130]

The same story played out across the North Atlantic in the 1980s. The Leninist problematic lost its purchase on internationalist campaigns. It ceased to resonate with new social movements that increasingly spoke a different language. It even lost the support of loyal anti-imperialist radicals. In this context, many radicals tried to find a new path. At first, they sought to go beyond Leninism through its own terms.[131] When that proved too difficult, they began to experiment with different approaches altogether. In this regard, it is no coincidence that the 1980s would become the era of the linguistic turn, the discursive turn, the cultural turn, the gender turn: in short, the turn away from the inherited ideas of Leninism.

Although some of those radicals who remained loyal to the old language denounced the heterodox efforts of the 1980s as accomplices of a broader attack on the left, these competing ideas were less a cause than a symptom of the radical left's defeat. It was, in other words, the exhaustion of Marxism, Leninism, socialism, communism, and radicalism more broadly that made possible the proliferation of these other ideas.[132] While it is true that some would go on to abandon revolutionary change altogether, it is worth recognizing that many of these figures began their journey out of a genuine desire to find a way to maintain their radical convictions in the wake of Leninism's failure. It is no coincidence that some of the most important thinkers in this regard – Alain Badiou, Étienne Balibar, Cornelius Castoriadis, Angela Davis, Silvia Federici, Michel Foucault, Stuart Hall, Félix Guattari, Ernesto Laclau, Sylvain Lazarus, Claude Lefort, Jean-François Lyotard, Chantal Mouffe, Antontio Negri, Huey Newton, Jacques Rancière, and Rossana Rossanda – had all passed through Leninism in some way or another. Nor should the presence of so many French names come as a surprise, since that was where Leninism, and its traumatic collapse, had such a profound impact.

Even before the fall of the Berlin Wall, then, the Leninist basis of the anti-imperialist politics that had animated millions of people for so many decades was falling apart. A problematic was collapsing, a long cycle was reaching an end, and an entire political matrix of ideas, symbols, theories, practices, references, cultures, and institutions was coming undone. What this meant concretely was that if earlier moments of crisis demanded a kind of recalibration, this one was so thorough that it required a refoundation of radical internationalist politics as such. But even if they had the will, this was not something radicals could simply do by thinking harder. It required the coming together of revolutionary movements across the globe in a long process of political invention. But with the right on the march everywhere, an imperialist reaction in full force, revolutionary movements in serious trouble, anti-imperialists weakened, their inherited theoretical system deteriorating, and rivals taking advantage of the impasse, this was a herculean task. What millions of people once considered the best way to change the world fell into ruin.

Coda
Return of the Repressed

Although facing many obstacles in the years following the 1970s, individualist human rights eventually achieved supremacy. By the 1990s, Jan Eckel argues, "human rights reached their peak proclamatory value and institutional consolidation."[1] Rights groups ballooned in influence. Governments expanded human rights posts. International tribunals tried autocrats for rights violations. The United Nations made human rights the centerpiece of international standards. Human rights became so synonymous with internationalist efforts to improve the world that to criticize them was tantamount to advocating suffering.[2]

Despite their wildly divergent politics, backgrounds, and ambitions, tens of millions of people came to see the world almost exclusively through the lens of human rights. Activists demanding social change, people of color combating racism, women fighting for bodily autonomy, indigenous communities resisting settler colonialism, scholars explaining historical reality, journalists covering political events abroad, politicians enticing voters, and governments justifying foreign interventions all spoke in terms of human rights. Neither true nor false, human rights were internalized as the norm, seen by all as simply the ways things are, and have always been.

But in the very early 2000s the principle of human rights found itself at the center of a series of crises. Perhaps the most heinous of these was the US government's mobilization of human rights to legitimize its brutal invasion of Iraq. Whatever Saddam Hussein's crimes, the United States pushed the limits of international law, ruined millions of lives, and destabilized an entire region. For all those who allowed themselves to believe that the old imperial order was long gone, imperialism struck back with a new human face. In the eyes of many, the idea of human rights began to lose its luster. No longer seen as a timeless reality, human rights rapidly became an object of historical inquiry. One after another scholars raced to make sense of modern human rights history.[3] While some of this earlier work remained relatively positive, with writers emphasizing that human rights had given the oppressed a language, helped win many progressive campaigns, and saved lives, many scholars increasingly focused on the limits of human rights.[4] They highlighted their hypocrisies, pointed to their close connection with neoliberalism, exposed them as a cover for imperialism, criticized rights groups for using biased sources to misinform the public, and excoriated rights campaigns for failing to improve the world.

Things only went from bad to worse. With North Africa gripped by political turmoil in 2011, the radical turned human rights advocate Bernard-Henri Lévy arranged a high-profile meeting between US Secretary of State Hillary Clinton and Mahmoud Jibril of the Libyan National Transitional Council in Paris. As Muammar Gaddafi's forces encircled the Council's base in Benghazi, and a presumed bloodbath appeared imminent, Clinton urged President Barack Obama to intervene. Having promised a new direction after the Bush years, America's first Black president was initially reluctant to let the United States get bogged down in yet another war, but some of his top advisors – such as Samantha Power, superstar academic, human rights activist, Pulitzer Prize-winning author, and the founding executive director of the Carr Center for Human Rights Policy at Harvard's Kennedy School – convinced him to join the French in bombing Gaddafi's forces in Libya. Military intervention allowed the rebels not only to survive, but also to defeat Gaddafi's own strongholds.

Despite warning signs, the champions of human rights declared an early victory. Daniel Cohn-Bendit, who had called for "regime change" in Libya, praised the action.[5] Bernard Kouchner upheld Libya as an example of not only the right, but also the legal responsibility, to intervene in the domestic affairs of a state to "protect civilians, over and above borders and sovereignty."[6] In an article titled "Thank You, America!" liberal commentator Nicholas Kristof wrote that Libya showed how "military force can advance human rights."[7] American political scientist Anne-Marie Slaughter judged the Libyan intervention a win–win, an ideal case where supporting the US government's specific strategic interests on the one hand and upholding the universal values of human rights on the other were nicely synchronized. Libya was paraded as the model for liberal human rights internationalism, an international effort of activists, politicians, philosophers, humanitarians, and human rights proponents that proved, as Slaughter put it, how the "west" could make tough choices and come out on top. The "sceptics," she concluded, "were proved badly wrong."[8]

But what should have been a triumph for human rights soon gave way to a humanitarian cataclysm. Soon after, Libya devolved into a failed state, a land of terrorists, millions of refugees, and a booming slave trade. If the Bush administration's invocation of human rights could be explained away as a cynical manipulation of rights discourse after other justifications for the invasion of Iraq fell flat, the administration that perpetrated the Libyan operation was full of committed supporters of human rights – and led by a man who had voted against the Iraq War – who justified their actions in terms of humanitarian benevolence. If human rights had triumphed in part by taking advantage of anti-imperialism's failures, then the failures of human rights were now becoming difficult to ignore.

The growing rejection of human rights was only one aspect of a generalized crisis across the North Atlantic. By the 2010s, fissures appeared in every sphere of life, each one compounding the others, putting the entire political, cultural, and intellectual order into question. Millions began to challenge inherited assumptions, established institutions, and entrenched political forces. Ours is a time of renewed social movements – on the left, right, and everything in between. If the neoliberal matrix of which human rights ultimately became a part emerged as the hegemonic solution to the multilayered crisis of the 1970s, we are now witnessing that solution's own crisis.[9] Today, the political field has been blown wide open, creating a new opportunity for competing visions of the future. In this context, people are searching for alternative ways of doing politics, not just domestically but internationally. Hundreds of thousands of new activists are once again seeking to change a world in which inequality runs rampant, powerful states invade smaller countries, tens of millions of people suffer from the worst kinds of exploitation, and huge swaths of the globe continue to live on the edge of destruction.

As they tackle the enormous global challenges that lie ahead, many of these newly politicized activists are returning to the revolutionary struggles of the twentieth century for guidance. This book adds to these efforts by revisiting a particularly generative moment of internationalist politics. It traces a history of anti-imperialism, analyzes the reasons for its popularity, explores its guiding assumptions, inventories its conceptual arsenal, profiles some of its partisans, surveys its repertoire of solidarity, tracks its transformations over time, investigates its complex encounters with rivals, explains some reasons for its collapse, and shows how its fall created the conditions that allowed human rights to assume the hegemonic internationalist mantle.

For those looking for concrete examples of different ways to practice solidarity, this study meticulously reconstructs the antiwar initiatives of the 1960s, one of the most vibrant examples of radical internationalism in recent history. For those seeking inspiration, this book's exploration of international resistance to US intervention in Vietnam highlights a particularly stirring instance of a struggle that succeeded against staggering odds. For those in search of conceptual tools, its analysis of a transformative decade showcases a set of concepts that may also help make sense of our own age of crisis. For those hoping to better understand how we got here, it explores a crucial moment of change in the 1970s that created the conditions of possibility for our own conjuncture. And for those wishing to anatomize what was until very recently the dominant way that progressive activists thought about improving the world, it dissects one of the more consequential episodes in the consolidation of individualist human rights as a hegemonic force.

But this book hopes to offer more than just lessons. It aims to suggest a way to think about how we might relate to the revolutionary past itself. Those of us who care about making the world a better place are faced with a vexing problem: Some of the most popular, inspiring, and effective attempts to change the world were intimately tied to the anti-imperialist radical left, and above all Leninism, a project that not only fell far short of its goals, but whose undeniable failures in some cases led to terrible suffering. For that reason, anyone who wishes to draw on the past to inform their politics in the present cannot ignore those glaring failures. Acting in the present depends not just on learning from the past, but also on acknowledging the uncomfortable truth that we stand in a long line of people whose personal, political, and intellectual efforts to change the world had a hand in making possible a whole series of catastrophes. The only way to move forward is to find a way to relate to this dark history.

Addressing this turbulent past is perhaps even more urgent today than in the immediate aftermath of Leninism's collapse in the 1980s because our distance from those events has exacerbated a creeping amnesia. An entire generation is now turning to radical politics without any living memory of this history. In some ways, this collective forgetting has been salutary: It has allowed a new cohort of activists to see with fresh eyes, enabled them to act without guilt, and authorized them to cheerfully salvage whatever they wish from the wreckage of an alien revolutionary past, unburdened by the weight of its failures. But simply forgetting about a problem is not the same as solving it. Ignoring – or repressing – these failures will certainly lead to further problems down the road. Even those activists who believe that they need not bother themselves with such ancient artifacts as Leninism and think they can create something entirely new from scratch will eventually find themselves in trouble. This is quite simply because any attempt to change the world without explaining past failures risks replicating the same mistakes.

To be sure, there are already many strategies for thinking through our relationship to this difficult history, but most are inadequate. Take, for example, perhaps the most fashionable approach today:

rehabilitating the radical movements of the past by expunging their association with the far left as a whole. Progressives now uphold Nelson Mandela as a peaceful reformer but hide his history as a communist revolutionary allied with the likes of Fidel Castro. Liberal feminists reclaim International Women's Day but conveniently forget its provenance in international socialism. Antiracists praise the Black Panther Party but downplay its vociferous criticism of identitarianism, to say nothing of the BPP's explicit struggle for world communism. Postcolonial writers turn to thinkers like C. L. R. James, Claudia Jones, Kwame Nkrumah, and Amílcar Cabral but often say little about how these figures developed their ideas in deep dialogue with Leninism, and even less about how quite a few were outright communist militants.

Of course, recovering radical struggles that were unaffiliated with the red left is important, and there is nothing wrong with drawing on those that were in order to develop a non-Leninist theory of internationalist politics in the present. But it is another thing entirely to distort the fact that so many of these liberation movements did draw on elements of Leninism specifically and the communist left more broadly. Indeed, many of the figures involved in those movements would be the first to admit that some of the novelties often ascribed to them today were already at play in these leftist traditions. By denying these connections, this approach does not simply falsify history, it undermines its own political ambitions: Any attempt to reactivate the ideas of the past necessitates confronting their limits, and so erasing the irrefutable entanglement of these movements with projects like Leninism only hampers the otherwise admirable goal of reinventing emancipatory politics for our own time.

A second approach to the past is to rescue the red flag by shifting attention to the many far left alternatives to Leninism. This means, for instance, returning to Marxist thinkers like Otto Bauer or Rosa Luxemburg, dissident revolutionary currents like anarchism or councilism, or forgotten radical internationalist episodes like the Communist Workers' International. But, as valuable as it may be to take a second look at these heterodox projects today, this approach also misses the target. Since many of these alternatives stemmed from similar sources, and often shared many foundational assumptions with the very Leninism they claimed to oppose, some of the factors that led to the failures of Leninism were also present in those currents that claimed they would have done things differently if given the opportunity. Moreover, this approach struggles to explain exactly why so many people across the globe consciously chose Leninism instead of these other alternatives. It is no coincidence that the majority of leftist revolutionaries in such places as Iran, Angola, Vietnam, and South Africa in the 1970s were not reading Karl

Renner, Anton Pannekoek, or Guy Debord, but V. I. Lenin. Leninism was not merely more popular than these other currents, it was also in many ways the most effective political strategy for combating colonialism, imperialism, and capitalism in a coordinated internationalist manner. With some partial exceptions, none of these alternative far left currents could match the successes of Leninism. From Cuba to Albania, Yugoslavia to China, Vietnam to Russia, the only movements with the capacity to challenge imperialism, overthrow the old order, and begin the transition to an egalitarian future were in some way tied to Leninism. Refocusing attention on marginal episodes without confronting this reality only amounts to avoiding the problem.

A third option is to recognize the historical centrality of Leninism, but to downplay its failures. In its most extreme form, this means pretending that the horrors of the past never happened. In more moderate versions, this means maintaining that a great omelet cannot be made without many broken eggs. More commonly, it means arguing that while Leninism, and communism more generally, was not without its casualties, the death toll from all the invasions, genocides, mass murders, and world wars orchestrated by the colonial, imperialist, and capitalist powers of the modern world has been greater. Leninism may have not have been entirely successful, in other words, but it is hard to believe that capitalism has done much better. If ideologues constantly point to the past to convince us that any attempt to change the world will only lead to disaster, the argument goes, then it is necessary to point out that it is the status quo itself which is already a disaster. There is certainly some truth to this line of reasoning – it is difficult for any honest person to believe that this capitalist world of war, disease, corrupt governments, spiraling inequality, resurgent fascism, and ecological apocalypse is somehow a success. But as politically exigent as it may be to reframe the question of failure, this approach does nothing to help us explain, make sense of, and come to terms with the fact that millions of people who once hoped to change a similar state of affairs ended up doing the opposite. Demonstrating that our progenitors killed fewer people than their enemies does very little to advance emancipatory politics. It does not simply brush the problem under the rug but ends up excusing otherwise inexcusable crimes.

A fourth approach is to accept that Leninism failed, and even that individual Leninists perpetrated atrocities, but to show that none of this was Leninism's fault. According to this view, those radicals who espoused Leninism faced such enormous opposition that in many cases they succeeded in coming to power only through devastating crises such as world wars. Although these crises created indispensable opportunities, they also severely limited what revolutionaries could accomplish.

Instead of realizing their grandiose plans to improve the world, they first had to confront the chaotic conditions that allowed them to come to power in the first place: devastation, starvation, displacement, and instability. They had to redirect energy to countering domestic subversion and foreign intervention. They had to make compromises, bend their ideals, and embrace stopgap measures. This arduous revolutionary process left many Leninists impatient and militaristic, and their politics grew rigid and authoritarian. In other words, if Leninism failed, the reasons have nothing to do with the project itself, which means it is ripe for revival today.

Like the other approaches, this one also has its merits. With so many myths obscuring the complex history of the twentieth century, it is important to correct the historical record by showing that Leninism, and in fact the far left in all its forms, had emancipatory goals and attempted to realize them, but was never given a fair chance. Yet one cannot blame everything on bad luck, merciless enemies, or uncontrollable circumstances. Revolutionaries also had a hand in their own defeat. Refusing to confront the internal failings of Leninism does not merely constrain our ability to understand the history of how and why the broader radical left collapsed so dramatically; it also does a disservice to all those who care about egalitarian politics today. As uncomfortable as it may be, anyone who wants to change the world today must take a cold, sober look at how, when, and where radicals themselves went wrong in the past. This in turn means having the courage to ruthlessly criticize Leninism even while sympathizing with its aims.[10]

Yet another approach is to acknowledge that these Leninist projects failed, and to even accept that revolutionaries were themselves partly responsible for those failures, but to contend that they nevertheless achieved a great deal. They may not have reached their ultimate goals, but these movements successfully expelled imperialists, constructed independent states, held heterogeneous polities together, developed productive forces, raised the quality of life for many people, and gave millions a sense of pride after centuries of humiliation. Although it is important to draw attention to these accomplishments, and imperative to insist that Leninism was not an absolute historical failure, attempting to redeem Leninism in this fashion ends up minimizing its ambitions in a way that misrepresents what was so powerful – and historically attractive – about it in the first place. Leninism was not just about winning national independence, but uniting national liberation struggles across the globe into a vast international movement that could build world communism, that is, a world free of all states, nations, classes, borders, oppressions, inequalities, dominations, and hierarchies. Leninism's great appeal lay precisely in its assurance that nation-building was the means to realizing this universalist project of communism-building.

For that reason, we cannot assess Leninism by artificially dividing it into a nation-building side that is said to have succeeded in spite of the failure of its communist-building side. Quite the contrary, it was the successes of the former that helped make possible the failures of the latter. The very achievements of nation-state modernization that many cite as examples of Leninism's lasting successes, in other words, were often won at the expense of the overarching goal of universal emancipation. Essentializing the nation may have furthered the goal of building a modern nation-state, but it ended up undermining the communist goal of abolishing the nation. Constructing expansive states may have ensured independence, but it ended up undermining the communist goal of abolishing the state. Making people work harder to rapidly develop productive forces may have helped create a powerful country, but it ended up undermining the communist goal of abolishing work. Glorifying the proletariat through affirmative action programs may have integrated more people into a modernizing polity, but it ended up undermining the communist goal of abolishing classes. Since the promise of Leninism was to combine nation-building with communism-building in a harmonious whole, to argue that the nation-building side succeeded but the communism-building side failed is actually to admit that the project of Leninism itself failed. There was, in other words, not a "successful" Leninism that can be saved and an "unsuccessful" Leninism to be discarded, but rather a single contradictory process of failure.

If these different ways of engaging with Leninism's complex history amount to erasure, avoidance, denial, exoneration, or misrepresentation, the approach taken in this book is that of reconciliation. We cannot stand outside this problem but must subjectively place ourselves inside it. This means recognizing that Leninism was one of the most powerful, influential, and effective ways that millions of people tried to change the world, but also accepting that it failed everywhere to realize its goals, that this had much to do with the problematic itself, that these failures sometimes resulted in calamity, and that as heirs to this tradition we too are partly responsible.[11] The only way out, in other words, is through. The approach of this book, then, has been to work deliberately within the terms of the Leninist problematic to explore how several of its core elements crumbled, which in turn sheds light on the overall exhaustion of the problematic itself, yielding insights into the collapse of the radical left as a whole.[12] This is why my exploration of the dramatic transformations in internationalist politics during the 1960s and 1970s has concentrated so heavily on the history of problems internal to the radical left and, specifically, its guiding ideas.

To be clear, I am not suggesting that ideas were the sole driving force in this history. Nor am I suggesting that if only radicals had developed the right theories they could have avoided defeat. The history of the left was very much about millions of people making quick decisions in response to changing circumstances. Nevertheless, ideas such as the right of nations to self-determination played a central role in the collapse of the radical left as such, largely because they acted not as abstruse notions limited to rarefied intellectual debate, but as living concepts that shaped the way that millions of activists interpreted the world, framed problems, and imagined available choices. Nowhere was this clearer than in the Leninist movements, which saw ideas as central to political struggle, constantly made practical decisions in accordance with theoretical precepts, and placed great emphasis on theoretical production. It was Lenin himself who insisted: "Without revolutionary theory there could be no revolutionary movement."[13]

There is also a pressing political reason for this emphasis on intellectual history. While we certainly cannot control the events of the past, or even the circumstances of the present, we can control the sorts of ideas that we choose to reactivate. For those of us seeking to rethink emancipatory politics today, confronting the core ideas that played a role in the collapse of Leninism is mandatory. This means rigorously studying concepts like class, unity, party, state, rights, strategy, history, difference, revolution, transition, democracy, universalism, socialist construction, seizure of power, and the dictatorship of the proletariat. While I have tried to engage with several aspects of the Leninist problematic, it would have been impossible – not to mention a test of the reader's patience – to address all these concepts in a single volume. I therefore chose to devote this book to exploring just one constellation of ideas that includes the nation, nation-state, nationalism, imperialism, anti-imperialism, internationalism, and the right to self-determination.

There are many reasons for focusing on these particular ideas, but perhaps the most important is that they have received relatively less sustained attention in critical assessments of Leninism's failures than other core ideas such as class, party, and state.[14] It is in part because they have escaped the scathing criticism usually reserved for other aspects of Leninism that these ideas remain very much alive. While progressives today automatically reject the vanguard party, the dictatorship of the proletariat, and the absolute objective centrality of class, many have effectively – and in quite a few cases unknowingly – rehabilitated other classically Leninist ideas like the right of nations to self-determination. Against the backdrop of widespread skepticism toward globalized neoliberal capitalism, as well as international institutions like the United Nations, the

World Bank, and the European Union, national self-determination has even made something of a comeback. It is now invoked by those who support the Palestinian people, indigenous sovereignty in North America, the Venezuelan government, or Southern European efforts to fight the European "Troika," to name only a few examples. The renewed appeal of these ideas demands that they be confronted with an urgency that other elements of the Leninist problematic do not.[15]

The point, however, is neither to condemn these old, abandoned ideas nor to expose the ones that have managed to survive. It is instead to understand why those who once fought to create a new world free from all oppression, domination, and exploitation invented them in the first place. It is to reconstruct the political problems that they were intended to solve. It is to determine whether they succeeded in adequately addressing these problems, solved them in a way that created new problems, or simply failed altogether. It is to explain why the political matrix that gave them meaning is now saturated. And it is to discover what all this means for us.

In this way, this book has sought to contribute to the collective reassessment of our shared revolutionary history, without which we cannot rethink emancipatory politics today. Taking stock of previous attempts to change the world allows us to draw new lessons, avoid repeating old mistakes, and find healthy ways of reconciling ourselves to the disasters of the past. But more than that, coming to terms with these failed attempts can help us to begin again. Leninism's blueprint for winning an egalitarian future is exhausted, but its tragic failures have illuminated many crucial political problems that are still very much in need of resolution. It is only by working through these failures – instead of ignoring them, explaining them away, or pretending they never happened – that we can invent a new emancipatory political matrix for our time. The real work has only just begun.[16]

Notes

Introduction

1 Heather Marie Stur, *Saigon at War: South Vietnam and the Global Sixties* (Cambridge: Cambridge University Press, 2020), 32–40.

2 For internal debates leading to the offensive, see Lien-Hang T. Nguyen, *Hanoi's War: An International History of the War for Peace in Vietnam* (Chapel Hill: University of North Carolina Press, 2012), especially Parts 1 and 2.

3 Edwin E. Moïse, *The Myths of Tet: The Most Misunderstood Event of the Vietnam War* (Lawrence: University Press of Kansas, 2017).

4 Sheila Rowbotham, *Promise of a Dream: Remembering the Sixties* (London: Verso, 2001), 164.

5 Tariq Ali, *Street Fighting Years: An Autobiography of the Sixties* (London: Verso, 2005), 246.

6 Martin Klimke, *The Other Alliance: Student Protest in West Germany and the United States in the Global Sixties* (Princeton: Princeton University Press, 2010), 91–96.

7 Salar Mohandesi, "Bringing Vietnam Home: The Vietnam War, Internationalism, and May '68," *French Historical Studies* 41, no. 2 (April 2018): 219–51.

8 Grant Evans and Kelvin Rowley, *Red Brotherhood at War: Vietnam, Cambodia and Laos since 1975*, 2nd ed. (London: Verso, 1990).

9 Jana K. Lipman, *In Camps: Vietnamese Refugees, Asylum Seekers, and Repatriates* (Berkeley: University of California Press, 2020).

10 Barbara J. Keys, *Reclaiming American Virtue: The Human Rights Revolution of the 1970s* (Cambridge, MA: Harvard University Press, 2014).

11 For a personal account of the campaign to save the "boat people," see Bernard Kouchner, *L'île de Lumière* (Paris: Ramsay, 1980).

12 Perry Anderson, *In the Tracks of Historical Materialism* (London: Verso, 1983), 32.

13 Robert Brier, *Poland's Solidarity Movement and the Global Politics of Human Rights* (Cambridge: Cambridge University Press, 2021), 108.

14 For an excellent study of Paris as a historical site of internationalist politics, see Michael Goebel, *Anti-Imperial Metropolis: Interwar Paris and the Seeds of Third World Nationalism* (Cambridge: Cambridge University Press, 2015).

15 Robert Horvath, "'The Solzhenitsyn Effect': East European Dissidents and the Demise of Revolutionary Privilege," *Human Rights Quarterly* 29, no. 4 (November 2007): 907.

16 See, among many others, Kristin Ross, *May '68 and Its Afterlives* (Chicago: University of Chicago Press, 2002).

17 See, among many others, Max Elbaum, *Revolution in the Air: Sixties Radicals Turn to Lenin, Mao and Che* (London: Verso, 2002).

18 Che Guevara, "Vietnam Must Not Stand Alone," *New Left Review* 43 (May–June 1967): 80.

19 Quoted in Christoph Kalter, *The Discovery of the Third World: Decolonization and the Rise of the New Left in France, c. 1950–1976*, trans. Thomas Dunlap (Cambridge: Cambridge University Press, 2016), 278.

20 I wish to emphasize, however, that, while this book certainly brings Vietnamese actors back into the history of international antiwar activism, it is primarily about activists in the North Atlantic, who were transnationally connected to a certain set of Vietnamese figures, and does not presume to be a history of Vietnam proper. To undertake the latter would require a deeper engagement with Vietnamese history, the rich historiography of modern Vietnam, and a wider range of Vietnamese sources, all of which would have pushed this already lengthy study well beyond its limits.

21 Le Duan, *Forward under the Glorious Banner of the October Revolution* (Hanoi: Foreign Languages Publishing House, 1967), 61.

22 Nguyet Nguyen, "Antiwar Transnationalism: People's Diplomacy in the Vietnam War" (Ph.D. diss., American University, 2019).

23 For the concept of "encounters," see Louis Althusser, "The Underground Current of the Materialism of the Encounter," in Louis Althusser, *Philosophy of the Encounter: Later Writings, 1978–1987*, trans. G. M. Goshgarian (London: Verso, 2006), 163–207.

24 For a few examples of these other pathways, see Horvath, "'The Solzhenitsyn Effect'"; Brier, *Poland's Solidarity Movement*; Eleanor Davey, *Idealism beyond Borders: The French Revolutionary Left and the Rise of Humanitarianism, 1954–1988* (Cambridge: Cambridge University Press, 2015); and Patrick William Kelly, *Sovereign Emergencies: Latin America and the Making of Global Human Rights Politics* (Cambridge: Cambridge University Press, 2018).

25 "To be radical is to grasp the root of the matter," wrote Karl Marx in his introduction to the "Contribution to the Critique of Hegel's Philosophy of Law," reprinted in *Marx & Engels Collected Works*, vol. III (London: Lawrence & Wishart, 1975), 182.

26 For the notion of collective characters living through a process of subjectivation, see Nanni Balestrini, "Q&A," *The Nation* 303, no. 23–24 (December 5–12, 2016): 5.

27 For internationalism, see Fred Halliday, "Three Concepts of Internationalism," *International Affairs* 64, no. 2 (Spring 1988): 187–98; Tom Nairn, "Internationalism and the Second Coming," *Daedalus* 122, no. 3 (Summer 1993): 155–70; Perry Anderson, "Internationalism: A Breviary," *New Left Review* 14 (March–April 2002): 5–25; Mark Mazower, "An International Civilization? Empire, Internationalism and the Crisis of the Mid-Twentieth Century," *International Affairs* 82, no. 3 (May 2006): 553–66; and Glenda Sluga, "Rediscovering Internationalism," *Current History* 113, no. 766 (November 2014): 305–11.

28 For the concept of the "problematic," see Louis Althusser, *For Marx*, trans. Ben Brewster (London: Verso, 2005), 32 and 69.

29 For an insightful, though obviously biased, exploration of the philosophical basis of this kind of human rights discourse, see Alain Badiou, *Ethics: An Essay on the Understanding of Evil*, trans. Peter Hallward (London: Verso, 2002), 4–17.

30 To take one example, Julian Bourg's otherwise excellent book *From Revolution to Ethics: May 1968 and Contemporary French Thought* (Montreal: McGill-Queen's University Press, 2007), 6. For a criticism of this approach, see Warren Breckman, "From Revolution to Ethics: May 1968 and Contemporary French Thought. By Julian Bourg," *Journal of Modern History* 81, no. 1 (March 2009): 207–09.

31 Samuel Moyn, *The Last Utopia: Human Rights in History* (Cambridge, MA: Belknap Press of Harvard University Press, 2010).

32 For a classic account, see Charles DeBenedetti and Charles Chatfield, *An American Ordeal: The Antiwar Movement of the Vietnam Era* (Syracuse: Syracuse University Press, 1990).

33 Bethany S. Keenan, "'Vietnam Is Fighting for Us': French Identities and the US–Vietnam War, 1965–1973" (Ph.D. diss., University of North Carolina, Chapel Hill, 2009).

34 Nicolas Pas, "Sortir de l'ombre du Parti communiste français. Histoire de l'engagement de l'extrême-gauche française sur la guerre du Vietnam, 1965–1968" (Mémoire de DEA, Institut d'études politiques, 1998).

35 Sabine Rousseau, "Du Vietnam héroïque à la défense des droits de l'homme," in *68: Une histoire collective, 1962–1981*, eds. Philippe Artières and Michelle Zancarini-Fournel (Paris: La Découverte, 2008), 481–86.

36 Harish C. Mehta, "'People's Diplomacy': The Diplomatic Front of North Vietnam during the War against the United States, 1965–1972" (Ph.D. diss., McMaster University, 2009).

37 Judy Tzu-Chun Wu, *Radicals on the Road: Internationalism, Orientalism, and Feminism during the Vietnam Era* (Ithaca: Cornell University Press, 2013).

38 Robin D. G. Kelley, *Freedom Dreams: The Black Radical Imagination* (Boston: Beacon Press, 2002).

39 Gerd-Rainer Horn, *The Spirit of '68: Rebellion in Western Europe and North America, 1956–1976* (Oxford: Oxford University Press, 2007).

40 Klimke, *The Other Alliance.*

41 Kalter, *The Discovery of the Third World.*

42 Cynthia A. Young, *Soul Power: Culture, Radicalism, and the Making of a US Third World Left* (Durham: Duke University Press, 2006).

43 Ross, *May '68 and Its Afterlives.*

44 Alessandro Russo, *Cultural Revolution and Revolutionary Culture* (Durham: Duke University Press, 2020).

45 Moyn, *The Last Utopia.*

46 Mark Philip Bradley, *The World Reimagined: Americans and Human Rights in the Twentieth Century* (Cambridge: Cambridge University Press, 2016).

47 Jan Eckel, *The Ambivalence of Good: Human Rights in International Politics since the 1940s*, trans. Rachel Ward (Oxford: Oxford University Press, 2019).

48 Keys, *Reclaiming American Virtue.*

49 Davey, *Idealism beyond Borders.*

Overture

1 Sophie Quinn-Judge, *Ho Chi Minh: The Missing Years, 1919–1941* (Berkeley: University of California Press, 2002), Chapter 1.
2 For more on the First World War and French Indochina, see Kimloan Vu-Hill, *Coolies into Rebels: Impact of World War I on French Indochina* (Paris: Les Indes savantes, 2011).
3 "Claims of the Annamite People," in *Vietnam and America: A Documented History*, eds. Marvin E. Gettleman et al. (New York: Grove Press, 1995), 19.
4 William Duiker, *Ho Chi Minh: A Life* (New York: Hyperion, 2000), 62–64.
5 Hồ Chí Minh, "The Path Which Led Me to Leninism," in Hồ Chí Minh, *Selected Writings, 1920–1969* (Hanoi: Foreign Languages Publishing House, 1977), 251.
6 It is worth noting that the role of Leninism in the Vietnamese revolution has been hotly debated since at least the Vietnam War itself. The ferocity of the debate is largely a consequence of the political stakes. On the one side are liberals, who seek to reclaim the Vietnamese liberation struggle by divorcing it from Leninism, in the same way, for instance, that the "doves" claimed during the war that the National Liberation Front was an independent formation free from communism. On the other side are the conservatives, who seek to denounce the liberation struggle by proving its thorough association with Leninism, in the same way, for instance, that the "hawks" claimed during the war that the National Liberation Front was fully controlled by communists in Hanoi. In this way, shared assumptions about Leninism have tended to bind scholarly positions to specific political stances. I try to take a different approach here: This book argues that the thinking of many Vietnamese leaders was deeply shaped by Leninism but rejects the political conclusions of the conservatives.
7 The debates that eventually resulted in those positions later codified as the Leninist problematic were complex, involved many figures, and followed uneven timelines. Lenin's interventions on national self-determination, for example, preceded his exposition of the theory of imperialism. All this makes any historical reconstruction, particularly in so short a space, difficult. In order to make this history as accessible as possible, I have therefore limited my scope, simplified some of the terms, and reordered the narrative according to concepts rather than strict chronology.
8 Jules Ferry, "Speech before the French National Assembly," reprinted in Ralph A. Austen, ed., *Modern Imperialism: Western Overseas Expansion and Its Aftermath, 1776–1965* (Lexington: Heath, 1969), 73.
9 Eugen Weber, *Peasants into Frenchmen: The Modernization of Rural France, 1870–1914* (Stanford: Stanford University Press, 1976).
10 For French Indochina, see Pierre Brocheux and Daniel Hémery, *Indochina: An Ambiguous Colonization, 1858–1954*, trans. Ly Lan Dill-Klein et al. (Berkeley: University of California Press, 2011).
11 John Darwin, *After Tamerlane: The Global History of Empire since 1405* (London: Bloomsbury, 2008), 328.
12 Richard B. Day and Daniel Gaido, "Introduction," in *Discovering Imperialism: Social Democracy to World War I*, eds. Richard B. Day and Daniel Gaido (Chicago: Haymarket Books, 2011), 11–13.

13 Eduard Bernstein, "German Social Democracy and the Turkish Troubles," reprinted in *Marxism and Social Democracy: The Revisionist Debate, 1896–1898*, eds. H. Tudor and J. M. Tudor (Cambridge: Cambridge University Press, 1988), 51–61.

14 Day and Gaido, "Introduction," 20–23.

15 *Cinquième Congrès socialiste international tenu à Paris du 23 au 27 septembre 1900. Compte rendu analytique officiel* (Paris: Société nouvelle de librairie et d'édition, 1901), 107.

16 Belfort Bax, "The International Congress and Colonial Policy," *Justice*, September 14, 1907, 3.

17 Belfort Bax, "Some Reflections on the Paris Congress," *Justice*, October 13, 1900, 4.

18 Material in the following survey was previously published in Salar Mohandesi, "Imperialism," in *The SAGE Handbook of Marxism*, vol. I, eds. Beverley Skeggs et al. (London: Sage, 2022), 432–35. Copyright 2022, Salar Mohandesi. Republished by permission of the publisher.

19 John Atkinson Hobson, *Imperialism: A Study* (Cambridge: Cambridge University Press, 2011).

20 For an excellent collection of early leftist writings on imperialism, see Day and Gaido, eds., *Discovering Imperialism*.

21 For overviews of early Marxist theories of imperialism, see Wolfgang J. Mommsen, *Theories of Imperialism*, trans. P. S. Falla (New York: Random House, 1980); Anthony Brewer, *Marxist Theories of Imperialism: A Critical Survey*, 2nd ed. (London: Routledge, 1990); and John Milios and Dimitris P. Sotiropoulos, *Rethinking Imperialism: A Study of Capitalist Rule* (New York: Palgrave Macmillan, 2009).

22 Karl Kautsky, "Ultra-Imperialism," reprinted in *New Left Review* 59 (January–February 1970): 41–46.

23 V. I. Lenin, "Imperialism, the Highest Stage of Capitalism," in V. I. Lenin, *Collected Works*, vol. XXII (Moscow: Progress Publishers, 1974), 294.

24 Ibid., 265–67.

25 Ibid., 266.

26 For criticisms of Lenin's pamphlet, see Brewer, *Marxist Theories of Imperialism*, 116–23.

27 For a genealogy of this term, see Eric D. Weitz, "Self-Determination: How a German Enlightenment Idea Became the Slogan of National Liberation and a Human Right," *American Historical Review* 120, no. 2 (April 2015): 462–96.

28 Eric Blanc, "Anti-Imperial Marxism: Borderland Socialists and the Evolution of Bolshevism on National Liberation," *International Socialist Review* 100 (Spring 2016): 111–40.

29 For a good overview of Marxist debates over the "national question," see Georges Haupt, Michael Löwy, and Claudie Weill, eds., *Les Marxistes et la question nationale, 1848–1914*, 2nd ed. (Paris: L'Harmattan, 1997).

30 Rosa Luxemburg, "The National Question and Autonomy," in *The National Question: Selected Writings by Rosa Luxemburg*, ed. Horace B. Davis (New York: Monthly Review Press, 1976), 173.

31 Ibid., 134.

32 Ibid., 130–31.

33 Rosa Luxemburg, *The Crisis in the German Social-Democracy* (New York: Fertig, 1969), 95.
34 Luxemburg, "The National Question," 110.
35 Ibid.
36 Ibid., 110–11.
37 Ibid., 190.
38 Ibid., 134.
39 V. I. Lenin, "The Right of Nations to Self-Determination," in V. I. Lenin, *Collected Works*, vol. XX (Moscow: Progress Publishers, 1977), 399.
40 See, for example, Michael Löwy, "Marxists and the National Question," *New Left Review* 96 (March–April 1976): 96–97.
41 V. I. Lenin, "The Discussion on Self-Determination Summed Up," in Lenin, *Collected Works*, vol. XXII, 356. Unless otherwise indicated, all emphasis in quotations is in the original text.
42 For an exploration of this thinking, see Matthieu Renault, *L'Empire de la révolution. Lénine et les musulmans de Russie* (Paris: Syllepse, 2017).
43 For an overview of the concept of the "bourgeois revolution," see Neil Davidson, *How Revolutionary Were the Bourgeois Revolutions?* (Chicago: Haymarket Books, 2012).
44 Lenin, "Right of Nations to Self-Determination," 406.
45 Ibid., 399.
46 Luxemburg, *The Crisis in the German Social-Democracy*, 95.
47 V. I. Lenin, "The Revolutionary Proletariat and the Right of Nations to Self-Determination," in V. I. Lenin, *Collected Works*, vol. XXI (Moscow: Progress Publishers, 1974), 409.
48 Ibid.
49 V. I. Lenin, "The Socialist Revolution and the Right of Nations to Self-Determination," in *Collected Works*, vol. XXII, 144.
50 V. I. Lenin, "The Junius Pamphlet," in *Collected Works*, vol. XXII, 312.
51 Even those who side with Luxemburg admit as much. See Horace B. Davis, "Introduction: The Right of National Self-Determination in Marxist Theory – Luxemburg vs. Lenin," in *The National Question*, 10 and 12.
52 V. I. Lenin, "Decree on Peace," in V. I. Lenin, *Collected Works*, vol. XXVI (Moscow: Progress Publishers, 1977), 249–53.
53 Arno Mayer, *Political Origins of the New Diplomacy, 1917–1918* (New Haven: Yale University Press, 1959); Erez Manela, *The Wilsonian Moment: Self-Determination and the International Origins of Anticolonial Nationalism* (Oxford: Oxford University Press, 2007); and Adom Getachew, *Worldmaking after Empire: The Rise and Fall of Self-Determination* (Princeton: Princeton University Press, 2019), Chapter 2.
54 Manela, *Wilsonian Moment*, 45–53.
55 Susan Pedersen, *The Guardians: The League of Nations and the Crisis of Empire* (Oxford: Oxford University Press, 2015).
56 Manela, *Wilsonian Moment*, Part 3.
57 V. I. Lenin, "Preliminary Draft Theses on the National and Colonial Questions," in V. I. Lenin, *Collected Works*, vol. XXXI (Moscow: Progress Publishers, 1974), 144–51.

58 V. I. Lenin, "Report on the National and Colonial Questions," in *Workers of the World and Oppressed Peoples, Unite! Proceedings and Documents of the Second Congress, 1920*, vol. I, ed. John Riddell (New York: Pathfinder, 1991), 276–77.

59 M. N. Roy, "Supplementary Theses on the National and Colonial Questions," in *Workers of the World*, 284.

60 For the Trotskyist interpretation, see Leon Trotsky, *The Permanent Revolution*, trans. Max Shachtman (New York: Pioneer Publishers, 1931). For the Maoist one, see Mao Zedong, *On New Democracy* (Beijing: Foreign Languages Press, 1967).

61 V. I. Lenin, "The Terms of Admission into the Communist International," in *Collected Works*, vol. XXXI, 209.

62 It is worth noting that this emphasis on emancipatory nationalist internationalism goes at least as far back as Karl Marx and Friedrich Engels. As the latter once remarked, "Generally speaking, an international movement of the proletariat is possible only as between independent nations." See "Engels to Karl Kautsky. 7 February 1882," in *Marx and Engels Collected Works*, vol. XLVI (London: Lawrence & Wishart, 1992), 191–92.

63 Ewa Czerwińska-Schupp, *Otto Bauer (1881–1938): Thinker and Politician*, trans. Maciej Zurowski (Leiden: Brill, 2017), Chapter 4.

64 See, for example, Otto Bauer, "The Nation," in *Mapping the Nation*, ed. Gopal Balakrishnan (London: Verso, 2012), 39–77.

65 V. I. Lenin, "To Maxim Gorky," in V. I. Lenin, *Collected Works*, vol. XXXV (Moscow: Progress Publishers, 1973), 84. I have chosen to go with Robert C. Tucker's translation in *Stalin as Revolutionary, 1879–1929: A Study in History and Personality* (New York: Norton, 1973), 152.

66 James M. Blaut, *The National Question: Decolonizing the Theory of Nationalism* (London: Zed Books, 1987), 146–47.

67 J. V. Stalin, "Marxism and the National Question," in J. V. Stalin, *Works*, vol. II (Moscow: Foreign Languages Publishing House, 1953), 307.

68 Ibid., 13.

69 Alfred J. Rieber, "Stalin, Man of the Borderlands," *American Historical Review 106*, no. 5 (December 2001): 1651–91.

70 Leon Trotsky, *Stalin: An Appraisal of the Man and His Influence*, trans. Charles Malamuth (New York: Harper & Brothers, 1941), 154–59.

71 For an excellent overview of these debates, see Jeremy Smith, *The Bolsheviks and the National Question, 1917–1923* (London: Palgrave Macmillan, 1999).

72 Jeremy Smith highlights some of these differences in "Stalin as Commissar for Nationality Affairs, 1918–1922," in *Stalin: A New History*, eds. Sarah Davies and James Harris (Cambridge: Cambridge University Press, 2009), 45–62.

73 Terry Martin, "An Affirmative Action Empire: The Soviet Union as the Highest Form of Imperialism," in *A State of Nations: Empire and Nation-Making in the Age of Lenin and Stalin*, eds. Ronald Grigor Suny and Terry Martin (Oxford: Oxford University Press, 2001), 69–72.

74 Terry Martin, *The Affirmative Action Empire: Nations and Nationalism in the Soviet Union, 1923–1939* (Ithaca: Cornell University Press, 2001).

75 Hồ Chí Minh, "Lenin and the Colonial Peoples," in Hồ Chí Minh, *Selected Writings*, 38.

76 Terry Martin, "Borders and Ethnic Conflict: The Soviet Experiment in Ethno-Territorial Proliferation," *Jahrbücher für Geschichte Osteuropas* 47, no. 4 (September 1999): 538–55.

77 Francine Hirsch, *Empire of Nations: Ethnographic Knowledge and the Making of the Soviet Union* (Ithaca: Cornell University Press, 2005).

78 Terry Martin, "Modernization or Neo-traditionalism? Ascribed Nationality and Soviet Primordialism," in *Russian Modernity: Politics, Knowledge, and Practices, 1800–1950*, eds. David L. Hoffmann and Yanni Kotsonis (London: Palgrave Macmillan, 2000), 161–82.

79 See, for example, V. I. Lenin, "The State and Revolution," in V. I. Lenin, *Collected Works*, vol. XXV (Moscow: Progress Publishers, 1974), 387–497.

80 For Stalin's theory, see, for example, "Concerning Questions of Leninism," in J. V. Stalin, *Works*, vol. VIII (Moscow: Foreign Languages Publishing House, 1954), 64–80.

81 For a summary of this historical episode, see Sheila Fitzpatrick, *The Russian Revolution*, 4th ed. (Oxford: Oxford University Press, 2017), 112–20.

82 Jeremy Smith, *Red Nations: The Nationalities Experience in and after the USSR* (Cambridge: Cambridge University Press, 2013), especially Chapter 5. For Soviet patriotism, see David Brandenberger, *National Bolshevism: Stalinist Mass Culture and the Formation of Modern Russian National Identity, 1931– 1956* (Cambridge, MA: Harvard University Press, 2002).

83 See also Perry Anderson's remarks on the relationship between "socialism in one country" and the breakdown of communist internationalism in "Internationalism: A Breviary," *New Left Review* 14 (March–April 2002): 21.

84 Cited in Duiker, *Ho Chi Minh*, 97.

85 See, for example, J. V. Stalin, "The Foundations of Leninism," in J. V. Stalin, *Works*, vol. VI (Moscow: Foreign Languages Publishing House, 1953), 71–196.

86 Ibid., 73.

87 Lenin, "Imperialism," in Lenin, *Collected Works*, vol. XXII, 187 and 195–96.

88 Recognizing this goes a long way to explaining the unity of communism and nationalism in so many historical cases. For the Eastern European case, see, for example, Martin Mevius, "Reappraising Communism and Nationalism," *Nationalities Papers* 37, no. 4 (July 2009): 377–400.

89 For an interesting exploration of this "symptomatic aporia" with a focus on class, or "classism," see Alessandro Russo, "The Sixties and Us," in *The Idea of Communism*, vol. III, *The Seoul Conference*, eds. Alex Taek-Gwang Lee and Slavoj Žižek (London: Verso Books, 2016), 169.

90 For the League, see, among others, Vijay Prashad, *The Darker Nations: A People's History of the Third World* (New York: New Press, 2007), 16–30; Fredrik Petersson, "Hub of the Anti-Imperialist Movement: The League against Imperialist and Berlin, 1927–1933," *Interventions: International Journal of Postcolonial Studies* 16, no. 1 (2014): 49–71; and Michele Louro et al., eds., *The League against Imperialism: Lives and Afterlives* (Leiden: Leiden University Press, 2020).

91 For an exploration of interwar anti-imperialist internationalisms, see Manu Goswami, "Imaginary Futures and Colonial Internationalisms," *American Historical Review* 117, no. 5 (December 2012): 1461–85.

92 Michele L. Louro, *Comrades against Imperialism: Nehru, India, and Interwar Internationalism* (Cambridge: Cambridge University Press, 2018), 22–23.

93 For a detailed criticism of the USSR's promotion of national liberation to advance its own geopolitical interests against communist internationalism, see Loren Goldner, "'Socialism in One Country' Before Stalin, and the Origins of Reactionary 'Anti-Imperialism': The Case of Turkey, 1917–1925," reprinted in Loren Goldner, *Revolution, Defeat and Theoretical Underdevelopment: Russia, Turkey, Spain, Bolivia* (Leiden: Brill, 2016), 52–116.

94 Jay Taylor, *The Generalissimo: Chiang Kai-Shek and the Struggle for Modern China* (Cambridge, MA: Belknap Press of Harvard University Press, 2009), 34 and 42–47.

95 For the League and its tensions, see Michael Goebel, *Anti-Imperial Metropolis: Interwar Paris and the Seeds of Third World Nationalism* (Cambridge: Cambridge University Press, 2015), 199–215.

96 See, for example, Clive J. Christie, *Revolution and Ideology in Southeast Asia 1900–1980* (Richmond: Curzon Press, 2001).

97 See, for example, Hue-Tam Ho Tai, *Radicalism and the Origins of the Vietnamese Revolution* (Cambridge, MA: Harvard University Press, 1996).

98 Pierre Asselin, *Vietnam's American War: A History* (Cambridge: Cambridge University Press, 2018), 35.

99 William J. Duiker, *The Rise of Nationalism in Vietnam, 1900–1941* (Ithaca: Cornell University Press, 1976), 13–14.

100 See, especially, Tuong Vu, *Vietnam's Communist Revolution: The Power and Limits of Ideology* (Cambridge: Cambridge University Press, 2017), especially Chapters 2 and 3.

101 Alec Holcombe, *Mass Mobilization in the Democratic Republic of Vietnam, 1945–1960* (Honolulu: University of Hawai'i Press, 2020), 10.

102 Ho Chi Minh, "Consolidation and Development of Ideological Unity among Marxist-Leninist Parties," in Ho Chi Minh, *Selected Works*, vol. IV (Hanoi: Foreign Languages Publishing House, 1962), 184.

103 Scholars such as David Biggs, Andrew Hardy, Shawn McHale, Edward Miller, Lien-Hang T. Nguyen, and Hue-Tam Ho Tai have all tried to complicate the teleological and often black-and-white history of communism in Vietnam.

104 The most recent, forceful, and well-researched representative of this perspective is Vu, *Vietnam's Communist Revolution*.

105 Ho Chi Minh, "The Imperialist Aggressors Can Never Enslave the Heroic Vietnamese People," in Ho Chi Minh, *Selected Works*, vol. III (Hanoi: Foreign Languages Publishing House, 1961), 312.

106 For the construction of the authoritarian party-state in the 1940s and 1950s, see, for example, Holcombe, *Mass Mobilization*.

107 For land reform, see, among others, Edwin E. Moise, *Land Reform in China and North Vietnam: Consolidating the Revolution at the Village Level* (Chapel Hill: University of North Carolina Press), 1983; Balazs Szalontai, "Political and Economic Crisis in North Vietnam, 1955–1956," *Cold War History* 5, no. 4 (November 2005): 395–426; Alex-Thai D. Vo, "Nguyễn Thị Năm

and the Land Reform in North Vietnam, 1953," *Journal of Vietnamese Studies* 10, no. 1 (February 2015): 1–62; and Holcombe, *Mass Mobilization*.

108 See, for example, Chen Jian, "China and the First Indo-China War, 1950–1954," *China Quarterly* 133 (March 1993): 85–110; Qiang Zhai, *China and the Vietnam Wars, 1950–1975* (Chapel Hill: University of North Carolina Press, 2000), Chapters 1 and 2; and Christopher E. Goscha, "Vietnam, the Third Indochina War and the Meltdown of Asian Internationalism," in *The Third Indochina War: Conflict between China, Vietnam and Cambodia, 1972–1979*, eds. Odd Arne Westad and Sophie Quinn-Judge (New York: Routledge, 2006), 157–58.

109 Cited in Vu, *Vietnam's Communist Revolution*, 109.

110 Frantz Fanon, *The Wretched of the Earth*, trans. Richard Philcox (New York: Grove Press, 2004), 30–31.

111 Truong Chinh, *The August Revolution* (Hanoi: Foreign Languages Publishing House, 1958), 54.

112 This thinking is implicit in the Program of the National Liberation Front of South Vietnam, and even more so in the revised version, which aimed to encourage national minorities to "settle down to sedentary life" and to "catch up with the general standard of the people." See "Political Program of the South Viet Nam National Front for Liberation," reprinted in Robert F. Turner, *Vietnamese Communism: Its Origins and Development* (Stanford: Hoover Institution Press, 1975), 438. For a survey of nationalities policies in Vietnam, see Walker Connor, *The National Question in Marxist–Leninist Theory and Strategy* (Princeton: Princeton University Press, 1984), Chapter 5.

113 For the internationalism of Vietnamese communists in Southeast Asia, see Goscha, "Vietnam," 159–62.

114 Hồ Chí Minh, "Testament," in Hồ Chí Minh, *Selected Writings*, 362.

115 Duiker, *Ho Chi Minh*, 560.

116 For a theoretical exploration of this contradiction more generally, see Michael Neocosmos, *Thinking Freedom in Africa: Toward a Theory of Emancipatory Politics* (Johannesburg: Wits University Press, 2016), Chapter 4.

1   Internationalism

1 Stephen Smale, "Talk at Mutualité," May 26, 1966, 1 in Stephen Smale Papers, BANC MSS 99/373 c, carton 3, Bancroft Library, University of California, Berkeley, United States (hereafter Bancroft).

2 Since France only had "economic" relations with the Democratic Republic of Vietnam (DRV) at this time, Mai Văn Bộ was technically the chief representative of the DRV's commercial delegation. That said, he effectively served as a diplomat, a role that would become more formalized in the coming years. See Nguyet Nguyen, "Antiwar Transnationalism: People's Diplomacy in the Vietnam War" (Ph.D. diss., American University, 2019), 110–15.

3 Smale, "Talk at Mutualité," 2.

4 Material in the following survey was previously published in Salar Mohandesi, Bjarke Skærlund Risager, and Laurence Cox, eds., *Voices of 1968: Documents from the Global North* (London: Pluto Press, 2018), 1–34. Copyright 2018, Salar Mohandesi, Bjarke Skærlund Risager, and Laurence Cox. Reproduced with permission of the Licensor through PLSclear.

5 Robert Gildea, James Mark, and Niek Pas, "European Radicals and the 'Third World': Imagined Solidarities and Radical Networks, 1958–1973," *Cultural and Social History* 8, no. 4 (December 2011): 449–71.
6 Julien Hage, "Feltrinelli, Maspero, Wagenbach. Une nouvelle génération d'éditeurs politiques d'extrême gauche, histoire comparée, histoire croisée, 1955–1982" (Ph.D. diss., Université de Versailles-Saint-Quentin-en-Yvelines, 2010). For the French case, see Christoph Kalter, *The Discovery of the Third World: Decolonization and the Rise of the New Left in France, c. 1950–1976*, trans. Thomas Dunlap (Cambridge: Cambridge University Press, 2016), especially Chapter 4.
7 See, for example, Daniel A. Gordon, *Immigrants and Intellectuals: May '68 and the Rise of Anti-Racism in France* (Pontypool: Merlin Press, 2012); Burleigh Hendrickson, "March 1968: Practicing Transnational Activism from Tunis to Paris," *International Journal of Middle East Studies* 44, no. 4 (November 2012): 755–74; and Quinn Slobodian, *Foreign Front: Third World Politics in Sixties West Germany* (Durham: Duke University Press, 2012).
8 The literature on the social problems of the 1960s is massive. For a brief survey, see Ronald Fraser et al., eds., *1968: A Student Generation in Revolt* (New York: Pantheon Books, 1988), 15–32.
9 Arthur Marwick, *The Sixties: Cultural Revolution in Britain, France, Italy, and the United States, c. 1958–c. 1974* (Oxford: Oxford University Press, 1998), Part 2; Gerd-Rainer Horn, *The Spirit of '68: Rebellion in Western Europe and North America, 1956–1976* (Oxford: Oxford University Press, 2007), Part 1; and Jeremi Suri, "The Rise and Fall of an International Counterculture, 1960–1975," *American Historical Review* 114, no. 1 (February 2009): 45–68.
10 Mohandesi et al., *Voices of 1968*, 10–11.
11 Kristin Ross, *May '68 and Its Afterlives* (Chicago: University of Chicago Press, 2002).
12 Van Gosse, *Where the Boys Are: Cuba, Cold War America and the Making of a New Left* (London: Verso, 1993).
13 Elaine Mokhtefi, *Algiers, Third World Capital: Freedom Fighters, Revolutionaries, Black Panthers* (London: Verso, 2018). For Algeria as "Mecca," see Jeffrey James Byrne, *Mecca of Revolution: Algeria, Decolonization, and the Third World Order* (Oxford: Oxford University Press, 2016).
14 Christophe Bourseiller, *Les Maoïstes. La folle histoire des gardes rouges français* (Paris: Plon, 1996). For the Cultural Revolution, see Alessandro Russo, *Cultural Revolution and Revolutionary Culture* (Durham: Duke University Press, 2020).
15 Fraser et al., eds., *1968*, 33–74.
16 For the US decision to support France, see Mark Atwood Lawrence, *Assuming the Burden: Europe and the American Commitment to War in Vietnam* (Berkeley: University of California Press, 2005).
17 Dwight D. Eisenhower, *Mandate for Change, 1953–1956* (Garden City, NY: Doubleday & Co., 1963), 372.
18 The literature is enormous but, for a survey that briefly juxtaposes the competing modernizations of the two states, see Christopher Goscha, *Vietnam: A New History* (New York: Basic Books, 2016), Chapter 10.

19 Michael E. Latham, "Redirecting the Revolution? The USA and the Failure of Nation-Building in South Vietnam," *Third World Quarterly* 27, no. 1 (2006): 27–41.

20 For Diệm, see Edward Miller, *Misalliance: Ngo Dinh Diem, the United States, and the Fate of South Vietnam* (Cambridge, MA: Harvard University Press, 2013).

21 The best account of these internal debates remains Lien-Hang T. Nguyen, *Hanoi's War: An International History of the War for Peace in Vietnam* (Chapel Hill: University of North Carolina Press, 2012).

22 For political competition in South Vietnam, see, among others, Jessica M. Chapman, *Cauldron of Resistance: Ngo Dinh Diem, the United States, and 1950s Southern Vietnam* (Ithaca: Cornell University Press, 2013); Geoffrey C. Stewart, *Vietnam's Lost Revolution: Ngô Đình Diệm's Failure to Build an Independent Nation, 1955–1963* (Cambridge: Cambridge University Press, 2017); and Heather Marie Stur, *Saigon at War: South Vietnam and the Global Sixties* (Cambridge: Cambridge University Press, 2020).

23 Robert K. Brigham, *Guerrilla Diplomacy: The NLF's Foreign Relations and the Viet Nam War* (Ithaca: Cornell University Press, 1999), 18.

24 Fredrik Logevall, "'There Ain't No Daylight': Lyndon Johnson and the Politics of Escalation," in *Making Sense of the Vietnam Wars: Local, National, and Transnational Perspectives*, eds. Mark Philip Bradley and Marilyn B. Young (Oxford: Oxford University Press, 2008), 91–108.

25 For two good overviews of the American War in Vietnam, see George C. Herring, *America's Longest War: The United States and Vietnam, 1950–1975* (New York: McGraw Hill, 2014), and Pierre Asselin, *Vietnam's American War: A History* (Cambridge: Cambridge University Press, 2018).

26 "SDS to Sponsor Vietnam March," *SDS Bulletin* 3, no. 4 (January 1965): 1, 14.

27 Paul Booth, "March on Washington," *SDS Bulletin* 3, no. 7 (May 1965): 10.

28 "15,000 White House Pickets Denounce Vietnam War," *New York Times*, April 18, 1965.

29 Fred Halstead, *Out Now! A Participant's Account of the American Movement against the Vietnam War* (New York: Monad Press, 1978), 41.

30 Paul Potter, "The Incredible War," in *Voices of 1968*, 41.

31 Melvin Small, *Antiwarriors: The Vietnam War and the Battle for America's Hearts and Minds* (Wilmington, DE: Scholarly Resources, Inc., 2002), 3–9.

32 For an overview of American radicals in the 1960s and 1970s, see Howard Brick and Christopher Phelps, *Radicals in America: The US Left since the Second World War* (Cambridge: Cambridge University Press, 2015).

33 For the SWP's antiwar work, see Halstead, *Out Now!*

34 Bay Area Vietnam Day Committee, *Did You Vote For War?*, 23, Social Protest Collection, Bancroft.

35 Tom Wells, *The War Within: America's Battle over Vietnam* (Berkeley: University of California Press, 1994), 13.

36 For SNCC, see, among others, Clayborne Carson, *In Struggle: SNCC and the Black Awakening of the 1960s* (Cambridge, MA: Harvard University Press, 1981).

37 For some of these debates, see Brick and Phelps, *Radicals in America*, 141.

38 Potter, "Incredible War," 40.

39 Ibid., 41.

40 Ibid.

41 Thomas Powers, *The War at Home: Vietnam and the American People, 1964–1968* (New York: Grossman, 1973), 77.

42 Paul Potter, *A Name for Ourselves: Feelings About Love, Authentic Identity, Love, Intuitive Politics, Us* (Boston: Little, Brown, 1971), 101.

43 Brick and Phelps, *Radicals in America*, 130.

44 Martin Klimke, *The Other Alliance: Student Protest in West Germany and the United States in the Global Sixties* (Princeton: Princeton University Press, 2010), 41.

45 Barry Sheppard, *The Party: The Socialist Workers Party, 1960–1988*, vol. I (Chippendale, Australia: Resistance Books, 2005), 135–36.

46 Penny Lewis, *Hardhats, Hippies, and Hawks: The Vietnam Antiwar Movement as Myth and Memory* (Ithaca: Cornell University Press, 2013), 102. Lewis notes, however, that while organized labor, especially the AFL-CIO, was certainly prowar in the early years American workers were more likely to oppose the war than were their middle-class counterparts.

47 For the disproportionate influence of radicals, see, for example, Small, *Antiwarriors*, 29.

48 Halstead, *Out Now!*, 146.

49 Many of the speeches that day were republished as *We Accuse* (Berkeley: Diablo Press, 1965).

50 See the collection Bay Area Vietnam Day Committee, *Did You Vote For War?*

51 Diane C. Fujino, *Samurai among Panthers: Richard Aoki on Race, Resistance, and a Paradoxical Life* (Minneapolis: University of Minnesota Press, 2012), 109.

52 For SDS's decision to focus elsewhere, leaving antiwar leadership open, see James Miller, *"Democracy Is in the Streets": From Port Huron to the Siege of Chicago* (New York: Simon & Schuster, 1987), 235–36. For SDS's antiwar work, and in particular the efforts of some individual SDSers to internationalize the movement, see Klimke, *The Other Alliance*, 41–49.

53 Sheppard, *The Party*, 134.

54 For the VDC's history, see W. J. Rorabaugh, *Berkeley at War: The 1960s* (New York: Oxford University Press, 1989), Chapter 3.

55 Jean-Paul Sartre, "Pourquoi je refuse d'aller aux États-Unis," *Le Nouvel Observateur*, April 1, 1965.

56 It is interesting to note that Iyanaga, Schwartz, Smale, and Russell were all famous mathematicians, and that these figures used their professional societies to organize against the war.

57 Laurent Schwartz to Stephen Smale, May 14, 1965, Stephen Smale Papers, carton 4, Bancroft.

58 "News from the Vietnam Day Committee," n.d., Social Protest Collection, BANC MSS 86/157 c, carton 3, reel 9, Bancroft.

59 Fujino, *Samurai among Panthers*, 110.

60 *The International Protest Movement against American Intervention in the War in Vietnam*, report prepared by the International Secretariat of the National Committee to End the War in Vietnam and the Vietnam Day Committee, 1966, ii, Social Protest Collection, Bancroft.

61 Elaine Pierce, "British Commonwealth Countries," ibid., 23.

62 Ben C. Ramos and S. Pollard, "Europe," ibid., 17.

63 Madeleine Rebérioux to Stephen Smale, June 28, 1965, Stephen Smale Papers, carton 3, Bancroft.

64 Nicolas Pas, "Sortir de l'ombre du Parti communiste français. Histoire de l'engagement de l'extrême-gauche française sur la guerre du Vietnam, 1965–1968" (Mémoire de DEA, Institut d'études politiques, 1998), 20.

65 "Semaine universitaire en France contre la guerre du Vietnam," *Le Monde*, November 6, 1965.

66 *The International Protest Movement*, ii.

67 Halstead, *Out Now!*, 141–45.

68 Fujino, *Samurai among Panthers*, 110.

69 Richard Aoki, "International Protest," *VDC News* 1, no. 4 (October 11, 1965): 2.

70 Michael Kazin, "Book Discussion: The Other Alliance: Student Protest in West Germany and the United States in Global Sixties," Wilson Center, Washington, DC, April 21, 2010, www.wilsoncenter.org/event/book-discussion-the-other-alliance-student-protest-west-germany-and-the-united-states-the. Martin Klimke shows that, even in the West German case, international contacts between the two sides were more important for the Germans than they were for the Americans. See Klimke, *The Other Alliance*.

71 The examples are legion, but for a few examples of US radicals drawing inspiration from the French, see Brick and Phelps, *Radicals in America*, 139, and Charles DeBenedetti and Charles Chatfield, *An American Ordeal: The Antiwar Movement of the Vietnam Era* (Syracuse: Syracuse University Press, 1990), 97. For comparisons between French opposition to the Algerian War and American opposition to the Vietnam War, see David L. Schalk, *War and the Ivory Tower: Algeria and Vietnam* (Oxford: Oxford University Press, 1991).

72 "Le Vietnam à Berkeley," *Avant-Garde Sorbonne* 1, November 1965, 9.

73 See Slobodian, *Foreign Front*, Chapter 3; Klimke, *The Other Alliance*, Chapter 2.

74 Pas, "Sortir de l'ombre," 56–60; Bethany S. Keenan, "'Vietnam Is Fighting for Us': French Identities and the US–Vietnam War, 1965–1973" (Ph.D. diss., University of North Carolina, Chapel Hill, 2009), 65–71.

75 "Manifestation contre la guerre jeudi prochain à la Mutualité," *Le Monde*, May 21, 1966.

76 Grey Anderson, *La guerre civile en France, 1958–1962. Du coup d'État gaulliste à la fin de l'OAS* (Paris: La Fabrique, 2018).

77 Schalk, *War and the Ivory Tower*; David Porter, *Eyes to the South: French Anarchists and Algeria* (Oakland: AK Press, 2001); and Sylvain Pattieu, *Les camarades des frères. Trotskistes et libertaires dans la guerre d'Algérie* (Paris: Syllepse, 2002).

78 See, for example, Hervé Hamon and Patrick Rotman, *Les porteurs de valises. La résistance française à la guerre d'Algérie* (Paris: Albin Michel, 1979), and Jacques Charby, ed., *Les porteurs d'espoir. Les réseaux de soutien au FLN pendant la guerre d'Algérie: Les acteurs parlent* (Paris: La Découverte, 2004).

79 Danièle Joly, *The French Communist Party and the Algerian War* (London: Macmillan, 1991).

80 Richard F. Kuisel, *Seducing the French: The Dilemma of Americanization* (Berkeley: University of California Press, 1993).

81 See Christian Nünlist, Anna Locher, and Garret Martin, eds., *Globalizing de Gaulle: International Perspectives on French Foreign Policies, 1958–1969* (Lanham: Rowman & Littlefield, 2010).

82 "Cinq mille personnes ont participé aux 'Six heures du monde pour le Vietnam,'" *Le Monde*, November 30, 1966.

83 Alain Ruscio, "L'opinion française et la guerre d'Indochine (1945–1954). Sondages et témoignages," *Vingtième Siècle. Revue d'histoire* 29 (January–March 1991): 39–41.

84 Kalter, *The Discovery of the Third World*.

85 Marc Lazar, "Le parti communiste français et l'action de solidarité avec le Vietnam," in *La guerre du Vietnam et l'Europe, 1963–1973*, eds. Christopher Goscha and Maurice Vaïsse (Brussels: Bruylant, 2003), 241–52.

86 See especially Pas, "Sortir de l'ombre."

87 Michelle Zancarini-Fournel, "Le champ des possibles," in *68. Une histoire collective, 1962–1981*, eds. Philippe Artières and Michelle Zancarini-Fournel (Paris: La Découverte, 2008), 38–43.

88 Centre Information Vietnam, "Manifeste pour un soutien politique au peuple vietnamien," February 1967, F delta 701, La contemporaine, Nanterre, France.

89 For the Union of Communist Youth (Marxist-Leninist), see Bourseiller, *Les Maoïstes*, 54–63, 77–88; Julian Bourg, "The Red Guards of Paris: French Student Maoism of the 1960s," *History of European Ideas* 31, no. 4 (2005): 472–90; and Christian Delacroix, "L'engagement radical de la rue d'Ulm," in *68: Une histoire collective*, 125–31.

90 For the formation of the Vietnam Base Committees, see Pas, "Sortir de l'ombre," 73–87, and Keenan, "'Vietnam Is Fighting for Us,'" 99–104.

91 For the Revolutionary Communist Youth, see A. Belden Fields, *Trotskyism and Maoism: Theory and Practice in France and the United States* (New York: Praeger, 1988), 49–51; Alain Krivine, *Ça te passera avec l'âge* (Paris: Flammarion, 2006), 91–94; and Daniel Bensaïd, *An Impatient Life: A Political Memoir*, trans. David Fernbach (London: Verso, 2013), 35–41, 52.

92 Éditorial, *Avant-Garde Jeunesse* 1, May–June 1966, 2.

93 Pas, "Sortir de l'ombre," 116, 161–62. For the Revolutionary Communist Youth's efforts outside Paris, see Ludivine Bantigny, "Hors frontières. Quelques expériences d'internationalisme en France, 1966–1968," *Monde(s)* 11, no. 1 (May 2017): 153.

94 Laurent Schwartz, "Il faut crever l'écran," *Le Nouvel Observateur*, November 16–22, 1966.

95 For an example of the Vietnam Base Committees' critical attitude toward other initiatives, see "L'ancien et le nouveau comité," *Victoire pour le Vietnam* 3, November–December 1967, 2.

96 For the National Vietnam Committee's composition, see Pas, "Sortir de l'ombre," 90–101.

97 Ken Coates, "Mass Rally in Paris Backs War Crimes Tribunal," *World Outlook* 4, no. 40 (December 16, 1966): 13–14.

98 Laurent Schwartz, *A Mathematician Grappling with His Century*, trans. Leila Schneps (Basel: Birkhäuser Verlag, 2001), 413. For PACS, see Bethany S. Keenan, "'At the Crossroads of World Attitudes and Reaction': The Paris American Committee to Stopwar and American Antiwar Activism in France, 1966–1968," *Journal of Transatlantic Studies* 1, no. 11 (March 2013): 62–82. Jolas also worked with NLF representatives in Paris, briefing them on the US antiwar movement, assisting with outreach, and organizing events, such as the 1968 Paris Women's Conference. See Judy Tzu-Chun Wu, *Radicals on the Road: Internationalism, Orientalism, and Feminism during the Vietnam War Era* (Ithaca: Cornell University Press, 2013), 210.

 99 "Communiqué à la presse," January 19, 1967, 1 in F delta 151/7, La contemporaine.

100 "Halte à l'agression impérialiste au Viêt-Nam," supplément à *Avant-Garde Sorbonne* 1, November 1965, 4, F delta 2089, La contemporaine.

101 Alain Krivine, "Éditorial," *Avant-Garde Jeunesse* 2, November–December 1966, 2.

102 For Soviet foreign policy during the war, see Ilya V. Gaiduk, *The Soviet Union and the Vietnam War* (Chicago: Ivan R. Dee, 1996).

103 Quoted in Fraser et al., eds., *1968*, 135–36.

104 For the Sino-Soviet Split, see Lorenz M. Lüthi, *The Sino-Soviet Split: Cold War in the Communist World* (Princeton: Princeton University Press, 2008).

105 Jeremy Friedman, *Shadow Cold War: The Sino-Soviet Competition for the Third World* (Chapel Hill: University of North Carolina Press, 2015).

106 Chen Jian, "China's Involvement in the Vietnam War, 1964–1969," *China Quarterly* 142 (June 1995): 356–87.

107 Tuong Vu, *Vietnam's Communist Revolution: The Power and Limits of Ideology* (Cambridge: Cambridge University Press, 2017), 166.

108 For "global Maoism," see Julia Lovell, *Maoism: A Global History* (New York: Knopf, 2019).

109 "The International Situation and the Tasks of Revolutionary Marxists," *International Socialist Review* 27, no. 2 (Spring 1966): 48.

110 Ernest Tate, *Revolutionary Activism in the 1950s and 60s*, vol. II, *Britain 1965–1969* (London: Resistance Books, 2014), 25–26. For Trotskyism in France, see, among others, Jacques Roussel, *Les enfants du prophète. Histoire du mouvement trotskiste en France* (Paris: Spartacus, 1972); Fields, *Trotskyism and Maoism*, Chapter 2; and Jean-Jacques Marie, *Le trotskysme et les trotskystes* (Paris: Armand Colin, 2009).

111 "The International Situation," 48.

112 Krivine, *Ça te passera avec l'âge*, 91.

113 "Organisations participantes," October 16, 1966, 1, Box 47, Folder 4, Socialist Workers Party Records, Hoover Institution, Stanford University, Stanford, United States (hereafter SWP Records).

114 Mary-Alice Waters in "Report on European Trip," November 4, 1966, 1, Box 46, Folder 13, SWP Records.

115 "Liège, 16.10.1966," October 16, 1966, Box 47, Folder 4, SWP Records.

116 "Liège, 15 Octobre 1966," *Avant-Garde Jeunesse* 2, November–December 1966, 2.

117 "Première conférence internationale de la jeunesse," *Avant-Garde Jeunesse* 4, February 1967, 2. See also Tate, *Revolutionary Activism*, 184.
118 "Basic Political Resolution Adopted by the Conference of the Vanguard Youth Organizations of Europe for the Coordination of Aid to the Vietnamese Revolution and the Struggle against NATO," March 12, 1967, 1, Box 22, Folder 3, SWP Records.
119 Ibid., 3.
120 Ibid.
121 For Japan, see Thomas R. H. Havens, *Fire across the Sea: The Vietnam War and Japan, 1965–1975* (Princeton: Princeton University Press, 1987). For Johnson's efforts, see Robert M. Blackburn, *Mercenaries and Lyndon Johnson's "More Flags": The Hiring of Korean, Filipino, and Thai Soldiers in the Vietnam War* (Jefferson, NC: McFarland, 1994); Fredrik Logevall, "The American Effort to Draw European States into the War," in *La guerre du Vietnam*, 3–16; and Jonathan Colman and J. J. Widén, "The Johnson Administration and the Recruitment of Allies in Vietnam, 1964–1968," *History* 94, no. 4 (October 2009): 483–504.
122 For a good history, see Eugenie M. Blang, *Allies at Odds: America, Europe, and Vietnam, 1961–1968* (Lanham: Rowman & Littlefield, 2011).
123 Yuko Torikata, "Reexamining de Gaulle's Peace Initiative on the Vietnam War," *Diplomatic History* 31, no. 5 (November 2007): 909–38, and Pierre Journoud, *De Gaulle et le Vietnam, 1945–1969. La réconciliation* (Paris: Tallandier, 2011).
124 "Comité universitaire pour le Vietnam," 1967, 1, F delta 151/6, La contemporaine.
125 "Basic Political Resolution," 3.
126 Conference of Vanguard Youth Organizations of Western Europe, *Information Bulletin*, n.d., 8, "IWCT: General correspondence (by country)," Series 377, Box 10.9, Bertrand Russell Fonds, McMaster University, Hamilton, Canada.
127 Ibid., 15.
128 Mark T. Berger, "After the Third World? History, Destiny and the Fate of Third Worldism," *Third World Quarterly* 25, no. 1 (2004): 9–39.
129 The literature on the Tricontinental Conference is vast, but see Robert J. C. Young, "Postcolonialism: From Bandung to the Tricontinental," *Historein* 5 (2005): 11–21. For a more recent view, see Anne Garland Mahler, *From the Tricontinental to the Global South: Race, Radicalism, and Transnational Solidarity* (Durham: Duke University Press, 2018).
130 Robert J. C. Young, *Postcolonialism: An Historical Introduction* (Oxford: Blackwell, 2001), Part 4.
131 John Callaghan, *The Far Left in British Politics* (Oxford: Blackwell, 1987), 122.
132 Ross, *May '68*, 35–40, and Kalter, *The Discovery of the Third World*, 162–65.
133 Christian G. Appy, *Patriots: The Vietnam War Remembered from All Sides* (New York: Viking, 2003), 142–43, and Brick and Phelps, *Radicals in America*, 92–93.
134 For one example, see Nicola Pizzolato, "Transnational Radicals: Labour Dissent and Political Activism in Detroit and Turin (1950–1970)," *International Review of Social History* 56, no. 1 (April 2011): 1–30.
135 This is not to say there was no radical antiwar solidarity during the First Indochina War, only that it was comparatively very weak. For French opposition to the war, see Alain Ruscio, *Les communistes français et la guerre*

d'Indochine, 1944–1954 (Paris: L'Harmattan, 1985), and Alain Ruscio, "Les intellectuels français et la guerre d'Indochine. Une répétition générale?" *Les Cahiers de l'IHTP* 34 (June 1996): 113–32.

136 Pierre Asselin, "Forgotten Front: The NLF in Hanoi's Diplomatic Struggle, 1965–1967," *Diplomatic History* 45, no. 2 (April 2021): 333–34.
137 See, for example, *Solidaridad. Bulletin du comité de solidarité avec le peuple dominicain*, no. 1, Décembre 1965, F delta 2089, La contemporaine.
138 See, for example, several of the speeches reprinted in *We Accuse.*
139 Nick Turse, *Kill Anything that Moves: The Real American War in Vietnam* (New York: Metropolitan Books, 2013).
140 Aijaz Ahmad, *In Theory: Classes, Nations, Literatures* (London: Verso, 1992), 28.
141 "Basic Political Resolution," 1.
142 Kalter, *The Discovery of the Third World*, 271–75.
143 Lisandro Otero, "The Vietnamese Miracle," n.d., 14, Box 130, Folder 1, Liberation News Service Records, Temple University, Philadelphia, United States.
144 Mai Văn Bộ, *Tấn công Ngoại giao và Tiếp xúc Bí mật: Hồi ký* (Ho Chi Minh City: Nhà xuất bản Thành phố Hồ Chí Minh, 1985), 56–57.
145 *Le Courrier du Vietnam* 69, July 27, 1966, 1.
146 "Founding Program of the National Liberation Front of South Vietnam," in *Vietnam and America: A Documented History*, ed. Marvin E. Gettlemen et al. (New York: Grove Press, 1995), 192.
147 Schwartz, *A Mathematician*, 395.
148 "Nous Vaincrons, les agresseurs américains seront certainement battus," *Le Courrier du Vietnam* 56, April 28, 1966, 3.
149 See, among others, Brigham, *Guerrilla Diplomacy*, and Asselin, "Forgotten Front."
150 Asselin, "Forgotten Front," 346.
151 Ibid., 349.
152 On these diverse struggles, see, for example, Wu, *Radicals on the Road.*
153 Bantigny, "Hors frontières," 146.
154 See Brigham, *Guerrilla Diplomacy*; Harish C. Mehta, "'People's Diplomacy': The Diplomatic Front of North Vietnam during the War against the United States, 1965–1972" (Ph.D. diss., McMaster University, 2009); Nguyen, "Antiwar Transnationalism"; and Asselin, "Forgotten Front."
155 Schwartz, *A Mathematician*, 397.
156 "Un message du FNL au CVN," *Vietnam* 2, December 1967, 7.
157 "La conférence de Bruxelles," *Avant-Garde Jeunesse* 5, April–May 1967, 18.

2   Anti-Imperialism

1 Laurent Schwartz, "La victoire du Viet-Nam c'est...," *Pour le Viet-Nam* 1, n.d., 1 in F delta 236/4, La contemporaine, Nanterre, France.
2 "M. Humphrey. Les liens de mon pays avec l'Europe sont profonds et réels," *Le Monde*, April 9–10, 1967.
3 Bethany S. Keenan, "'Vietnam Is Fighting for Us': French Identities and the US–Vietnam War, 1965–1973" (Ph.D. diss., University of North Carolina, Chapel Hill, 2009), 108–17.

4 Max Paul Friedman, *Rethinking Anti-Americanism: The History of an Exceptional Concept in American Foreign Relations* (Cambridge: Cambridge University Press, 2012), 190–94. For the West German episode, see Martin Klimke, *The Other Alliance: Student Protest in West Germany and the United States in the Global Sixties* (Princeton: Princeton University Press, 2010), 155–58.

5 Friedman, *Rethinking Anti-Americanism*, 191–93.

6 "Solidarité avec les combattants vietnamiens," 1967, F delta 2089, La contemporaine.

7 "Humphrey à Paris," *Avant-Garde Jeunesse* 5, April–May 1967, 5.

8 Eugenie M. Blang, "A Reappraisal of Germany's Vietnam Policy, 1963–1966: Ludwig Erhard's Response to America's War in Vietnam," *German Studies Review* 27, no. 2 (May 2004): 341–60.

9 Quoted in Friedman, *Rethinking Anti-Americanism*, 191.

10 On this point, see, among others, Eugenie M. Blang, *Allies at Odds: America, Europe, and Vietnam, 1961–1968* (Lanham: Rowman & Littlefield, 2011).

11 "Humphrey à la porte," 1967, F delta 2089, La contemporaine.

12 Collectif de diffusion des comités de base, *Lisons et diffusions les textes vietnamiens*, n.d., 2, F delta 2089, La contemporaine.

13 For a longer history of transnational exchanges between Germans and American GIs, particularly African Americans, see Maria Höhn and Martin Klimke, *A Breath of Freedom: The Civil Rights Struggle, African American GIs, and Germany* (New York: Palgrave Macmillan, 2010).

14 Klimke, *The Other Alliance*, 182–87.

15 Max Watts, "American RITA GIs in the Paris of May 1968," *Le blog de mai*, May 3, 2008, http://mai68.over-blog.org/article-19253262.html.

16 "Lettre de la SDS," *Vietnam* 3, February 1968, 7; Dick Perrin with Tim McCarthy, *GI Resister: The Story of How One American Soldier and His Family Fought the War in Vietnam* (Victoria: Trafford, 2001), 85 and 106.

17 Klimke, *Other Alliance*, 84.

18 This paragraph draws on Bethany S. Keenan, "'At the Crossroads of World Attitudes and Reaction': The Paris American Committee to Stopwar and American Anti-War Activism in France, 1966–1968," *Journal of Transatlantic Studies* 1, no. 11 (March 2013): 69–71.

19 Moshik Temkin, "American Internationalists in France and the Politics of Travel Control in the Era of Vietnam," in *Outside In: The Transnational Circuitry of US History*, eds. Andrew Preston and Doug Rossinow (Oxford: Oxford University Press, 2017), 259–60.

20 Perrin, *GI Resister*, 73–77.

21 "Rita...," *ACT* 1, no. 3, 1968, 1, GI Press Collection, 1964–1977, Wisconsin Historical Society, Madison, United States.

22 Perrin, *GI Resister*, 83.

23 "L'ADC. Notre lutte," *Second Front Review*, Édition française, 1, n.d., 10–12, GI Press Collection.

24 "Déclaration du FLN sur la désertion," ibid., 35.

25 Gregory Nevala Calvert, Oral Interview, July 1987, 93, "Student Movements of the 1960s," Columbia Center for Oral History, Rare Book and Manuscript Library, Columbia University Libraries, New York, United States.

26 Klimke, *The Other Alliance*, 76.
27 Watts, "American RITA GIs."
28 Calvert, Interview, 224.
29 Ibid., 225.
30 Ibid.
31 The following draws heavily on the excellent work of Nicolas Pas, "Sortir de l'ombre du Parti communiste français. Histoire de l'engagement de l'extrême-gauche française sur la guerre du Vietnam, 1965–1968" (Mémoire de DEA, Institut d'études politiques, 1998), 118–25.
32 "Les visages d'une même lutte," *Pour le Viet-Nam* 1, 4.
33 "Défendre l'héroïque Vietnam," March 31, 1965, cited in Pas, "Sortir de l'ombre," 119.
34 Conference of vanguard youth organizations of Western Europe, *Information Bulletin*, n.d., 10, "IWCT: General correspondence (by country), Series 377, Box 10.9, Bertrand Russell Fonds, McMaster University, Hamilton, Canada (hereafter BRA II).
35 "Deux cents volontaires français prêts à lutter contre les Américains au Vietnam," *Le Monde*, February 16, 1967.
36 "Entrevue avec les Vietnamiens," *Le Volontaire* 4, September 1967, 3.
37 Le Dinh Nhan to J. Grimblat, June 7, 1967, reprinted ibid., 4.
38 Gilbert Marquis interview with Nicolas Pas, April 21, 1998, in Pas, "Sortir de l'ombre," 124.
39 Tariq Ali, *Street Fighting Years: An Autobiography of the Sixties* (London: Verso, 2005), 176.
40 Quoted in "Les visages d'une même lutte."
41 "Hanoi Termed Open on US Volunteers," *New York Times*, July 19, 1968.
42 Conference of vanguard youth organizations, *Information Bulletin*, 10.
43 "Entrevue avec les Vietnamiens," 3.
44 This arrangement held a certain benefit for the radicals as well. It could demonstrate the depth of their opposition to the United States, the seriousness of their commitment to the Vietnamese cause, and the selflessness of their internationalism.
45 Marquis in Pas, "Sortir de l'ombre du Parti Communiste Français," 124.
46 For "people's diplomacy," see Robert K. Brigham, *Guerrilla Diplomacy: The NLF's Foreign Relations and the Viet Nam War* (Ithaca: Cornell University Press, 1999); Harish C. Mehta, "'People's Diplomacy': The Diplomatic Front of North Vietnam during the War against the United States, 1965–1972" (Ph.D. diss., McMaster University, 2009); Judy Tzu-Chun Wu, *Radicals on the Road: Internationalism, Orientalism, and Feminism during the Vietnam War Era* (Ithaca: Cornell University Press, 2013); Jessica M. Frazier, *Women's Antiwar Diplomacy during the Vietnam War Era* (Chapel Hill: University of North Carolina Press, 2017); Nguyet Nguyen, "Antiwar Transnationalism: People's Diplomacy in the Vietnam War" (Ph.D. diss., American University, 2019); and Pierre Asselin, "Forgotten Front: The NLF in Hanoi's Diplomatic Struggle, 1965–1967," *Diplomatic History* 45, no. 2 (April 2021): 330–55.
47 Cited in Nguyen, "Antiwar Transnationalism," 6.
48 Asselin, "Forgotten Front," 335.

49 Pierre Asselin, *Vietnam's American War: A History* (Cambridge: Cambridge University Press, 2018), 144.

50 Ibid., 145.

51 Given their rivalries, the convergence is striking. For example, the Union of Communist Youth (Marxist-Leninist) could denounce their rivals while simultaneously advocating an alternative that fell within the same parameters of ideological struggle. See *Victoire pour le Vietnam* 1, June 1967.

52 For Maspero, see Kristin Ross, *May '68 and Its Afterlives* (Chicago: University of Chicago Press, 2002), 82–88; Julien Hage, "François Maspero, éditeur (p)artisan," *Contretemps* 13 (2005): 100–08; and Christoph Kalter, *The Discovery of the Third World: Decolonization and the Rise of the New Left in France, c. 1950–1976*, trans. Thomas Dunlap (Cambridge: Cambridge University Press, 2016), 193–207.

53 Nguyen, "Antiwar Transnationalism," 175–205.

54 Ralph Schoenman, "Memorandum Concerning Discussions in Prague and Budapest with the National Liberation Front," n.d., Working Correspondence with Vietnamese (May 1966), Series 375, Box 10.5, BRA II.

55 "Summary Report of Series of Meetings between Members of the Central Committee of the National Liberation Front and the Personal Representatives of Bertrand Russell," n.d., 1, Working Correspondence with Vietnamese (May 1966), Series 375, Box 10.5, BRA II.

56 Ralph Schoenman to Pham Van Dong, March 11, 1966, Working Correspondence with Vietnamese (May 1966) and Bertrand Russell to Ho Chi Minh, June 9, 1966, Working Correspondence with Vietnamese (December 1966) both in Series 375, Box 10.5, BRA II.

57 "Summary Report of Series of Meetings," 1–2.

58 Harish C. Mehta, "North Vietnam's Informal Diplomacy with Bertrand Russell: Peace Activism and the International War Crimes Tribunal," *Peace & Change* 37, no. 1 (January 2012): 68–69.

59 Ralph Schoenman to Nguyen Duy Tinh, April 2, 1966, 2 and Bertrand Russell to Pham Van Dong, April 5, 1966, 1, both in Working Correspondence with Vietnamese (May 1966), Series 375, Box. 10.5, BRA II.

60 Claude Cadart to Ralph Schoenman, December 19, 1966, 2, French Office, Series 374, Box 10.5, BRA II.

61 Pas, "Sortir de l'ombre," 189–96; Simone de Beauvoir, *All Said and Done*, trans. Patrick O'Brian (New York: G. P. Putnam's Sons, 1974), 339–41; and Laurent Schwartz, *A Mathematician Grappling with His Century*, trans. Leila Schneps (Basel: Birkhäuser Verlag, 2001), 401–13.

62 Mehta, "People' Diplomacy," 231.

63 Conference of vanguard youth organizations, *Information Bulletin*, 9.

64 "Aims and Objectives of the International War Crimes Tribunal," in *Against the Crime of Silence: Proceedings of the Russell International War Crimes Tribunal*, ed. John Duffett (New York: O'Hare Books, 1968), 14–16.

65 Jean-Paul Sartre, "Imperialist Morality," *New Left Review* 41 (January–February 1967): 6.

66 Lelio Basso, "Summary of the First Two Charges," in *Against the Crime of Silence*, 297.

67 Incidentally, much of the recent scholarship on the war has tried to decenter the United States and recenter Vietnamese actors by reinterpreting the conflict as primarily a civil war between Vietnamese. For just one example, see Jessica Chapman, "Teaching the Vietnam War from the Vietnamese Perspective," *OAH Magazine of History* 18, no. 5 (October 2004): 33–35. For a criticism of this approach, see Christian G. Appy, "What Was the Vietnam War About?," *New York Times*, March 26, 2018.

68 Cited in Keenan, "Vietnam Is Fighting for Us," 205.

69 Jean-Paul Sartre, "Inaugural Statement to the Tribunal," in *Against the Crime of Silence*, 45.

70 Ho Chi Minh, "Text of Telegram from Ho Chi Minh to Preliminary Meeting of International War Crimes Tribunal," November 12, 1966, Working Correspondence with Vietnamese (December 1966), Series 375, Box 10.5, BRA II.

71 Pham Van Dong, "Message du Premier Ministre Pham Van Dong à M Jean Paul Sartre," *Le Courrier du Vietnam* 139, November 27, 1967, 3.

72 Mehta, "North Vietnam's Informal Diplomacy," 69, 78–85.

73 Keenan, "Vietnam Is Fighting for Us," 205–12, and Mehta, "People's Diplomacy," 261–62.

74 Mehta, "People's Diplomacy," 96.

75 Karen Wald, "Tribunal: Implications for the American Anti-War Movement," May 11, 1967, 1, Box 1, Folder 31, International War Crimes Tribunal Records, Tamiment Library and Robert F. Wagner Labor Archives, New York University, New York, United States.

76 Carl Oglesby, "Greetings to the Tribunal from American Supporters," in *Against the Crime of Silence*, 322.

77 Ibid. This was actually one of the primary motivations for forming the Tribunal in the first place. See Bertrand Russell to Pham Van Dong, January 25, 1966, in *The Selected Letters of Bertrand Russell: The Public Years, 1914–1970*, eds. Nicholas Griffin and Alison Roberts Miculan (New York: Routledge, 2001), 383–86.

78 Oglesby, "Greetings to the Tribunal," 322.

79 Mehta, "People's Diplomacy," 221–22.

80 Beauvoir, *All Said and Done*, 344–48.

81 Bertrand Russell to Ho Chi Minh, October 20, 1966, Working Correspondence with Vietnamese (December 1966), Series 375, Box 10.5, BRA II.

82 Bertrand Russell to Ho Chi Minh, October 3, 1966, 1, Working Correspondence with Vietnamese (December 1966), Series 375, Box 10.5, BRA II.

83 Ho Chi Minh to Bertrand Russell, November 7, 1966, Working Correspondence with Vietnamese (December 1966), Series 375, Box 10.5, BRA II.

84 See, for example, Asselin, *Vietnam's American War*, Chapters 3–4, and especially Lien-Hang T. Nguyen, *Hanoi's War: An International History of the War for Peace in Vietnam* (Chapel Hill: University of North Carolina Press, 2012), Chapters 1–3.

85 See, for example, Laurent Schwartz to Bertrand Russell, July 14, 1967, and Bertrand Russell to Laurent Schwartz, October 17, 1967, both in Members' Correspondence (July–December 1967), Series 371, Box 10.2, BRA II.

86 Bertrand Russell to Vladimir Dedijer, May 14, 1967, Members' Correspondence (May 1967), Series 371, Box 10.2, BRA II.

87 Beauvoir, *All Said and Done*, 354–59, and Schwartz, *A Mathematician*, 409–10.

88 Ethel H. Minor to International War Crimes Tribunal, June 9, 1967, Members' Correspondence (June 1967), Series 371, Box 10.2, BRA II.

89 Bertrand Russell, "Introduction," in *Against the Crime of Silence*, 5.

90 See, among others, Donald Sassoon, *One Hundred Years of Socialism: The West European Left in the Twentieth Century* (London: I. B. Tauris, 2010), 384–86.

91 Carl Oglesby, "Notes on a Decade Ready for the Dustbin," *Liberation* 14, nos. 5–6 (August–September 1969): 6.

92 Klimke, *The Other Alliance*, 77 and Kirkpatrick Sale, *SDS* (New York: Vintage Books, 1974), 390–92.

93 For the general turn to Marxism in the United States, see Max Elbaum, *Revolution in the Air: Sixties Radicals Turn to Lenin, Mao and Che* (London: Verso, 2002), Chapters 2 and 3.

94 Material in this passage was previously published in Salar Mohandesi, Bjarke Skærlund Risager, and Laurence Cox, eds., *Voices of 1968: Documents from the Global North* (London: Pluto Press, 2018), 20–21. Copyright 2018, Salar Mohandesi, Bjarke Skærlund Risager, and Laurence Cox. Reproduced with permission of the Licensor through PLSclear.

95 Quoted in Ronald Fraser et al., eds., *1968: A Student Generation in Revolt* (New York: Pantheon Books, 1988), 108.

96 As Immanuel Wallerstein once wrote, "it is probable that more people read Lenin on *Imperialism: The Last Stage of Capitalism* than read the *Manifesto*": Immanuel Wallerstein, "The Concept of National Development, 1917–1989: Elegy and Requiem," *American Behavioral Scientist* 35, nos. 4–5 (March–June 1992): 519.

97 For surveys of this wave of new thinking, see Anthony Brewer, *Marxist Theories of Imperialism: A Critical Survey*, 2nd ed. (London: Routledge, 1990), Chapters 7 and 8; John Milios and Dimitris P. Sotiropoulos, *Rethinking Imperialism: A Study of Capitalist Rule* (London: Macmillan, 2009), Chapter 2; and Murray Noonan, *Marxist Theories of Imperialism: A History* (London: I. B. Tauris, 2017), Chapters 3, 4, and 5.

98 Milios and Sotiropoulos, *Rethinking Imperialism*, 1.

99 Nguyen, "Antiwar Transnationalism," 187–90.

100 Le Duan, *Hold High the Revolutionary Banner of Creative Marxism, Lead Our Revolutionary Cause to Complete Victory!* (Peking: Foreign Languages Press, 1964), 7–8.

101 Ho Chi Minh, *Ho Chi Minh on Revolution: Selected Writings, 1920–1966*, ed. Bernard B. Fall (New York: Praeger, 1967), 24–25.

102 See, for example, Le Duan, "Leninism and Vietnam's Revolution," in *On the Socialist Revolution in Vietnam*, vol. I (Hanoi: Foreign Languages Publishing House, 1965), 9–56.

103 See, for example, Benny Lévy in *Les maos en France*, ed. Michèle Manceaux (Paris: Gallimard, 1972), 187.

104 "Au Vietnam. Patriotes contre agresseurs" *Servir le peuple* 1, July 1, 1967, 7.

105 *Vietnam, Laos, Cambodge. Même combat! Cahier "Rouge"* no. 14 (Paris: François Maspero, 1970), 3.

106 For Trotskyist debates on the Stalinism of Vietnamese communists, see Ludivine Bantigny, "Hors frontières. Quelques expériences d'internationalisme en France, 1966–1968," *Monde(s)* 11, no. 1 (May 2017): 153–54.

107 A good example is "Third Worldism or Socialism," in *Ceylon: The JVP uprising of April 1971* (London: Solidarity, n.d.), 35–40.

108 "Two Local Wars," reprinted in *Situationist International Anthology*, ed. Ken Knabb (Berkeley: Bureau of Public Secrets, 2006), 254.

109 Mario Tronti, "A New Type of Political Experiment: Lenin in England," reprinted in Mario Tronti, *Workers and Capital*, trans. David Broder (London: Verso, 2019), 71.

110 Ali, *Street Fighting*, 188.

111 Beauvoir, *All Said and Done*, 410.

112 See also Elbaum, *Revolution in the Air*, 85–90.

113 Ibid., 83–84.

114 Sabine Rousseau, *La Colombe et le napalm. Des chrétiens français contre les guerres d'Indochine et du Vietnam, 1945–1975* (Paris: CNRS Éditions, 2002).

115 For a good overview, see Jan Eckel, *The Ambivalence of Good: Human Rights in International Politics since the 1940s*, trans. Rachel Ward (Oxford: Oxford University Press, 2019).

116 Universal Declaration of Human Rights, General Assembly Resolution 217 (111), December 10, 1948.

117 Declaration on the Granting of Independence to Colonial Countries and Peoples, General Assembly Resolution 1514 (XV), December 14, 1960. For human rights and the United Nations, see Roger Normand and Sarah Zaidi, *Human Rights at the UN: The Political History of Universal Justice* (Bloomington: Indiana University Press, 2008).

118 See, especially, Roland Burke, *Decolonization and the Evolution of International Human Rights* (Philadelphia: University of Pennsylvania Press, 2010).

119 The relationship between human rights and decolonization is hotly debated. For a good treatment, see Jan Eckel, "Human Rights and Decolonization: New Perspectives and Open Questions," *Humanity* 1, no. 1 (Fall 2010): 111–35.

120 Golnar Nikpour, "Claiming Human Rights: Iranian Political Prisoners and the Making of a Transnational Movement, 1963–1979," *Humanity* 9, no. 3 (Winter 2018): 363–88. For the Conference itself, see Burke, *Decolonization*, Chapter 4.

121 For human rights and liberal elites in the US context, see Daniel Sargent, "Oasis in the Desert? America's Human Rights Rediscovery," in *The Breakthrough: Human Rights in the 1970s*, eds. Jan Eckel and Samuel Moyn (Philadelphia: University of Pennsylvania Press, 2014), 131, and Sarah B. Snyder, *From Human Rights to Moscow: How Human Rights Activists Transformed US Foreign Policy* (New York: Columbia University Press, 2018).

122 For human rights "vernaculars" in the United States, see Mark Philip Bradley, *The World Reimagined: Americans and Human Rights in the Twentieth Century* (Cambridge: Cambridge University Press, 2016).

123 Malcolm X., "The Ballot or the Bullet," in *Malcolm X Speaks: Selected Speeches and Statements*, ed. George Breitman (New York: Grove Press, 1990), 35 and 38.

124 For an impassioned plea to remain attentive to the messy plurality of human rights discourses of the past, see Robert Brier, "Beyond the Quest for a 'Breakthrough': Reflections on the Recent Historiography on Human Rights," in *Mobility and Biography*, ed. Sarah Panter (Berlin: De Gruyter, 2016), 155–74.

125 See, for example, Jessica Whyte, *The Morals of the Market: Human Rights and the Rise of Neoliberalism* (London: Verso, 2019).

126 For Amnesty International's origins, see Tom Buchanan, "'The Truth Will Set You Free': The Making of Amnesty International," *Journal of Contemporary History* 37, no. 4 (October 2002): 575–97.

127 Peter Benenson, "The Forgotten Prisoners," *Observer*, May 28, 1961.

128 Peter Benenson, *Persecution 1961* (Harmondsworth: Penguin, 1961), 152.

129 For an exploration of these internal debates, with a focus on the US section, see Sarah Snyder, "Exporting Amnesty International to the United States: Transatlantic Human Rights Activism in the 1960s," *Human Rights Quarterly* 34, no. 3 (August 2012): 779–99.

130 Sartre, "Inaugural Statement," 42.

131 Do Xuan Sang, "Le Tribunal international Bertrand Russell tiendra sa 2ème session officielle à Copenhague," *Le Courrier du Vietnam* 138, November 20, 1967, 2.

132 Ho Chi Minh, "Telegram."

133 Eleanor Davey, *Idealism beyond Borders: The French Revolutionary Left and the Rise of Humanitarianism, 1954–1988* (Cambridge: Cambridge University Press, 2015), 87–94.

134 Russell, "Opening Statement to the Second Tribunal Session," in *Against the Crime of Silence*, 315.

135 Oglesby, "Notes on a Decade," 6.

136 Barbara Keys, "Anti-Torture Politics: Amnesty International, the Greek Junta, and the Origins of the US Human Rights Boom," in *The Human Rights Revolution: An International History*, eds. Akira Iriye, Petra Goedde, and William I. Hitchcock (New York: Oxford University Press, 2012), 201–22.

137 Mary Ann Heiss, "Privileging the Cold War over Decolonization: The US Emphasis on Political Rights," in *Decolonization, Self-Determination, and the Rise of Global Human Rights Politics*, eds. A. Dirk Moses, Marco Duranti, and Roland Burke (Cambridge: Cambridge University Press, 2020), 132–50.

138 Brad Simpson, "The United States and the Curious History of Self-Determination," *Diplomatic History* 36, no. 4 (September 2012): 675–94.

139 See, for example, Lyndon Johnson, "Remarks to Committee Members on the Need for Additional Appropriations for Military Purposes in Viet-Nam and the Dominican Republic," May 4, 1965, in *Public Papers of the Presidents of the United States: Lyndon B. Johnson, 1965* (Washington, DC: US Government Printing Office, 1972), 491.

140 Tom Buchanan, "Amnesty International in Crisis, 1966–1967," *Twentieth-Century British History* 15, no. 3 (2004): 267–89.

141 Jan Eckel, "The International League for the Rights of Man, Amnesty International, and the Changing Fate of Human Rights Activism from the 1940s through the 1970s," *Humanity* 4, no. 2 (Summer 2013): 193.
142 Bradley, *The World Reimagined*, 123–24.

3   Revolution

1 Jean-Luc Godard, Joris Ivens, William Klein, Claude Lelouch, Chris Marker, Agnès Varda, and Alain Resnais, *Loin du Vietnam*, France, 1967.
2 Ibid.
3 "Loin du Vietnam," *Cinéma*, January 1968, 37; Kristin Ross, *May '68 and Its Afterlives* (Chicago: University of Chicago Press, 2002), 87–89. For Chris Marker's film projects at Besançon, see Trevor Stark, "'Cinema in the Hands of the People': Chris Marker, the Medvedkin Group, and the Potential of Militant Film," *October 139* (Winter 2012): 117–50, and Donald Reid, "Well-Behaved Workers Seldom Make History: Re-Viewing Insubordination in French Factories during the Long 1968," *South Central Review* 29, no. 1 (2012): 68–85.
4 Salar Mohandesi, "Bringing Vietnam Home: The Vietnam War, Internationalism, and May '68," *French Historical Studies* 41, no. 2 (April 2018): 219–51.
5 Maxwell C. Stanford, "Revolutionary Action Movement (RAM): A Case Study of an Urban Revolutionary Movement in Western Capitalist Society" (MA thesis, Atlanta University, 1986), 99.
6 Robin D. G. Kelley, *Freedom Dreams: The Black Radical Imagination* (Boston: Beacon Press, 2002), 72–91.
7 Ibid., 16–17.
8 Asad Haider, "The Shadow of the Plantation," February 12, 2017, *Viewpoint Magazine*, https://viewpointmag.com/2017/02/12/the-shadow-of-the-plantation.
9 Harry Haywood, *Negro Liberation* (New York: International Publishers, 1948).
10 Harry Haywood, *Black Bolshevik: Autobiography of an Afro-American Communist* (Chicago: Liberator Press, 1978), 279.
11 Communist International, *The 1928 and 1930 Comintern Resolutions on the Black National Question in the United States* (Washington, DC: Revolutionary Review Press, 1975), 28.
12 See, for example, Haywood, *Negro Liberation*, 146.
13 Nikhil Pal Singh, *Black Is a Country: Race and the Unfinished Struggle for Democracy* (Cambridge, MA: Harvard University Press, 2004), Chapter 5.
14 Peniel E. Joseph, *Waiting 'til the Midnight Hour: A Narrative History of Black Power in America* (New York: Henry Holt and Company, 2006), 30–32.
15 Harold Cruse, "Revolutionary Nationalism and the Afro-American," reprinted in *Rebellion or Revolution?* (Minneapolis: University of Minnesota Press, 2009), 76.
16 Cruse, "*Revolutionary Nationalism*," 94.

17 "People Get Ready (An Analysis by RAM: Revolutionary Action Movement)," n.d. [likely 1965], 1, in Muhammad Ahmad (Max Stanford) – Writings, 1965, Folder: 010629–001–0289, The Black Power Movement, Part 3: Papers of the Revolutionary Action Movement, 1962–1996, available from (among other places) www.lexisnexis.com/documents/academic/upa_cis/16313_blackpowermovempt3.pdf.

18 Charles Simmons, "Declaration of the Afroamerican Student Movement," n.d., in Publications – "The Razor," Folder: 010629–014–0108, The Black Power Movement, Part 3: Papers of the Revolutionary Action Movement, 1962–1996.

19 Black Women Enraged, "Black Women!!," n.d., SNCC Records, Box 141, Folder 1, Martin Luther King, Jr. Center, Atlanta, United States (hereafter King Center).

20 "Greetings to Our Militant Vietnamese Brothers," *Black America*, Fall 1964, 21.

21 "On Vietnam," *Soulbook: The Quarterly Journal of Afroamerica* 2, no. 3 (Summer–Fall 1967): 181.

22 "Dr. King and the Viet Cong," *Black Vanguard* 1, no. 5 (August 1965): 53.

23 "Cockroach for Council," *Black Vanguard* 1, no. 5 (August 1965): 54.

24 "The 12 Point Program of RAM (Revolutionary Action Movement)," in Stanford, "Revolutionary Action Movement," 204–06.

25 See, for example, Robert F. Williams, "USA: The Potential of a Minority Revolution" *The Crusader* 5 no. 4 (May–June 1964): 1–7. For more on Robert F. Williams, see Timothy B. Tyson, *Radio Free Dixie: Robert F. Williams and the Roots of Black Power* (Chapel Hill: University of North Carolina Press, 1999), especially Chapters 7–10.

26 Robert F. Williams, "Speech: Delivered at the International Conference for Solidarity with the People of Vietnam against US Imperialist Aggression for the Defense of Peace," reprinted in *The Crusader* 6, no. 3 (March 1965): 5.

27 "A New Philosophy for a New Age," *Black America*, Summer–Fall 1965, 10.

28 "The Relationship of Revolutionary Afro-American Movement to the Bandung Revolution," ibid., 11.

29 Ibid.

30 John Wilson, "Statement by John Wilson, Conference – talks between Vietnamese and Americans," September 1967, 1–2, SNCC Records, Box 59, Folder 298, King Center.

31 Ibid., 4.

32 The literature on the Black Panther Party has become enormous. For just one example of their internationalism, see Sean L. Malloy, *Out of Oakland: Black Panther Party Internationalism during the Cold War* (Ithaca: Cornell University Press, 2017).

33 "Le deuxième front contre l'impérialisme américain," *Le Courrier du Vietnam* 73, August 29, 1966, 6.

34 Tom Wells, *The War Within: America's Battle over Vietnam* (Berkeley: University of California Press, 1994), 53–55.

35 The clearest articulation of the SWP's position is Fred Halstead, *Out Now!: A Participant's Account of the American Movement against the Vietnam War* (New York: Monad Press, 1978).

36 One of the clearest statements of this position can be found in "Revolutionaries Must Fight Nationalism," reprinted in *Revolution Today: USA. A Look at the Progressive Labor Movement and the Progressive Labor Party* (New York: Exposition Press, 1970), 279–97.

37 Che Guevara, "Message to the Tricontinental," reprinted in *Che Guevara Reader: Writings on Politics and Revolution*, ed. David Deutschmann (Melbourne: Ocean Press, 2003), 352.

38 Daniel Bensaïd, *An Impatient Life: A Political Memoir*, trans. David Fernbach (London: Verso, 2013), 54.

39 Ibid., 358.

40 Ibid., 358–59.

41 Ibid., 361–62.

42 "'Créer 1, 2, 3 … Vietnam': Les Vietnamiens à l'OLAS," *Vietnam* 1, October 1967, 8.

43 Joseph, *Waiting*, 191–93, and Sarah Seidman, "Tricontinental Routes of Solidarity: Stokely Carmichael in Cuba," *Journal of Transnational American Studies* 4, no. 2 (2012): 1–25.

44 Stokely Carmichael, "Solidarity with Latin America," reprinted in *Stokely Speaks: From Black Power to Pan-Africanism* (New York: Random House, 1971), 104.

45 "OLAS General Declaration," reprinted in *International Socialist Review* 28, no. 6 (November–December 1967): 55.

46 "Political Program of the South Viet Nam National Front for Liberation," reprinted in Robert F. Turner, *Vietnamese Communism: Its Origins and Development* (Stanford: Hoover Institution Press, 1975), 441.

47 Ibid., 442.

48 Le Duan, *Forward under the Glorious Banner of the October Revolution* (Hanoi: Foreign Languages Publishing House, 1967).

49 Ibid., 29.

50 Alain Krivine, "Éditorial," *Avant-Garde Jeunesse* 2, November–December 1966, 2.

51 William S. Turley, *The Second Indochina War: A Concise Political and Military History* (Lanham: Rowman & Littlefield, 2008), 124.

52 Nicolas Hatzfeld and Cédric Lomba, "La grève de Rhodiaceta en 1967," in *Mai–Juin 68*, eds. Dominique Damamme et al. (Paris: Les Éditions de l'Atelier, 2008), Chapter 6.

53 "Le combat des travailleurs contre Rhodiaceta," *Garde Rouge* 5, April 1967, 5.

54 W. Châtelet, "Grève à Rhodiaceta," *Avant-Garde Jeunesse* 5, April–May 1967, 15.

55 Xavier Vigna, *L'Insubordination ouvrière dans les années 68. Essai d'histoire politique des usines* (Rennes: Presses Universitaires de Rennes, 2007).

56 "Vive la lutte du peuple afro-américain," *Servir le Peuple* 3, August 1, 1967, 4.

57 Pierre Rousset, "Le long été chaud des USA," *Avant-Garde Jeunesse* 7, October 1967, 21.

58 Peniel E. Joseph, *Stokely: A Life* (New York: Basic Civitas, 2014), 225–29.

59 Quoted in Jacques Amalric, "Le 'Pouvoir noir' à la Mutualité," *Le Monde*, December 8, 1967.

60 Quoted in Joseph, *Stokely*, 227.

61 Laurent Schwartz, *A Mathematician Grappling with His Century*, trans. Leila Schneps (Basel: Birkhäuser Verlag, 2001), 399.

62 Bensaïd, *An Impatient Life*, 54.

63 "Appel de la conférence de Bruxelles pour la victoire du Vietnam," *Avant-Garde jeunesse* 9, January–February 1967, 28.

64 Ludivine Bantigny, "Hors frontières. Quelques expériences d'internationalisme en France, 1966–1968," *Monde(s)* 11, no. 1 (May 2017): 145.

65 Timothy Scott Brown, *West Germany and the Global Sixties: The Anti-Authoritarian Revolt, 1962–1978* (Cambridge: Cambridge University Press, 2013), Chapter 1.

66 For a general overview of the German antiwar movement, see Jost Düffler, "The Anti-Vietnam War Movement in West Germany," in *La guerre du Vietnam et l'Europe, 1963–1973*, eds. Christopher Goscha and Maurice Vaïss (Brussels: Bruylant, 2003), 287–306.

67 Brown, *West Germany and the Global Sixties*, Chapter 2.

68 Martin Klimke, *The Other Alliance: Student Protest in West Germany and the United States in the Global Sixties* (Princeton: Princeton University Press, 2010), 91–96.

69 SDS Westberlin and Internationales Nachrichten-und Forschungsinstitut. INFI, eds., *Der Kampf des vietnamesischen Volkes und die Globalstrategie des Imperialismus, Internationaler Vietnam-Kongreß 17./18. Februar 1968, Westberlin* (Berlin: Peter von Maikowski, 1968), 140–41.

70 Ibid., 90.

71 Ibid., 123.

72 Tariq Ali, *Street Fighting Years: An Autobiography of the Sixties* (London: Verso, 2005), 242.

73 Ibid., 247.

74 Bensaïd, *An Impatient Life*, 56.

75 Alain Krivine, *Ça te passera avec l'âge* (Paris: Flammarion, 2006), 96, 99, and Geneviève Dreyfus-Armand and Laurent Gervereau, eds., *Mai 68. Les mouvements étudiants en France et dans le monde, Catalogue de la BDIC* (Paris: BDIC, 1988), 140.

76 "21 février, journée du Vietnam héroïque," *Avant-Garde Jeunesse* 10–11, February–March 1968, 14.

77 Ibid.

78 "Berlin. La jeunesse européenne pour le Vietnam," *Vietnam* 4, March 1968, 7.

79 The Maoists in the Vietnam Base Committees carried out these actions independently of the other antiwar groups, which they denounced as "false friends" of Vietnam. Again, it is worth noting that, despite the sectarian split, their general strategy that day remained roughly the same.

80 "21 Février," *Vietnam* 4, March 1968, 8. See also "Le 21 février sera la journée du Vietnam héroïque," February 1968; "Tout pour la victoire," February 1968; and "Vive la victorieuse guerre du peuple vietnamien," n.d., all in F delta 2089, La contemporaine, Nanterre, France.

81 "Après les attentats anti-américains de Paris. M. Boulte, l'un des dirigeants du comité 'Vietnam national' et plusieurs lycéens sont arrêtés," *Le Monde*, March 23, 1968.

82 For the March 22 Movement, see, among others, Jean-Pierre Duteuil, *Nanterre 1965–66–67–68. Vers le mouvement du 22 mars* (Mauleon: Acratie, 1988).

83 For a detailed, though biased, study of this sequence of events, see Michael Seidman, *The Imaginary Revolution: Parisian Students and Workers in 1968* (New York: Berghahn Books, 2004), Chapters 1–3.

84 The literature on the May events is simply too large to engage with here, but for an interesting recent study see Ludivine Bantigny, *1968. De grands soirs en petits matins* (Paris: Seuil, 2018). An intriguing philosophical reflection can be found in Alain Badiou, "May '68 Revisited, 40 Years On," in Alain Badiou, *The Communist Hypothesis*, trans. David Macey and Steve Corcoran (London: Verso, 2015), 33–51.

85 Jean-Paul Sartre, "Itinerary of a Thought," *New Left Review* 58 (November–December 1969): 62.

86 Ligue Communiste, "Washington, Tokyo, Berlin, Londres, Amsterdam … Paris: FNL Vaincra!," n.d., 2, F delta 151/11, La contemporaine.

87 Nicolas Pas, "'Six Heures pour le Vietnam': Histoire des Comité Vietnam français, 1965–1968," *Revue Historique* 302, no. 1 (January–March 2000): 177–84.

88 Laurent Jalabert, "Aux origines de la génération 68. Les étudiants français et la guerre du Vietnam," *Vingtième Siècle: Revue d'histoire*, no. 55 (July–September 1997): 78.

89 Sartre, "Itinerary of a Thought," 63.

90 Alain Geismar, Serge July, and Erlyne Morane [Herta Alvarez and Evelyne July], *Vers la guerre civile* (Paris: Éditions et publications premières, 1969), 21.

91 Ibid., 22–23.

92 Quoted in Ross, *May '68*, 91. Translation modified.

93 "Berlin–Louvain–Rome–Londres–Paris," May 9, 1968, F delta 1061 (4) Part 1, La contemporaine.

94 Roger Gregoire and Fredy Perlman, *Worker–Student Action Committees: France, May 68* (Kalamazoo: Black and Red, 1969), 37.

95 Ali, *Street Fighting Years*, 273.

96 H. R., "Viet Nam. De la guérilla rurale à la guérilla urbaine," *La Nouvelle Avant-Garde* 1, June 1968, 13.

97 For a good collection of oral histories documenting diverse perspectives on the May events, see Mitchell Abidor, *May Made Me: An Oral History of the 1968 Uprising in France* (London: Pluto Press, 2018).

98 Christophe Bourseiller, *Les Maoïstes. La folle histoire des gardes rouges français* (Paris: Plon, 1996), 89–104.

99 The group condemned the May events as a trap, forbidding its own militants from participating and urging students to go to the factories and popular neighborhoods to unite with the workers, the only class who could make the revolution. See Union of Communist Youth (Marxist-Leninist), "Et maintenant, aux usines!" May 7, 1968, F delta 1061 (4) Part 1, La contemporaine.

100 The Union of CommunistYouth (Marxist-Leninist) was forced to postpone the demonstration because of the police presence, but they claimed the original plan was nevertheless "entirely correct." See "Le peuple vietnamien vaincra!," May 9, 1968, 4602, and "La manifestation du dimanche 12 mai est reporté," n.d., 4603, both in "Les tracts de mai 1968," Bibliothèque Nationale de France, Paris, France.

101 "Luttes étudiantes, luttes ouvrières," supplement to *Avant-Garde Jeunesse* 12, May 18, 1968, 6.

102 "L'exemple du peuple vietnamien," *La Cause du peuple. Journal de front populaire* 21, June 29–30, 1968, 6.

103 "Soulèvement générale des peuples du monde," *La Cause du peuple. Journal communiste révolutionnaire prolétarien*, n.s. no. 1, November 1, 1968, 10.

104 For the challenges of translation across borders in the context of antiwar activism in France, see Bantigny, "Hors frontières," 139–59.

105 Manus McGorgan, "Vive La Révolution and the Example of Lotta Continua: The Circulation of Ideas and Practices Between the Left Militant Worlds of France and Italy Following May '68," *Modern & Contemporary France* 18, no. 3 (August 2010): 319.

106 "Interview with Alain Krivine," in *France: The Struggle Continues* (NewYork: Committee to Defend the French Students, September 1968), 22, in New Left Collection, Box 19, Folder 2, Hoover Institution, Stanford University, Stanford, United States.

107 Ibid., 22.

108 Ali, *Street Fighting Years*, 305.

109 "Interview with Alain Krivine," 22.

110 Sergio Bologna, "1968: Memoirs of a Workerist," trans. Alessandra Guarino, *Viewpoint Magazine*, January 12, 2016, https://viewpointmag.com/2016/01/12/1968-memoirs-of-a-workerist.

111 Quoted in Ronald Fraser et al., eds., *1968: A Student Generation in Revolt* (New York: Pantheon Books, 1988), 251.

112 Robert Lumley, *States of Emergency: Cultures of Revolt in Italy from 1968 to 1978* (London: Verso, 1990).

113 Quoted in Fraser et al., eds., *1968*, 279.

114 Ali, *Street Fighting Years*, 296.

115 Ibid.

116 Editorial, "1968: The Ice Cracks," *International Socialism* 35 (Winter 1968/1969): 2.

117 Tony Cliff and Ian Birchall, "France – the Struggle Goes On," in Tony Cliff, *International Struggle and the Marxist Tradition: Selected Writings*, vol. I (London: Bookmarks, 2001), 213.

118 Peter B. Levy, *The New Left and Labor in the 1960s* (Urbana: University of Illinois Press, 1994), 111.

119 "People Are Mobilized to Fight the Repression," in *France: The Struggle Continues*, 29.

120 Klimke, *The Other Alliance*, 73.

121 Kirkpatrick Sale, *SDS* (New York: Vintage Books, 1974), 405.

122 Carl Davidson, "Inter-Organizational," *New Left Notes* 3, no. 20 (June 10, 1968): 6.

123 Ibid., 11.

124 Ibid., 6.
125 "Minutes of the New NIC," *New Left Notes* 3, no. 21 (June 24, 1968): 8.
126 Barbara Ehrenreich and John Ehrenreich, "NC Notes – in Absentia," *New Left Notes* 3, no. 23 (July 29, 1968): 2.
127 John Ehrenreich and Barbara Ehrenreich, "European Student Movements: Part One – Germany," ibid., 8.
128 Quoted in Fraser et al., eds., *1968*, 288.
129 Klimke, *The Other Alliance*, 79.
130 Sale, *SDS*, 451.
131 "Minutes of the National Convention," *New Left Notes* 3, no. 21 (June 24, 1968): 4.
132 Gerd-Rainer Horn, *The Spirit of '68: Rebellion in Western Europe and North America, 1956–1976* (Oxford: Oxford University Press, 2007), 155–57.
133 Fraser et al., eds., *1968*, 321.
134 Bensaïd, *An Impatient Life*, 81.
135 Carl Oglesby, "Notes on a Decade Ready for the Dustbin," *Liberation* 14, nos. 5–6 (August–September 1969): 6.
136 See, for example, Schwartz, *A Mathematician*, 401.
137 Bethany S. Keenan, "'Vietnam Is Fighting for Us': French Identities and the US–Vietnam War, 1965–1973" (Ph.D. diss., University of North Carolina, Chapel Hill, 2009), 277–96.
138 See, for example, Pas, "'Six heures pour le Vietnam,'" 182–84.
139 Perlman and Gregoire, *Worker–Student Action Committees*, 94.
140 Keenan gestures at this argument in "'Vietnam Is Fighting for Us,'" 290–91.
141 For just one example, see "ITALIE, Fiat. L'Indochine est dans ton usine," *Tout! 1*, September 23, 1970, 2.
142 "Femmes de la région parisienne," n.d., F delta 151/184, La contemporaine.
143 Des groupes du MLF, "20 janvier. Journée internationale pour le Vietnam: Des groupes de femmes y participent, voilà pourquoi," n.d., F delta 151/65, La contemporaine.
144 Helen E. Anderson, "Fighting for Family: Vietnamese Women and the American War," in *The Columbia History of the Vietnam War*, ed. David L. Anderson (New York: Columbia University Press, 2011), 297.
145 "An Open Letter from Vietnamese Mothers to Mothers and Children-Loving People in the World," Hanoi, May 1, 1967, 1, "IWCT Printed Materials (-78)," Series 385, Box 10.30, Bertrand Russell Fonds, McMaster University, Hamilton, Canada.
146 See, among many, Sandra C. Taylor, *Vietnamese Women at War: Fighting for Ho Chi Minh and the Revolution* (Lawrence: University of Kansas Press, 1999).
147 Anderson, "Fighting for Family," 298–99.
148 Judy Tzu-Chun Wu, *Radicals on the Road: Internationalism, Orientalism, and Feminism during the Vietnam War Era* (Ithaca: Cornell University Press, 2013), especially Chapters 7–9.
149 Vivian Rothstein in Christian G. Appy, *Patriots: The Vietnam War Remembered from All Sides* (New York: Penguin, 2003), 275.
150 Ibid, 277–78.
151 "Sisterhood Is Powerful!" *Le Torchon brûle* no. 1, 1971, 7.

152 Nguyet Nguyen, "Antiwar Transnationalism: People's Diplomacy in the Vietnam War" (Ph.D. diss., American University, 2019), 26–35, 167–75.
153 Lien-Hang Nguyen, "Revolutionary Circuits: Towards Internationalizing America in the World," *Diplomatic History* 39, no 3 (2015): 414.
154 See especially Wu, *Radicals on the Road*, Chapters 7–9, and Jessica M. Frazier, *Women's Antiwar Diplomacy during the Vietnam War Era* (Chapel Hill: University of North Carolina Press, 2017), Chapters 3–4.
155 "L'Imagination au pouvoir. Les affiches de Lip," quoted in Keenan, "'Vietnam Is Fighting for Us,'" 290. For Lip, see Donald Reid, *Opening the Gates: The Lip Affair, 1968–1981* (London: Verso Books, 2018).
156 Tuong Vu, *Vietnam's Communist Revolution: The Power and Limits of Ideology* (Cambridge: Cambridge University Press, 2017), 171–72 and 200–01.
157 See, for example, Wu, *Radicals on the Road*, 206 and 218.
158 "Une lettre du Premier Ministre Pham Van Dong," *Vietnam* no. 1, October 1967, 7.
159 Wu, *Radicals on the Road*, 194.
160 Vu, *Vietnam's Communist Revolution*, 198.
161 Nguyen, "Antiwar Transnationalism," 7–8.
162 Ibid., 91–93, 105–06, 162, and 172.
163 Bill Ayers, *Fugitive Days: A Memoir* (Boston: Beacon Press, 2008), 103.

4   Repression

1 Simone de Beauvoir, *All Said and Done*, trans. Patrick O'Brian (New York: G. P. Putnam's Sons, 1974), 434.
2 Jean-Paul Sartre, "The Maoists in France," in *Life/Situations: Essays Written and Spoken*, trans. Paul Auster and Lydia Davis (New York: Pantheon Books, 1977), 164.
3 Timothy Scott Brown, *West Germany and the Global Sixties: The Anti-Authoritarian Revolt, 1962–1978* (Cambridge: Cambridge University Press, 2013), Chapter 6.
4 See, among others, Max Elbaum, *Revolution in the Air: Sixties Radicals Turn to Lenin, Mao and Che* (London: Verso, 2002), Parts 1 and 2.
5 Geoff Eley, *Forging Democracy: The History of the Left in Europe, 1850–2000* (Oxford: Oxford University Press, 2002), 458. For the radical ecosystem in Italy, see Paul Ginsborg, *A History of Contemporary Italy: Society and Politics, 1943–1988* (New York: Palgrave Macmillan, 2003), Chapter 9.
6 For an example within antiwar internationalism, see Jessica M. Frazier, *Women's Antiwar Diplomacy during the Vietnam War Era* (Chapel Hill: University of North Carolina Press, 2017), 93–95.
7 See, for example, the organization's statement in *Triple Jeopardy: Racism, Imperialism, Sexism*, 1, no. 1 (September–October 1971), 16. For historical context, see Kimberly Springer, *Living for the Revolution: Black Feminist Organizations, 1968–1980* (Durham: Duke University Press, 2005).
8 Gerd-Rainer Horn, *The Spirit of '68: Rebellion in Western Europe and North America, 1956–1976* (Oxford: Oxford University Press, 2007), 160–63.
9 See, for example, Elbaum, *Revolution in the Air*, 88–90.

10 Alain Geismar, Serge July, and Erlyne Morane, *Vers la guerre civile* (Paris: Éditions et publications premières, 1969), 16.

11 Horn, *The Spirit of '68*, 159.

12 This dynamic was not unique to the North Atlantic. For a fascinating exploration of "pluralization" in the context of the Cultural Revolution, see Alessandro Russo, *Cultural Revolution and Revolutionary Culture* (Durham: Duke University Press, 2020), especially Part 3.

13 Daniel Bensaïd, *An Impatient Life: A Political Memoir*, trans. David Fernbach (London: Verso, 2013), 109. The phrase ultimately comes from Régis Debray.

14 For a detailed exploration of how mass action provoked states into developing new practices for maintaining order, see Luca Provenzano, "Under the Paving Stones: Militant Protest and Practices of the State in France and the Federal Republic of Germany, 1968–1977" (Ph.D. diss., Columbia University, 2020).

15 Raymond Marcellin, *L'Ordre public et les groupes révolutionnaires* (Paris: Plon, 1969).

16 Julian Bourg, *From Revolution to Ethics: May 1968 and Contemporary French Thought* (Montreal: McGill-Queen's University Press, 2007), 65.

17 The literature on state repression in these years is vast, but see especially Tracy Tullis, "A Vietnam at Home: Policing the Ghettos in the Counterinsurgency Era" (Ph.D. diss., New York University, 1999), and Stuart Schrader, *Badges without Borders: How Global Counterinsurgency Transformed American Policing* (Oakland: University of California Press, 2019).

18 Seth Rosenfeld, "Of Spies and Radicals," *Inside: The Daily Cal's Weekly Magazine*, June 4, 1982, 7. See, in particular, the collection of FBI documents in "Stephen Smale FBI File," Stephen Smale Papers, BANC MSS 99/373 c, carton 3, Bancroft Library, University of California, Berkeley, United States.

19 Seth Rosenfeld, *Subversives: The FBI's War on Student Radicals, and Reagan's Rise to Power* (New York: Farrar, Straus and Giroux, 2012), 317–20.

20 The committee condemned the FBI's operations in no uncertain terms: "Many of the techniques used would be intolerable in a democratic society even if all of the targets had been involved in violent activity, but COINTELPRO went far beyond that." See *Final Report of the Select Committee to Study Governmental Operations with Respect to Governmental Operations, Book Three* (Washington, DC: US Government Printing Office, 1976), 3.

21 Tom Wells, *The War Within: America's Battle over Vietnam* (Berkeley: University of California Press, 1994), 203–12.

22 Bill Moyers quoted ibid., 203.

23 Ibid., 315.

24 See, for example, Kenneth O'Reilly, *"Racial Matters": The FBI's Secret File on Black America, 1960–1972* (New York: Free Press, 1989).

25 Quoted in Joshua Bloom and Waldo E. Martin, Jr., *Black against Empire: The History and Politics of the Black Panther Party* (Berkeley: University of California Press, 2013), 210.

26 Ibid., Part 3.

27 "Interview with Scandinavian Rep. of Black Panther Party: Connie Matthews," *Black Panther*, October 18, 1969, 9. For Panther internationalism more generally, see among others, Bloom and Martin, Jr., *Black against*

Empire, Chapter 14, and Robyn Spencer, "Merely One Link in the Worldwide Revolution: Internationalism, State Repression, and the Black Panther Party, 1966–1972," in *From Toussaint to Tupac: The Black International since the Age of Revolution*, eds. Michael O. West, William G. Martin, and Fanon Che Wilkins (Chapel Hill: University of North Carolina Press, 2009), 225.

28 Quoted in Edmund White, *Genet: A Biography* (New York: Alfred A. Knopf, 1993), 535.

29 Ibid., 521–40.

30 Ibid., 536.

31 Jean Genet, "May Day Speech," in *The Declared Enemy: Texts and Interviews*, ed. Albert Dichy, trans. Jeff Fort (Stanford: Stanford University Press, 2004), 38–39.

32 "A propos d'une dissolution," *Cahiers Prolétariennes 1. Elargir la résistance* (January 1971): 13.

33 Benny Lévy in *Les maos en France*, ed. Michèle Manceaux (Paris: Gallimard, 1972), 210.

34 For example, it was only by asking Jean-Paul Sartre, who was virtually immune to arrest, to serve as editor that radicals could continue publishing *La Cause du people*, among other papers.

35 "A propos d'une dissolution," 23.

36 Bourg, *From Revolution to Ethics*, 72–75.

37 For sequestrations, see Xavier Vigna, *L'Insubordination ouvrière dans les années 68. Essai d'histoire politiques des usines* (Rennes: Presses Universitaires de Rennes, 2007), 103–07.

38 Daniel A. Gordon, *Immigrants and Intellectuals: May '68 and the Rise of Anti-Racism in France* (Pontypool: Merlin Press, 2012), Chapter 3.

39 Christophe Bourseiller, *Les Maoïstes. La folle histoire des gardes rouges français* (Paris: Plon, 1996), 113, 121.

40 Georges Marion, "Bruay-en-Artois. À propos de justice populaire," *Rouge* 157 (May 13, 1972): 7.

41 Michel Foucault, "On Popular Justice: A Discussion with Maoists," in *Power/Knowledge: Selected Interviews and Other Writings, 1972–1977*, ed. Colin Gordon, trans. Colin Gordon et al. (New York: Pantheon Books, 1980), 1.

42 Hervé Hamon and Patrick Rotman, *Génération, vol. II. Les années de poudre* (Paris: Seuil, 1988), 175–79.

43 Acting as a kind of "international political Red Cross," this organization was originally created by the Comintern in the early 1920s but dissolved before the Second World War.

44 Manifeste Secours Rouge, June 2, 1970, F delta rés 576/5/8, La contemporaine, Nanterre, France.

45 Secours Rouge, "Projet de résolution. Sur l'orientation politique du Secours Rouge," 1971, 3–4, F delta rés 576/5/8, La contemporaine. It should be noted, however, that these branches naturally adapted to the specific needs of each national context. In West Germany, which witnessed a higher level of domestic terrorism, Rote Hilfe, as Secours Rouge was known there, was particularly geared toward providing assistance to those militants involved in leftist terrorist organizations.

46 Ibid., 4.

47 "Pour une politique juste vis-à-vis des camarades emprisonnés," [1970], 4, F delta rés 576/5/5/1, La contemporaine.

48 Secours Rouge, "Communiqué du Secours Rouge," 1970, F delta rés 576/5/5/1, La contemporaine.

49 Bourg, *From Revolution to Ethics*, 76–78.

50 Daniel Defert, "The Emergence of a New Front," reprinted in *Intolerable: Writings from Michel Foucault and the Prisons Information Group (1970–1980)*, eds. Kevin Thompson and Perry Zurn, trans. Perry Zurn and Erik Beranek (Minneapolis: University of Minnesota Press, 2021), 37.

51 For Gilles Deleuze's role, see *François Dosse, Gilles Deleuze and Félix Guattari: Intersecting Lives*, trans. Deborah Glassman (New York: Columbia University Press, 2010), 309–13. For Genet, see White, *Genet*, 567–69.

52 "GIP Manifesto," reprinted in *Intolerable*, 64.

53 For the workers' inquiry model, see Asad Haider and Salar Mohandesi, "Workers' Inquiry: A Genealogy," *Viewpoint Magazine* 3, September 2013, https://viewpointmag.com/2013/09/27/workers-inquiry-a-genealogy.

54 See Julian Bourg's excellent work, *From Revolution to Ethics*, Chapters 2, 5, 6, 7.

55 "Pour l'union des prisons et des bases d'appui," n.d., 2, F delta rés 576/5/5/1, La contemporaine.

56 Michel Foucault and John K. Simon, "Michel Foucault on Attica: An Interview," *Social Justice* 18, no. 3 (45) (Fall 1991): 32.

57 Bourg, *From Revolution to Ethics*, 77–95.

58 Defert, "The Emergence of a New Front," 45.

59 Robert Lumley, *States of Emergency: Cultures of Revolt in Italy from 1968 to 1978* (London: Verso, 1990), Part 3.

60 Italo Sbrogiò, "The history of the workers' committee of Porto Marghera," talk delivered on June 9, 2006 in Marghera, reprinted in *Porto Marghera: The Last Firebrands*, 39, pamphlet accompanying the film by the same name, dir. Manuela Pellarin, 2004.

61 For the concept of social reproduction in this context, see Mariarosa Dalla Costa, "The Power of Women and the Subversion of the Community," 1972, reprinted in *Women and the Subversion of the Community: A Mariarosa Dalla Costa Reader*, ed. Camille Barbagallo (Oakland: PM Press, 2019), 13–49.

62 "Take Over the City," trans. Ernest Dowson, *Radical America* 7, no. 2 (March–April 1973): 79–112.

63 Ginsborg, *Contemporary Italy*, 322–25.

64 "Depuis la réunion, des camarades du GIP ont rencontré ...," April 1971, reprinted in *Le Groupe d'information sur les prisons. Archives d'une lutte, 1970–1972*, eds. Philippe Artières, Laurent Quéro, and Michelle Zancarini-Fournel (Paris: IMEC, 2003), 104.

65 See, for example, the issue on housing, *Secours Rouge* 2, February 1972, F delta rés 576/5/8, La contemporaine. For other links with Continuous Struggle, see Manus McGrogan, "Vive la Révolution and the Example of Lotta Continua: The Circulation of Ideas and Practices Between the Left Militant Worlds of France and Italy Following May '68," *Modern & Contemporary France* 18, no. 3 (August 2010): 309–28.

66 "Intolerable 3: The Assassination of George Jackson," in *Intolerable*, 156.
67 "La bataille d'Attica," *La Cause du peuple–J'accuse* 9, September 23, 1971, 9.
68 "Intolerable 3," 156–57.
69 Ibid., 157.
70 "Nous levons une armée populaire au cœur du nouveau fascisme," *La Cause du peuple–J'accuse* 9, 10–11.
71 Jean Genet, "Introduction," trans. Richard Howard, *Soledad Brother: The Prison Letters of George Jackson* (New York: Bantam Books, 1970), 8.
72 See, for example, "La prison. Enjeu d'un combat," *La Cause du peuple–J'accuse* 1, May 24, 1971, 7.
73 "Intolerable 3," 156.
74 Le peuple en colère, "Camarades," [1971], 2, F delta rés 576/5/5/1, La contemporaine.
75 "La prison. Enjeu d'un combat," 6.
76 Alberto Toscano, "The Intolerable-Inquiry: The Documents of the Groupe d'information sur les prisons," *Viewpoint* 3, September 2013, https://viewpointmag.com/2013/09/25/the-intolerable-inquiry-the-documents-of-the-groupe-dinformation-sur-les-prisons.
77 Foucault and Simon, "Michel Foucault on Attica," 32. It is worth noting that Foucault's own thinking was deeply shaped by his encounter with the Black Panthers; see Brady Thomas Heiner, "Foucault and the Black Panthers," *City* 11, no. 3 (2007): 313–56.
78 See, for example, "La prison. Enjeu d'un combat," 6–7.
79 For more on this "bifurcated" strategy – violent militancy on the one hand and legalistic democratic unity on the other – in the ex-Proletarian Left, see Jean-Paul Étienne, "La Gauche prolétarienne (1968–1973): illégalisme révolutionnaire et justice populaire" (Ph.D. diss., Université Paris-VIII, 2003).
80 Vernon E. Davis, *The Long Road Home: US Prisoner of War Policy and Planning in Southeast Asia* (Washington, DC: Historical Office, Office of the Secretary of Defense, 2000), 197.
81 Ibid., 133.
82 See, for example, Jim Stockdale and Sybil Stockdale, *In Love and War: The Story of a Family's Ordeal and Sacrifice during the Vietnam Years* (Annapolis: Naval Institute Press, 1990), especially Chapter 10; Michael J. Allen, *Until the Last Man Comes Home: POWs, MIAs, and the Unending Vietnam War* (Chapel Hill: University of North Carolina Press, 2009), 24–29.
83 For the POW/MIA issue, see Allen, *Until the Last Man*. For a fascinating but polemical account, see H. Bruce Franklin, *MIA or Mythmaking in America* (New Brunswick: Rutgers University Press, 1993). For Nixon's approaches to the Vietnam War, see Jeffrey Kimball, *Nixon's Vietnam War* (Lawrence: University Press of Kansas, 1998). For the prowar coalition, see Sandra Scanlon, *The Pro-War Movement: Domestic Support for the Vietnam War and the Making of Modern American Conservatism* (Amherst: University of Massachusetts Press, 2013).
84 Davis, *The Long Road Home*, 202.
85 Stockdale and Stockdale, *In Love and War*, 320.
86 Franklin, *MIA*, 50.

87 H. Bruce Franklin, "Missing in Action in the Twenty-First Century," in *Four Decades On: Vietnam, the United States, and the Legacies of the Second Indochina War*, eds. Scott Laderman and Edwin A. Martini (Durham: Duke University Press, 2013), 266–70.

88 Allen, *Until the Last Man*, 43–44.

89 Tom Wilber and Jerry Lembcke, *Dissenting POWs: From Vietnam's Hoa Lo Prison to America Today* (New York: Monthly Review Press, 2021).

90 Richard Nixon, "Address to the Nation about a New Initiative for Peace in Southeast Asia," October 7, 1970, in *Public Papers of the Presidents of the United States: Richard Nixon, 1970* (Washington, DC: US Government Printing Office, 1971), 827.

91 Richard Nixon, "Panel Interview at the Annual Convention of the American Society of Newspaper Editors," April 16, 1971, in *Public Papers of the Presidents of the United States: Richard Nixon, 1971* (Washington, DC: US Government Printing Office, 1972), 541.

92 Ronald Reagan quoted in Scanlon, *The Pro-War Movement*, 236.

93 Nixon, "Panel Interview," 540.

94 Jonathan Schell quoted in Franklin, "Missing in Action," 272.

95 Richard Nixon, "Proclamation 4038: National Week of Concern for Americans Who Are Prisoners of War or Missing in Action" March 19, 1971, in *The Code of Federal Regulations of the United States of America* (Washington, DC: US Government Printing Office, 1972), 37.

96 Nixon, "Address to the Nation," 827.

97 Allen, *Until the Last Man*, 60–61.

98 Quoted in Michael J. Allen, "'Help Us Tell the Truth about Vietnam': POW/MIA Politics and the End of the American War," in *Making Sense of the Vietnam Wars: Local, National, and Transnational Perspectives*, eds. Mark Philip Bradley and Marilyn B. Young (Oxford: Oxford University Press, 2008), 265.

99 The proposal was made in "For World Peace," *Black Panther* 3, no. 28 (November 1, 1969): 12–13, and the quotation comes from "Prisoners of War for Political Prisoners," *Black Panther* 4, no. 5 (January 3, 1970): 9.

100 "Prisoners of War for Political Prisoners," 9.

101 Allen, *Until the Last Man*, Chapter 1.

102 Press Release, January 15, 1970, 1, in Committee of Liaison with Families of Servicemen Detained in North Vietnam Records, 1969–1973 (DG 227), Box 5, (Press Releases), Peace Collection, Swarthmore College, Swarthmore, United States (hereafter Peace Collection).

103 "POW group Won't Boycott Cora Weiss," Associated Press, October 18, 1972, in Committee of Liaison with Families of Servicemen Detained in North Vietnam Records, 1969–1973 (DG 227), Box 3, (League of Families), Peace Collection.

104 "Press Release Issued Thursday Sept. 17 after 379 Letters from POW's Were Seized Night before from Robert Scheer at Kennedy," September 17, 1970, 1, in Committee of Liaison with Families of Servicemen Detained in North Vietnam Records, 1969–1973 (DG 227), Box 5, (Press Releases), Peace Collection.

105 William S. Turley, *The Second Indochina War: A Concise Political and Military History* (Lanham: Rowman & Littlefield, 2008), Chapter 6.

106 Sophie Quinn-Judge, *The Third Force in the Vietnam War: The Elusive Search for Peace 1954–1975* (London: I. B. Taurus, 2017), 125.

107 Turley, *Second Indochina War*, 156.

108 Troung Nhu Tang with David Chanoff and Doan Van Toai, *A Vietcong Memoir* (New York: Vintage Books, 1986), Chapters 12 and 13. For the "Third Force," see Quinn-Judge, *The Third Force*, and Heather Marie Stur, *Saigon at War: South Vietnam and the Global Sixties* (Cambridge: Cambridge University Press, 2020).

109 Ngo Vinh Long, "Legacies Foretold: Excavating the Roots of Postwar Viet Nam," in *Four Decades On: Vietnam, the United States, and the Legacies of the Second Indochina War*, eds. Scott Laderman and Edwin A. Martini (Durham: Duke University Press, 2013), 19–21.

110 Takashi Oka, "Thieu Denounces 'Immediate Peace,'" *New York Times*, July 16, 1970.

111 For an eyewitness study of these relationships, see Paul Quinn-Judge, "Inside Saigon: Eye-Witness Report," *Commonweal*, September 26, 1975, 429–32, in Box 127, Folder 2, Series 1: Vietnam, Liberation News Service Records, Temple University, Philadelphia, United States (hereafter LNSR).

112 Van Nguyen-Marshall, "Student Activism in Time of War: Youth in the Republic of Vietnam, 1960s–1970s," *Journal of Vietnamese Studies* 10, no. 2 (2015): 57.

113 *After the Signing of the Paris Agreements: Documents on South Vietnam's Political Prisoners*, June 1973, 3–5, Box 128, Folder 3, LNSR. For Catholic politics, see Stur, *Saigon at War*, Chapter 7.

114 Frazier, *Women's Antiwar Diplomacy*, 107–09.

115 Copy of Open Letter to Spiro Agnew, 1, Women Strike for Peace Records, 1961–1966 (DG 115), Series C,2, Box 2, (Con Son Prison), Peace Collection.

116 Don Luce, "The Tiger Cages in Vietnam," *Historians against the War* 3 (2006): 10.

117 *After the Signing of the Paris Agreements*, 35, LNSR.

118 Frazier, *Women's Antiwar Diplomacy*, 107–13.

119 Stur, *Saigon at War*, 227–34.

120 Ngo Vinh Long, "Vietnamese in America – 'Why We Fight Thieu,'" *Thời Báo Gà* no. 21, February 1972, 2, in Box 128, Folder 6, LNSR. Vietnamese activism in the United States was relatively small-scale up to this point. There were few Vietnamese in the country, many were students handpicked by the South Vietnamese state, and most were initially not political. That said, they grew more radical in the United States, eventually organizing a Vietnamese American antiwar force, especially after the tragic murder of Nguyễn Thái Bình, a leading figure who participated in the consulate occupation. See Nguyet Nguyen, "Antiwar Transnationalism: People's Diplomacy in the Vietnam War" (Ph.D. diss., American University, 2019), Chapter 4.

121 Long, "Legacies Foretold," 24–25.

122 Jean-Pierre Debris and André Menras, "Thieu's Political Prisoners," n.d., 1, in Committee of Liaison with Families of Servicemen Detained in North Vietnam Records, 1969–1973 (DG 227), Box 3, (SVN Political Prisoners), Peace Collection.

123 See, for example, their fascinating interview with Studs Terkel on March 9, 1973, https://studsterkel.wfmt.com/programs/jean-pierre-debris-and-andres-menras-discuss-their-experiences-political-prisoners-vietnam.

124 Emergency Project for Saigon Political Prisoners, "Their Lives Are in *Our* Hands," n.d., 2 in Committee of Liaison with Families of Servicemen Detained in North Vietnam Records, 1969–1973 (DG 227), Box 3, (SVN Political Prisoners), Peace Collection.

125 "What about the Other POWs?," *Black Panther* 9, no. 23 (March 24, 1973): 9, 11.

126 Flora Lewis, "Vietnam Peace Pacts Signed; America's Longest War Halts," *New York Times*, January 28, 1973.

127 Richard Nixon, "Remarks at a Reception for Returned Prisoners of War," May 24, 1973, in *Public Papers of the Presidents of the United States: Richard Nixon, 1973* (Washington, DC: US Government Printing Office, 1975), 558.

128 Turley, *Second Indochina War*, 209–11.

129 Wells, *The War Within*, Chapter 10.

130 Sabine Rousseau, "Du Vietnam héroïque à la défense des droits de l'homme," in *68. Une histoire collective, 1962–1981*, eds. Philippe Artières and Michelle Zancarini-Fournel (Paris: La Découverte, 2008), 484–86.

131 Debris and Menras, "Thieu's Political Prisoners," 11.

132 For the ISF, see Laurent Jalabert, "Un movement contre la guerre du Vietnam. Le Front Solidarité Indochine, 1971–1973," in *Vietnam, 1968–1976. La sortie de la guerre*, eds. Pierre Journoud and Cécile Menétrey-Monchau (Brussels: Peter Land, 2011), 221–28.

133 Front Solidarité Indochine, "Vietnam 1973," 1973, F delta 236/22, La contemporaine.

134 Bureau national, "Circulaire hebdomadaire," October 27, 1972, 1–2, F delta 292, La contemporaine.

135 Ibid.

136 M. R. "Une victoire historique," *Solidarité Indochine* 9, February 1973, 2.

137 "Message du GRP au FSI," reprinted in *Rouge* 192, February 17, 1973, 17.

138 For example, Front Solidarité Indochine, *Saïgon. Les prisonniers* (Paris: Maspero, 1973), O col 2213/6, La contemporaine.

139 "Lundi 26 Février. Journée de solidarité avec les prisonniers au Sud-Vietnam," *Rouge* 193, February 24, 1973, 17. For League support, see Appel, n.d., and Circulaire du Bureau National FSI, January 26, 1972, 1, both in F delta rés 761/12/4, La contemporaine.

140 CILA and MNSPI, *Les Prisonniers politique au Sud Vietnam*, December 20, 1973, 34, F delta rés 613/68, La contemporaine.

141 "Une réunion européenne des mouvements de solidarité," *Rouge* 195, March 9, 1973, 17.

142 "Conférence de Presse du FSI," n.d., F delta rés 761/12/4, La contemporaine.

143 Statement reprinted as "L'Europe anti-impérialiste avec Indochine," *Solidarité Indochine* 10, March 1973, 8.

144 "Un mois européen de solidarité," *Rouge* 198, March 30, 1973, 19.

145 "L'Europe anti-impérialiste," 8.

146 "Qui était à Milan?," *Rouge* 205, May 18, 1973, 19, and "Bilan de la Manifestation européenne de Milan," May 18, 1973, 1, F delta 292, La contemporaine.

147 "L'heure du soutien," *Rouge* 204, May 11, 1973, 12.

148 For the full list of participants, see "Organizzazioni aderenti alla manifestazione," *Lunga Marcia* nos. 3–4, May–August 1973, 9.

149 "La Manifestazione internazionale di Milano," *Lunga Marcia* 3–4, 7–8, and "La Manifestation internationale de Milan," *Indochine en lutte* 5–6, June–July 1973, 8.

150 "Indochine. L'heure est au soutien!," 1973, F delta 151/117, La contemporaine.

151 "La Manifestation internationale de Milan," 8.

152 Phan Van Ba, "Messaggio di solidarietà del governo rivoluzionario provvisorio della repubblica del sud Vietnam alla manifestazione del 12 maggio a Milano," *Lunga Marcia* 2–3, 8.

153 "Le 12 Mai à Milan ! Manifestation internationale," *Rouge* 203, May 4, 1973, 19, and "Le stalinisme n'est pas morte," *Rouge* 205, May 18, 1973, 18.

154 See, for example, *Le Courrier du Vietnam* 364, March 13, 1972.

155 See, for example, the campaign to pressure Francisco Franco to free Basque militants: Rapport du comité d'initiative, September 1971, 6, F delta rés 576/5/8, La contemporaine.

156 Comité de Défense des Prisonniers Politiques Argentins, "Argentine 72. Oppression, répression, tortures," 1972, 4, F delta 2089, La contemporaine. For struggles in the Southern Cone during this time, see, among many others, Aldo Marchesi, *Latin America's Radical Left: Rebellion and Cold War in the Global 1960s* (Cambridge: Cambridge University Press, 2017).

157 "Conférence de presse. Pour la libération de tous les détenus au Sud," *Rouge* 194, March 2, 1973, 18.

158 "L'Europe anti-impérialiste," 8.

159 "Le Gabbie di tigre non bastano più," *Lunga Marcia* 2–3, 11.

160 See, for example, Peoples Action Union for Peace and Justice, "There Are Still 200,000 POWs in Vietnam," n.d., 1, Women Strike for Peace Records, 1961–1966 (DG 115), Series B,1, Box 10, (Political Prisoners), Peace Collection.

161 Wells, *The War Within*, 572.

162 "You Can Save Lives," in *No Peace/No Honor: An Indochina Peace Campaign Report*, n.d., 4, in Box 127, Folder 7, LNSR.

163 Emergency Project, "Their Lives Are in *Our* Hands," 1.

164 Conférence Internationale pour la Libération des prisonniers politiques du Sud-Vietnam, "Liste des organisations et mouvements participant à la conférence internationale pour la libération des prisonniers politiques du sud-Vietnam," April 1973, 1, F delta rés 613/65, La contemporaine.

165 For a brief summary of the event from the perspective of the radicals, see "Conférence internationale pour la libération des prisonniers politiques du Sud-Vietnam," *Rouge* 201, April 20, 1973, 14.

166 Sabine Rousseau, "1973. Conférences alternatives et Troisième force," in *Vietnam, 1968–1976*, 229–38.

167 Ibid., 232; "En bref," *Sud Viet Nam en lutte* 203, June 25, 1973, 7.

168 "Sample Letters," n.d., Women Strike for Peace Records, 1961–66 (DG 115), Series B,1, Box 16, (Amnesty File), Peace Collection.

169 Amnesty International, *Report on Torture* (London: Duckworth, 1973), 7.

170 Ibid., 1, 27.

171 Amnesty International, *Epidemic: Torture*, September 10, 1973.

172 "Instructions for Writing Letters," n.d., Women Strike for Peace Records, 1961–66 (DG 115), Series B,1, Box 16, (Amnesty File), Peace Collection.

173 "Instructions," n.d., Women Strike for Peace Records, 1961–66 (DG 115), Series B,1, Box 16, (Amnesty File), Peace Collection.

174 "Sample Letters."

175 For more on the ways that Amnesty, as well as other human rights organizations, creates a sense of objectivity, see Richard A. Wilson, "Representing Human Rights Violations: Social Contexts and Subjectivities," in *Human Rights, Culture and Context: Anthropological Perspectives*, ed. Richard A. Wilson (London: Pluto Press, 1997), 134–60.

176 "Le Gabbie di tigre," 13.

177 "Briser l'enfer concentrationnaire Sud-Vietnamien. 15,000 incarcérations par mois!," *Solidarité Indochine* 10, March 1973, 6.

178 Amnesty International, *Amnesty International Report 1968–1969* (London, 1969), 29.

179 Nguyen Ngoc Lan, "Reflections on the Universal Declaration of Human Rights," in Chan Tin, "Letter from Saigon," 1973, 32, Box 128, Folder 5, LNSR.

180 For a fuller exploration of the conditions of possibility for the rise of human rights in the 1970s, specifically within the US context, see Mark Philip Bradley, *The World Reimagined: Americans and Human Rights in the Twentieth Century* (Cambridge: Cambridge University Press, 2016), Chapter 5.

181 Sarah Snyder, "Exporting Amnesty International to the United States: Transatlantic Human Rights Activism in the 1960s," *Human Rights Quarterly* 34, no. 3 (August 2012): 792.

182 *Saïgon. Les prisonniers*, 44.

183 "La répression au sud se poursuit, le soutien doit continuer," *Solidarité Indochine* 11, November 1973, 4.

184 Of course, AI was not immune to internal division; see Snyder, "Exporting Amnesty International."

185 Jan Eckel, *The Ambivalence of Good: Human Rights in International Politics since the 1940s*, trans. Rachel Ward (Oxford: Oxford University Press, 2019), 175–83.

186 Kenneth Cmiel, "The Emergence of Human Rights Politics in the United States," *Journal of American History* 86, no. 3 (December 1999), 1240.

187 Lowell Livezey, "US Religious Organizations and the International Human Rights Movement," *Human Rights Quarterly* 11 (1989): 14–81.

188 Indochina Peace Campaign, *Women under Torture*, August 1973, 31–34, Box 128, Folder 4, LNSR.

189 Sabine Rousseau, *La Colombe et le napalm. Des chrétiens français contre les guerres d'Indochine et du Vietnam, 1945–1975* (Paris: CNRS Éditions, 2002), 280.

190 The literature on Chilean solidarity is enormous. For a study of diverse actors in the Americas, see Patrick William Kelly, *Sovereign Emergencies: Latin America and the Making of Global Human Rights Politics* (Cambridge: Cambridge University Press, 2018). For European solidarity, see Kim Christiaens, Idesbald Goddeeris, and Magaly Rodríguez García, eds., *European Solidarity with Chile, 1970s–1980s* (Frankfurt am Main: Peter Lang, 2014). For the development of human rights, see Jan Eckel, "'Under a Magnifying Glass': The International Human Rights Campaign against Chile in the Seventies," in *Human Rights in the Twentieth Century*, ed. Stefan-Ludwig Hoffmann (Cambridge: Cambridge University Press, 2010), 321–41.

191 Vania Markarian, *Left in Transformation: Uruguayan Exiles and the Latin American Human Rights Network, 1967–1984* (New York: Routledge, 2005), 86.

192 For an interesting exploration of the complex overlaps and the multiplicity of actors involved in just one of these transformative episodes, see Anna Konieczna and Rob Skinner, eds., *A Global History of Anti-Apartheid: "Forward to Freedom" in South Africa* (London: Palgrave Macmillan, 2019).

193 Quoted in Tom Buchanan, "'The Truth Will Set You Free': The Making of Amnesty International," *Journal of Contemporary History* 37, no. 4 (October 2002): 593.

5   Crisis

1 Quoted in A. J. Langguth, *Our Vietnam: The War 1954–1975* (New York: Simon & Schuster, 2000), 667. For Bùi Tín's own recollection of this event, see *Following Ho Chi Minh: The Memoirs of a North Vietnamese Colonel*, trans. Judy Stowe and Do Van (Honolulu: University of Hawaii Press, 1995), 84–86.

2 Kevin M. Kruse and Julian E. Zelizer, *Fault Lines: A History of the United States since 1974* (New York: W. W. Norton, 2019), Chapters 1–4.

3 Simon Reid-Henry, *Empire of Democracy: The Remaking of the West since the Cold War, 1971–2017* (New York: Simon & Schuster, 2019), Part 1.

4 Stuart Hall, "The Great Moving Right Show" and "Gramsci and Us," in *The Hard Road to Renewal: Thatcherism and the Crisis of the Left* (London: Verso, 1988), 39–56 and 161–73.

5 Marco Boato, "La generazione del Vietnam," *Lotta Continua* 8, no. 5, January 9, 1979, 2.

6 Ibid.

7 Luc Boltanski and Ève Chiapello, *The New Spirit of Capitalism*, trans. Gregory Elliot (London: Verso, 2005), Part 2.

8 Geoff Eley, *Forging Democracy: The History of the Left in Europe, 1850–2000* (Oxford: Oxford University Press, 2002), Chapter 23.

9 Louis Althusser, "The Crisis of Marxism," *Marxism Today* 22, no. 7 (July 1978): 215–20, 227. For another contemporary perspective, see Nicos Poulantzas, "Is There a Crisis of Marxism?," reprinted in *The Poulantzas Reader: Marxism, Law, and the State*, ed. James Martin (London: Verso, 2008), 376–86.

10 Ernesto Laclau and Chantal Mouffe, *Hegemony and Socialist Strategy: Towards a Radical Democratic Politics*, 2nd ed. (London: Verso, 2014), viii.

11 For an excellent study that situates the crisis of Marxism, and of the far left more generally, within a fully global scope, see Ernest Wamba dia Wamba, "The 'Crisis of Marxism' and Some of Its Implications," *Philosophy and Social Action* 16, no. 1 (1990): 7–22.

12 See, among others, Vijay Prashad, *The Poorer Nations: A Possible History of the Global South* (London: Verso, 2012).

13 Chen Jian, "China's Changing Policies toward the Third World and the End of the Global Cold War," in *The End of the Cold War and the Third World: New Perspectives on Regional Conflict*, eds. Artemy Kalinovsky and Sergey Radchenko (London: Routledge, 2011), 101–21.

14 Eleanor Davey, "French Adventures in Solidarity: Revolutionary Tourists and Radical Humanitarians," *European Review of History/Revue européenne d'histoire* 21, no. 4 (2014): 582–84.

15 Olivier Todd, "Comment je me suis laissé tromper par Hanoi," *Réalités* 332 (September 1973): 36–41.

16 Gérard Chaliand, *Mythes révolutionnaires du tiers monde. Guérillas et socialismes* (Paris: Seuil, 1976).

17 Claudie Broyelle, Jacques Broyelle, and Evelyne Tschirhart, *Deuxième retour de Chine* (Paris: Seuil, 1977).

18 François Ponchaud, *Cambodia Year Zero*, trans. Nancy Amphoux (London: Allen Lane, 1978).

19 Rony Brauman, *Penser dans l'urgence: Parcours critique d'un humanitaire. Entretiens avec Catherine Portevin* (Paris: Seuil, 2006), 55.

20 Michael Christofferson, *French Intellectuals against the Left: The Antitotalitarian Moment of the 1970s* (New York: Berghahn Books, 2004), Chapter 2.

21 Eleanor Davey, *Idealism beyond Borders: The French Revolutionary Left and the Rise of Humanitarianism, 1954–1988* (Cambridge: Cambridge University Press, 2015), 132.

22 Quoted in Ronald Fraser et al., eds., *1968: A Student Generation in Revolt* (New York: Pantheon Books, 1988), 332.

23 "Contre l'abstention des révolutionnaires," *Libération*, May 15, 1974.

24 Daniel Cohn-Bendit, "Tribune libre. Abstention piège à cons," *Libération*, May 18–19, 1974.

25 This passage draws heavily on Christofferson, *French Intellectuals*, Chapter 3.

26 Ibid., 195.

27 See, among others, ibid., especially Chapter 5; Julian Bourg, *From Revolution to Ethics: May 1968 Contemporary French Thought* (Montreal: McGill-Queen's University Press, 2007), Part 4; and Kristin Ross, *May '68 and Its Afterlives* (Chicago: University of Chicago, 2002), 169–81.

28 Davey, *Idealism beyond Borders*, Chapter 4.

29 Jacques Julliard, "Le tiers monde et la gauche," *Le Nouvel Observateur*, June 5, 1978.

30 Ibid.
31 Maxime Szczepanski-Huillery, "'L'idéologie tiers-mondiste.' Constructions et usages d'une catégorie intellectuelle en 'crise,'" *Raisons politique* 18 (2005): 31–32.
32 Samir Amin, *Imperialism and Unequal Development* (New York: Monthly Review Press, 1977), 11.
33 Jean Daniel and André Burguière, eds., *Le tiers monde et la gauche* (Paris: Seuil, 1979), 14.
34 For more on the uses of this polemical concept, see Szczepanski-Huillery, "L'idéologie tiers-mondiste," 27–48.
35 Ross, *May '68*, 167.
36 Ibid, 163–64.
37 Paige Arthur, *Unfinished Projects: Decolonization and the Philosophy of Jean-Paul Sartre* (London: Verso, 2010), 210–13.
38 Julliard, "Le tiers monde et la gauche."
39 Ibid.
40 Ibid.
41 Lasse Heerten, *The Biafran War and Postcolonial Humanitarianism: Spectacles of Suffering* (Cambridge: Cambridge University Press, 2017), Chapters 1–2.
42 Davey, *Idealism beyond Borders*, 172–76.
43 Max Récamier and Bernard Kouchner, "De retour du Biafra. Deux médecins français témoignent," *Le Monde*, November 27, 1968.
44 Heerten, *The Biafran War*, 321–22.
45 Peter Redfield, *Life in Crisis: The Ethical Journal of Doctors Without Borders* (Berkeley: University of California Press, 2013), 58.
46 The literature on MSF is voluminous. For a few examples, see Anne Vallaeys, *Médecins sans frontières. La biographie* (Paris: Fayard, 2004); Redfield, *Life in Crisis*; and Renée C. Fox, *Doctors Without Borders: Humanitarian Quests, Impossible Dreams of Médecins Sans Frontières* (Baltimore: Johns Hopkins University Press, 2014).
47 Bernard Kouchner quoted in Davey, *Idealism beyond Borders*, 174.
48 Ibid., 175.
49 Michael Barnett, *Empire of Humanity: A History of Humanitarianism* (Ithaca: Cornell University Press, 2011), 151.
50 Eleanor Davey, "The Language of ingérence: Interventionist Debates in France, 1970s–1990s," in *Human Rights and Humanitarian Intervention: Legitimizing the Use of Force in the 1970s*, eds. Norbert Frei et al. (Göttingen: Wallstein, 2017), 46–63.
51 Rony Brauman, "The Médecins sans Frontières Experience," in *A Framework for Survival: Health, Human Rights, and Humanitarian Assistance in Conflicts and Disasters*, ed. Kevin M. Cahill (New York: Council on Foreign Relations, 1993), 209.
52 Davey, *Idealism beyond Borders*, 213.
53 Cited ibid.
54 Barnett, *Empire of Humanity*, 146–47, 154.
55 Paul Berman, *Power and the Idealists: Or, the Passion of Joschka Fischer and Its Aftermath* (Brooklyn: Soft Skull Press, 2005), 231–32.
56 Julliard, "Le tiers monde et la gauche."

57 For examples of critical replies to Julliard's position, see the contributions of Samir Amin, Yves Lacoste, Claude Liauzu, and Guy Sitbon in *Le tiers monde et la gauche*. For one example of a radical attempt to fight the anti-Marxist tide while trying to reinvent Marxist thinking in light of these challenges, see Nicos Poulantzas, *State, Power, Socialism* (London: Verso, 2014).

58 For Southeast Asia as a particularly explosive site in the Global Cold War, see Bradley R. Simpson, "Southeast Asia in the Cold War," in *The Cold War in the Third World*, ed. Robert J. McMahon (Oxford: Oxford University Press, 2013), 48–66.

59 Ben Kiernan, *How Pol Pot Came to Power: Colonialism, Nationalism, and Communism in Cambodia, 1930–1975*, 2nd ed. (New Haven: Yale University Press, 2004).

60 Grant Evans and Kelvin Rowley, *Red Brotherhood at War: Vietnam, Cambodia and Laos since 1975*, 2nd ed. (London: Verso, 1990), 6–10, 81–92.

61 Christopher E. Goscha, "Vietnam, the Third Indochina War and the Meltdown of Asian Internationalism," in *The Third Indochina War: Conflict between China, Vietnam and Cambodia, 1972–1979*, eds. Odd Arne Westad and Sophie Quinn-Judge (London: Routledge, 2006), 164–69.

62 Ben Kiernan, *The Pol Pot Regime: Race, Power, and Genocide in Cambodia under the Khmer Rouge, 1975–1979*, 3rd ed. (New Haven: Yale University Press, 2008). For a detailed but biased account of the split between Cambodia and Vietnam, see Stephen J. Morris, *Why Vietnam Invaded Cambodia: Political Culture and the Causes of War* (Stanford: Stanford University Press, 1999), especially Part 1.

63 Noam Chomsky and Edward S. Herman, "Distortions at Fourth Hand," *The Nation*, June 25, 1977, 789–94.

64 Lien-Hang T. Nguyen, "The Sino-Vietnamese Split and the Indochina War, 1968–1975," in *The Third Indochina War*, 13–14.

65 Chen Jian, "China, the Vietnam War, and the Sino-American Rapprochement, 1968–1973," in *The Third Indochina War*, 53–54.

66 For Chinese aid to the Khmer Rouge, see Andrew Mertha, *Brothers in Arms: Chinese Aid to the Khmer Rouge, 1975–1979* (Ithaca: Cornell University Press, 2014).

67 For the lasting conflict between the two, see Xiaoming Zhang, *Deng Xiaoping's Long War: The Military Conflict between China and Vietnam, 1979–1991* (Chapel Hill: University of North Carolina Press, 2015).

68 Thu-huong Nguyen-vo, *Khmer–Viet Relations and the Third Indochina Conflict* (Jefferson: McFarland & Company, 1992), 138.

69 Kenton Clymer, "Jimmy Carter, Human Rights, and Cambodia," *Diplomatic History* 27, no. 2 (April 2003): 257.

70 For a good analysis of this conflict, see Evans and Rowley, *Red Brotherhood at War*.

71 Daniel Bensaïd, "Le deuxième chute de Phnom Penh," *Rouge* 835, January 9, 1979, 1.

72 José Sanchez, "Cambodge. La cerise et le noyau," *Tribune socialiste* 809, January 12–17, 1979, 13.

73 Bensaïd, "Le deuxième chute" and "Les troupes vietnamiennes doivent quitter le Cambodge," *Rouge* 837, January 12–14, 1979, 5.

74 Catherine Quiminal, *L'invasion du Cambodge par le Vietnam: éléments d'histoire et points de repère* (Marseille: Éditions Potemkine, 1979).
75 Pierre Klaufer, "A propos de Vietnam-Cambodge," *Rouge* 848, January 29, 1979, 9.
76 Jean-Pierre Champagny, "Après plusieurs mois de provocations vietnamiennes soutenues par l'URSS: L'armée chinoise riposte aux agressions," *Le Quotidien du peuple* 857, February 20, 1979, 7.
77 Jian, "China's Changing Policies," 105–11.
78 Jennifer Altehenger, "Social Imperialism and Mao's Three Worlds: Deng Xiaoping's Speech to the UN General Assembly, 1974," in *Revolutionary Moments: Reading Revolutionary Texts*, ed. Rachel Hammersley (London: Bloomsbury Academic, 2015), 175–81.
79 "Chairman Mao's Theory of the Differentiation of the Three Worlds Is a Major Contribution to Marxism–Leninism," *Peking Review* 20, no. 45 (November 4, 1977): 24.
80 Ibid., 29–33.
81 For an incisive discussion of the general theoretical gesture of dividing the globe into "three worlds," see Aijaz Ahmad, *In Theory: Classes, Nations, Literatures* (London: Verso, 1992), Chapter 8.
82 Christophe Bourseiller, *Les Maoïstes. La folle histoire des gardes rouges français* (Paris: Plon, 1996), 256–60.
83 For the October League, which became the Communist Party (Marxist-Leninist), see Max Elbaum, *Revolution in the Air: Sixties Radicals Turn to Lenin, Mao and Che* (London: Verso, 2002), 102–03, 228–34.
84 "War and Revolution on the Rise: Report from Europe – Part 1," *The Call*, 5, no. 20, September 20, 1976, www.marxists.org/history/erol/ncm-3/western-europe-1.htm.
85 "Saluons la création du Parti communiste marxiste-léniniste," *L'Humanité rouge* 713, June 23, 1977, 2.
86 Carl Davidson, "Should we speak out on Hanoi's atrocities?," *The Call* 8, no. 28, July 16, 1979, www.marxists.org/history/erol/ncm-5/davidson-baez.htm.
87 "Rapport sur la situation actuelle et nos tâches," *L'Humanité rouge* 1168, November 16, 1979, 3.
88 "Cambodge. Les méthodes de Hanoï pour exterminer un peuple," *L'Humanité rouge* 1181, December, 5, 1979, 5.
89 Jean-Paul Gay, "Les non-alignés maintiennent leur refus du 'fait accompli' vietnamien au Cambodge," *Le Quotidien du peuple*, May 19–21, 1979, 11.
90 Reprinted as "Appel pour le soutien au Cambodge contre l'agression Vietnamienne," *Kampuchea Vaincra!: Journal du Comité Kampuchea*, no. 1, February 1979, 4.
91 "Appel," *Kampuchea Vaincra!*, 2. It should be noted, however, that the pro-Chinese and Maoists were not united in their efforts, even if they all supported the Khmer resistance against Vietnam. Alain Badiou's Maoist group, for example, created its own rival base committee. See "Pour un Comité Kampuchéa Vaincra!," supplement to *ML* no. 33–34, n.d., F delta rés 613/66, La contemporaine, Nanterre, France.

92 "World Kampuchea Conference a Great Success," *Class Struggle: Political Paper of the Revolutionary Communist League of Great Britain* 3, no. 25, December 12–26, 1979, 8.

93 "Une audience qui s'élargit," *L'Humanité rouge* 1168, November 16, 1979, 2.

94 "Nouvelle initiative pour exiger le retrait des troupes vietnamiennes," *L'Humanité rouge* 1172, November 22, 1979, 2.

95 "Extraits de l'intervention de Jan Myrdal à la tribune de la conférence," *Solidarité Cambodge*, February 1980, 4.

96 Mouvement Solidarité Cambodge, Communiqué, January 12, 1980; *Kampuchea Conference: Tokyo 1981*, June 1981; and *Kampuchea Conference: Paris 1982*, June 1982, all in F delta rés 613/66, La contemporaine.

97 "Plate-Forme. Mouvement Solidarité Cambodge," *Solidarité Cambodge*, 7.

98 Evan Gottesman, *Cambodia after the Khmer Rouge: Inside the Politics of Nation Building* (New Haven: Yale University Press, 2003), 82–83.

99 William Shawcross, *The Quality of Mercy: Cambodia, Holocaust and Modern Conscience* (New York: Simon & Schuster, 1983), 96; Jamie Frederic Metzl, *Western Responses to Human Rights Abuses in Cambodia, 1975–1980* (London: Palgrave Macmillan, 1996), 144; and Gottesman, *Cambodia after the Khmer Rouge*, 80.

100 Shawcross, *The Quality of Mercy*, 183–84; Metzl, *Western Responses*, 146; Rony Brauman, "Refugee Camps, Population Transfers, and NGOs," in *Hard Choices: Moral Dilemmas in Humanitarian Intervention*, ed. Jonathan Moore (Lanham: Rowman & Littlefield, 1998), 179; and Clymer, "Jimmy Carter," 275–76.

101 On the general challenges aid agencies faced in Cambodia, see Barnett, *Empire of Humanity*, 149–51; Brauman, "Refugee Camps," 177–81; and Fiona Terry, *Condemned to Repeat? The Paradox of Humanitarian Action* (Ithaca: Cornell University Press, 2002), Chapter 4.

102 "Plate-Forme," *Solidarité Cambodge*, 7. See, also, "Solidarité Cambodge: Programme d'aide médicale et sanitaire, 1981–82," February 1981, F delta rés 613/66, La contemporaine.

103 See, for example, Claude Liria, "Le people khmer ne doit pas mourir!," *L'Humanité rouge* 1137, October 2, 1979, 2; "Soutien sans réserve au peuple cambodgien!," *L'Humanité rouge* 1159, November 2–4, 1979, 4; and "Soutien-Cambodge," *L'Humanité rouge* 1203, April 26–May 7, 1980, 4.

104 "Soutien sans réserve."

105 Claude Lira, "Témoignage de 'Médecins sans frontières' sur la situation au Cambodge," *L'Humanité rouge* 1164, November 10–11, 1979, 2.

106 "'Médecins sans frontières' appelle à une 'marche pour la survie,'" *Le Monde*, December 20, 1979.

107 Terry, *Condemned to Repeat*, 146.

108 Quoted in Davey, *Idealism beyond Borders*, 165.

109 Quoted in Shawcross, *The Quality of Mercy*, 205.

110 Quoted in Davey, *Idealism beyond Borders*, 165.

111 Quoted in Shawcross, *The Quality of Mercy*, 193.

112 Metzl, *Western Responses*, 162–68.

113 Clymer, "Jimmy Carter," 275–78.

114 Ibid., 264–65.

115 Christopher Goscha, *Vietnam: A New History* (New York, Basic Books, 2019), 372–85.

116 See Troung Nhu Tang with David Chanoff and Doan Van Toai, *A Vietcong Memoir* (New York: Vintage Books, 1986).

117 For an excellent analysis of the limits of national liberation struggles as a mode of politics, see Michael Neocosmos, *Thinking Freedom in Africa: Toward a Theory of Emancipatory Politics* (Johannesburg: Wits University Press, 2016), Chapter 4.

118 "Chairman Mao's Theory," 20.

119 Ibid., 23.

120 Ibid.

121 "Aggression Against Democratic Kampuchea Condemned," *Beijing Review* 22, no. 5, February 2, 1979, 22–26; "Counterattack in Defense of Our Frontiers," *Beijing Review* 22, no. 8, February 23, 1979, 9–11; and "On the Vietnamese Authorities' Rejection of Negotiations," *Beijing Review* 22, no. 9, March 2, 1979, 18.

122 Nguyen Huu Thuy, "Vietnam–China: The Root of the Problem," in *Vietnamese Studies 58: Viet Nam 1975–1979* (Hanoi: Xunhasaba, 1979), 100 and 117.

123 Phan Hien, Speech delivered to the 34th Session of the UN General Assembly, September 28, 1979, 9, in Sino-Vietnamese Conflict, TAM PE 029, Box 20, Tamiment Library and Robert F. Wagner Labor Archives, New York University, New York, United States.

124 Nguyen Huu Thuy, "Vietnam–China," 147.

125 Hoang Nguyen, "Problems of Foreign Policy," in *Vietnamese Studies 58*, 84.

126 Nguyen Huu Thuy, "Vietnam–China," 147.

127 Ieng Sary, Speech to the 26th Plenary Meeting, 34th Session of the United Nations General Assembly, October 9, 1979, Official Records, A/34/PV.25, 581.

128 Benedict Anderson, *Imagined Communities: Reflections on the Origin and Spread of Nationalism* (London: Verso, 2016), 1.

129 Alessandro Russo, *Cultural Revolution and Revolutionary Culture* (Durham: Duke University Press, 2020), 239.

130 Ibid., 3.

6   Human Rights

1 David Macey, *The Lives of Michel Foucault: A Biography* (New York: Pantheon Books, 1993), 437–38.

2 Michel Foucault, "Confronting Governments: Human Rights," in *The Essential Works of Foucault, 1954–1984: Power*, ed. James D. Faubion, trans. Robert Hurley et al. (New York: New Press, 2000), 474–75.

3 For an analysis of Foucault's later thinking on the problem of rights, see Jessica Whyte, "Human Rights: Confronting Governments?: Michel Foucault and the Right to Intervene," in *New Critical Legal Thinking: Law and the Political*, eds. Mathew Stone, Illan rua Wall, and Costas Douzinas (New York: Routledge, 2012), 11–31.

4 Mai Văn Bộ, *Hà Nội – Paris: Hồi ký Ngoại giao của Mai Văn Bộ* (Ho Chi Minh City: Nhà xuất bản Văn nghệ Thành phố Hồ Chí Minh, 1993), 231.

5 Quoted in Nayan Chanda, *Brother Enemy: The War after the War* (New York: Collier Books, 1986), 234.

6 For SRV attitudes toward the ethnic Chinese population, see, among others, ibid., 231–47.

7 W. Courtland Robinson, *Terms of Refuge: The Indochinese Exodus and the International Response* (London: Zed Books, 1998), 32.

8 See, for example, Gisèle L. Bousquet, *Behind the Bamboo Hedge: The Impact of Homeland Politics in the Parisian Vietnamese Community* (Ann Arbor: University of Michigan Press, 1991), especially Chapter 6.

9 For East European dissidents, human rights, and French politics, see Robert Horvath, "'The Solzhenitsyn Effect': East European Dissidents and the Demise of Revolutionary Privilege," *Human Rights Quarterly* 29, no. 4 (November 2007): 879–907.

10 "Invité du mois. Doan Van Toai," *La Libre Belgique*, December 24–25, 1979.

11 Vo Van Ai, "Isle of Light: A Look Back at the Boat People and the European Left," *World Affairs* 176, no. 6 (March–April 2014): 40.

12 Doan Van Toai and Michel Voirol, *Le goulag vietnamien* (Paris: Robert Laffont, 1979).

13 "Crimes de paix," *Le Monde*, October 5, 1978.

14 Roland-Pierre Paringaux, "La violation des droits de l'homme au Vietnam," *Le Monde*, October 5, 1978.

15 "Entretien avec Jacques Broyelle," in Louis-Winoc Christiaens, "La Défense des droits de l'homme en France à travers les comités politiques (1969–1979). Un cas pratique: le comité 'Un bateau pour le Vietnam,' 1979" (Mémoire de DEA, Université Charles de Gaulle, Lille III, 1990), 82.

16 Bernard Kouchner, *L'île de Lumière* (Paris: Ramsay, 1980), 28.

17 Olivier Weber, *French Doctors. Les 25 ans d'épopée des hommes et des femmes qui ont inventé la médecine humanitaire* (Paris: Robert Laffont, 1995), 206.

18 Kouchner, *L'île de Lumière*, 29.

19 See, for example, "Un Bateau pour le Vietnam," *Tribune Socialiste* no. 356, January 25, 1968, 16.

20 Kouchner, *L'île de Lumière*, 35.

21 Quoted in Horvath, "'The Solzhenitsyn Effect,'" 904.

22 "Un appel du comité 'Un bateau pour le Vietnam,'" *Le Monde*, November 22, 1978.

23 For a list of signatories, see Christiaens, "La Défense des droits de l'homme en France," 123–24.

24 Eleanor Davey, *Idealism beyond Borders: The French Revolutionary Left and the Rise of Humanitarianism, 1954–1988* (Cambridge: Cambridge University Press, 2015), 193–98.

25 Paul Berman, *Power and the Idealists: Or, the Passion of Joschka Fischer and Its Aftermath* (Brooklyn: Soft Skull Press, 2005), 237.

26 "Entretien avec Jacques Broyelle," 86.

27 Weber, *French Doctors*, 215.

28 Davey, *Idealism beyond Borders*, 198–200.

29 For the complex history of humanitarian universalism, internationalism, and interventionism in France, see Bertrand Taithe, "Reinventing (French) Universalism: Religion, Humanitarianism and the 'French Doctors,'" *Modern and Contemporary France* 12, no. 2 (2004): 147–58.

30 Yến Lê Espiritu, *Body Counts: The Vietnam War and Militarized Refuge(es)* (Berkeley: University of California Press, 2014).

31 "Entretien avec Ilios Yannakakis," in Christiaens, "La Défense des droits de l'homme en France," 98.

32 "Entretien avec Jacques Broyelle," 90.

33 Weber, *French Doctors*, 242.

34 James Traub, "A Stateman without Borders," *New York Times Magazine*, February 3, 2008.

35 "Entretien avec Jacques Broyelle," 89–90.

36 Kouchner, *L'île de Lumière*, 407.

37 Rupert Neudeck, *Die Menschenretter von Cap Anamur* (Munich: C. H. Beck, 2002); Lora Wildenthal, "Humanitarianism in Postcolonial Contexts: Some Western European Examples from the 1960s to the 1980s," in *Colonialism and Beyond: Race and Migration from a Postcolonial Perspective*, eds. Eva Bischoff and Elisabeth Engle (Zurich: LIT, 2013), 104–06 and 115–17; and Frank Bösch, "Refugees Welcome? The West German Reception of Vietnamese 'Boat People,'" *Studies in Contemporary History* 14 (2017): 2–29.

38 Joan Baez, *And a Voice to Sing With: A Memoir* (New York: New American Library, 1988), 179.

39 Barbara J. Keys, *Reclaiming American Virtue: The Human Rights Revolution of the 1970s* (Cambridge, MA: Harvard University Press, 2014), 195.

40 Rozanne Weissman, "Ginetta Sagan: The 'Little Mouse' that Roars," *Air California Magazine*, September 1978, 38.

41 Keys, *Reclaiming American Virtue*, 199.

42 Doan Van Toai, Curriculum Vitae, n.d., Box 6, Folder 5–6, Ginetta Sagan Papers, Hoover Institution, Stanford University, Stanford, United States (hereafter Hoover).

43 Doan Van Toai and David Chanoff, *The Vietnamese Gulag* (New York: Simon & Schuster, 1986), 340.

44 Baez, *And a Voice to Sing With*, 274.

45 Ginetta Sagan, "Human Rights Violation in Vietnam," circa 1979, 1, Box 6, Folder 2, Ginetta Sagan Papers, Hoover.

46 Baez, *And a Voice to Sing With*, 274.

47 Berman, *Power and the Idealists*, 240.

48 See, for example, the paper trail in Box 15, Folders 5, 7, 8, 11–14, Ginetta Sagan Papers, Hoover.

49 Baez, *And a Voice to Sing With*, 279.

50 Jana K. Lipman, *In Camps: Vietnamese Refugees, Asylum Seekers, and Repatriates* (Berkeley: University of California Press, 2020), 84 and 262.

51 "Open Letter to the Socialist Republic of Vietnam," *New York Times*, May 30, 1979.

52 "Cinq mille personnes ont participé aux 'Six Heures du monde pour le Vietnam,'" *Le Monde*, November 30, 1966.

53 Ibid.

54 Joan Baez, "The Toll of Violence in Vietnam," *Washington Post*, June 12, 1979.

55 Joan Baez and Ginetta Sagan, draft letter to Father Ando, n.d., 1, Box 15, Folder 12–14, Ginetta Sagan Papers, Hoover.

56 Weissman, "Ginetta Sagan," 38.

57 Ibid.

58 Jimmy Carter to Ginetta and Leonard Sagan, July 26, 1975, Box 9, Folder 11, Ginetta Sagan Papers, Hoover.

59 Weissman, "Ginetta Sagan," 38.

60 Baez, *And a Voice to Sing With*, 282–83.

61 Jimmy Carter, "Inaugural Address," January 20, 1977, in *Public Papers of the Presidents of the United States: Jimmy Carter, 1977*, vol. I (Washington, DC: US Government Printing Office, 1977), 1.

62 Ibid., 2–3.

63 For competing ideas of human rights in US political discourse after the Vietnam War, see Keys, *Reclaiming American Virtue*, especially Chapters 4–10. The following paragraphs draw heavily on Keys's excellent work.

64 Ibid., 261.

65 These internal tensions are explored ibid., 259–64.

66 For the Vietnam War as a trauma that "crippled faith in America's virtuous power," see John Kane, *Between Virtue and Power: The Persistent Moral Dilemma of US Foreign Policy* (New Haven: Yale University Press, 2008), Chapter 15.

67 Judith Kumin, "Orderly Departure from Vietnam: Cold War Anomaly or Humanitarian Innovation?," *Refugee Survey Quarterly* 27, no. 1 (2008): 110.

68 Robert D. Schulzinger, *A Time for Peace: The Legacy of the Vietnam War* (Oxford: Oxford University Press, 2006), 13–14.

69 For Soviet–American relations more generally, see Odd Arne Westad, ed., *The Fall of Détente: Soviet–American Relations during the Carter Years* (Oslo: Scandinavian University Press, 1997).

70 Scott Kaufman, *Plans Unraveled: The Foreign Policy of the Carter Administration* (Dekalb: Northern Illinois University Press, 2008), 142–44.

71 Ibid., 32–35.

72 Jimmy Carter, "Human Rights Violations in Cambodia," April 21, 1978, in *Public Papers of the Presidents of the United States: Jimmy Carter, 1978*, vol. I (Washington, DC: US Government Printing Office, 1979), 767.

73 For Vietnamese in the diaspora embracing human rights at this time, see Lipman, *In Camps*, 82–86.

74 Walter F. Mondale with David Hage, *The Good Fight: A Life in Liberal Politics* (New York: Scribner, 2010), 212.

75 Ibid., 213.

76 Henry Scott Stokes, "US to Double Its Refugee Quota to 14,000 a Month," *New York Times*, June 29, 1979.

77 *Indochinese Refugee Assistance Program: Report to Congress*, US Department of Health, Education, and Welfare, Social Security Administration, Office of Refugee Affairs, December 31, 1979, 3.

78 Lipman, *In Camps*, 79–89.

79 Speech by Vice President Walter F. Mondale to the United Nations Conference on Indochinese Refugees, Geneva, July 21, 1979, 1, 153.L.14.3B, Walter F. Mondale Vice Presidential Papers, Minnesota Historical Society, Saint Paul, United States.

80 Ibid.

81 Ibid., 2.

82 Ibid., 3.

83 Ibid., 2.

84 Ibid., 4.

85 See Ngô Vinh Long, "The socialization of South Vietnam," in *The Third Indochina War: Conflict between China, Vietnam and Cambodia, 1972–1979*, eds. Odd Arne Westad and Sophie Quinn-Judge (London: Routledge, 2006), 132; Nick Turse, *Kill Anything that Moves: The Real American War in Vietnam* (New York: Metropolitan Books, 2013), 11–14; and Pierre Asselin, *Vietnam's American War: A History* (Cambridge: Cambridge University Press, 2018), 237.

86 Espiritu, *Body Counts*, 40.

87 Cyrus Vance, "Statement by the Secretary of State (Vance) before the Subcommittee on Immigration, Refugees, and International Law of the House Judiciary Committee, July 31, 1979," in *American Foreign Policy: Basic Documents, 1977–1980* (Washington, DC: US Department of State, 1983), 941.

88 Mondale, *The Good Fight*, 216.

89 See, for example, *Those Who Leave: The "Problem of Vietnamese Refugees"* (Hanoi: Vietnam Courier, 1979).

90 Ibid., 5.

91 Robinson, *Terms of Refuge*, 17.

92 Kumin, "Orderly Departure from Vietnam," 110–17.

93 Ibid., 104.

94 Quoted ibid., 115.

95 Robinson, *Terms of Refuge*, 58.

96 Ibid.

97 *Those Who Leave*, 33.

98 Ngo Ba Thanh, "Defence of Human Rights or US Policy of Interference in the Internal Affairs of Other Countries?," reprinted in *Vietnam: Which Human Rights? A Dossier* (Hanoi: Vietnam Courier, 1980), 106.

99 Ibid.

100 Ibid., 107.

101 *Those Who Leave*, 33.

102 Ngo Ba Thanh, "Defence of Human Rights," 118.

103 Ibid., 112 and 114.

104 Ibid., 119.

105 For migration, mobility, and demography, see Andrew Hardy, *Red Hills: Migrants and the State in the Highlands of Vietnam* (Honolulu: University of Hawai'i Press, 2002), Part 3.

106 D. R. SarDesai, *Vietnam: Past and Present*, 4th ed. (Boulder: Westview Press, 2005), 128–33.

107 "Wilfred Burchett Answers Joan Baez," *Washington Post*, June 27, 1979.
108 Don Luce, "The Boat People: America Can Best Help Them by Recognizing Its Complicity," *The Progressive*, September 1979, 27–29.
109 Laurent Schwartz, "Nous solidariser avec le Vietnam mais défendre aussi les victimes," *Tribune Socialiste* 809, January 12–17, 1979, 12.
110 Michel Thomas, "Boat People. Des victimes de la guerre américaine," *Rouge* 873, June 29–July 5, 1979, 5.
111 Jean-Francois B., "En première ligne contre ceux qui assassinent l'espoir communiste," *Rouge* 876, July 20–27, 1979, 10.
112 Ibid., 11.
113 Gabriel M., "Le droit de dénoncer hanoi," *Rouge* 876, July 20–27, 1979, 12.
114 Ibid., 11–12.
115 Laurent Schwartz, *A Mathematician Grappling with His Century*, trans. Leila Schneps (Basel: Birkhäuser Verlag, 2001), 439.
116 Ibid, 434–35.
117 Ibid, 435. For this mission, see *Report of an Amnesty International Mission to the Socialist Republic of Viet Nam, 10–21 December 1979*, Amnesty International Publications, June 1981.
118 Schwartz, "Nous solidariser," 12.
119 Emily K. Hobson, *Lavender and Red: Liberation and Solidarity in the Gay and Lesbian Left* (Oakland: University of California Press, 2016), Chapters 4 and 5.
120 Mike Davis, *Prisoners of the American Dream: Politics and Economy in the History of the US Working Class* (London: Verso, 2018), 284–87.
121 Steve Striffler, *Solidarity: Latin America and the US Left in the Era of Human Rights* (London: Pluto Press, 2019), 137.
122 Van Gosse, "Active Engagement: The Legacy of Central American Solidarity," *NACLA Report on the Americas* 28, no. 5 (March–April 1995): 24.
123 Daniel Bensaïd, *An Impatient Life: A Political Memoir*, trans. David Fernbach (London: Verso, 2013), 197.
124 V. I. Lenin, "The Three Sources and Three Component Parts of Marxism," in *V. I. Lenin Collected Works*, vol. XIX (Moscow: Progress Publishers, 1977), 23.
125 Alain Badiou, *Can Politics Be Thought?*, trans. Bruno Bosteels (Durham: Duke University Press, 2018), 40–69.
126 Odd Arne Westad, *The Cold War* (New York: Basic Books, 2017), Chapter 21.
127 Vijay Prashad, *The Darker Nations: A People's History of the Third World* (New York: New Press, 2007), Part 3.
128 Melanie Beresford, "Economic Transition, Uneven Development, and the Impact of Reform on Regional Inequality," in *Postwar Vietnam: Dynamics of a Transforming Society*, ed. Hy V. Luong (Lanham: Rowman & Littlefield, 2003), 57–64.
129 For debates over reform, see Tuong Vu, *Vietnam's Communist Revolution: The Power and Limits of Ideology* (Cambridge: Cambridge University Press, 2017), 245–58.

130 The literature on Đổi Mới is expansive; some useful works include William S. Turley and Mark Selden, eds., *Reinventing Socialism: Doi Moi in Comparative Perspective* (Boulder: Westview Press, 1993); Melanie Beresford and Đặng Phong, *Economic Transition in Vietnam: Trade and Aid in the Demise of a Centrally Planned Economy* (Cheltenham: Edward Elgar, 2000); and Peter Boothroyd and Pham Xuan Nam, eds., *Socioeconomic Renovation in Viet Nam: The Origin, Evolution, and Impact of Doi Moi* (Ottawa: International Development Research Centre, 2000).

131 Alain Badiou, *The Communist Hypothesis*, trans. David Macey and Steve Corcoran (London: Verso, 2015), 43.

132 Ellen Meiksins Wood, *The Retreat from Class: A New "True" Socialism* (London: Verso, 1986).

Coda: Return of the Repressed

1 Jan Eckel, *The Ambivalence of Good: Human Rights in International Politics since the 1940s*, trans. Rachel Ward (Oxford: Oxford University Press, 2019), 344.

2 For another account that centers the 1990s, see Stefan-Ludwig Hoffmann, "Human Rights and History," *Past & Present* 232, no. 1 (August 2016): 279–310.

3 Mark Philip Bradley, "American Vernaculars: The United States and the Global Human Rights Imagination," *Diplomatic History* 38, no. 1 (January 2014): 2.

4 For just two early examples, see David Rieff, *A Bed for the Night: Humanitarianism in Crisis* (New York: Simon & Schuster, 2002), and Wendy Brown, "'The Most We Can Hope For ...': Human Rights and the Politics of Fatalism," *South Atlantic Quarterly* 103, nos. 2–3 (Spring–Summer 2004): 451–63.

5 Daniel Cohn-Bendit, "EU Must Support Democratic Transition in Libya," Press Release, March 9, 2011, www.cohn-bendit.eu/en/ct/85.

6 Bernard Kouchner, "Libya: The Morality of Intervention," trans. Harry Forster, *The Guardian*, March 24, 2011.

7 Nicholas Kristof, "Thank You, America!," *New York Times*, August 31, 2011.

8 Anne-Marie Slaughter, "Why Libya Sceptics Were Proved Badly Wrong," *Financial Times*, August 24, 2011.

9 The relationship between human rights and neoliberalism is now the subject of intense debate. For an excellent recent account, see Jessica Whyte, *The Morals of the Market: Human Rights and the Rise of Neoliberalism* (London: Verso, 2019).

10 As Karl Marx once explained, "it is all the more clear what we have to accomplish at present: I am referring to *ruthless criticism of all that exists*, ruthless both in the sense of not being afraid of the results it arrives at and in the sense of being just as little afraid of conflict with the powers that be." See *Marx & Engels Collected Works*, vol. III (London: Lawrence & Wishart, 1975), 142.

11 The injunction to put oneself in "a position of immanence" to the crisis comes from Alain Badiou, *Can Politics Be Thought?*, trans. Bruno Bosteels (Durham: Duke University Press, 2018), 58–64.

12 For a sophisticated theoretical exposition of this general approach, see Sylvain Lazarus, *Anthropology of the Name*, trans. Gila Walker (London: Seagull Books, 2015), especially 25–26.

13 V. I. Lenin, "What Is to Be Done?" in *V. I. Lenin Collected Works*, vol. V (Moscow: Progress Publishers, 1977), 389.

14 For one interesting historical exploration of the crisis of the Leninist "party-state," see, for example, Alessandro Russo, *Cultural Revolution and Revolutionary Culture* (Durham: Duke University Press, 2020).

15 For a good investigation of the limits of national self-determination, see Jörg Fisch, *The Right of Self-Determination of Peoples: The Domestication of an Illusion*, trans. Anita Mage (Cambridge: Cambridge University Press, 2015).

16 For a similar approach to the past, see Alessandro Russo, "The Sixties and Us," in *The Idea of Communism*, vol. III, *The Seoul Conference*, eds. Alex Taek-Gwang Lee and Slavoj Žižek (London: Verso Books, 2016), 137–78.

Index

African American radicalism. *see* Black
 radicals
Agnew, Spiro, 179
AI. *see* Amnesty International (AI)
Algeria, 51, 67, 75
Algerian War, 63, 73, 88
Ali, Tariq, 87, 100, 125, 128, 130
Alliance of National, Democratic, and
 Peace Forces, 178
American Deserters Committee, 84
Amin, Samir, 204
Amnesty International (AI)
 anti-imperialist convergences, 190–94
 crisis in (1967), 109
 as key player in human rights
  ascendance, 104–105
 and political prisoners, 188–89
 Vietnamese refugee crisis, 229, 237,
  239, 252
Anderson, Benedict, 226
Anderson, Helen E., 137
anticolonialists, divisions among
 (1920s–1930s), 41–42, *see also* anti-
 imperialist internationalism
anticommunism
 and conservative human rights position,
  102
 and hesitancy of traditional American
  radical left, 57
 problems of challenging, 53
 self-determination as counterpose to
  communism, 109
 using Vietnamese human rights crisis to
  support, 242
anti-imperialism, 80–110
 US New Left's adoption of, 57
 Biafran dilemma for radicals, 207
 continued popularity (1970s), 161–63
 convergences with human rights at end
  of Vietnam War, 187–94
 vs. human rights activism, 238–39
 and national liberation, 38

post-Paris Peace Accords activism
 against repression in RVN, 183–85
post-Vietnam War decline of, 230
proposal for rethinking, 267
shift to civil rights focus after 1968, 160
shift to human rights as basis for
 internationalism, 3
trajectory of activism after US
 withdrawal, 181–85
anti-imperialist internationalism. *see also*
 national self-determination
antiwar soldiers in Europe, 83–85
beginnings of Vietnam's, 18–19
and competing internationalisms,
 101–106
contributions, 14–15
convergences with human rights, 12
European opposition to Vietnam War,
 81–83
and French conquest of Vietnam,
 20–22
impasse in response to Vietnamese
 refugee crisis, 250–52
as integral to 1960s internationalism,
 10, 106–10
international brigades in Vietnam War
 opposition, 85–88
of Leninism, 37–40
Leninist revival during Vietnam War,
 95–101
national self-determination as focus of,
 24–29
North Atlantic collapse of, 202–203,
 253–57
post-Vietnam War crisis of, 195–227
and postwar Vietnam, 222–27
reliance on Leninist problematic, 8–9
shift to human rights, 7–13
success of nation-building at expense of
 communist-building, 265
Third Indochina War, 210–15, 224–26
Vietnam as inspiration for, 1–3

324